READER'S DIGEST

The world's last mysteries

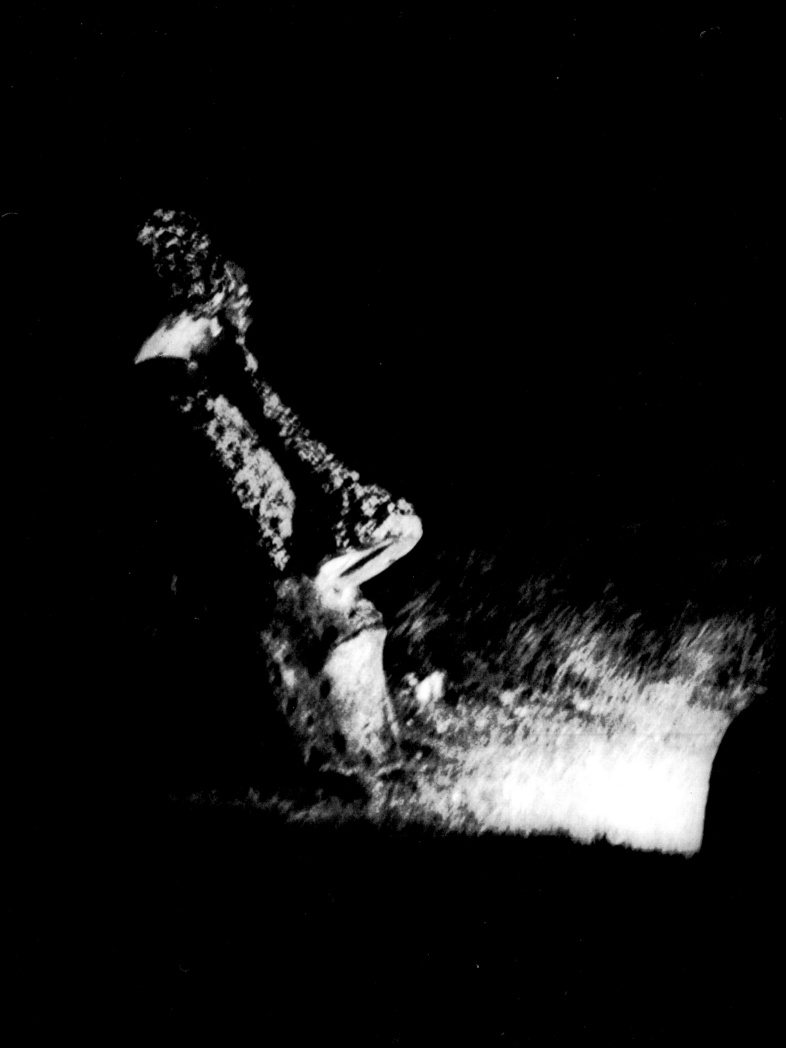

The world's last mysteries

THE READER'S DIGEST ASSOCIATION, INC.

Pleasantville, New York/Montreal

Contents

DIGGING UP THE PAST

Archaeology has been called 'a sentimental science' because of its mixture of passionate excitement and painstaking scientific methods. In the European world, this science was born in the 18th century with the excavation of Pompeii, and its early development coincided with the dawning of the romantic movement in the arts. Artists, pre-occupied with emotion and imagination, were drawn to wild and picturesque places, including ruins. Before that time nobody had much use for, or even interest in, the debris of history.

Thus, early in its life, archaeology – the study of antiquity from whatever evidence can be found – gained a double aura of science and romance. As men began to probe and question their past, often hoping to find clues to the future, they increasingly came to realise that a wealth of civilisations had preceded them. The probings of science began to replace the myths with reason. And yet many of the discoveries made by science proved to be so extraordinary and so enigmatic that even now many new finds are posing more questions than answers.

This book begins with some of European man's most cherished myths – the Utopian vision of Atlantis, the search for an Eldorado whose wealth was beyond imagining, the discovery of a green and fruitful New World – and shows what science now suggests is the reality behind each of these stories.

New techniques have produced fascinating evidence about much of our mysterious prehistory. The carbon-14 dating method, which determines the age of man-made objects by measuring the decay of radioactivity in them, has revolutionised our thinking about the peoples who raised the stone monuments at Stonehenge and throughout Europe. It has also helped to reveal the technological sophistication that Middle and South American civilisations achieved hundreds of years before the Spanish conquest.

Yet mysteries remain, despite the pace of modern discoveries. The final chapters in the story of humanity are far from being written. Who built the five cities of Tiahuanaco on the roof of the Andes? Why was Zimbabwe created, and by whom? Where was the final refuge of the last Inca king? How did the elaborate civilisations of the Mayas and the Khmers crumble? Who traced the mysterious lines in the desert at Nazca, in Peru, and for what possible reason?

Paradoxically, as science advances its store of knowledge, more and more efforts are required of man's imagination in order to breathe life into statistics and give direction to the new technology.

This is where the vital romantic vision comes in. Heinrich Schliemann, the 19th-century German archaeologist, had this vision to an extraordinary degree. Longing from boyhood to discover the site of Homer's Troy, he successfully set out to make a fortune in business with the sole aim of realising his childhood dream. And early this century the American Hiram Bingham would never have found the lost city of the Incas at Machu Picchu without an indomitable belief in his quest that overcame every obstacle.

Sometimes this romanticism leads to futility and even absurdity. Some men are still searching for Eldorado. Others seek an easy answer to all the world's mysteries by postulating that in prehistoric times gods from other worlds visited this planet. For reasons that are not explained, these visitors from space are said to have built Stonehenge, raised pyramids in Middle America and erected giant statues on Easter Island.

But there are still real mysteries that man can wonder about. One of the greatest concerns an explosion in Siberia in 1908, where the evidence of what happened points to almost unimaginable possibilities in the realm of the unknown.

As for the future, the wonders are limitless. There is hardly a serious scientist on earth who will deny the possibility of life somewhere amongst all the galaxies of the universe.

It seems that mystery and imagination are as vital as reason for man in the hunt for truth. As Albert Einstein wrote in 1930: 'The most beautiful thing we can experience is the mysterious; it is the source of all true art and science. He to whom this emotion is a stranger, who can no longer pause to wonder and stand rapt in awe, is as good as dead: his eyes are closed.'

THE EDITORS

In search of
fabled lands

Voyage to Atlantis

*Did the lost continent of Atlantis really exist,
or is the account of an island paradise
destroyed just a moral tale? The story of Atlantis was
first told by the Greek philosopher Plato as a
parable to show how heaven punishes those who worship
false gods. But at the same time he
hints that the story is true – the memory of a
terrible cataclysm passed down by word of
mouth for hundreds of years. Myth or reality,
the legend of Atlantis has inspired a search
that echoes down the centuries.*

It is 3,500 years ago and the long, lazy Aegean summer is drawing to its close. It is dusk and the rays of the dying sun pick out a tiny island so nearly a perfect circle in its outline, so compellingly lovely with its ochre-coloured volcano rising out of a violet sea, that even among the islands of the Aegean it is outstanding for its beauty.

The swallows streak through the sky, darting and wheeling in the blaze of the setting sun. The branches of the olive trees quiver in the light evening breeze. The island's harbour is quiet, now that the business of

---

The day when the sea swallowed Atlantis has haunted men's imaginations over the centuries. Modern research into the disappearance has concentrated on trying to find the site of a massive, and probably volcanic, catastrophe described by the Greek philosopher Plato in two of his Dialogues.

the day is over. The fishermen are going home with their shining, silvery catches. The narrow streets begin to fill with people, laughing and talking. In the doorways of the little houses women sit gossiping and from dozens of tiny workshops all over the town comes the cheerful whirr of the potter's wheel. In the orchards and vineyards, the men are strolling home after the day's labour.

The shadows lengthen as night comes. Then a strange, choking heat engulfs the town. The sea turns to the colour of lead. From deep within the earth comes a muffled rumbling, intermittent at first but soon continuous. Panic seizes the islanders. They sense that the great volcano, whose 5,000-ft peak dominates their lives, is about to erupt and that the god who controls the earth-shaking forces inside the volcano has awoken from his long sleep.

What they could not have known, as they stumbled

from their houses clutching a few frantically snatched treasures, was that their town, their island and ultimately their whole civilisation was about to be destroyed by what, according to the evidence gathered by vulcanologists and seismologists of a later day, has come to rate as one of the most violent volcanic cataclysms the world has seen.

First came a choking plume of dark smoke. Then a terrible rain of blazing pumice stone, followed by ash, poured down in between explosions blasting up from the cone. At the height of the cataclysm, the volcano itself exploded under enormous internal pressures. With a bang that was heard from one end of the Mediterranean to the other and must have sounded like the end of the world, most of the island was blasted into dust.

Finally, the magma chamber beneath the volcano emptied, spewing out millions of tons of solid rock and, as a result, the great volcano collapsed in on itself, forming a steep-sided caldera or crater, 37 miles in circumference. Into this void poured the sea, bringing even more horrors in its wake. These were the giant tsunamis, tidal waves which are set off by earthquakes or volcanic eruptions and are perhaps the most terrifying forces in nature. Waves as high as 650 ft radiated from the island to strike nearby coasts with a force that has never been equalled.

This is how scientists today see the sequence of events that destroyed the island 3,500 years ago. An explosion that they estimate produced a destructive force equivalent to 500–1,000 atomic bombs.

A terrible darkness, caused by the thick fall of ash,

One of the details mentioned by Plato in his description of Atlantis is that a dangerous but popular pastime among the nobles was capturing wild bulls with ropes. This scene, depicted on one of two gold cups found at Vaphio, in Greece, shows the ritual game. The cup was made about 1500 BC.

descended on the Aegean, plunging the whole area into a night that was to last for weeks. The ash itself continued to fall for some time and today deposits of it, called tephra, lie more than 200 ft deep on what remains of the island which the ancient Greeks called Kallisté.

Scientists now believe that what happened to Kallisté may be the solution to a riddle that has perplexed historians and geographers since the days of the Greek philosopher Plato (c. 427–347 BC).

Plato, one of the fathers of western thought, is our sole direct source for the legend of Atlantis. His fragmentary account of the continent that was swallowed up by the sea still excites the modern mind.

Plato's Atlantis was a kind of paradise – a vast island 'larger than Libya and Asia put together' – with magnificent mountain ranges, lush plains which teemed with every variety of animal, including elephants, and luxuriant gardens where the fruit was 'fair and wondrous and in infinite abundance'. The earth was rich with from their numbers, kept up a multitudinous sound of human voices, and din and clatter . . . night and day'.

At the heart of the city were the great palace and the temple, which was even more sumptuous: 'All the outside, with the exception of the pinnacles, they covered with silver, and the pinnacles with gold. In the interior of the temple the roof was of ivory, curiously wrought everywhere with gold and silver and orichalc; and all the other parts, the walls and pillars and floor, they coated with orichalc. In the temple they placed statues of gold: there was the god himself standing in a

---

Over the ages, innumerable places have been suggested as the site of Atlantis. At one time or another, practically every country in the world has been identified as the lost paradise. Modern scientists have narrowed the search down to two main possibilities: the Atlantic, either in the Azores or the Bahamas; and the Mediterranean, at Santorini or Crete.

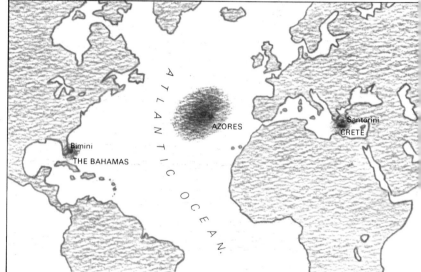

The man who can master the wealth of evidence about Atlantis, and come up with the final answer, has not yet emerged. But many commentators have placed it in the area of the Azores. If they are correct, then perhaps the lost paradise looked like this wood, in the Azores island of São Miguel.

---

precious metals, especially the one prized most highly by the ancients, the fabulous, iridescent orichalc, an alloy of copper – perhaps brass.

The capital of Atlantis, built in the very centre of the island, was remarkable for the scale and splendour of its public buildings which were designed in an architecturally harmonious blend of white, black and red stone. Even more extraordinary, perhaps, was the plan on which the city had been laid out. It was arranged in five zones built in perfect concentric circles. Its various ports were served by a system of canals. Plato says that the capital's canal and its nearby port were 'full of vessels and merchants coming from all parts, who,

chariot – a charioteer with six winged horses – and of such a size that he touched the roof of the building with his head; around him there were a hundred Nereids riding on dolphins . . .'

This charioteer was none other than the God of the Sea and Shaker of the Earth, Poseidon. When he and his divine brothers Zeus and Hades divided the world between them, Atlantis fell to Poseidon's lot. He became the all-powerful lord of the island which he peopled with his sons, a virtuous race touched with divinity. The ten kings of Atlantis were immensely rich and powerful but ruled wisely over the enormous colonial empire they built.

Numberless generations of Atlanteans lived in peace under a system of laws which had been handed down to them by Poseidon and whose justness commanded universal admiration. These laws were 'inscribed by the first kings on a pillar of orichalc, which was situated in the middle of the island, at the temple of Poseidon'.

This engraving, by the French 19th-century designer Edouard Riou, is called the Great Asian Flood. But whatever its title, the picture contains all the elements of the destruction of Atlantis. There is a glimpse of a city vanishing beneath the waves, with a few people and animals making a vain effort to survive on the last remnants of high ground.

But in the end, Atlantean society began to decay. The people started to worship the false gods of wealth, idleness and luxury. Plato, ever a pessimist about human nature, writes: 'When the divine portion began to fade away, and became diluted too often and too much with the mortal admixture, and the human nature gained the upper hand, they then, being unable to bear their fortune, behaved in an unseemly manner, and to him who had an eye to see, grew visibly debased, for they were losing the fairest of their precious gifts; but to those who had no eye to see the true happiness, they appeared glorious and blessed at the very time when they were full of avarice and unrighteous power.'

It was during this era of corruption that the Atlanteans embarked on a war of world conquest, launching huge fleets against other islands and enslaving the inhabitants of the coastal settlements of the Mediterranean. The only power that could stand against them was Athens, the city dedicated to Athena, goddess of wisdom, industry and war. The Athenian hoplites, or heavy infantry, succeeded in stemming the tide of invasion and won a brilliant victory.

But this setback was not enough. The gods had prepared a terrible retribution for the men who betrayed the ancient faith of Atlantis. Plato takes up the story: 'Afterwards there occurred violent earthquakes and floods; and in a single day and night of misfortune ... the island of Atlantis disappeared into the depths of the sea.'

According to Plato's version, all this happened in remote antiquity, some 12,000 years ago. He located Atlantis in the Great Ocean, the Western Sea whose swelling waves rose beyond the Pillars of Hercules which we know today as the Straits of Gibraltar. Many of the arguments that have subsequently raged about the existence and geographical position of Atlantis stem from this space-time location.

What was the origin of Plato's story, and how literally are we to take it? What were the circumstances under which he wrote it and what was its purpose?

Only 100 years ago, the cities of Troy and Mycenae were considered as mythical as Atlantis. Scholars were convinced that the *Iliad*, Homer's epic poem about the siege of Troy, was based purely on legend and imagination. But the lonely quest of a self-taught German, Heinrich Schliemann (1822–90), was to upset all the official dogmas. Convinced that the *Iliad* was based on historical fact, Schliemann used it as his guide to the lost world of Troy. His great adventure has become a model for many champions of Atlantis. In the words of Prince Michael of Greece: 'The rehabilitation of Homer and the belated but definitive victory of those who believed him may give food for thought to those who doubt the existence of Atlantis.'

But can Plato be vindicated in the way Homer was? The story of Atlantis differs from that of Troy in one important respect: it was not part of any ancient oral

The modern science of vulcanology – the study of volcanoes – has opened new avenues in the search for Atlantis. According to legend, Greek warriors who fought against Atlantis were swallowed by the angry earth. Taking this to be a reference to a volcanic eruption or an earthquake, scholars began to look in crevassed areas like this – the sites of ancient cataclysms.

Scientists have gained an insight into the disaster that could have wiped out Atlantis by studying underwater volcanoes. This eruption created the island of Surtsey off Iceland in 1963. A similar upheaval could have led to the sinking of Atlantis.

tradition. It was not a legend passed down, by word of mouth, from generation to generation, over the centuries. It was the work of one man, Plato.

The story appears in two of Plato's celebrated Dialogues – *Timaeus* and *Critias*. These Dialogues were, in essence, transcriptions from the philosophical debates in which the intellectual citizens of Athens constantly engaged. The driving force behind these question-and-answer discussions had been Plato's master, Socrates. The subjects ranged from the Immortality of the Soul to the Ideal City.

Plato used to liven up the discussion of these dry, abstract ideas by presenting them in the form of

Plato, who was born in Athens about 427 BC, gave the world its first literary references to Atlantis, insisting on the truth of his story of a paradise destroyed. This bronze bust of the philosopher is in an archaeological museum in Naples. Plato died in Greece in about 347 BC; but his ideas, and his description of the lost city, are as vivid as ever.

15

allegories, parables and other literary devices. He invented a wealth of stories to make his logical arguments more palatable and more vivid. Is it not possible, indeed likely, that the tale of Atlantis was just one of these fictions, dreamed up to illustrate a philosophical point?

In the Dialogues, the narrator of the Atlantis story is Critias, Plato's cousin and, like Plato, a follower of Socrates. On three separate occasions Critias stresses that the story is true, and Socrates himself is quoted as having said it had 'the very great advantage of being a fact and not a fiction'.

Critias also claims that he heard the story from his

The theory that Atlantis lay somewhere in the Atlantic was given a powerful boost in 1968 with the discovery of these colossal underwater stone walls, off the island of North Bimini in the Bahamas.

great-grandfather Dropides and that Dropides in his turn had heard it from none other than Solon. If this is true, then here is a source to make even the most sceptical pause, for Solon was famous throughout Greece for his honesty. The most celebrated law-giver of classical times, he was regarded as the wisest of the Seven Sages of Greece. He lived from about 640 BC to 558 BC, two centuries before Plato wrote down the Atlantis story – not a particularly long period for such a tale to be kept alive by word of mouth.

Solon did not claim that the story was original. He himself heard it during a trip to Egypt in about 590 BC. In Saïs, an ancient city in the Nile Delta, he met the priests of the goddess Neith. They were highly educated men and Solon, always eager to learn new things, questioned them about ancient times. One old priest recounted the heroic deeds of his own Athenian ancestors 9,000 years before, and the tragic fate of the island of Atlantis. Solon was astonished by the story and translated it into Greek, intending to turn it into an epic poem, for he was a distinguished poet as well as a

statesman. But he did not live long enough to achieve this ambition.

It seems to have been the Egyptians then, those meticulous historians obsessed with the past, with their tablets and sacred archives, who had preserved the story of Atlantis. Given that Atlantis really existed, this Egyptian connection is important: it means that the Egyptians had not only heard of Atlantis but also perhaps that they had extensive trade relations with the island power.

If this link with ancient Egypt is valid, it would appear that the issue has been clouded by Plato himself. The likelihood is that the great philosopher handed on the legend very much in the form that he himself had heard it, adapting and altering it according to purely literary demands, as he was perfectly entitled to do.

It is important to emphasise that Plato's intentions, in recounting the Atlantis legend, were philosophical rather than historical. Many commentators fail to point out that in the Dialogues Plato is concerned with the wisdom, noble institutions and influence of Athens rather than Atlantis. The doomed Atlanteans are a convenient contrast to the ancestors of Solon and Plato himself. These Athenians of old were the people whom Plato calls 'the upright men', who created something like the ideal state the philosopher projects in his *Republic*. The story of the corruption of Atlantis is a backcloth against which the virtues of this philosophical state stand out more clearly.

Some classical writers, however, did not take Plato's parable very seriously. His pupil Aristotle held that it was no more than a poetic fiction, invented to enhance the narrative, and that Plato had created Atlantis simply in order to sink it conveniently at the end of the story. Many other writers adopted the same attitude.

But other scholars had doubts. Crantor, who lived some time around 300 BC and was the first commentator on Plato's works, maintained that the account of Atlantis was accurate in every detail. It is believed that Crantor even went to Egypt to check Solon's sources at first hand. A few centuries later the Stoic philosopher and scholar Posidonius (c. 135–50 BC) cited Plato's belief that the story was not a pure invention.

Truth or fiction? It is an argument that has raged for some 23 centuries, that has stimulated the most extravagant fantasies and given birth to numerous and elaborate pseudo-sciences. Atlantis has become the happy hunting ground for the promoters of bogus religions, for occultists and black magicians, for spiritualists, clairvoyants and science-fiction writers. It has also engaged the attention of serious archaeologists.

What is the eternal fascination of Atlantis, the lost continent? It is the stuff of many myths: an idyllic land, lying to the west, in the path of the setting sun . . . the Garden of the Hesperides where the apple trees bore golden fruit . . . the Elysian fields . . . the land of the Hyperboreans – all these were located in the vast Western Sea that was thought to have swallowed

Atlantis. In the Middle Ages and the Renaissance the legendary Happy Islands, the Islands of the Blessed and St Brendan's Island were similarly situated. When geography is a product of the imagination, the possibilities are boundless and the pre-modern mind filled the oceans with fabulous islands, lands of milk and honey where the living and the dead were reunited in eternal bliss.

History and legend contain many accounts of islands that were swallowed by the sea – King Arthur's mysterious Isle of Avalon is an example. And the idea is not entirely fanciful. Volcanic islands which rise out of the sea and then disappear do genuinely occur in the Atlantic, particularly in the Azores and near Iceland.

Plato is clear that Atlantis was in the Atlantic, and a number of the more serious investigators have searched for it there, believing that there was once a vast continent in the middle of the ocean. According to this theory, the Azores, the Cape Verde Islands, the Canaries and Madeira were the mountain peaks of Atlantis and are all that remain visible of a lost continent.

Atlantis as a reality was rescued from legend in the 15th century, the age of European exploration and discovery. The cartographers of the time included it on their maps, though imagination was their only reference point. When America was discovered, it was frequently identified with Atlantis, in spite of the obvious objection that it was clearly dry land and had not been submerged.

Such errors and inconsistencies did nothing to discourage the renewed interest in the lost continent. The

quest for the historical Atlantis had begun. A bewildering proliferation of theory and counter-theory culminated, in the 19th century, in the birth of a new 'science' – Atlantology.

An early eminent Atlantologist was the American politician and member of the US Congress Ignatius Donnelly. In 1882 Donnelly published his masterwork, *Atlantis: The Antediluvian World*, which became a best-seller and the bible of Atlantology.

Donnelly's thesis was based on certain similarities he observed between the pre-Columbian civilisations of America and ancient Egyptian culture. Among these he cited the building of pyramids, the art of embalming, the development of a 365-day calendar and the tradition of the Flood. He believed that the two civilisations had a common origin, a continent which existed between the Old and New Worlds before the Flood. After the continent sank, two cultures developed, one in the East, one in the West.

Donnelly borrowed wholesale from contemporary science in constructing his theory. Archaeology, mythology, linguistics, ethnology, geology, zoology, botany – they were all brought in and mixed, with considerable literary skill and remarkable erudition, to support his argument. This scientific hodge-podge was

The Lake of the Seven Cities, on the island of São Miguel, in the Azores, is a favourite of many Atlantis-hunters. The lake lies in an old volcanic crater; and somewhere beneath the ash and silt on its bottom, according to their theory, is Poseidopolis, the Atlantean capital. The Greeks gave the city its name after its legendary patron and destroyer – Poseidon.

to have a brilliant future, providing an enduring source for a long line of disciples.

Donnelly's supporters had an arsenal of theories to bolster up their case. Atlantology appeared to provide the answers to so many hallowed enigmas. The mysterious breeding habits of eels, for instance, which make a long and perilous journey from Europe across the Atlantic to lay their eggs in the Sargasso Sea, were explained by past experience in the rivers of Atlantis.

Atlantis was said to be the original home of the Basques, who are racially and linguistically different from all other Europeans, and of the scattered tribes of white Indians who were occasionally found in places such as Venezuela. The Guanches, cave-dwelling aborigines of the Canary Islands who were wiped out in the Spanish conquest of the islands, could only have been descendants of the Atlanteans. They were white-skinned, tall and had an indecipherable written language. The bearded, white pre-Columbian god who was called Kukulcan by the Mayas, Quetzalcóatl by the Toltecs and Viracocha by the Incas brought civilisation

Birth of an island

If it is hard to believe that a large island can, in effect, be obliterated from the face of the earth, it is no less remarkable that the forces which in one case bring about destruction can also create new land where none existed before. In a majestic reversal of what may have happened to Atlantis, the world watched in November 1963 as a new Atlantic island was born – an island of fire. The planet's volcanic birth pangs were first spotted by the crew of a fishing-boat off the south coast of Iceland. The skipper radioed a report of a billowing black cloud 200 ft high. Within three hours scientists and journalists began arriving at the scene of the eruption.

By then the cloud was 12,000 ft high; and about once every 30 seconds explosions at its centre sent ash, dust and 'bombs' of superheated rock arcing 500 ft into the air. At the edge of the inferno, waves were breaking on something just under the surface – the summit cone of a new mountain.

That night, the volcano's cone pushed clear of the boiling sea. By the following morning it was 33 ft high. As the convulsions went on, the roaring island continued to grow. Five days later, it was 200 ft tall and more than one-third of a mile long. And its steaming flanks and summit were still growing.

The Icelanders named the infant island Surtsey, after the fire demon Surtur in Norse mythology. Surtur was a powerful giant, and Surtsey soon proved it was worthy of its super-human namesake. When the eruptions quieted down in August 1965, after 21 months of intermittent rumblings accompanied by spectacular lightning displays, the island was 550 ft high, 1⅓ miles long and about a square mile in area; it went on growing for two more years.

For scientists, Surtsey was a living laboratory – the first known island to appear in the North Atlantic for the past 200 years. Vulcanologists could study close up how the pressure of molten rock from deep inside the earth bent and squeezed and burst the crust to reach the surface. Biologists could watch in detail how the first forms of life – such as lichens – finally won a place in what would seem an unpromising environment. Nobody knows how long Surtsey will last. The volcano that gave it life may some day cause it to share the fate of the island which Plato called Atlantis.

over the sea from the east – could he have come from anywhere but Atlantis?

How do Donnelly's theories hold up in the light of modern science, especially of oceanic geology which has become so much more sophisticated in the past 30 years? Many of the analogies Donnelly drew were disturbing enough to cause furious controversy at the time; but today it is clear that his scholarship was riddled with errors. He attempted to show that virtually every enigma and puzzle in the world was in some way related to Atlantis and, in trying to prove everything, laid himself open to the criticism that he had proved nothing.

The fundamental base on which all Donnelly's theories are constructed – that Atlantis was in the mid-Atlantic – has now been substantially refuted. Oceanographic studies of the sea-bed and the formation of continents show that nowhere in all the Atlantic's 36 million sq. miles is there evidence that a cataclysm on the scale of Atlantis has ever occurred or that any such continent has ever existed. There is an enormous submerged mountain range which runs approximately 12,500 miles from north to south, emerging at the Azores. But although this is a volcanic range, it is 'in expansion' – rising towards the surface – whereas Atlantis would be subsiding.

It has taken modern methods and modern equipment to refute Donnelly. But in 1912 the Atlantis story was still capable of exciting the imagination of a credulous public. In the United States it was the hey-day of sensationalist journalism. On October 20, a banner headline in William Randolph Hearst's *New York American* proclaimed, 'How I Found the Lost Atlantis, The Source Of All Civilisation'. The author of the article bore the name of Dr Paul Schliemann, described as a grandson of the discoverer of Troy.

The article claimed that he was in possession of secret documents left by his celebrated grandfather which contained extraordinary revelations about the lost continent of Atlantis of profound importance for the civilised world. It was a dramatic, not to say melodramatic, story. The papers were in a sealed envelope with the following inscription: 'This can be opened only by a member of [the Schliemann] family who solemnly vows to devote his life to the researches outlined therein.' Paul Schliemann swore the oath and opened the mysterious envelope.

The first instruction it contained directed him to break open an owl-headed vase which had been stored with the papers. Inside the vase Schliemann found a curious, square-shaped coin, made of some unknown white alloy engraved with Phoenician writing: 'Issued in the Temple of Transparent Walls.'

With mounting excitement, Schliemann examined his grandfather's notes and came across a reference to a great bronze vase which had been unearthed at Troy and which bore the intriguing inscription: 'This was the gift of Cronos, King of Atlantis.'

Schliemann said that he then set off on a round-the-world trip in search of further evidence. He claimed to

have discovered two manuscripts which confirmed Plato's account of Atlantis sinking beneath the Atlantic Ocean. One, preserved in London, was of Mayan origin; the other, housed in a Tibetan monastery, was a Chaldean document more than 4,000 years old. They proved that civilisation had existed before the Flood.

Schliemann's article ended with promises of further amazing revelations. His story created an international sensation. It had all the ingredients of a classic suspense story, with an added ingredient of ancient mystery. But it turned out to be a story without an ending. The promised revelations never materialised. Paul Schliemann simply disappeared and has not been heard of since.

For hoaxers like Paul Schliemann, practical jokers, charlatans and cranks of every kind, the Atlantis story has an irresistible attraction. But while occultists and visionaries on the fringe of the cult dominate the headlines, there is an equally large number of serious students who receive little publicity. They include historians, geologists, novelists, politicians, botanists, oceanographers, archaeologists, poets, linguists and even one Nobel Prize winner, the British scientist Frederick Soddy who won the chemistry prize in 1921.

Atlantis appears able to command the most varied imaginations. It has caused rivers of ink to flow. A German archaeological journalist, C. W. Ceram, recently counted almost 20,000 volumes on the subject.

One of the more bizarre episodes in the Atlantis saga concerns the American prophet and clairvoyant Edgar Cayce (1877–1945). Cayce, a successful commercial photographer, had a remarkable reputation as

Like an inland sea, the flooded crater of Santorini stretches away to the horizon – a total of 32 square miles. Soaring cliffs nearly 1,000 ft high mark the rim – and plunge steeply another 1,300 ft below the surface. In the centre of the picture are lava islands, thrown up by eruptions in 197 BC and AD 1707.

Santorini's necklace of islands is only the debris of the single large island which, according to some theorists, was once the home of Atlantis. This sketch map shows how the islands look now and, on the same scale, how the concentric walls and canals described by Plato might have fitted on the site.

The multi-coloured cliffs of Santorini loom over the sea beneath a fringe of whitewashed houses. Here, at the island's western tip, near the town of Ia, the layered russets and blacks of lava and ash deposits are reminiscent of the red, white and black stones of which Atlantis is said to have been built.

a faith healer and, when in a hypnotic trance, saw extraordinary visions. A great many of these concerned Atlantis. Cayce claimed that a number of his 'clients' were reincarnated Atlanteans, and that they had one outstanding characteristic in common – a rare understanding of technical matters.

His picture of what Atlantis was like, which emerged in the course of hundreds of trances between 1923 and 1944, was remarkably similar to Plato's although he was thought not to have read the Dialogues. His Atlantis was a civilisation of advanced material and spiritual standards in which both science and technology had reached highly sophisticated levels. The Atlanteans had mastered all sources of energy, notably atomic energy, and understood the principles of flight. Their world had been destroyed in three separate nuclear holocausts which occurred in 50,000 BC, 28,000 BC and 10,000 BC. This last date corresponds approximately with Plato's dating of the catastrophe that overwhelmed Atlantis. Cayce was able to reveal, however, that most Atlanteans escaped annihilation because they had foreseen the coming disasters. These people spread eastwards into Egypt and westwards to Mexico and Peru, and the heritage of their culture was in some measure preserved.

Cayce's visions were full of obscurities and idiosyncrasies, but two essential elements can be discerned. First, the Atlantis he described as lying between the Gulf of Mexico and the Straits of Gibraltar bears a remarkable resemblance to the United States as it is in the last quarter of the 20th century. He also emphasised that it was the scientists and technologists of Atlantis who brought about their own destruction

through the misuse of the dangerous knowledge they had acquired. Is it possible that Cayce's vision was in fact a premonition: that he was looking not at the remote past but at the immediate future of industrialised America? His message does appear to be a clear warning to modern society.

Cayce's ideas seem positively moderate in comparison with some theories. Some enthusiasts place Atlantis firmly in the realm of science-fiction, transforming the island's ancient mariners into extra-terrestrial beings and equipping them with space ships, laser guns and cosmic rays.

The fanciful seekers of Atlantis have rediscovered the lost continent in a bewildering variety of locations, including the Andes, Tibet, Australia, the Caucasus, South Africa, the Amazon basin, Spitzbergen, Libya, the Basque country, India, Morocco, the Gobi Desert, Egypt, Mexico, Ceylon, China, Tunisia, Sweden, the Sahara, Siberia, the North Sea and the Pacific Ocean.

It is hardly surprising that, in the face of such inane ideas, the scientific establishment tends to treat any mention of Atlantis with a scepticism bordering on outright hostility.

An observation in the Bahamas in 1958 later led to a new discovery which was to provide further fuel for Atlantis fantasists, as well as some new puzzles to perplex serious scholars. Dr J. Manson Valentine, an American zoologist and a veteran deep-sea diver, noticed some strange structures on the sea-bed, but their pattern was clearly visible only from the air. They were curious geometric structures – regular polygons, circles, triangles, rectangles and dead straight lines extending over several miles.

In 1968 Dr Valentine found a giant 'wall' several hundred yards long submerged in the waters off the small island of North Bimini. The wall had two branches, running at right-angles, in a perfectly straight line. The construction, which was precisely perpendicular, was of massive stone blocks over 16 ft square. As he explored further, a much more complex structure was revealed which, with its quays and double jetty, resembled a drowned harbour.

The veteran French engineer and diver Dimitri Rebikoff arrived at the site. A pioneer of underwater photography and inventor of the *Pegasus* torpedo, Rebikoff carried out a complete survey of the area, using the most up-to-date methods.

In no time, the clear, blue waters of the Bahamas were teeming with divers and with equal swiftness controversy about the walls began to rage. Some observers stated positively that they were of natural origin. Just as definite were the arguments which

proclaimed an unprecedented archaeological site whose huge man-made structures revealed the existence of an advanced civilisation in remote antiquity.

But who had hewn these enormous stones? The experts were extremely cautious in identifying the builders. The pre-Columbians – Olmecs and Mayas – were suggested, but ruled out. Other candidates were the architects of Tiahuanaco. Parallels were drawn with Stonehenge and the mysterious outlines in the sands of the Nazca desert. But these theories amounted to little more than puzzled guesses.

Dr Valentine's new findings provoked further waves of speculation. Once again, extra-terrestrial beings were suggested. It was pointed out that North Bimini lies within the Bermuda Triangle, a part of the ocean which is famous for mysteries. And inevitably, of course, there was talk of Atlantis.

The geology of the area showed that the submersion of the Bahama plateau had been caused by the melting

---

Among the Atlantic sites that have been suggested for the lost continent are the volcanic Canary Islands off the north-west coast of Africa. This is the eerie lunar landscape of Las Cañadas, a barren plain of lava and pumice in the main crater of Tenerife, the largest island in the Spanish-owned group.

of the polar glaciers which raised the level of the world's oceans. This would give a probable date for the North Bimini ruins of 8000 to 7000 BC and would upset all the current theories about the peopling of the Americas and the origin of its civilisations.

The questions raised by the North Bimini finds were further obscured by one of those curious coincidences which unfailingly crop up whenever the subject of Atlantis is raised.

Edgar Cayce, it appeared, had prophesied the whole affair. He had predicted that Atlantis would rise from the waters of North Bimini and this resurrection would occur in 1968 or 1969. The great temples of Atlantis, he said, would be found 'buried under the silt of centuries and the waves of the sea'.

Serious scientists, searching for a rational explanation of the discoveries, reacted characteristically and understandably to this posthumous intervention by the American seer (who had died in 1945). They rejected any theory connected with Plato's Atlantis. Indeed, if the ruins had been submerged as a result of the slow melting of the polar glaciers, where was the sudden, mighty catastrophe that engulfed the continent? Opinions about North Bimini remain inconclusive. The general view seems to be that the structures are 'probably artificial' and date from 'a fairly distant period'.

Can North Bimini be so simply dismissed in the quest for Atlantis? What if Plato or Solon had located the island in the wrong sea? What if Solon had misinterpreted the information he received from the Egyptian priests?

They had used the expression 'The True Sea', but this did not necessarily mean the Atlantic. Similarly, the Greeks could have been wrong in assuming that the 'straits' referred to were the Pillars of Hercules.

There are other straits, closer to the Nile Delta. Although Egyptians are thought to have made remarkable voyages on papyrus rafts, they were not basically a seafaring people and their knowledge of the oceans was largely second-hand from maritime traders such as the Phoenicians and the Cretans.

Such doubts about the geographical reliability of the Egyptian account of Atlantis might suggest North Bimini as a location for the island. At the same time, they prompt another train of thought. It would be natural for the Egyptians, with scanty knowledge of the seas, to place a vast and mysterious continent like Atlantis in some remote ocean, and unlikely that they would accept that it was very much closer to home – in the Aegean. Without any real information to go on, did the Egyptians just assume that Atlantis was a place thousands of miles beyond their own horizons? Such a simple, understandable misapprehension could, by diverting the attention of scholars away from the Aegean, have created the blind alley down which generations of earnest Atlantis seekers have stumbled.

The massive volcanic eruption on the island of Kallisté certainly corresponds with the catastrophe described by Plato. And there is solid evidence that an advanced and decadent society was flourishing in the eastern Mediterranean before the tragedy.

It was in 1967 that the eminent Greek archaeologist Spyridon Marinatos began excavating at what has come to be known as 'The Pompeii of the Aegean' – the remains of an ancient city buried under the tephra on the island of Kallisté. Now known as Santorini or Thera, it is the southernmost of the Cyclades Islands.

Two years earlier the American scientists Dragoslav Ninkovich and B. C. Heezen had made a remarkably accurate reconstruction of the cataclysm at Santorini

3,500 years ago. They compared it with a more recent eruption, that of Krakatoa in the Sunda Strait between Java and Sumatra, in August 1883.

The sequence of events in this explosion is well documented and follows a pattern almost identical to that of Santorini. The Krakatoa eruption was heard nearly 3,000 miles away. The cloud of ash rose to a height just under 50 miles with a fall-out covering 300,000 sq. miles. The main difference is that forces unleashed at Santorini were four times those of Krakatoa. It is possible to get a picture of the scale of the destruction by considering that the tidal waves at Krakatoa, which reached a height of only 115 ft compared with over 650 ft at Santorini, still caused the deaths of some 36,000 people.

At Santorini, the absence of any human remains, beyond a few bones and charred teeth, suggests that the inhabitants had time to flee before the island blew apart – just as, according to Pliny, many of the citizens of Pompeii escaped. It is doubtful, however, that any of the people of Santorini survived the devastating after-effects of the eruption. The death that overtook them would have been particularly hideous. Trapped in their overcrowded boats by floating chunks of pumice stone, they would have been burned alive in the rain of exploding rock and burning ash and finally swallowed up by the giant waves.

It is impossible to say how long the destruction lasted, whether it was a matter of days or weeks. But it is known that its effects were felt throughout the eastern part of the Mediterranean basin. The ash, blown towards the south-east by the summer winds, was deposited over an area of more than 100,000 sq. miles, being carried as far as 435 miles from the volcano itself. Oceanographers have been able to determine the extent of the dispersal from samples of sediment taken from the bed of the Mediterranean between 1945 and 1965. The tell-tale Santorini tephra was found at a point 87 miles from the volcano, at a depth of 9,850 ft, in a layer approximately 7 ft thick.

Ash reached the coast of Asia Minor, Palestine and Egypt. The Nile Delta was severely affected. Some scientists have suggested that the wider effects of the Santorini eruption may have been the basis for certain biblical stories. The Ten Plagues of Egypt might have been related to the fall-out of volcanic ash. The parting of the Red Sea which allowed the Hebrews to escape from the pharaoh was possibly related to the tidal waves. The sea would have retreated from the shore before the arrival of the tsunamis, which would have been powerful enough to sweep away an army.

The volcanic crater of Santorini is one of the most remarkable natural sites in the Mediterranean. In the centre, where the volcano used to stand, there are two blocks of black lava called Palea Kameni and Nea Kameni, meaning 'The Old Burnt Island' and 'The New Burnt Island'. These came into being long after the cataclysm, but a few wisps of smoke can sometimes be seen rising from them, the last vestiges of volcanic activity in the area. The landscape is reminiscent of the surface of the moon, pitted, calcined, jagged and sinister. Santorini and its sister isles, Therasia and

---

Could this extraordinary fresco be a picture of the Atlanteans? It shows ships on an expedition to North Africa – and according to legend the Atlanteans were great seafarers. The destination is indicated by the people and animals in the painting. The fresco was uncovered in a house at Akrotiri, the ancient city found buried under volcanic debris on Santorini in 1967.

Moses and the Israelites watch from high ground as the Red Sea, which had parted to allow their escape from Egypt, crashes down on Pharaoh's army. Some students of Atlantis now wonder whether the Bible story may be based on fact, and that the parting of the waters was caused by the gigantic waves triggered by the eruption which destroyed Santorini.

The glory that was Crete

When a cataclysmic volcanic eruption engulfed the Greek island of Santorini 3,500 years ago, it did more than give birth to the legend of Atlantis. It destroyed one of the world's earliest great civilisations – that of Minoan Crete.

The first settlers arrived in Crete about 5000 BC, probably from Asia Minor or the eastern Mediterranean. They crossed the sea in primitive sailing boats, and sea-power became the basis of their civilisation. But, unlike many other societies, the Minoans seem to have been totally peaceful. They used their power to build up a web of trade routes, selling wine, olive oil and luxury ornaments in return for tin from Spain, gold and pearls from Egypt, and ivory from North Africa.

Knossos, the capital city, was built a little inland from Crete's north-eastern coast. Twice it was destroyed by earthquakes, and twice rebuilt. But at its height, Knossos and the nearby port town may have housed 50,000 people – making it the largest city in the eastern Mediterranean.

The golden age of Minoan Crete lasted almost 500 years, from about 1950 BC until the eruption at Santorini, nearly 70 miles away, created a tidal wave which devastated most of the island. In those centuries the islanders decorated their cities, worshipped their kindly gods and created some of the most beautiful workmanship the world has ever seen.

In many ways the Minoans were far ahead of their time. They built complex systems of drainage and used piped water when, elsewhere in the known world, most people had to rely on wells. And women were treated as the equals of men at a time when they were usually regarded as possessions.

Their religion, in fact, centred around a woman – a barebreasted mother-goddess. It seems to have been a remarkably happy system of beliefs. In one spectacular ceremony, young Cretans would somersault over a bull's horns, symbolising perhaps the power of man over nature. The bull was never harmed in these rituals. Instead, it seems to have been revered as a symbol of male potency, and perhaps as a reminder of the terrifying power of the earthquakes which sometimes shook the island.

It was almost certainly accounts of this bull-leaping that gave rise, in later Greek tales, to the legend of the Minotaur or Bullman. In the legend, Theseus slays the beast. But when Santorini tossed its head, the glory of Minoan Crete could not survive, and a fabled realm collapsed almost overnight.

Aspronisi, are all that remain of the once fertile island that may have been Atlantis.

Although the entire Aegean area is relatively free of volcanic activity today, it is still subject to frequent earthquakes. On July 9, 1956, at 5 o'clock in the morning, Santorini suffered another tragedy. A sudden, short earth tremor shook the island. The quake measured 7·8 on the Richter scale and was followed by tidal waves more than 80 ft high. The result was 50 people killed, 200 injured and 2,400 homes destroyed. The scars of this disaster are visible today, particularly in the strangely gloomy town of Ia.

Ia's atmosphere of decay is in sharp contrast to the mood of Akrotiri, at the other end of the island.

The sun shines on a street corner in Akrotiri for the first time in almost 3,500 years. The city, which was buried in a rain of ash from the eruption of Santorini in about 1500 BC, was rediscovered only in 1967. Now, as the digging goes on, scientists are wondering: was this Atlantis?

Akrotiri, currently Greece's most famous excavation site, is alive with the spirit of exploration. It lies in a small ravine where the relative shallowness of the tephra layer, about 30 ft, has made digging possible. Compared with Pompeii, the Bronze Age site at Akrotiri is hardly spectacular; but the romance of Atlantis is a powerful attraction, and every year

like Amnisos, which served the capital, Knossos, pulverising towns and palaces and claiming countless victims. The whole of the eastern part of the island was buried in a thick downpour of ash which destroyed the crops and poisoned the soil for years afterwards.

Knossos itself, which was well inland, was spared; but the other cultural centres of the east were abandoned and there was a great migration to the western side of the island which had been less affected by the great waves. Even so, the Cretan economy had been so suddenly and so brutally disrupted that it was never to recover. The Golden Age of Minoan civilisation was at an end, destroyed in a day by the unimaginable elemental forces unleashed at Santorini.

The Egyptians were of course aware of these events which were, after all, linked to disasters striking their own country. They would have known that a small island had been swallowed up by the sea and that the large island, Crete, which they knew very well, had been devastated. The Cretans, called Keftiou by the Egyptians, had for years maintained profitable trading relations with Egypt. To the Egyptians it would have appeared that the seafaring Cretans had suddenly disappeared. Their ships were no longer seen in the Nile ports. As far as Egypt was concerned the rich island to the north-west had ceased to exist, and the memory of its extinction was bound up with that of the great catastrophe which had shaken the eastern end of the Mediterranean. The legend of Atlantis was born.

And what of the advanced culture, the Utopian civilisation that is so central to the myth of Atlantis? There is a striking similarity between Plato's picture of Atlantis and the ancient Minoan society rediscovered at Knossos in Crete by the British archaeologist Sir Arthur Evans in the early 1900s.

Before the Santorini disaster destroyed its way of life, Crete had been a prosperous island empire, perhaps the leading sea power in the Mediterranean. Crete was the scene of the first and most original flowering of refined civilisation in the West. Cretan ships plied between all the ports of the Mediterranean. The Cretans were fearless navigators, prudent traders and highly accomplished builders and town planners.

They are best known today for the spectacular practise of bull-leaping, a sport or possible cult. They had baths, main drainage and other sophisticated aids to material comfort. Their island was large, mountainous and fertile but prone to earthquakes. It was a kind of crossroads in the ancient world, unchallenged in prosperity. Then suddenly, after 500 years, this brilliant maritime power, at the height of its glory, disappears mysteriously into oblivion.

The parallels with Plato's Atlantis are obvious

thousands of visitors clamber up the 587 steps of the Stairway of Phira to view the diggings.

On a clear day in autumn or winter, it is possible to see Crete, 68 miles to the south, from the site at Akrotiri. Crete did not escape the major effects of the Santorini cataclysm. Tidal waves hit the island within half an hour of leaving Santorini. It is possible to calculate the speed at which they travelled since this is relative to the depth of the sea. Between Santorini and Crete there is an average depth of 3,280 ft and it is possible, therefore, that the tsunamis travelled at speeds up to as much as 220 mph.

These great walls of water, 300 ft high by the time they reached Crete, lashed the densely populated north coast of the island, sweeping through great ports

enough; but neither Plato nor Solon could have been expected to recognise them. The ancient Minoan civilisation was unknown to Classical Greece. In Homer there is only an image of a much later civilisation on Crete: 'There is a certain land, Crete, in the midst of the wine-dark ocean, lovely and fertile, circled by the sea. Many men are in it, innumerable, and 90 cities are there; one tongue is mingled with others . . .' Even so, there is a flavour of Atlantis about this description.

Only 100 years ago, Knossos, Phaestos and Haghia Triada, the great centres of Minoan civilisation, were unknown to the world. The Minoans were as forgotten as they had been in Plato's time. Even when Evans made his remarkable finds, no one at first recognised the points of similarity between this rediscovered culture and Atlantis. No one, that is, except a certain K. T. Frost, who published his theories in an article in *The Times* of London on February 19, 1909.

The Minoan hypothesis was apparently not mentioned again until 1939 when a piece by Spyridon Marinatos appeared in the journal *Antiquity*. The discoveries made during the excavation of the port of Amnisos alerted Marinatos to the possibility that the destruction of the Minoan civilisation was linked with the eruption of Santorini. His theory did not take solid shape until, in 1967, he began making his own discoveries on Santorini itself.

It would seem then that the two pictures – of the splendid Cretan culture that flourished and was suddenly extinguished and which we know existed, and of Atlantis, the Lost Continent of legend – fit together: Kallisté, the Atlantis of legend, was simply an outpost of the brilliant Cretan civilisation. There are some discrepancies of detail, but these can quite reasonably be attributed to poetic licence on Plato's part. The great circular capital of Atlantis, for instance, probably never existed and was included by the philosopher because the circle is a symbol of perfection.

There remains, however, the knotty problem of date. It is possible that Plato made the error of multiplying his dates by ten and that when he said that Atlantis existed 9,000 years before his time, he meant 900 years. This would make more sense: 900 years before Solon's journey to Egypt would place the destruction of Atlantis in approximately the year 1500 BC. Moreover, there were no known advanced cultures developing in 12,000 BC.

Is it now possible, therefore, to regard Atlantis as a myth no longer, but as an historical problem that has been solved?

In one sense the Atlantis myth can never die, since it has so many equivalents in the mythologies of other countries. In India, for instance, the epic poems *Mahabharata* and *Ramayana* contain their versions of Atlantis. Egypt, too, has its own independent lost continent in the Middle Empire legend of the Castaway or Dragon island.

Even the impressive scientific evidence supporting the Santorini explanation has been challenged. There is a theory building up in favour of the North Sea island of Hellgoland as the site of Atlantis.

The most one can say is that, so far, Santorini seems the most likely solution to the riddle of Atlantis, but that it has by no means been proved beyond all doubt. Atlantis remains what it has always been – one of the world's most enduring mysteries.

MAY VEBER

The search for Eldorado, land of gold

The lure of gold has led to many strange adventures – few stranger than those which befell the men who sought Eldorado, the realm of the golden king. For centuries fortune-hunters searched the jungles and mountains of South America, performing feats of courage and endurance – and terrible acts of cruelty – in their obsessive quest for gold. But what were they seeking? A golden city? A golden land? A golden man? Or was it just a golden myth?

Since ancient times, the minds of men have been filled with dreams of gold. It glittered in the vanished treasures of Solomon and the Queen of Sheba. It was picked up by the handful in the river which ran through the medieval African kingdom of Prester John. Marco Polo, in his book of travels, told of meeting the Great Khan in a palace as big as a town, and decorated with gold. Golden roofs shone beside rivers as wide as seas; and the golden lands were Cipangu (the name used by early travellers for Japan) and Cathay (China).

All day and every day the conquistadores *pressed on through dense forest, clearing the way ahead of them with machetes. Sometimes they came to a river. If this happened towards evening they would emerge into the light blinking and dazzled. Then, perhaps, they thought they could see in the golden hues of sunset a reflection of Eldorado.*

For all the enchantment of these lands, the most compelling of all the myths about gold was to come not out of Asia, but out of the New World. It was the legend of Eldorado, the fabulous land of gold. Many men were to lose fortune, reputation, life itself, in the vain pursuit of this glittering prize. For they were searching for something that did not exist – a land that seems to have been based not even on a legend but on the misinterpretation of a legend.

Vivid evidence of the craze for gold, which raged like a fever in the veins of white men in the New World, came in 1530 when the adventurer Francisco Pizarro, tough and illiterate, set sail from Panama with some 180 men to plunder the treasures of the Inca empire in Peru. The Spaniards may have been ridiculously few in number, but they were bold, well disciplined, well armed and well mounted. And in Pizarro they had a commander of genius. When he captured the Inca

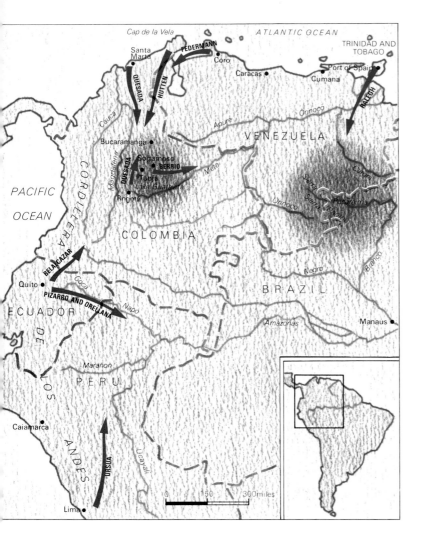

This was the vast territory covered by explorers in search of Eldorado. For a century it was criss-crossed by their routes. The two areas which attracted the most attention were the Cundinamarca plateau of Colombia, and the mountain range of Parima around the borders of Venezuela and Brazil.

emperor, Atahualpa, it must have seemed that even the greed of the *conquistadores* was about to be satisfied. For the Inca bargained for his life by promising to fill the room in which he was being held to a height of 8 ft with precious objects of gold and an adjacent room twice over with silver.

The first room measured 22 by 17 ft, and the Inca kept his side of the bargain, filling it with treasure to the level of his raised hand. Pizarro melted down the gold and silver but, isolated as he was in a hostile land, dared not release the emperor from captivity. Finally, he gave in to the demands of his captains, and had the Inca garrotted. The search for gold in Peru had begun as it was to continue – in treachery and murder.

The more gold the Spaniards found, the more they believed that even greater treasures must surely lie waiting for them somewhere through the dense jungles, across the wild rivers, beyond the towering moun-

tains. They dreamed of a land where gold was as common as pebbles; and the Indians they captured stoked these fantasies, telling them that if only they would venture a little further north or south, or east, or west, they would find the wonders they sought.

Most of the stories, not surprisingly, were richly embellished as they passed from one credulous group of adventurers to another. Others appeared to be pure invention. Juan Martín de Albujar, sole survivor of an ill-fated Spanish expedition, turned up with an astonishing tale of being held captive in a secret Inca capital and then sent away with fabulous gifts of gold – unfortunately lost en route home.

In 1535 Sebastián de Belalcázar, veteran of the Inca conquest and founder of Quito, the capital of Ecuador, met an Indian who told of a far-off tribe whose king sprinkled his body with gold dust before swimming in a sacred mountain lake. On hearing this story, Belalcázar coined the name that was to become engraved on the minds of adventurers for centuries. He called the mysterious king El Dorado – the Golden Man.

In some accounts this became Eldorado, the golden land. And so a hundred separate stories and legends became confused into one hypnotic legend. The search for Eldorado was underway.

The hazards of the search

Among the first to fall under the spell of Eldorado was Gonzalo Jiménez de Quesada, who in 1536 led 900 men inland from Santa Marta on Colombia's northern coast. Quesada, an austere, pious man, was a well-trusted official; and the governor of the province had set him the task of exploring the south by following the Magdalena river.

Quesada's expedition struggled through forest so dense that it formed a living wall of vegetation and each step had to be carved out with machetes and then widened. The men sank to their waists in the swamps. Snakes and alligators were a constant peril, and the party was decimated by fever, malaria, and the attacks of hostile natives. They were at the end of their strength when suddenly the countryside changed: the valley became fertile, and maize, beans and nuts were under cultivation. Quesada and his companions had reached the land of the Chibchas.

As the *conquistadores*, by now reduced to fewer than 200 men, entered the Chibcha villages that were strewn across Colombia's Cundinamarca plateau, they found salt which they were told the Indians bartered for the gold of Eldorado. 'Find salt and you will find gold' became the rallying call of the expedition.

The Chibchas had three rulers. After the Spaniards had routed the army of the king of the southernmost state, the invaders found some gold and a few emeralds. But, an Indian told them, if it was gold and emeralds they sought, they should go north, where there was an abundance of both. With that Quesada's expedition turned north, quickly subdued the second of the Chibcha kings and found plenty of the 'little green stones' the Indian had spoken of. Quesada eventually collected several thousand of the gems.

In the Chibcha village of Sogamoso the Spaniards encountered a temple dedicated to the sun god. Inside were the mummified remains of numerous Chibcha kings. Emeralds filled their eye sockets and gold ornaments covered their desiccated bodies. Predictably enough, the Chibchas claimed that they had obtained the gold from another Indian tribe in exchange for bars of salt, and they told the Spaniards of a lake called Guatavita, a few days' march away. At Guatavita, so the story went, a strange annual ceremony took place – the ceremony of the Golden Man.

The Indians said that the king of the region, decked in gold ornaments and with powdered gold sprinkled over his body, set out from the shore on a balsa-wood raft. The Spaniards listened fascinated as the Chibchas described how the smoke from bonfires ringing the shore drifted across the lake. As the assembled multitude sounded various instruments, the king slipped into the water and the gold dust was washed from his body. Simultaneously, priests and nobles threw precious ornaments into the lake as an offering to the sun.

The Spaniards immediately set out for the lake with an Indian guide. They found it to be a deep, dark expanse of water set in the crater of an extinct volcano almost 9,000 ft above sea level. There were a few huts, but of the Golden Man and his people there was no sign. The treasure – if there was any – was on the bottom of the lake.

Quesada was not just a gold-hunter but a would-be builder of empires. Before leaving to make fresh conquests, he founded the city of Santa Fé de Bogotá – now the capital of Colombia – on a site 8,500 ft up, which reminded him of the plain of Granada in his native Spain. He called the land New Granada.

But Quesada was in for a surprise. He was not the only European to reach the plateau of Bogotá. Two other parties of Europeans were approaching. One was led by Sebastián de Belalcázar, the conqueror of Ecuador and the first man to speak of El Dorado. He had left Quito at about the same time as Quesada set out from Santa Marta, and had gone up the Cauca valley by way of Pasto and Popayán. Reaching the land

The Andes: a formidable barrier which bristles with peaks and volcanoes. It is a land of bleak heights gashed by majestic valleys. In their relentless pursuit of Eldorado, such men as Belalcázar and Quesada braved all these hazards.

of the Chibcha Indians, he too sought the king who sailed on Lake Guatavita.

The second party of white men in New Granada was led by a German named Nicolaus Federmann. He had arrived in South America under the employ of the German banking house of Welser, which had established a colony at Coro on the Gulf of Venezuela with the authority of the Holy Roman Emperor, Charles V, who was also king of Spain. Federmann's force, numbering some 400 men, had set out from Coro to explore the interior of the Welser domain. But for three and a half years Federmann and his men had roamed about the mountains along the Apure river and over the adjoining plains and had found nothing.

Rival conquerors

After having wandered in search of riches for several years, the three expeditions were about to converge upon the Cundinamarca plateau in the same month of 1539. Even more curious – though the three original forces had been of different sizes and Quesada and Federmann had endured terrible hardships while Belalcázar had enjoyed a relatively easy progress – each of the three armies now numbered exactly 166 men.

The three captains warily greeted one another through intermediaries, set up their camps at respectful distances from one another and finally agreed to meet at Bogotá. There they arrived at a gentleman's agreement. Quesada gave Federmann some 40 pounds of gold and emeralds (Belalcázar asked for no compensation), and the three men agreed to return to Spain and let the Council of the Indies divide among them the governorships of the territories they had explored. However, none of the three was to be completely satisfied. Federmann died in obscurity, Belalcázar returned to his earlier conquests but died in disrepute, while Quesada had still another scene to play in the Eldorado drama.

Two years later, in 1541, another German expedition left Coro, led by Philip von Hutten. He eventually reached a fair-sized city called Macatoa. There he was told of a rich tribe nearby called the Omaguas. Hutten travelled on into their land where he was met with a volley of arrows, but he turned back filled with optimism. The little that he had seen of the region – rich towns and splendid houses – made him think he had discovered Eldorado. But this was his last expedition.

While Hutten was in the interior a dispute developed about the concession under which Charles V had bestowed on the house of Welser all the territory of Venezuela between Cape de la Vela and Cumaná. While men of law engaged in courteous dispute in a lawsuit instigated by the Welsers at the Spanish court, a Spanish adventurer, Juan de Carvajal, seized control of the colony. As Hutten was approaching Coro in 1545, Carvajal had him seized and beheaded. Ten years later, the military reality was recognised in law; the Welsers lost their case and territory.

Quito was one of the clearing houses for rumours

El Dorado, the Golden Man, is not a myth. This model shows him on a balsa raft, as he is rowed slowly out into the waters of Lake Guatavita. When it reaches the middle, the Golden Man himself will dive in. This solid gold model raft – similar to one taken from Lake Siecha in the 19th century – was found by two farm workers in a cave near Bogotá in 1969.

about Eldorado and a favourite starting point for expeditions in search of golden lands. In 1541, five years after Belalcázar's expedition set out from there, Gonzalo Pizarro, brother of Francisco, conqueror of Peru, left Quito at the head of 350 Spaniards and 4,000 Indians. He was looking not only for gold but also for cinnamon, which was said to be abundant in the kingdom of Eldorado. The expedition climbed the mountains and then descended into the tropical forests to the east. Shortly thereafter Gonzalo Pizarro was joined by another soldier of fortune, Francisco de Orellana. Together they came upon a river called the Coca, where the expedition – by now desperately short of supplies – divided in two. Orellana took a party downstream in two canoes and a hastily constructed brigantine, while Pizarro made camp on the river bank to await his return.

In the next weeks Pizarro's men made several sorties in search of game and fruit, but this did little to alleviate the party's misery. A warm rain fell steadily on the camp and the forces became sadly reduced by hunger and fever. Pizarro finally returned to Quito, leaving behind three-quarters of his original force, dead of starvation or disease.

Meanwhile, Orellana travelled downstream until he reached a much larger river. This he followed all the way to the Atlantic. In the open waters of the ocean Orellana continued his fantastic journey, eventually reaching the Caribbean. From there he pressed on to Spain, where he related his epic tale to Charles V.

Although the emperor reacted somewhat coolly to the adventurer's tale – he feared the territory traversed belonged to Portugal – Charles did grant Orellana the governorship of a South American province to be known as New Andalusia. Plagued with difficulties in raising funds to colonise his province, Orellana died without ever retracing his route – and without ever finding the land of gold or cinnamon.

Women archers of the Amazon

But on his voyage down the great river, Orellana had come across a tribe whose long-haired women drew a bow better than any man. Chance had brought a myth into the realm of reality. Orellana gave the name Amazonas (later Amazon) to the river, because these warrior-women recalled for him the Greek legend of the Amazons.

The myth of gold can sometimes be useful to colonial rulers. This was so in the case of Luís Hurtado de Mendoza, viceroy of Peru, who in 1560 was trying to establish some order in a country torn by recent rebel-

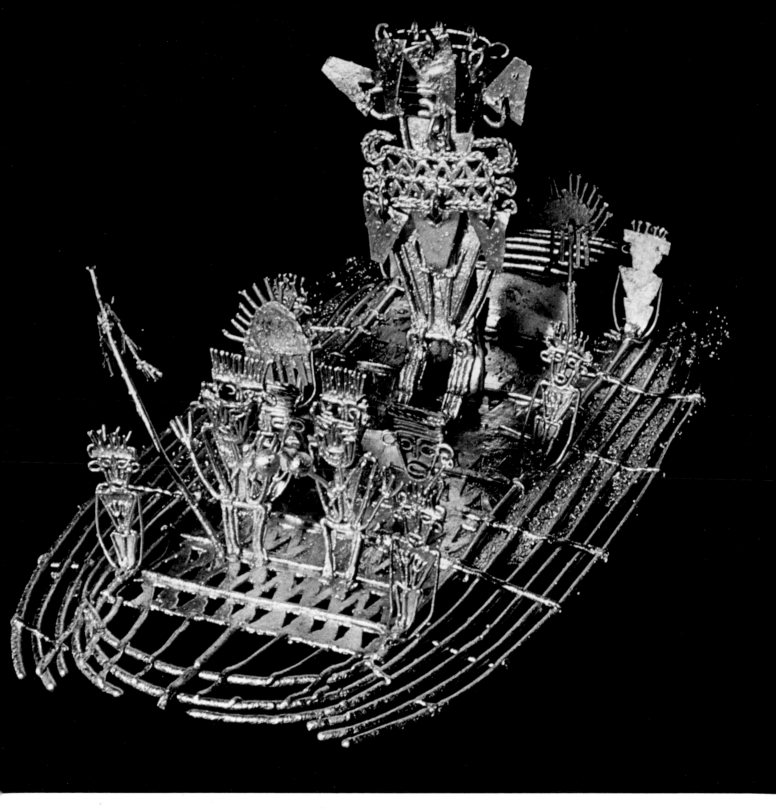

lions and filled with soldiers of fortune. To keep the malcontents from stirring new trouble, he encouraged the formation of a new expedition in search of the fabled Eldorado. So, 20 years after the abortive attempts of Gonzalo Pizarro and Francisco de Orellana, another expedition set out after the elusive goal.

It left Lima under the command of Pedro de Ursúa. Part of their route was to be the same as Orellana's. They followed tributaries until they reached the Amazon and started down its lengthy course. Soon after-

wards, the Spaniards fell to quarrelling amongst themselves. Lope de Aguirre, an ambitious and unscrupulous member of the expedition, entered into a conspiracy to overthrow Ursúa from command and permitted his assassination by fellow mutineers. Directly or indirectly, Aguirre was responsible for the deaths of some 80 members of the expedition, which eventually made its way to the Orinoco river and into Venezuela.

Back in Colombia, an old Eldorado hand, Quesada, continued to be haunted by the idea of a lake which he

A Spanish ship might have sailed down a tributary of the Amazon, such as this. The muddy waters meander endlessly between banks from which rise dense walls of vegetation. The conquistadores pressed on and on, always hoping that the next bank would be the one beyond which lay Eldorado.

financial loss was a staggering 200,000 gold pesos.

So, for nearly four decades expeditions had criss-crossed northern South America – from the Andean highlands of what is now Peru, Ecuador and Colombia to the forests of Venezuela and Brazil. Each expedition had lasted from two to five years. The cost had been huge; the treasure, practically nil.

Towards the end of the 16th century, the magnetic lure of Eldorado shifted from western to eastern South America: from Colombia to Guiana.

In 1584, Antonio de Berrío, governor of a vast tract of land between the Amazon and Orinoco rivers, where Eldorado was now thought to be, set off from Tunja in central Colombia to explore the hinterland of Guiana. He had become convinced that the Golden Man was to be found only at a lake surrounded by mountains. Berrío headed into eastern Guiana, reached the River Orinoco, had a boat built, took his men and animals across the river and headed into the mountains beyond. He was sure that this was the area to which the Incas had fled from Francisco Pizarro's invasion, taking with them part of their treasure. According to one current tale, fleeing Incas had founded Manoa, a city of gold. It was this city that Berrío sought. Berrío's expedition was unsuccessful, as was a second which lasted from 1585 to 1588. But on his first campaign, Indians told him of a mountain lake to the west where the Meta joined the Orinoco.

In 1591, Berrío launched a third expedition and travelled down the Orinoco. After a perilous journey in which he had to fight off frequent attacks by Indians, Berrío crossed Guiana from west to east, then sailed to the island of Trinidad where he established a settlement as a base for future expeditions to Eldorado.

It was on Trinidad, in 1595, that he met the redoubtable English adventurer Sir Walter Ralegh, who was searching for new sources of wealth for his queen, Elizabeth I. During some mighty drinking bouts between the Spaniards and the English, Ralegh picked up all the information he could about Berrío's expedition to Guiana, the Orinoco and the route to Manoa. It is not clear what happened to Berrío then, but it is possible that he was held prisoner by the English so that they could follow the trail that he had blazed. However, Berrío eventually turned up again, presumably having been freed by the English.

Armed with the information gained from the Spaniards, Ralegh set off into Guiana to explore the area which today makes up south-east Venezuela, Guyana and Surinam. He would write rapturously of Manoa, the 'imperial golden city' with countless palaces. He would also describe a vast inland lake, as big as the Caspian Sea, known as Lake Parima. Ralegh

thought must have treasures hidden in its depths. In 1568, the elderly Quesada received royal approval for a new expedition. Almost all his former companions were dead. But Quesada had Eldorado fever. He left Bogotá with a force of 2,800 men. They hunted in vain for three years before Quesada gave up.

When he arrived back at Bogotá he brought with him only 64 of the 1,300 Spaniards who had started out, only four Indian porters out of 1,500 who began the journey, and only 18 horses out of 1,100. The

had not actually seen any of this – as his writings make clear – but Berrío had, or knew men who claimed to have, and their enthusiasm proved infectious. From this time on men would speak of Lake Parima in much the same way that they once spoke of Lake Guatavita, where El Dorado was said to hold his rites.

It was after this expedition that Ralegh published his journal *The Discovery of the Empire of Guiana*. It is revealing to note just how little Ralegh knew of the land he was seeking.

'*The Empyre of* Guiana *is directly east from* Peru *towards the sea, and lieth under the Equinoctial line, and it hath more abundance of Golde then any part of* Peru, *and as many or more great Cities then ever* Peru *had when it florished most: it is governed by the same lawes, and the Emperour and people observe the same religion, and the same forme and pollicies in government as was used in* Peru, *not differing in any part: and as I have beene assured by such of the* Spanyardes *as have seene* Manoa *the emperiall Citie of* Guiana, *which the* Spanyardes *cal* el Dorado, *that for the greatnes, for the riches, and for the excellent seate, it farre exceedeth any of the world, at least of so much of the world as is knowen to the Spanish nation: it is founded upon a lake of salt water of 200 leagues long like unto* mare caspiú. *And if we compare it to that of* Peru, *and but reade the report of* Francisco Lopez *and others, it wil seeme more then credible, and because we may judge of the one by the other, I thought good to insert part of the 120 chapter of* Lopez *in his generall historie of the* Indies, *wherein he discribeth the court and magnificence of* Guaynacapa, *auncestor to the Emperour of* Guiana . . . *All the vessels of his home, table, and kitchin were of gold and silver, and the meanest of silver and copper for strength and hardnes of the mettal. He had in his wardroppe hollow statues of golde which seemed giants, and the figures in proportion and bignes of all the beastes, birdes, trees and hearbes, that the earth bringeth forth: and of all the fishes that the sea or waters of his kingdome breedeth. Hee had also ropes, budgets, chestes and troughs of golde and silver, heapes of billets of golde that seemed woode, marked out to burne.*'

The Urubamba river looks calm, and the current slack, as it flows through a gorge on the eastern slope of the Andes on its way to join the River Tambo, forming a main tributary of the Amazon. Many strongholds of the Incas were hidden in the gorges of the Urubamba. Was Eldorado hidden there too?

The golden king, El Dorado, is anointed with resin, then dusted with powdered gold. At the appointed hour, he will bathe in Lake Guatavita in honour of the sun god.

Lake Guatavita yielded little or no gold to the European adventurers who regularly tried to drain it in the centuries after Quesada's expedition first reached its shores. The wealth supposedly beneath its waters was never found.

After the death of Queen Elizabeth in 1603, and the succession of James I, Ralegh was convicted on trumped-up charges of treason and sentenced to death. The sentence was suspended and Ralegh remained in the Tower of London from 1603 to 1616. He was then released, though not pardoned, and allowed to lead a second expedition in search of Eldorado. This time, he claimed to have located gold mines. But in fact the expedition was as unsuccessful as all those that had gone before. Ralegh returned to England where the suspended sentence was imposed, and in 1618 he was beheaded.

But the golden king himself was not forgotten. The poet Juan de Castellanos, who was a soldier in the Spanish Indies, described him in 1601: 'This is the king who went without garments, in a boat upon a pool, anointed all over with essence of terebinthine [turpentine] over which a quantity of powdered gold had been cast in such a way as to cover him from head to foot, and which made him shine like a sun . . . In the evening, he bathed in the waters of the lake where all the gold with which he had been covered dissolved away.'

It was now the beginning of the 17th century. The road to Eldorado was littered with corpses of captains, soldiers and Indians. Except for a few nuggets of gold,

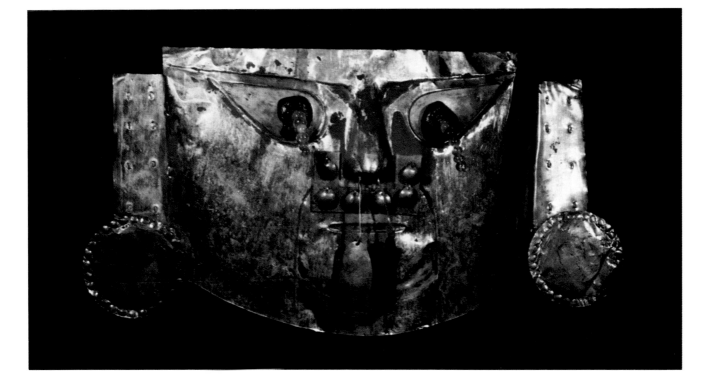

a sizeable haul of emeralds and some cinnamon, there was little to show for nearly a century of exploration. No one had found the Golden Man or discovered his treasure. No one had ever seen Lake Parima. Even so, the lake was confidently shown on maps.

In 1599, for example, the cartographer Jodocus Hondius, on a chart entitled 'New Map of the Country of Guiana Rich in Gold', showed a huge lake that he called Laguna Parima or Dorado. On its shores stood the imperial city of Manoa.

Following the publication of Ralegh's *Discovery of the Empire of Guiana*, Lake Parima was generally depicted by geographers as lying below the equator – in accordance with his description. In shape it was sometimes irregular and sometimes rectangular. A French cartographer, Pierre du Val d'Abbeville, showed Lake Parima astride the equator. To the west he had marked Eldorado and Manoa; to the north, Guiana. In the 18th century, mapmakers often referred to Lake Parima as the Golden Sea, but after that it ceased to appear on any map.

Right up to the end of the 18th century, expeditions in search of the lake continued. But as with all the previous quests, what the explorers sought always seemed to be over the next range of mountains or on the other side of the jungle.

One of the last Spanish expeditions in search of Eldorado was led by Diez de la Fuente. He set off into

Eldorado proved highly elusive, and the conquistadores were disappointed when they failed to find a land with pebbles of gold. But there was plenty of gold in the temples and tombs of the Indians of South America. Several centuries before the conquistadores arrived, the Mochica people of the river valleys on Peru's northern coast placed masks of gold encrusted with emeralds on the faces of their dead leaders.

the Caroní river region of south-east Venezuela, and there divided his expedition into three columns, one of which, under the command of Gonzalo Suárez Rondón, was convinced it would reach its destination. According to the Indians, they were only 20 days by boat or two days on foot from Lake Parima!

But a sudden attack by Indians forced the Spaniards to turn back even though they were so close to their

The Mochica people left many splendid examples of their highly sophisticated metalcraft. Having perfected the goldsmith's art, they created such unusual ceremonial objects as these golden hands with realistic fingernails.

goal. Suárez Rondón's subsequent explanations were vague, and it was then that people began to wonder whether Lake Parima really existed. The Spaniards gave up the search for Eldorado and at the same time abandoned most of Guiana, leaving it to the English, Dutch and French to divide up into colonies.

For a time, a sort of weariness kept explorers away from the dank, rustling hell of the jungles. But myths die hard. Sometimes the legend seemed more real than the truth. Chroniclers of the Lake Guatavita story tell us, perhaps without even believing it themselves, of hundreds of slaves labouring with makeshift tools to cut through the side of the enormous conical crater at an altitude of 9,000 ft in order to empty out the water it contained. The bottom became visible. Jewels glittered in the mud. A Spaniard stretched out his hand to pick up an emerald the size of an egg.

This is only one story among many, but this one is, at least, partly true. In 1580 Don Antonio Sepúlveda, a wealthy Spanish merchant from Bogotá, asked the

Spanish court for permission to dredge the lake, in return for which he was to pay the treasury one-fifth of the profits. Sepúlveda organised an army of Indian workers who cut a breach in the lake wall. Water rushed out and the level of the lake dropped 15 ft. An egg-sized emerald and several gold objects were recovered. Then the breach collapsed. Sepúlveda returned to Bogotá, where he died before he could mount a new expedition.

By the beginning of the 19th century the quest for Eldorado had passed to a new breed of adventurers, all of them men of science or representatives of business concerns. The first of these latter-day explorers was the Prussian polymath Alexander von Humboldt, whose interest in the Amazon basin was purely scientific. In the company of Aimé Bonpland, a French botanist with whom he had originally planned to tour the Nile Valley, Humboldt sailed for the Americas in 1799. In the course of their survey of Spanish possessions in South America the two would cover almost 6,000 miles, much of it on foot or muleback.

Humboldt shatters a myth

Humboldt and Bonpland spent 18 months in Venezuela, where their reconnaissance of the Orinoco basin took them deep into territory that had first been explored by men searching for Eldorado. When hostile natives forced Humboldt's men to turn back short of the source of the Orinoco river, they made their way to the nearby penal colony of Esmeralda, which stood on the very spot where the fabled Lake Parima was supposed to be. What they found, in place of the great inland sea described in Ralegh's journal, was a river with the same name. At flood stage the Parima river might possibly be mistaken for a small lake, but never for the vast body of water on which the imperial city of Manoa was said to stand. 'The Laguna Rupunuwini, or Parima of the voyage of Ralegh and of the maps of Hondius,' Humboldt concluded, 'is an imaginary lake.'

Humboldt and Bonpland's travels eventually took them to Cundinamarca, the Colombian plateau associated with many versions of the legend of the Golden Man. They made camp on the shores of Lake Guatavita, a water-filled volcanic crater which was as real as Lake Parima was imaginary. On a tour of the crater's perimeter Humboldt noted the spot where Sepúlveda's expedition had bored a breach in the crater wall in the 1580's, but the Prussian made no attempt to drain the lake.

Humboldt had no interest in the sunken treasure of Guatavita, but many others did – and reports of his journey to the holy lake of ancient legend touched off a

The Indians had no iron before the Spanish conquest. They did, however, have gold, and used it not only for decoration, but for everyday objects such as nails, eating utensils, combs and eyebrow tweezers. This vase, in the shape of a human figure, was made by a goldsmith of the Quimbaya Indians who lived on the Cauca river in Colombia.

new wave of expeditions to the site. It was calculated that if a thousand Indians had made the annual pilgrimage to Lake Guatavita for a century, and if each had thrown five gold trinkets into the water as some versions of the tale held, then nearly 500,000 gold objects lay at the bottom of the lake. Such a golden trove could run into millions of dollars. The race to find Eldorado was on again.

In 1912, for instance, a British company called simply Contractors, Ltd. arrived in Colombia with some $150,000 worth of equipment and a master plan for pumping Lake Guatavita dry. Using machinery that was considered highly sophisticated in its day, this group did succeed in exposing part of the lake bed, which proved to be composed of thick black mud and little else. In all, the gold recovered by these expeditions was hardly sufficient to repay a fraction of the cost of the expeditions themselves. Moreover, the most interesting find was more important for its historical rather than its monetary value and was made not at Guatavita but a half century earlier at nearby Lake Siecha – a tiny raft entirely of gold. On it stood figures

Cloud masses gather low in the sky over a landscape shaped by water. A golden glow lights the horizon. This was the kind of scene that beckoned men to Eldorado.

representing nobles and priests, and one who was indisputably intended to represent El Dorado himself.

The allure of El Dorado, the Golden Man, and Eldorado, the golden land, have lost their power over the minds of men, but they have been replaced by the reality of modern discoveries. For anthropologists there was the discovery between 1948 and 1950 of the Maquiritares and the Guaharibos, tribes living in the mountain range of the Sierra Parima. For modern prospectors there were discoveries of platinum, silver and emeralds in Colombia and gold, bauxite and manganese in Guiana. And above all there was the discovery of oil, the black gold of the 20th century, in the Lake Maracaibo basin of north-west Venezuela. Perhaps, after all, there is an Eldorado.

CASPAR MONTIBELLI

39

The land of the Queen of Sheba

*The Bible tells how the Queen of Sheba,
fascinated by stories of the glory of Solomon,
visited him with gifts of gold, jewels and rare spices.
When she left Jerusalem, this remarkable monarch vanished
from historical record. Did she really exist? Was she
a wise woman or a witch, noble mother of an empire,
or simply a seductress? For 30 centuries she has
inspired a variety of legends. If she did exist she
almost certainly came from Southern Arabia, where, in the
scorching plains, remains of the ancient kingdom
of Sheba are still visible today.*

The Queen of Sheba glides through history and legend like a beguiling shadow. Her story was first told, with infuriating brevity, in the 10th chapter of the First Book of Kings: 'And when the queen of Sheba heard of the fame of Solomon concerning the name of the Lord, she came to prove him with hard questions. And she came to Jerusalem with a very great train, with camels that bare spices, and very much gold, and precious stones.'

When she had questioned the king and been satisfied with his replies, she praised him for his wisdom

The fertile Yemini highlands – perhaps once the land of the Queen of Sheba – are sandwiched between the Arabian wasteland and the humid Red Sea coastal plain. The mountains attract rain, which is fed to cultivated terraces like these near the southern Yemen town of Ta'izz.

and presented him with her gifts of gold, spices and precious stones.

'And king Solomon gave unto the queen of Sheba all her desire, whatsoever she asked, beside that which Solomon gave her of his royal bounty. So she turned and went to her own country, she and her servants.'

The story is repeated, with minor alterations, in the 9th chapter of the Second Book of Chronicles. But in neither account does the Bible tell more than that she was a royal traveller of great wealth. It gives no details of her name, her appearance, her race or her country. In the Gospel of St Matthew, Jesus speaks of the queen of the south who 'came from the uttermost parts of the earth to hear the wisdom of Solomon!'

She is one of the most intriguing women in history, and has kept her secrets for 30 centuries. The biblical story of her visit to Solomon is told in a total of only 25 verses and almost certainly relates to a real historical event. But it is used simply to emphasise the power and wisdom of the king of Israel.

The Bible is generally a reliable witness. It is sometimes vague, when it considers the rise and fall of entire peoples in terms of mythology; often incomplete; seldom impartial, because it looks at history from the point of view of Israel, but never false. The people whose history is recounted in the Bible knew their most glorious period towards the middle of the 10th century BC. This period lasted 40 years, and covers half the First Book of Kings – the story of the reign of Solomon, written down, it is quite possible, only a short time after his death.

Wealth of Solomon's kingdom

At the time of the queen's visit, Solomon's power was at its peak. His garrisons held all the roads from the Euphrates to the Sinai Desert, and from the Red Sea to Palmyra. In the 10th chapter of the First Book of Kings it says: 'So king Solomon exceeded all the kings of the earth for riches and for wisdom. And all the earth sought to Solomon, to hear his wisdom, which God had put in his heart.'

Of all the emissaries to the king, only the Queen of Sheba is specifically recorded. When she arrived, Solomon's great temple and the royal city of Jerusalem were complete. She saw all the wealth of the kingdom and the wisdom of its king, and what she saw confirmed the reports she had not believed. Again, the 10th chapter of the First Book of Kings recounts: 'She gave the king a hundred and twenty talents of gold, and of spices very great store, and precious stones: there came no more such abundance of spices as these which the queen of Sheba gave to king Solomon.'

It is probable that her visit was for the purpose of negotiating commercial agreements, perhaps for the use of Israel's ports as a route to the Mediterranean for her country's goods. But the Book of Kings says nothing about the practical aims of her visit. She simply exchanges gifts and then departs.

The king whose legendary wisdom and power brought the Queen of Sheba to Jerusalem was no saint. Early in his career Solomon ruthlessly destroyed his rivals for power – among them his half-brother Adonijah, the eldest son of King David. And near the end of his reign, he angered God by his dissolute living and by allowing the worship of false gods. But never before did his reign did the Israelites know such peace, prosperity and unity. And never after it were such times to return.

Israel in Solomon's day stood at the centre of the land routes between Asia and Africa, and its ports linked the Atlantic-Mediterranean and the Red Sea-Indian Ocean routes. Solomon understood how much his nation would gain if he could take advantage of this strategic location. But first he had to establish internal peace, increase trade and acquire a fleet. Solomon ensured peace by raising a great army whose strength included 12,000 horsemen and 1,400 war chariots. When he had consolidated his rule over the tribes of his kingdom, he set about building alliances with his neighbours. One method of cementing foreign alliances has always been marriage, and among Solomon's many wives, the first was the daughter of the pharaoh of Egypt.

Use of Phoenician skills

Solomon looked to another neighbour, Tyre, for the means to extend commercial prosperity. His father had made an agreement with the Phoenician ruler, Hiram. In exchange for access to the Red Sea, the Phoenicians brought technical expertise to Israel. Merchants were sent to the port of Ezion-Geber, a biblical city on the Gulf of Aqaba which some archaeologists believe was on the site of modern Elat. Phoenician builders and seamen at Ezion-Geber constructed the long-distance boats which were their speciality, and mounted joint trading expeditions with the Israelites. Wood for the boats and building projects came from Lebanon where, with Hiram's consent, Solomon sent woodcutters to fell the great cedars. The timber was floated by sea to Jaffa.

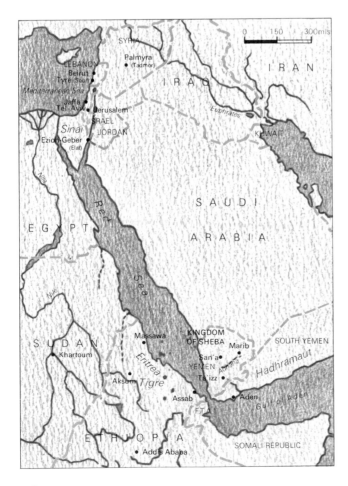

The Red Sea was a major trade route of biblical days, linking the ancient lands of Arabia, Ethiopia, the Yemen and Israel. King Solomon's merchant fleet was based at Ezion-Geber.

Artists throughout the Middle Ages were fascinated by the legend of the Queen of Sheba. This painting by the Italian Piero della Francesca shows the queen, with her retinue of ladies, being greeted by Solomon. The work hangs today in the chancel of the church of St Francis of Arezzo, in Tuscany.

Solomon's labour force was large, and some of the work was done by non-Jewish slaves. He sent 10,000 men a month to work in the mountains of Lebanon. At home, according to biblical reckoning, he had 70,000 hauliers and 80,000 quarrymen, working under the direction of 3,300 foremen, digging and transporting the stones for his great temple.

Solomon paid heavily for the Phoenicians' skills, ceding to Hiram 20 Galilean towns. But the joint commercial ventures launched at Ezion-Geber soon brought fabulous returns. The Phoenician fleet and Israeli merchant ships apparently returned from their long voyages to far distant shores heavily loaded with gold, silver, ivory and exotic animals. More wealth was collected in the form of gifts and tributes from foreign rulers and from the taxes levied on the camel caravans coming from Arabia and the East. In the Second Book of Chronicles, it is said that Solomon 'made silver and

gold at Jerusalem as plenteous as stones . . .'

Solomon amassed gold at a fantastic rate – perhaps several tons a year. There was so much that he used it to cover the walls of the great temple he had built to the glory of Jehovah. This huge structure of stone and Lebanese cedar had taken seven years to complete. On its walls, Solomon hung 200 shields and 300 bucklers of beaten gold. He sat on an elaborate throne of ivory overlaid with gold, and all his utensils and drinking vessels were of gold.

But the unity of his state and its wealth did not

The great dam at Marib was symbolic of Sheba at the height of its powers. It was built to store rainwater for the irrigation system that turned this harsh land into a fertile plain. The dam collapsed in AD 543. Now only these 60-ft-high anchorage points, and some irrigation channels, remain.

The ruins of this temple in the sands at Marib are known to the Yemenis as Haram Bilkis. The colonnade was part of a temple dedicated to Ilumquh, god of the moon. Hamdani, a 10th-century Arab historian, wrote that at one time kings would prostrate themselves there each day before carved images of the sun and the crescent moon.

endure. The Bible tells how God became angry with the wayward, luxury-loving king. When Solomon died, the northern tribes revolted and the kingdom was divided into two. Under the rule of Solomon's son Rehoboam, the sea route was lost and in the fifth year of his reign Jerusalem was attacked by the Egyptian king Shishak.

The temple was pillaged and all the treasures carried off. The last vestiges of the kingdom were destroyed more than three centuries later by Nebuchadrezzar, king of Babylon. Almost 3,000 years were to pass before remains of the great Israelite kingdom were uncovered. At Meggido archaeologists have found what may have been Solomon's legendary stables.

Legends of the Queen of Sheba

Although the Bible has little to say about the Queen of Sheba, tradition and folklore are much more informative. In the religious art of the Christian Middle Ages and Renaissance, the Queen of Sheba was a favourite subject. She is frequently found among the carvings and sculptures which adorn the Gothic cathedrals of France, England, Germany and Italy. Generally she appears as a queen, but sometimes she is represented as a sorceress. In French Gothic sculpture she is depicted as the *reine pedauque*, or web-footed queen, while a medieval German tradition takes this theme to extremes and transforms her into a goose.

A popular legend that grew up in the Middle Ages made her the prophetess of the True Cross. As told in the 13th-century *Legenda Aurea*, compiled by the Dominican bishop Jacobus de Voragine, the queen,

during her visit to Solomon, comes upon a bridge made from a plank that came from the Tree of Knowledge of Good and Evil which had been planted on Adam's grave. She had a vision of the Saviour who would hang on this wood, and she refused to step on the bridge, blessing it instead. Solomon had the plank buried, and it was later exhumed and became the cross of Christ.

In the 19th century, the Queen of Sheba played another role, this time in Gustave Flaubert's *Temptation of Saint Anthony* – a work begun in 1846, completed in 1874 and based on the legends of Anthony the Abbot. In Flaubert's story, the queen, as a personification of Lust, appears to the hermit Anthony in the desert near Thebes. She tempts him first with wealth and then with her own body. When she is rejected, she reveals a deformed foot under her splendid costume, and departs. Another French writer, Gérard de Nerval, was captivated by the queen whom he called Balkis, the 'Queen of the Morning', in his *Voyage en Orient*, written in 1851 after a visit to the Middle East.

In the Koran, the holy book of Islam, the queen is summoned to King Solomon's court after an exchange of letters between them. Solomon had learned of her existence from the hoopoe, a magical bird which served as his messenger. In Jewish tradition, a similar story is told in the *Targum Sheni*, an imaginative and much-embellished translation of the book of Esther. Again the hoopoe heralds the queen's visit. She meets the king in an apartment with a glass floor, which she thinks is water, and raises her skirts to reveal that she has hairy feet.

In later stories, the hairy feet become a hairy body which is the mark of a demon. Other Jewish legends identify the queen with Lilith, a demonic seductress borrowed from Assyrian and Babylonian myths.

Solomon marries the queen

In Islamic legend, Solomon solves the aesthetic problem of being wed to a hairy queen by having his genies invent a way of removing the hair, and when he has converted her to Islam, he marries her. She is called Bilkis in Islamic tradition, and is sometimes said to be the daughter of a genie. Today, visitors to the Yemen are told that the Temple of the Moon, a 4th century BC ruin near the ancient Sheban capital of Marib, is the Haram Bilkis, which means the palace of Bilkis the queen – the Queen of Sheba.

In our own century, the lure of the Queen of Sheba remains seductive. Her secular and sexual nature was a recurrent theme in the poetry of W. B. Yeats. She appears in *The Butterfly that Stamped* – one of Rudyard Kipling's *Just-So Stories* – and is an important symbol in John Dos Passos' novel *Three Soldiers*, of 1921. In 1934, the young French journalist André Malraux claimed to have discovered her white city while flying over the desert of southern Arabia. In a cable to his Paris newspaper, he described sighting 20 towers or temples still standing . . . on the north

Could this be the face of a god or priest from the days of the Queen of Sheba? This alabaster head was found at Marib, once part of the Sheban kingdom. It is in the museum at San'a, capital of the Arab Republic of Yemen, but experts are unable to date it. The eyes are of deep blue lapis-lazuli. Precious stones were so plentiful in the Yemen at the height of the kingdom of Sheba that, according to the Greek historian Diodorus Siculus, they were inlaid in furniture and ceilings.

The mountains of the Yemen soar more than 9,000 ft above the surrounding desert. In the regions above 4,000 ft there are temperate zones ideal for the cultivation of incense and myrrh. The Queen of Sheba took both to Solomon.

boundary of Rub'al Khali. Whatever it was that Malraux saw, no one has been able to confirm his story.

But while historical details about the Queen of Sheba are scant, ancient writings from many sources give very clear descriptions of the land of Sheba itself. It was one of the Arabian kingdoms bordering the Red Sea. Certainly it was well known to the prophets who came after Solomon.

Isaiah in the Old Testament spoke of 'the multitude of camels . . . dromedaries of Midian and Ephah; all they from Sheba shall come: they shall bring gold and incense; and they shall show forth the praises of the Lord'. Midian was located south-east of Sinai, on the coastal route to the Yemen: it was the site of a spring where the caravans stopped for water. In the 27th chapter of the Book of Ezekiel, the ancient land of Sheba is associated with the trade in spices, precious stones and gold.

The name Sheba actually goes back to Genesis where it was not a place but a person, a descendant of Noah's son, Shem, the father of the Semites: Sheba had 12 brothers, two of whom gave their names to the lost lands of Ophir and Havila. The names of the other brothers were also adopted by people and places in Arabia. One was Hazarmoth, a name that was attached to the large Arabian region now known as Hadhramaut. Hazarmoth and its neighbouring kingdoms of Sheba, Ma'in and Qataban were allied until the beginning of the 6th century AD.

Trade in frankincense and myrrh

Sheba was the largest of the four, a green place described in the Koran as 'two gardens'. Water for these 'gardens' was supplied by a giant dam built at Marib, the capital of Sheba. The dam and its complex system of canals and sluices carried water from the Wadi Dhana for 12 centuries. The dam was faced with enormous stones, so well fitted that their joints were almost invisible.

Trees yielding frankincense and myrrh were grown on the mountain slopes of the country, and trade in these products was the basis of Sheba's wealth. Diodorus Siculus, a Greek historian of the 1st century BC, described the riches of the capital city, including furnishings of ivory and gold inlaid with precious

46

stones, and engraved silver columns plated with gold.

Sheba and the neighbouring lands controlled the trade of the area. They took advantage of the monsoon winds – which, from February to August, blow towards India and the Far East and then reverse their course – using them as a natural navigational aid. The Arabians monopolised this trade route and kept the secret of the winds until it was discovered by the Greeks sometime around the beginning of the 1st century AD.

Overland routes were also established, and transport was by means of camel caravans. Domesticated more than 3,000 years ago, the camel could cover 25 miles in a day, putting Tyre, Palmyra and Jerusalem less than three months' march from Sheba by the coastal oasis route. Four camels could carry a ton of merchandise and go for three days without water. It was by these caravans that balm, myrrh and frankincense from Sheba were exported to the north, to Africa and the Roman Empire. There was an enormous demand for these substances, which were used in cosmetics and medicines and in religious ceremonials and burial rites.

Lost culture of Sheba

The natives of the kingdoms of Sheba, Ma'in, Qataban and Hazarmoth were Semites from the north, possibly the Euphrates. They worshipped the sun, the moon and Venus, which they called Ashtar, a name similar to the one used in Sidon, Tyre and Babylon. Their system of government by priest-kings was similar to the Sumerian system. Their writing and alphabet were similar to those of the Phoenicians.

Whatever their origins, these ancient Arabians were geographically isolated, a situation that worked to their advantage by protecting them from invasion. When Emperor Augustus sent a Roman army under Aelius Gallus, the prefect of Egypt, against the area in 25–24 BC, the invaders were driven into the desert, where many died from heat and thirst. It was four more centuries before the region finally fell to foreigners.

References to Sheba abound in classical writings, in Herodotus, Strabo, Pliny the Elder and Diodorus Siculus, as well as in the Assyrian annals and the Bible. The ruins of the dam at Marib and the inscriptions and architectural remains found in the Yemen corroborate

San'a, the capital of Yemen, is a city of earth and stone houses faced with painted bricks. An early Yemenite chronicler claims that there was once a 20-storey palace in the city.

these descriptions of the power of Sheba. But much of the mystery remains.

The queen made her journey to Jerusalem sometime in the 10th century BC, but as yet very little evidence of Sheban culture before the 8th century BC has been unearthed. Exploration has been hindered by Islamic attitudes, for Sheba was cursed by the Prophet Mohammed as a pagan land.

The great dam of Marib, which had been weakened by a long period of neglect, finally collapsed in AD 543. A hundred or so years later, the event was recorded in the Koran as an example of the revenge God wreaks on non-believers.

'"Eat of your Lord's provision, and give thanks to Him, a good land, and a Lord All-forgiving." But they turned away; so We loosed on them the Flood of Arim, and We gave them, in exchange for their two gardens,

The kings of Ethiopia claim direct descent from Menelik, son of Solomon and the Queen of Sheba, and this 19th-century picture from an Ethiopian manuscript illustrates the legend. At the feet of the queen is a lion, emblem of Judah and the rulers of Aksum, and elephant tusks are placed beside Solomon. But gifts of lions and ivory are not mentioned in the Bible as having been among the gifts they exchanged.

The legend of Menelik, son of Solomon and Sheba

The country which today claims the closest living link with the Queen of Sheba is Ethiopia. The last emperor, Haile Selassie, who was deposed in 1974 and died a year later, was said to be a direct descendant of a union between the queen and King Solomon. For more than 1,000 years this link with the legendary past played a central part in the crowning of the emperors of Ethiopia. At his coronation Haile Selassie rode his horse amid the din of clashing swords and banging drums, up to the gateway of the old capital, Aksum, 'the second Jerusalem'. There, under the sign of the Coptic cross, the last emperor of Ethiopia cut a symbolic cord and declared, 'I am the son of David and Solomon, and Ibna Hakim'.

Ibna Hakim, which means 'son of the wise', is another name for Menelik, the legendary child of Solomon and the Queen of Sheba. This version of the emperor's ancestry is a holy tradition reinforced as recently as 1931 when it was written into the national constitution. The story of Menelik is told in the legends known as the 'Kebra Nagast', or Glory of the Kings, compiled by an Ethiopian monk, Yetshak, early in the 14th century.

In Yetshak's account, the kingdom of Sheba extended across both banks of the Red Sea and it was from the region now known as Ethiopia that Makeda, the Queen of Sheba, travelled to visit the great and wise King Solomon. She was so impressed with what she saw and heard that she accepted the faith of the Jews. Solomon was equally taken with her beauty and intelligence, and he cunningly plotted her seduction. He held a banquet where many spicy foods were served and he told the queen that, while she was welcome to his hospitality, she must take nothing without his permission. During the night, made thirsty by the spicy meal, Makeda took a drink of water. Solomon accused her of violating his trust and, as payment, demanded her favours. The queen left Israel and, in due course, gave birth to a son, Menelik.

When the boy grew up, he went to Jerusalem to see his father. He was welcomed by Solomon and studied the laws and faith of the Hebrews. But finally he decided to return home. Before he went, Solomon's priest anointed him as the first Emperor of Ethiopia. Solomon was so taken with his son that he commanded the elders of Israel to send their first-born sons with Menelik and they took with them the Ark of the Covenant.

Thus, according to the legend, the divine presence moved from Zion to Aksum and the royal lineage of the Ethiopian emperors was established. The city of Aksum still houses the tomb of Menelik; and hidden somewhere within the ancient Church of St Mary of Zion, the sacred Ark of the Covenant is said to lie to this day.

The story of Menelik, spread first by Ethiopian priests and later by the Crusaders, had, by the 14th century, become part of the popular traditions of the whole Christian world. Politics and religion coincided here, for by accepting the claims of the Ethiopians, the Christian Europeans felt they were winning an ally against the infidels of the East.

To back up the Ethiopian claim, even geography was altered to suit the new faith. Up to the beginning of the 15th century, the Queen of Sheba's capital was popularly supposed to have been in Arabia. But in 1459, Fra Mauro, of the Monastery of Murano in Venice, produced a huge map of the world which showed the city of Sheba firmly located in Ethiopia.

In fact, there is strong evidence that, at one time, Sheba and Ethiopia were part of the same country. There are places where the Red Sea is only about 50 miles wide and for a long period there was constant traffic between the two shores. Shebans settled on the Ethiopian shore and remains of their great hewn stone temples to the moon god can be seen in Ethiopia today. Ancient Ethiopian manuscripts are written in an alphabet similar to that of Sheba, and excavations of a wall at Abba-Pantleon in Aksum have revealed inscriptions recording Sheban victories in Arabia.

Religious writings from 10th-century Egypt describe Ethiopia as the kingdom of Sheba. The two shores of the Red Sea retained their links until the 6th century AD when the Persians invaded Arabia. With the triumph of Islam in Arabia a century later, however, the Christian Ethiopians became completely cut off from their eastern neighbours.

---

two gardens bearing bitter produce . . . Thus We recompensed them for their unbelief.'

It appears that the Shebans – their economic strength destroyed by the collapse of their irrigation system and their society broken up into nomadic tribes – have still not been forgiven for their lack of faith. In modern times, there are several examples of the hostility of the Islamic inhabitants of Yemen towards their pagan predecessors, and this hostility has extended towards explorers and archaeologists.

When Thomas Joseph Arnaud, a French pharmacist, went to Marib in 1843 to collect tracings of ancient inscriptions, he was accused of being a sorcerer. On his flight over the mysterious 'white city' in 1934, André Malraux claimed that his aircraft was shot at. The Egyptian archaeologist Ahmed Fakhry tried to prevent Yemenite officials from removing stones from Marib in 1947, but he received only insults for his efforts.

In 1952–53, an American expedition led by Wendell Phillips and W. P. Albright was threatened and forced to flee its Marib excavations, leaving its equipment behind. Nevertheless, enough archaeological work has been accomplished to vindicate the story of a queen of Sheba.

There was a land of Sheba and it was a healthy trading state. It could well have had a queen, as did many other peoples in the area at that time. In the 3,000 years that she has kept her secrets she has appeared as a royal beauty, a temptress, a demon and in many other guises. That many of the stories that surround her violate the rules of time and logic has done nothing to diminish the lure of the mysterious Queen of Sheba.

ALEX MANTOUX

This painting on sheepskin depicts the basic features of the traditional Ethiopian legend of the Queen of Sheba. Angabo becomes king after killing a serpent, and later Makeda (the Ethiopian name for the Queen of Sheba) becomes queen. Tamrin, the merchant who managed her business affairs, tells her of Solomon's wisdom and she visits him. The final pictures show her son Menelik. The outlines of the pyramids are a reminder that in the Middle Ages the route from Aksum to Israel followed the course of the Nile.

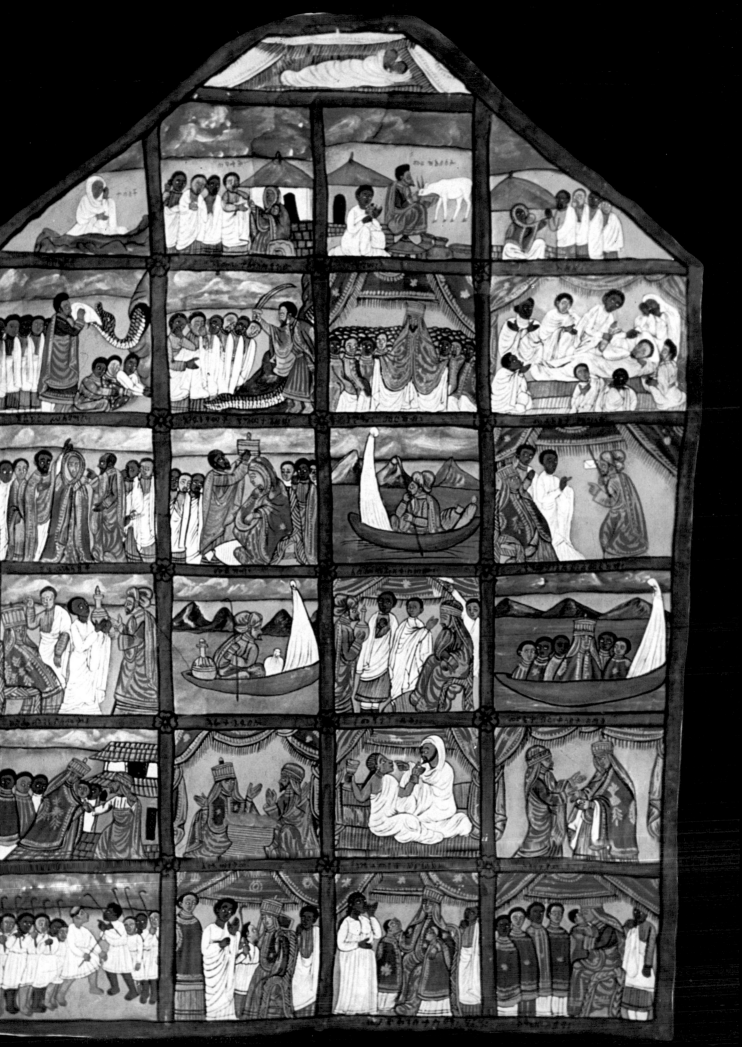

Who really discovered the New World?

Nearly 500 years before Columbus 'discovered' America, the Norsemen had already set foot on its shores. But some sceptics now doubt that they were the first Old World visitors to the New. There is increasing speculation that centuries before Leif Ericson made his landfall on Baffin Island, other navigators were braving the Atlantic — and Pacific — oceans. Whether or not any of these forgotten voyagers actually reached the Western Hemisphere will perhaps never be conclusively known.

Throughout recorded time, men have dreamed of lands beyond the horizon, of countries where fabulous treasures were to be won. Greek bards delighted generations of listeners with the adventures of Odysseus, perhaps inspired by voyages of Cretan sea kings of the Minoan Age, 1,500 years before the birth of Christ.

Stories of the Phoenician voyagers told by Herodotus, the Greek historian of the 5th century BC, were evidence that men could sail thousands of miles without falling off the earth's edge, as many feared. Intrepid monks from early Christian Ireland sailed

Sweeping down from Scandinavia in their dragon-prowed longships, the Vikings spread terror and death to western and southern Europe. But not all Norsemen were pirates. Some of their most daring voyagers were traders and settlers, who discovered new lands across the uncharted Atlantic.

about the North Sea in their curraghs, sharp-prowed boats made of ox hide stretched over a basket-like frame, and then struck across the Atlantic to Iceland. In the 6th century, St Brendan brought back tales of marvellous encounters on strange Atlantic isles – possibly the Azores. In the 9th and 10th centuries Scandinavian voyagers sailed through northern seas in their deep-hulled knarrs, inspiring Norse poets to tell of their exploits with hearth-side chants of Eric the Red and his son Leif the Lucky. Marco Polo's tales of gorgeous Cathay evoked the age-old vision of a direct sea route to the East, while Sir John Mandeville's *Travels*, a 14th-century best-seller throughout western Europe, told of dog-headed men and women, of unicorns and of Prester John's glittering realm of gold and emeralds, somewhere in Africa.

The century between 1450 and 1550 is justly known as the 'Age of Discovery', for it was then that this age-old longing for new lands was rewarded, with the discovery of the New World. But the great burst of excitement over America obscured the feats of earlier mariners. Modern archaeology is still uncovering evidence to suggest that earlier voyages were made. Perhaps even more is to be learned.

The ancestors of the American Indians, it is conjectured, crossed from Asia into the Americas more than 40,000 years ago by a land bridge, since vanished, over the Bering Strait. But if these were the only men to reach the New World before Columbus, an immediate problem arises: how was it that these first inhabitants remained in a primitive state throughout North America, while further south the people of Mexico, Yucatán and Peru created complex societies, with technical knowledge of a high order, centuries before the better-known civilisations of the Aztecs and the Incas? Much might be explained if the Indians of pre-Columbian America had known direct contact by sea with other cultures, which were able to penetrate theirs in a way that did not happen in the north.

Gods from an unknown world

Legends of god-like strangers are fairly common in the societies that came before the Incas and Aztecs. And it is fairly certain that in the eyes of primitive Indians any strangers bringing with them the arts of civilisation would have seemed like gods. But who were they, these gods from an unknown world? Men of many races have been suggested as candidates – among them the Phoenicians, the Norsemen, even the Chinese, whose fabled land of 'Fu-sang', across the eastern ocean, has been said to bear a passing resemblance to ancient Mexico.

The claims for the Phoenicians as the first voyagers from the Old World to discover the Americas start with the indisputable fact that they were the finest sailors of the ancient world. Herodotus tells how, around 600 BC, Pharaoh Necho of Egypt commissioned the intrepid mariners of Tyre and Sidon to circumnavigate Africa. The Phoenicians, originally the Canaanites of the Bible, were the obvious choice for such a mission. They were the traders and colonisers of antiquity, who established a far-flung network of commerce based on the gold and silver of Africa, the copper of Cyprus, the ivory of India and the iron, tin and lead of Spain.

It was these men who set sail down the Red Sea on the pharaoh's mission and returned three years later, claiming that in sailing round Libya (Africa) they had the sun on the right side. Herodotus scornfully dismissed this claim ('which some may believe, but I do not') but it was this statement which convinced later scholars that the Phoenicians had indeed voyaged around Africa. For it was clinching evidence that they had sailed south beyond the Tropic of Capricorn, where the sun crosses the sky in the north – to the right of ships heading west.

The Phoenicians of Carthage also sailed the Atlantic

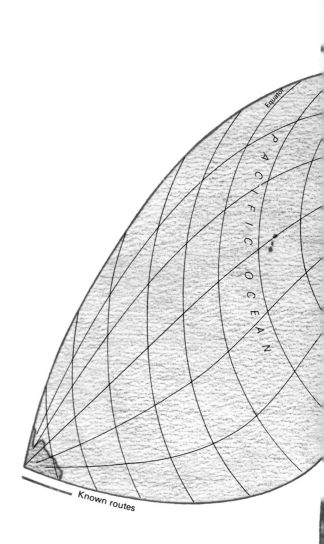

Known routes

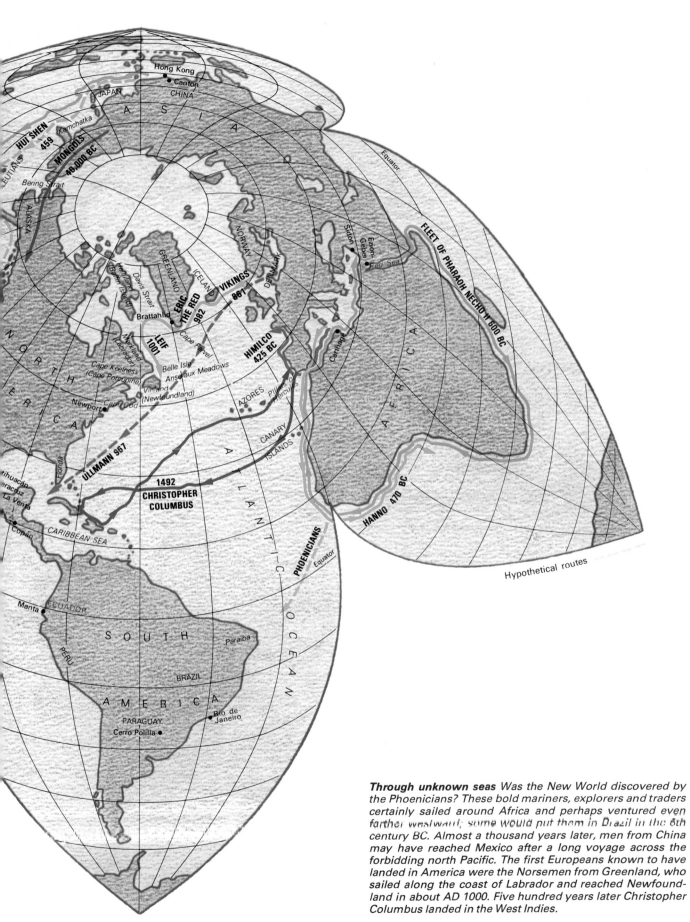

Hypothetical routes

Through unknown seas *Was the New World discovered by the Phoenicians? These bold mariners, explorers and traders certainly sailed around Africa and perhaps ventured even farther westward; some would put them in Brazil in the 6th century BC. Almost a thousand years later, men from China may have reached Mexico after a long voyage across the forbidding north Pacific. The first Europeans known to have landed in America were the Norsemen from Greenland, who sailed along the coast of Labrador and reached Newfoundland in about AD 1000. Five hundred years later Christopher Columbus landed in the West Indies.*

53

in triremes – galleys with three decks of rowers – going round Iberia and the Canaries, and possibly reaching the Azores, where it has been claimed that a hoard of Carthaginian coins was discovered in the 18th century.

It is also claimed that Necho's expedition may have ended in the first European landfall on the shores of South America. In defence of this theory, supporters cite the alleged discovery on a Brazilian plantation in 1872 of a stone with an inscription in unknown characters. A copy of it was sent to Ladislau Netto, Director of the National Museum in Rio de Janeiro, who pronounced it to be Phoenician and made a translation. European scholars scoffed, but in 1968 Cyrus H. Gordon, of Brandeis University in Massachusetts, supported Netto's interpretation. Nuances of Punic style unknown to 19th-century scholars, it was argued, showed its authenticity.

The translation reads: 'We are sons of Canaan from Sidon, the city of the king. Commerce has cast us on this distant shore, a land of mountains. We set [sacrificed] a youth for the exalted gods and goddesses in the eighteenth year of Hiram, our mighty king. We embarked from Ezion-Geber into the Red Sea and voyaged with ten ships. We were at sea together for two years around the land belonging to Ham [Africa] but were separated by a storm and we were no longer with our companions. So we have come here, twelve men and three women, on a new shore which I, the Admiral, control. But auspiciously may the exalted gods and goddesses favour us!'

During the last Ice Age the Bering Strait was an isthmus more than 600 miles wide with steppe-like vegetation. Siberian hunters ventured into this area from time to time in search of game. This huge land bridge linking the two continents was crossed by the first inhabitants of the New World possibly more than 40,000 years ago.

It is also possible to translate the phrase 'distant shore' in the above inscription as 'an island of iron' – and it may be more than sheer coincidence that the Brazilian state of Minas Gerais, near where the stone was supposedly found, contains enormous reserves of iron ore. It is also interesting to note that the Old Semitic word for iron is *brzl* – although etymologists are more inclined to trace the derivation of the word Brazil to a native wood that yields a bright red dye said to glow like the coals in a brazier.

Does the missing stone, with its disputed inscription, amount to evidence that the Phoenicians reached South America long before the birth of Christ? Probably not, for Samuel Eliot Morison, author of the definitive history of the discovery of America, dismissed the entire story as a transparent invention, pointing out that neither the stone nor the original copy of the inscription can be traced. Moreover, another expert, Frank M. Cross, also of Harvard, rejects the inscription on purely linguistic grounds, demonstrating that it is no more than a hodge-podge from different periods.

Another relic alleged to confirm a Phoenician land-fall in the Americas is the inscribed stone that was found at Bourne on Cape Cod, Massachusetts, in 1658. It has been translated as a proclamation of annexation: 'Hanno takes possession of this place' – presumably a reference to the Hanno of Carthage who set sail down the west coast of Africa in 425 BC in search of gold. Yale historian Robert Lopez rejected the Bourne Stone as 'an obvious hoax'.

Those who champion the Phoenicians as the true discoverers of America have advanced a number of other, equally dubious pieces of evidence in support of their theory. One of these is a map of the known world, executed in 1513 by the Turkish admiral and cartographer Piri Reis, that includes a remarkably accurate rendering of South America's eastern coast. It is said that Reis' map is based on charts that were housed in the giant library at Alexandria before its destruction by fire in 47 BC. Were this in fact the case, the information would almost certainly have been supplied to the Egyptian mapmakers by Phoenician sailors, who alone had first-hand knowledge of what lay beyond the Pillars of Hercules. A much more likely source of such information, however, was Portuguese navigators, for 1513 marks the midpoint of the 'Age of Discovery'.

Another classical source of Phoenician lore is the Greek author Diodorus Siculus, who wrote in the 1st century BC that the Phoenicians had discovered, in the sea beyond Africa, 'an island of considerable size, fruitful, much of it mountainous . . . through it flow navigable rivers'. To some this sounds like a reference to South America; to the Phoenician scholar Sabatino Moscati, it sounds more like an allusion to a nearer shore, possibly Madeira.

A comparison of the artefacts left by the ancient Mediterranean and Middle American civilizations has led to new speculation about contact between the two. Like the Egyptians, the Olmecs and Mayas wrote in hieroglyphs, developed a calendar and predicted the movements of the planets. They also built flat-topped pyramids similar to the imposing ziggurats of Mesopotamia, and they decorated these with bas-reliefs showing priests or rulers of Semitic aspect.

Another intriguing bit of evidence is botanical rather than archaeological. It is known that the Olmecs' successors wove garments from a strain of cotton that was once thought to be a cross between a wild American variety and the long-staple Egyptian type. It is highly improbable that cotton seeds from the Nile Valley floated across the Atlantic to Mexico and spontaneously generated on those distant shores; among other things, prolonged immersion in salt water would have killed the seeds. Could the seeds have reached America aboard a Phoenician galley?

The Chinese in America?

The next visitors could have been the Chinese, who recorded a trip made in AD 459 by Hui Shen and four other Buddhist monks who sought the earthly paradise of 'Fu-sang' across the eastern ocean. Their Chinese junk may have taken the great circle route across the north Pacific, swept along by the Kuroshio, a strong, warm current flowing eastwards from Japan across the Pacific. Having reached North America, the junk could then have worked its way down the coast to Mexico.

The Chinese found a cultivated people with 'a system of writing, but they have no fortresses or walled cities . . . and they do not wage war'. They also discovered the Fu-sang tree, which had 'sprouts like bamboo shoots that the people eat. The fruit is like a pear, but reddish. They spin thread from the bark and make coarse cloth and also a finer fabric. The wood is used to build houses, and the bark to make paper'.

Is this a Phoenician record, meaningless graffiti drawn by an Indian – or a hoax? The Bourne Stone was found in the 17th century at an Indian mission station in Massachusetts and bears engravings which some people believe to be a Punic inscription commemorating the voyage of Hanno, a Carthaginian prince of the 5th century BC.

To some these passages bring to mind the golden age of Teotihuacán, the first great metropolis of the Americas with its peaceful sun-worshipping inhabitants and its unwalled perimeter. The agave, native to tropical America, fits the description of the Fu-sang tree, except that it does not bear reddish fruit. The sprouts do resemble bamboo, however, and they are eaten. The plant itself furnishes a rough thread from which both coarse cloth and fine linen are made, and the fibre is used in paper-making. All this may be nothing more than coincidence, however, for Hui Shen's narrative also mentions horses, cattle and deer trained to draw carts. Before the Spanish conquest, the Indians of the region had neither wheeled vehicles nor domesticated livestock – and this presents what would seem to be an irrefutable contradiction.

In 1974 a man named Kuno Knöbl tried to test the credibility of such a voyage by sailing from Hong Kong to Mexico in a Chinese junk. He had been inspired by the similarity between the ancient Vietnamese practice of sending messages by means of corded knots and the Inca system of using knots instead of writing. The junk survived almost every sailing hazard but fell victim to a marine mollusc which infested the hull and devoured the ship.

Archaeological discoveries seem to confirm the existence of contacts between Asia and America. In Mexico an Austrian expert claims to have found pre-Columbian terracotta heads of markedly Chinese, Phoenician and Negroid aspect; and amid Maya ruins at Copán stands a great upright stone with what to some observers resembles a carved elephant head and turbaned mahout; near by there is another stone carved with what could be the features of a mandarin. But Mayan experts are far from agreed that these sculptures indicate a direct link with Asia.

Even so, the noted anthropologist Robert von Heine-Geldern has postulated the amazing theory of a 'vast maritime expansion' from China across the Pacific, starting in 700 BC. He predicts: 'Future research will probably indicate that Asiatic influences . . .

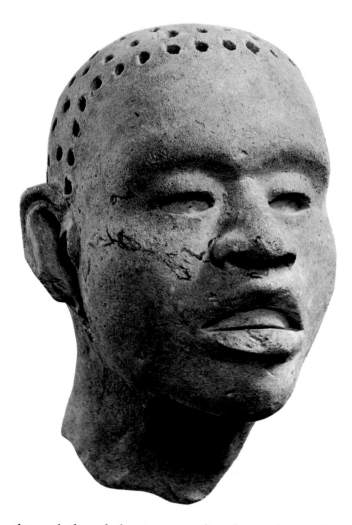

The Negroid features of this head from Veracruz, in Mexico, seem to testify to the presence in pre-Columbian America of black Africans, who were often galley slaves on Phoenician ships. Black slaves were first introduced by the Spaniards at the beginning of the 16th century.

Could this three-dimensional portrait by a pre-Columbian artist have been intended to portray a Phoenician? The delicate, elongated oval face, the large, aquiline nose and the pointed beard seem more Semitic than Indian. The head is crowned with a tiara and decorates an incense burner excavated at Iximché in Guatemala.

changed the whole structure of native society and transformed the ancient tribal cultures into civilisations more or less comparable to those of the Old World.'

One of the most intriguing of all speculations about the pre-Columbian discoverers of America centres around the enigmatic figure of Quetzalcóatl, the Plumed Serpent, God of Wind and Water.

Quetzalcóatl, according to one version of the legend, was a Toltec prince of Tóllan, 40 miles north of the later Aztec capital of Tenochtitlan (Mexico City), who reigned in the 10th century AD. Secluded in his palace, never gazing into a mirror, Quetzalcóatl aroused anger by offering butterflies as sacrifices to the gods, instead of human beings. Wizards tempted him to drink and to seduce a priestess, then gave him a mirror to study his corrupted or aged (opinions vary) face. His royal mystery destroyed, Quetzalcóatl rushed to the coast, near the modern Veracruz, and sailed away on a raft, vowing to reappear one day to recover his hoard of treasure and to rule his people.

When, 500 years later, Hernán Cortés and his band of bearded *conquistadores* landed from Cuba not far from the same spot, Montezuma II, the Aztec ruler, received first-hand reports of the visitors which accorded closely with Toltec tradition of Quetzalcóatl's

explorer and man of letters Jacques de Mahieu.

In 1970 Mahieu discovered what he claimed were traces of runes – characters inscribed in the old Germanic alphabet. With them were a helmeted and bearded figure carved in rock and what appeared to be outlines of Viking ships on a carved cross. From these, he formulated an elaborate theory that Norsemen, on their way to Iceland in AD 967, were blown off course to Mexico; that their leader, Ullmann, became the original Quetzalcóatl; and that over the next 300 years they established societies in Mexico and the Andean high plateau.

There are a number of objections to Mahieu's hypothesis, not least the fact that similar interpretations of possible rock weathering or scratches of unknown date have been made in America for many years without convincing results. But from the remote, rock-girt realm of the Incas comes a tale which may lend credence to Mahieu. In his *Royal Commentaries of the Incas*, Garcilaso de la Vega (1540–1616), son of an Inca princess, tells of the tradition of giants arriving by sea many centuries ago: 'A number of large cane

Some claim that the Chinese reached Mexico in the 5th century AD. A jade head with markedly Oriental features, carved by an Olmec sculptor and found at Tenango, has been taken to indicate that links may have existed in ancient times between Middle America and China.

return. According to the prediction, the god and his retinue would return as 'bearded white men, dressed in different colours and on their heads round coverings . . . mounted on beasts similar to deer and others on eagles which would fly like the wind'.

Was Quetzalcóatl a Viking?

The story of Quetzalcóatl is the most striking legend known of a strange foreign ruler in America, long before Columbus. And the descriptions of a prince aloof from his subjects, with no mirrors in his palace and an uncommon distaste for human sacrifice, might suggest an alien usurper supplanting a ruler whom his people did not know was dead, and who fled when his true identity was revealed. Many suggestions have been made as to this man's origins, and one of the most ingenious is that recently put forward by the French

This head was another mysterious find in Guatemala. Is it evidence that Asians discovered America before Columbus? Those who read this statue's features as Oriental are inclined to think so, for they doubt that an Indian artist could have reproduced the distinctive facial characteristics of a race with which he was totally unfamiliar.

57

rafts appeared one day . . . manned by males so tall that a normal person hardly came to their knees, though they were very well proportioned. All of them were bearded, wore their hair hanging down to their shoulders, and had eyes as big as saucers.'

Whether the Norsemen, bold sailors that they were, ever reached Mexico is clearly open to considerable doubt. What is no longer disputed is that these adventurous seamen did reach North America some 500 years before Christopher Columbus. The accounts of those voyages were preserved in the oral traditions of medieval Iceland, later collected under two titles: *Tale of the Greenlanders* and the *Saga of Eric the Red*. Both contain a wealth of detail that could only have come from first-hand reports.

The Norsemen began to settle in Iceland in the 9th century, and by AD 982 the new country had a sizable population. In that year the Icelander Eric the Red – already banished from Norway for killing a man – killed another man and set sail again to the west. He voyaged 450 miles, reaching after four days a land of grassy meadows and tree-covered slopes with seals and walruses frolicking in the fjords. Best of all, the land appeared empty, and Eric returned enthusing over 'Greenland' as he called it.

Eric recruited an expedition of some 25 ships, of which 14, carrying 400 colonists, with horses, cattle, sheep and goats, completed the passage. They settled at Brattahlid, or 'Steep Slope', the nucleus of Greenland's Eastern Settlement near Cape Farvel.

In AD 986, Bjarni Herjulfson set out from Iceland to join Eric. After wandering for many days beset by fog and north winds, the Icelanders sighted an unknown coast, wooded with low hills and quite unlike Greenland. Sailing north, they came to a flat, well-forested coastline, and further north still, mountains and glaciers. Though the men clamoured to go ashore, Bjarni refused to land anywhere, changing course and after four days finally reaching Greenland.

Bjarni had thrown away the opportunity to become the first white man to set foot in North America. But other Greenlanders were eager to explore the lands he had found. In 1001, Eric's son Leif bought Bjarni's ship, raised a crew of 35 men, and sailed away westwards. He came first to the mountains and glaciers last sighted by Bjarni – Baffin Island – and went ashore in their little boat, proclaiming: 'I shall call this Helluland' ('Land of Flat Rocks'). The ship continued down the coast, reversing Bjarni's voyage, until they sighted a level wooded country with miles of white beaches. Going ashore, Leif named the country Markland ('Land of Forests'); it is known today as Labrador.

Leif sailed on again until he found a place for settlement. A cape jutted out from the mainland opposite an island, and the Norsemen sailed up the channel between the cape and the island, beaching their ship in the shallows. They went ashore to where a stream flowed out of a lake, and when the tide rose they moved their ship up the river and into the lake. Here they built houses and passed the winter.

The lake gave them plenty of salmon; the winter was so mild that it seemed cattle could graze outside; and on the shortest day of the year the sun was up from breakfast to mid-afternoon. Then Leif's foster-father,

---

In the great hall of 'Leif's house' at L'Anse aux Meadows, situated beside a bay in Newfoundland, there was a huge central hearth with these long earth benches running round it. It was probably here that the comrades of Leif Ericson the Norseman met to feast and reminisce about the adventures that occurred on their voyage from Greenland to Newfoundland, somewhere around the year 1000.

Tyrker, made a surprising discovery: he found vines and grapes – and Leif named the country Vinland ('Land of Grape Vines'). When spring came, they loaded the afterboat with grapes and the ship itself with timber (both unavailable in Greenland and Iceland) and sailed for home.

The exploration of Vinland

Over the next few years four expeditions set out, and Leif's brother Thorvald wintered with 30 men in Vinland in 1004. Westward along the coast they found a fine wooded country and the gleaming white beaches they named Furdustrandir ('Wonder Beaches'). When their ship was driven ashore on a cape, and the keel was damaged, Thorvald named the place Cape Keelness. Exploring eastwards, they found three upturned, skin-covered kayaks, and under each three sleeping men. The Norsemen killed them all, except one who escaped to alert his people. The natives returned to attack the Norse ship and one of their arrows fatally wounded Thorvald. Dying, he told his men: 'Bury me here with a cross at my head and another at my feet and ever after you shall call it "Crossness".'

Thorstein, another brother, set out to bring home Thorvald's body, but his boat tossed about all summer in the stormy sea and finally returned to Greenland. When Thorstein died of the plague his widow, Gudrid, married an Icelandic trader, Thorfinn Karlsevni, and they spent three winters in Vinland with 250 Greenlanders, including Eric's illegitimate daughter Freydis, and assorted livestock brought in their three ships.

The first winter was hard, and they tried to add to their meagre rations by feasting off a whale beached in a storm, though its meat made them sick. But amid their privations, Gudrid gave birth to Snorri, the first white child born in North America, and according to the sagas the birth took place in the house built by Leif.

Exploring up and down the coast, the Norsemen landed at Hop ('Landlocked Bay') where they found wild grapes and wild wheat, and such an abundance of halibut that they caught them by simply digging trenches along the shore. Peaceful trading with the 'skraelings' or natives began when the Norsemen gave them goats' milk and clothing. But the mood soon turned to one of hostility and armed clashes. In one skirmish, Freydis panicked the foe by striking her naked breasts with her sword. But the Norsemen, outnumbered, fled to Greenland.

The final attempt to colonise Vinland was that made in 1014 by the redoubtable Freydis and two Norse brothers, leading a joint expedition of some 60 men and a few women in two ships. After reaching Vinland, Freydis turned on her partners. Resolving to seize their ships and belongings, she instigated the murder of 30 men and herself slew their women. Thus, with a bloodstained battle-axe, ended the recorded history of Norse settlements in North America.

The vague geography given in the sagas, and some contradictions between the narratives, have led to

Mastering the seas

Phoenician galley *This stoutly built ship was 100 ft or more in length, with a very high deck and curved prow. The body of the ship was of cypress and the oars of oak. The great cedar mast carried a huge square sail. The Phoenicians were the first to have their merchant fleet convoyed by warships. The bulwarks of these warships were hung with bronze shields and their long tapering prows were sheathed in bronze or iron. The Phoenician galley could carry up to 250 men, including the slaves who manned the 60 oars.*
Norse knarr *A broad-beamed merchant ship riding high in the water, the knarr was a solid, dependable ship for long voyages on the high seas. The mast was amidships and carried a square woollen sail. There was a single row of 15 to 20 oars and a crew of 35 to 40 men. The Vikings' fighting longship, or drakkar, though sleeker and faster, was better suited to coastal and river navigation.*

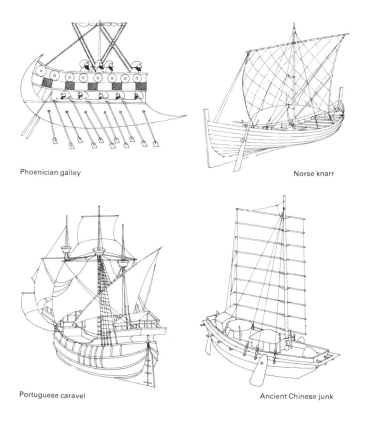

Phoenician galley

Norse knarr

Portuguese caravel

Ancient Chinese junk

Portuguese caravel *With its upswept hull and rounded stern, the caravel was designed for ocean voyages. It had three masts, and an enormous mainsail which allowed the ship to travel up to 80 nautical miles in 24 hours. The caravel was about 100 ft long, and by the end of the 15th century ships of advanced design carried a small forecastle. The navigators of this period had compasses, but still used the sun and stars to guide them.*
Ancient Chinese junk *This drawing is based on a model found in a Han tomb of the 1st century AD. The 00 ft hull was of pine and had seven watertight compartments. The cedar mast was 50 ft high and carried a sail of woven rushes. A mushroom-shaped roof covered the large aft cabin. No metal at all was used in its construction. Although a clumsy-looking craft, the junk could in fact sail as many as 100 nautical miles in 24 hours.*

Kept as a curiosity in the park at Newport, Rhode Island, this 26-ft-high stone tower has eight arches supported on pillars. Some people maintain that it is the work of Vikings, but it is more likely that it was built as a windmill late in the 17th century by Benedict Arnold, an ancestor of the famous traitor in the American War of Independence.

controversy over their authenticity and about the location of the sites described. The problem has been further obscured by claims for such dubious Norse 'relics' as the Kensington Rune Stone and the Newport Stone Tower. Allegedly dug up 3 miles from Kensington, Minnesota, by a Swedish farmer in 1898, the 200-lb Kensington Stone bore a runic inscription which, when translated, purported to be a message from 30 Viking explorers in 1362. Although it has been rejected as a fraud by Scandinavian experts, the Stone still has its supporters. The Tower, in Newport's Touro Park, is a 26-ft cylindrical structure with eight arches resting on columns, and is said to date from a Viking settlement on Rhode Island.

Though firmly placed in colonial times by archaeologists, the Tower, like the Stone, is still put forward as evidence by those who believe in Norse penetration of New England and the Middle West.

Modern authorities now agree on the location of Helluland, Markland and Vinland, the three main landfalls mentioned in the sagas. Helluland is Baffin Island, just 200 miles across the Davis Strait from Greenland's Western Settlement. Markland, with its wondrous white beaches, is on the coast of Labrador where the sands stretch for 30 miles. And the case for the northern tip of Newfoundland as Vinland has been virtually clinched by Helge Ingstad's excavations at L'Anse aux Meadows from 1961 to 1968.

Ingstad, a Norwegian authority on the Viking Age, was drawn to Newfoundland by early documents such as Adam of Bremen's description of Vinland in 1075, and an Icelandic map of 1590 which was the first to show the three Norse landfalls. He pinpointed L'Anse aux Meadows as Leif's site by its physical features: the strait between Cape Bauld and Belle Isle, the low, wooded hills, and Black Duck Brook winding from a lake where salmon spawned, through grassy meadows into a bay. Further along the coast looms Cape Porcupine, Thorvald's 'Cape Keelness'. Karlsevni's 'Hop' may be simply Leif's own settlement.

With his wife Anne Stine, and Icelandic and American archaeologists, Ingstad uncovered the sites of six houses built of turf and timber, the largest being 70 ft long and 55 ft wide and carbon dated to around AD 1000. It is similar in plan to Eric's dwellings at Brattahlid in Greenland, which have also been excavated. Most remains of the Norse occupation would have rotted away in the acid soil, but Ingstad's team did find a bronze ring-headed pin, a typical Norse clasp to fasten a mantle, and a soapstone spindle-whorl identical to those used in Greenland for spinning wool.

About 300 yds from the site stood a number of cairns from which bearings of the sun may have been taken. Iron slag and charcoal deposits gave evidence of iron working, using nearby bog iron, though the natives of this period – Algonquin Indians and Eskimos – had no knowledge of this craft.

Even the 'wild wheat' has been identified as lyme grass, a long wild grass looking like wheat and from the seeds of which flour could be made. L'Anse aux Meadows provides a neat solution in all except one respect. For grape vines do not grow in Newfoundland, although the grapes may have been the red and black currants, cranberries and gooseberries which abound there. Ingstad favours an alternative meaning of 'grazing land' for the Norse 'vin'. He points out that nowhere in the sagas is Vinland connected with grapes. But Ingstad's explanation hardly fits Leif's explicit description of loading his afterboat with grapes.

Sporadic contacts continued between Greenland and Vinland. Medieval bills of lading in Bergen refer to black bear, sable and marten furs – none of which are found in Greenland but may have been re-exported from Vinland. But by 1490 no European ship had called at Greenland for 80 years, and its people had vanished.

No one knew where they had gone, but a Portuguese expedition to Newfoundland in 1500 returned with a possible answer – that they had emigrated to Vinland. Gaspar Corte Real returned from this expedition with 57 natives, whom he described as 'white'. It may be that these were descendants of the Norsemen, who had gone native, intermarried with Indians, and taken to living in caves and wearing animal skins.

With Corte Real's voyage, the Portuguese achieved their first landfall in North America. They were such indefatigable sailors that this success was long over-due. For many years they had sailed all over the Atlantic. They discovered the Azores in 1432 and a feasible sea route to the Indies in 1488, to be traversed ten years later by Vasco da Gama. In 1500, while en route to the Indies, Pedro Alvarez Cabral discovered Brazil by accident, and in that same year Fernandes the Lavrador ('Landowner') rediscovered Greenland.

Portuguese writers, however, assert that the Court of Lisbon kept discoveries quiet to avoid encroachments by rival nations, especially Spain, and even claim that their navigators reached America before Columbus. They cite as evidence a voyage by Gaspar Corte Real's father, João Vaz Corte Real, in 1472, to the 'Land of Cod', or Newfoundland, and the Lavrador's claim to have started on a three-year tour of the Atlantic in April 1492 in which he beat Columbus across by a few days. However, all that seems certain are the Portuguese discoveries of 1500. Samuel Eliot Morison has exhaustively contested the whole theory of secret claims to pre-Columbian landfalls in the West, pointing out caustically that 'the only evidence of a Portuguese policy of secrecy with regard to the discovery of America is *lack of evidence of a Portuguese discovery of America*'.

The Portuguese historian Dr Antonio Baiao argues that 'the existence of other islands beyond the Azores was known or suspected in Portugal. It was in the wake of these indications that Columbus sailed'. And it was Columbus who carried off the prize, reaching the New World in September–October 1492, when he was 33 days out from the Canaries.

Ironically, the Florentine Amerigo Vespucci, after whom America was named, made no discoveries but owed his fame to a genius for self-advertisement, claiming falsely that he reached the American mainland before Columbus. Amerigo did sail as navigator on a Portuguese ship to explore the coast of Brazil, and his account of the voyage, *Mundus Novus*, gained a wide readership. Impressed by Amerigo's exploits, the German cartographer Martin Waldseemüller seized on his name to affix the Latin form 'America' on a 1507 map of the New World.

But Columbus' landfall was no accident, his journey was accurately recorded and his achievement led to the first permanent colonisation of the Americas. It is hardly surprising, then, that history credits him with discovering the New World.

BYRON LONGMAN

Leif the Norseman and his comrades left Greenland to look for a land which they had glimpsed on a previous voyage, and reached a wooded region with sandy beaches stretching as far as the eye could see. They landed, and Leif named the country Markland, meaning 'Land of Forests'. This part of Canada is today called Labrador. They then put out to sea again and sailed southwards to Newfoundland where they built shelters and spent the winter.

Age
of the
megaliths

Strange stones of western Europe

*Dolmens, cromlechs, menhirs, megaliths – there
are many names for the huge standing
stones which loom up in the
misty landscape of western Europe.
For long they were thought to be the work of
giants, but modern research has shown how
they were shaped and moved by
men of the Stone Age. But a central
mystery remains – what was the purpose
of the stones? Were they, perhaps, the
instruments of Europe's first scientists?*

Looming out of the mists from hillside, moor and forest glade, in a great arc around the coasts of Europe, from Sweden and the Shetland Islands in the north to Spain, Portugal and Malta in the south, stand the megaliths – great grey rocks, rough-hewn, streaked with age, often imposing, always mysterious. They range from single natural boulders to grandiose structures which would have demanded complex architectural planning and the labour of tens of thousands of men for centuries.

There has never been a systematic census of these

monuments, but it is estimated that there are at least 50,000 of them. Even that figure amounts to only a fraction of the total number erected, for countless megaliths (from two Greek words meaning 'great stones') have been destroyed by the forces of nature or by man.

The known and lost monuments once formed an enormous blanket of stone extending over western Europe. Today, often only the skeleton of the original can be seen. The bare grey stones were, in many cases, covered by great mounds of green turf and gleaming white quartz pebbles. Spread by their thousands along the coasts they must have been a dazzling and unparalleled sight.

Unparalleled indeed in human history. For there has never been anything like this rage, almost mania, for megalith-building, except perhaps during the centuries after AD 1000 when much the same part of

On a heath in Brittany the megaliths stand like ghosts. Cracked, tilted and stained by centuries of wind and rain, they are like thousands of other monuments which were first erected more than 4,000 years ago, and are scattered across Europe from the Shetland Islands to the central Mediterranean.

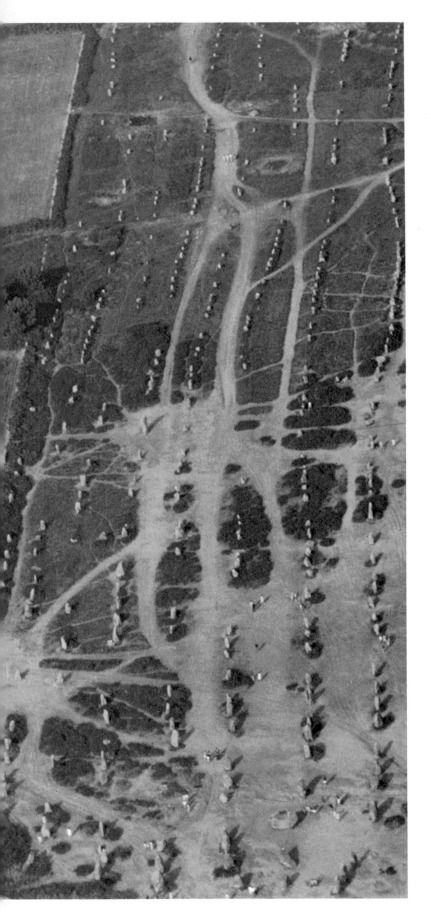

Europe was covered with what a monk of the time called a 'white mantle of churches'.

The age of megalith-building lasted from around 3500 BC to 1500 BC, and as far back as records go there has been speculation on the origin and meaning of these strange objects. In the Middle Ages, Christians viewed them as the work of demons, of wizards or of the giants who walked the earth before the Flood. In more rationalistic times it became fashionable to attribute them to the Druids, the priests of the Celts. Then careful investigation showed that they must have been built centuries before the Celts reached western Europe.

Learned men then developed the theory that the megaliths were crude copies of the more polished stone monuments of the Middle East and Homeric Greece, and that the designs had been brought by missionaries preaching a new religion, or by merchants following the trade routes which brought amber from the Baltic and tin from Cornwall to the Mediterranean world. Other students, less bound by fact or probability, insisted that the impetus for the building of the megaliths had come from the lost continent of Atlantis.

Who the builders were

Since there was no evidence to back up any of these theories, the air of mystery surrounding the monuments was not dispelled. The questions loomed as large and as puzzling as ever: who built these huge ungainly piles? And when, how and why?

Advances in knowledge in the last two decades make it possible for the first three questions to be answered, not with absolute precision – nothing can ever be absolutely precise in prehistory – but with reasonable accuracy.

The answer to the first question – who? – can be found by simply looking inside the monuments. Many of them are tombs and, where the climatic and soil conditions are right, these tombs have preserved the bones of the people who were buried in them. These bones have been examined in modern laboratories. They are the remains of the aboriginal inhabitants of the continent – peoples who may have lived there for thousands of centuries, perhaps with some slow admixture of immigrants from Asia. They were a sturdy folk, probably dark-haired, and some maintain that the present-day Basques, on the French and Spanish slopes of the Pyrénées, and the coastal areas of northern Spain, are their direct descendants.

Many of the tombs can be proved to be family vaults, because all or most of the skeletons in them show

These giant stones seem to be marching in serried ranks across the countryside at Carnac. According to local legend, a Roman legion which was pursuing a saint was turned to stone when the saint faced them and made the sign of the cross. The long lines of stones at Carnac contain 2,934 menhirs.

certain rare bone formations, undoubtedly caused genetically. It is only logical to assume that the tomb would have been built by the family buried within. It is also logical to assume that other structures of the same style, lacking bones, were built by the same sort of people.

The megaliths, then, were raised by some of the earliest Europeans. The reason that this simple fact took so long to be accepted was the peculiar inferiority complex which western Europeans had about their past. Their religion, their laws, their cultural heritage, their very numerals, all come from the east. The inhabitants, before civilisation came flooding in from the Mediterranean, were illiterate; they kept no records, they built no cities. It was easy to assume that they were simply bands of howling half-naked savages who painted their bodies, put bear-grease on their hair and ate their cousins.

It was simply unthinkable to most educated Euro-

This aerial view of Avebury in Wiltshire shows the main circle of megaliths. There are now some 100 standing stones in and around Avebury, but originally there were many more. This and other circles were largely destroyed to build the village, which runs through them. There are many other prehistoric sites in the vicinity, including Stonehenge.

The shaded areas show how the megaliths in Europe were in the main concentrated in coastal regions, which were more accessible for commerce and trade than inland areas.

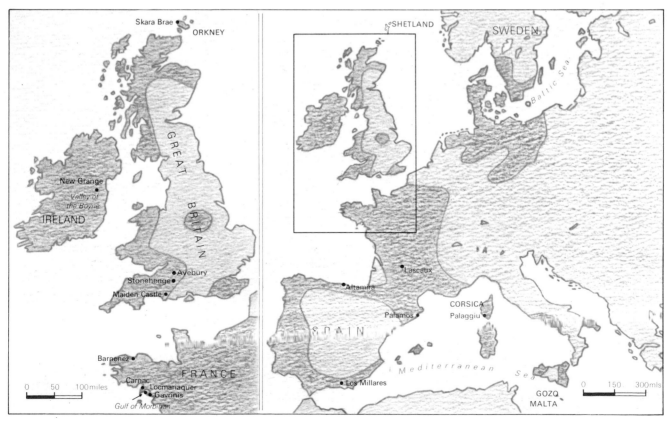

peans of the last century that these primitive ancestors were capable of imagining, let alone designing and building, such feats of engineering as Stonehenge, with its peg-and-socket lintels, or the cantilevered roofs of the tombs in the Valley of the Boyne in Ireland. It was assumed that the native population must have been guided, if not directed, by more civilised outsiders in the construction work.

All this disparagement of the ancestral Europeans was quite unfounded. Lacking in sophistication they may have been, but they were neither stupid nor uncreative. Some 20,000 years before Christ they knew how to make pigments from powdered rocks and earth, and had covered the walls of caves at Lascaux, in France, and Altamira, in Spain, with drawings of rare skill. They survived the ice ages, adjusted to changing climates, domesticated the dog, invented the bow and arrow, the harpoon and other devices. It used to be believed that agriculture, the domestication of goats and cattle and the smelting of ore were discovered in western Asia and only gradually spread westwards across Europe. But recent research indicates that all three practices may have arisen independently in different parts of Europe.

These early Europeans also developed navigational skills, travelling across the stormy waters of the Atlantic in frail craft made from animal skins stretched on wooden frames, to bring their families and their art of megalithic construction to such distant lands as the Shetlands, north of Scotland, and the Canary Islands, far out in the Atlantic.

In the 1960s it became possible to prove that the megaliths were not derived from the east but were developed at the western extremity of the continent, by the people who lived there. This stemmed from Willard Libby's earlier discovery that the rate of decay of the radioactive isotope carbon-14 in organic materials can be used to date them. Early radiocarbon datings of objects found at megalithic sites proved that they were very old, but not so old that they could not have been derived from models in the ancient east. Then it was found that these datings were incorrect. Checking with the rings of bristlecone pines in the mountains of California, thought to be the oldest living things on earth, enabled researchers to push back the date of the megaliths by several centuries.

It is now known that stone monuments were being built in Brittany almost 1,000 years before the pyramids were constructed in Egypt. Three separate monuments had been built and partially destroyed at Stonehenge before Mycenae, site of the oldest monumental sculpture in Greece, became recognisable as a city of importance.

How the stones were moved

The chronological details are still being debated, but it seems certain that in any case the megaliths of western Europe were built at a time when there was little if any contact between the people of these regions and those of the east.

However, this does not clear up the mystery of how the monuments were built by people living at a very low level of technological development – about that of the most primitive regions of the world today. Obviously it was no easy job, but neither was it beyond the capacity of men of average intelligence and strong motivation.

Contemporary anthropologists have observed megaliths being constructed in out-of-the-way places. In 1966, on Sumba, Indonesia, one of them saw 552 men hauling an 11-ton stone over the countryside to serve as the capstone of a grave.

A bas-relief of ancient Egypt illustrates how a gigantic alabaster statue weighing 60 tons was moved into place: it was carried on a sledge drawn by 90 men, with an overseer seated on the knees of the statue beating time as they heaved, three water-carriers to keep the hauling ropes from overheating, and a force of 60 soldiers with whips and clubs to see that the heaving was done efficiently.

Such a scene might well have been enacted as the huge stones of the megaliths were moved into place, sometimes from a distance of many miles. Probably there were no soldiers and no whips: all the evidence indicates that the Europe of the megalithic age was a remarkably peaceful place.

To haul and raise into place monster stones like the Grand Menhir at Locmariaquer, in Brittany, which originally weighed about 380 tons, must have required the muscle power of thousands of men. But most megalithic stones were much smaller.

The engineering problems of setting the stones up-

When the Grand Menhir of Locmariaquer was still standing it weighed about 380 tons. It may have been used as a sighting point in astronomical observations for a whole complex of megalithic structures round the Gulf of Morbihan in Brittany.

right without toppling them over, not to speak of placing lintel stones on the top of uprights, are considerable. But it is clear that with sufficient time and manpower these problems could be solved. The megalith-builders had plenty of time – 2,000 years. And they had plenty of manpower, too, even though the Stone Age population of Europe was quite thin by modern standards.

An age of leisure

A modern scholar, Stuart Piggott, has estimated that in Britain in those days the inhabitants did not need to work more than two hours a day on the average to keep themselves fed and sheltered. The land was swarming with game, and if farmland became depleted it was easy to burn down some forest and start anew. With the exception of sowing and harvest times, and the period when the hunting season was at its height, there was ample time for the kind of collective work needed to erect the megaliths.

So modern scientists have revealed who erected the megaliths, when and how. The reason why they were built, however, still remains a mystery. Whatever possessed these men to devote such time and effort for

Overlooking the Mediterranean, the temples of Mnajdra, whose fan-shaped ground plan is characteristic of Malta's megalithic structures, were built about 4,500 years ago. The huge stone blocks have been protected from the weather by cliffs and are surprisingly well preserved.

centuries and centuries to raising giant stones? What purpose did the megaliths serve?

It is easier to say what they were not for. They were not for defence. There are no megalithic fortifications left to see in western Europe, except for a wall round a village at Los Millares, in southern Spain. Immense circular earthwork embankments, known today as causewayed camps, which were a feature of the British life of the period, have gaps every so often in their circumference. These gaps, which were closed only by barriers of thorn or simple wooden gates, were better suited to penning in a herd of cattle than to keeping out invaders.

It seems clear, too, that the megaliths were not meant as living quarters. They were not palaces for an upper class, like so many structures of the later Bronze and Iron Ages all over Europe from Greece to Ireland. Some people in megalithic times may have been buried

69

more sumptuously than others, with faience (a fine glazed pottery) beads and golden bracelets in their graves, but there is no trace that they lived any differently. New Stone Age villages have been preserved at Skara Brae on the Orkney Islands, where they were made of stone and buried by drifting sand, and in some Alpine lakes, where they were made of wood which was preserved when lake levels rose and covered them. In these villages the houses are all of roughly the same size and shape, with no special ornaments or furnishings to suggest that some belonged to higher-class people than others.

It is almost certain that the megaliths were not settings for human sacrifices, though for some time this was considered to have been one of their chief functions. In the days when the megaliths were ascribed to the Druids, the romantic imagination ran riot with scenes of blood-curdling cruelty. The poet William Wordsworth, wandering by a megalithic site in the English countryside, could not help imagining 'the sacrificial altar, fed with living men, how deep the groans'.

More prosaic investigators have failed to turn up the slightest evidence that human sacrifice was ever performed at the megalithic monuments. For a while a piece of such evidence was thought to exist when a dismembered body with a hole in its skull was found in south west England, at Maiden Castle, which had been a fort in Celtic times and was probably a shrine in the New Stone Age.

However, experimental work on cutting human bones has shown that the body in question could not have been cut up by a stone knife, only by an iron one. And carbon-14 dating added the information that this unfortunate man must have died a good 2,000 years after the megalithic age had ended.

The absence of sacrifices does not mean that the megaliths were not used for religious purposes. Many of them were tombs, ranging from tiny family vaults to the huge underground labyrinth at Hal Saflieni on Malta, in which the bones of more than 7,000 bodies were interred. But many megalithic structures were clearly not tombs, and there is no reason to suppose that even those which were tombs were never used for other purposes as well.

On Malta, too, at the villages of Hagar Qim, Mnajdra, Hal Saflieni and Tarxien, are found huge elaborate structures, some rough-hewn, some of polished limestone; some with painted walls, some with intricate carvings. They are called temples because of their dark inner recesses, which look like shrines, and flat stones which resemble altars. On the nearby island of Gozo is another temple of even more imposing proportions. The local people have named it *Ggantija* (the Work of the Giants). The temple's façade, rising to a height of 26 ft and consisting of close-fitting slabs of limestone, is one of the earliest architecturally conceived exteriors in the world – built about 4,500 years ago.

If the example of primitive people living today is relevant, the megaliths may have been used for a variety of social and religious purposes. Extensive remains of animal bones show that they were used for feasts. They may have been used for periodic tribal meetings, for processions, for dances, and perhaps for rudimentary markets, like the fairs of later ages. They may have been monuments to great men or records of great events. They may conceivably have expressed certain theological ideas – in the same way as Christian churches are often laid out in the form of a cross – but there is no way of knowing what these theological ideas could have been.

Were they observatories?

They could also have been used for astronomical observation, and this is currently the most passionately debated aspect of the subject. It has long been known that Stonehenge was built in such a way that the rising sun would be visible on a sight-line to a stone called the Heel Stone at dawn on the year's longest day, June 21. This was an impressive, but isolated, phenomenon.

Then it was discovered, a dozen or so years ago, that the tomb under the great turf-covered stone mound at New Grange on the River Boyne in Ireland had an astronomic orientation as well. The tomb itself, which bears a superficial resemblance to the much more recent beehive tombs in the Mycenaean cities of Greece, is approached through a 70-ft-long passage, lined and roofed by gigantic stone slabs, a little lower than the height of a man. For a brief period at the winter solstice, when the days are shortest, the rising sun shines all the way down this passage and its reflection bouncing off the elaborately spiral-carved stones illuminates the whole 20-ft-high vault of the tomb chamber itself.

Since then many scholars, the chief of whom are the American astronomer Gerald S. Hawkins, Professor Sir Fred Hoyle, and Alexander Thom, a professor of engineering science at Oxford University, have made elaborate studies which tend to indicate that the builders of the megaliths had truly profound astronomical and mathematical insights, greater than those of any until the Greeks or, perhaps, until Copernicus and Newton.

The stones, according to these scholars, are placed with such ingenuity and sophistication that they can be used not only as sight-lines to heavenly bodies at crucial periods of the year, but also as a giant calculating machine or computer which will, among other things, provide accurate predictions of eclipses of the sun and the moon.

Such information would have been of great practical value to a farming and seafaring people. It might also, of course, have provided a class of learned astronomer-priests with immense prestige and power, and this might explain how they were able to get such prodigies of labour to be willingly performed by the ordinary people.

Despite the impressive evidence collected by the professors, there remains a good deal of doubt among experts as to whether megalithic man really rose to such heights of scientific learning. For one thing, some of the stones on whose placement all the arguments rest have in the past been toppled or have fallen over. Modern scholars have conscientiously sought to restore them to their original positions; but as one of these scholars, Professor Richard Atkinson of Cardiff University, points out, an error of an inch or two in their work on earth might make for light-years of error in calculations involving outer space.

An uneasy feeling remains: if these old builders

A monumental main door (a modern reconstruction) leads into the maze of chambers and corridors which made up the temple of Tarxien in Malta, now in ruins.

Tarxien: a Stone Age
temple in Malta

1

16

15

14

13

3

12

11

10

9

7

8

5

4

6

3

2

0 1 2 3 4 5   10 yards

For centuries Maltese peasants around the village of Tarxien lived with a constant irritation. Their ploughs kept being damaged by huge stones just under the ground. Not unnaturally, the peasants broke up these stones whenever they came across them—and it was not until 1913 that it crossed one farmer's mind that the stones might be more than just a nuisance. He mentioned them to the island's national museum, and archaeologists soon mounted a major excavation. Their work revealed the remains of the temple reconstructed here: one of Europe's largest ancient monuments.

Only the lower walls and foundations were still intact. But research has enabled an artist to reconstruct what it must have been like when it was being used—about 5,000 years ago—in ceremonies probably linked with ancestor-worship. This drawing shows only part of the temple complex, for the whole covers about 20 acres. Several rooms have been excavated, including the two halls of one temple (left and centre), one hall of another (above), and the beginning of a third (extreme right).

The roof [1], cut away to show the building's structure, seems to have been made of beams and brushwood covered with clay or plaster. A forecourt [2] led into the temple, which had thick walls faced with limestone slabs [3] fitted together without mortar. The walls were topped by stone bricks [4] and cornices [5].

The main doorway [6] led to the central chamber of the first temple [7], dominated by a giant statue [8], probably a fertility goddess. To the statue's right was an altar [9] with spiral carvings—perhaps representing the goddess' eyes—found at several places in Tarxien. Animal bones and a flint knife were found at the altar; a nearby stone vase [10] may have held sacrificial instruments.

Large doorways [11, 15] led into curved recesses [12, 16], another [10] into the temple's second chamber [14] which had three recesses [16, 17, 18]. From one [18], another passage [19] linked the first temple with the main hall of the second [20]. The two stone pots [21] may have been for incense or animal sacrifices. Sacrificial altars [22] flanked the passage [23] to another temple (not shown). A doorway [24] led to the third temple [25] and a stairway [26] ending in a strange platform—its purpose still unknown.

Back outside through the doorway [27] is another riddle—a curious slab-roofed shelter [28]. Its floor is pitted with small holes matching round stone balls found nearby. But their purpose—ritual, perhaps, or a simple game—remains a mystery of the megaliths.

The funeral chamber under the New Grange burial mound in Ireland is covered by a vaulted cantilevered roof some 20 ft high. The stones are arranged in horizontal layers one above the other, overlapping on the inside edge, each stone being held in position by the one above.

were so immensely clever, if they knew about Pythagorean triangles (as Professor Thom says), and the precession of the equinoxes (as Professor Hoyle maintains), how is it that they did not invent anything else: the wheel or the alphabet or the city-state – anything indeed but the technology needed to predict eclipses?

Colin Renfrew, Professor of Archaeology at Southampton University, believes that the building of megaliths was a result of profound changes in social and economic organisation. These were caused by the so-called Neolithic (New Stone Age) Revolution, the introduction of agriculture and stock-breeding into nomadic groups of hunters and fishers. These groups then settled down, becoming much more populous because they could produce much more food. As they did so, communities which had once been isolated found themselves in fairly close contact with one another. Each community would then have felt a need to express its own individuality, to mark out its own territory. A highly visible object would have been ideal for such a purpose.

The tribespeople may have started by raising cairns of stones over their dead. As they grew more prosper-

The hypogeum, or underground tomb, of Hal Saflieni in Malta is a labyrinth dug out of the limestone rock in which over 7,000 bodies have been found. The roof of this chamber is cut into the rock to resemble a cantilevered vault; a small room off the chamber is known as the holy of holies.

ous and acquired greater technological sophistication they would have started raising big stones. It would have enhanced a community's prestige to have bigger and better stones than anyone else. They would also have formed a convenient rallying-point for all the energies of the tribe, whose scattered members could come there periodically to bury their dead, to worship whatever gods they had, to take counsel together, to get drunk together, to exchange axes, pottery, jewellery – and brides.

This is all perfectly plausible, but like most plausible explanations it does not really explain anything. After all, the New Stone Age Revolution spread over many other parts of the world. The practice of building megaliths also emerged in other parts of the inhabited world. But why did it appear first on the furthest fringes of Europe? And why was it carried on there on a scale greater than anywhere else in the world?

The 50,000 or so monuments known today are only a fraction of what must have existed in the heyday of the megalithic culture. Uncounted numbers have been destroyed over the ages by the forces of nature: by the erosion of wind and rain; by the shifting of coastlines, like the one which drowned some megaliths in what is now the Gulf of Morbihan in Brittany; by thunderbolts like the one which is believed to have overthrown and shattered the biggest of them all, the Grand Menhir at Locmariaquer.

The handiwork of devils

More, perhaps, have been destroyed by the hand of man. The early Christians saw in the old stones the remnants of ancient superstitions. They saw these colossal monuments as the handiwork of devils, and counted it as meritorious to mutilate or shatter them. Some menhirs in Brittany have crosses carved on their tops to symbolise the triumph of the new faith. Others were simply destroyed.

Still others were used as quarries, convenient sources of supply for building houses and roads. The giant stone circles of Avebury in southern England, which the 17th-century antiquarian John Aubrey said 'as much exceed Stonehenge in grandeur as a cathedral doth an ordinary parish Church' were largely destroyed after his day in order to build the picturesque village which runs through them.

There are many records of the wilful destruction of megaliths. In the 18th and 19th centuries gentlemen in England used to go out and picnic while their servants pillaged New Stone Age barrows looking for relics. Modern agricultural equipment, and especially the bulldozer, has enabled farmers to move easily prehis-

Extraordinary patterns of scrolls, spirals and zigzags cover the surface of these dressed stones forming the passageway to the funeral chamber of a burial mound on the island of Gavrinis off the coast of Brittany. Generations of archaeologists have been unable to decipher these designs.

toric monuments lying in the middle of their fields. In 1968 a road contractor looking for gravel half-destroyed the mounds at Barnenez on the north coast of Brittany, which may well contain among its 11 remaining megalithic tombs the oldest man-made structure still existing on the face of the earth.

The megaliths of western Europe are not only the earliest recorded – built thousands of years earlier than any similar gigantic works in Tibet, Japan, Africa or Easter Island – they are also far more complex. Nothing in other megalithic centres surpasses the luxuriant sprawl of spirals, chevrons and other geometric shapes on the walls of the tombs at New Grange, in Ireland, or on the Isle of Gavrinis in the Gulf of Morbihan, in Brittany. There is nothing like the sheer number and variety of forms to be found at such sites: the circles, the ovals, the alignments, the table-top dolmens, the tombs, the temples. There is nothing like the mechanical precision of these monuments, which Professor Thom's studies indicate were all built on multiples of a standard unit of measurement called by him the megalithic yard (2·72 ft).

For 2,000 years and more, men worked on these monuments. Then gradually they stopped. After about 1500 BC no more megaliths were put up anywhere in Europe. Here is another unsolved mystery.

Professor Hoyle suggests one rather melodramatic explanation. If, as he believes, there was a caste of astronomer-priests maintaining a hold on the people by their ability to predict the movement of heavenly bodies, there was a built-in danger in their system. The heavens are not static. The fixed stars and the movements of the sun and moon across them change very slightly in position as time goes by, and the cumulative effect over the centuries can be great. A stone circle that predicts eclipses and other astronomical events accurately today will be slightly inaccurate in 100 years' time; it will take some extremely fine mathematical calibrations to read it correctly.

Hoyle suggests that while technology improved all through the megalithic period, intellectual power declined. The priests went on lazily following in the steps of their predecessors without making the constant effort needed to keep up to date.

Downfall of the priests

It is easy to imagine the result. One fine day all the population comes dutifully to the great shrine. The high priest solemnly commands the sun to hide its face, but the sun does no such thing. The whole band of priests takes to howling and gashing themselves with knives, as the priests of Baal did in front of King Ahab in the Book of Kings when they promised to bring fire down from heaven. The sun is still there – the eclipse will not take place until the following week. Before that time the enraged populace will have slaughtered their former guides the way Ahab's people did the priests of Baal. From that day it would be difficult to persuade volunteers to put up another megalith.

Perhaps the end of megalith-building came under less lurid conditions than this. Perhaps it was simply another change in the socio-economic climate. The population of Europe was changing in the 2nd millennium BC. The peaceful farmer-herders of the New Stone Age were giving way to the quarrelsome warrior bands of the Bronze Age, the vainglorious heroes of Irish legend and the Homeric epics. These people were more interested in building forts and palaces than in the quiet pastoral life and communal building efforts of the megalith-builders.

At all events no one trundled the huge stones around any more. Successive invaders – Celts, Germans, Romans, Goths, Saxons, Danes, Vikings, down to the tourists of the last century – passed by and looked up in wonder. Modern archaeology has cast a little light; but the central mystery of what caused this great surge of building to take place will probably never be solved.

ROBERT WERNICK

The monument at Palamos in southern Spain combines the two main types of megalithic construction – the menhir, or single upright stone, and the dolmen, one or two large flat blocks supported on raised stones.

The Stone Age shepherds of Palaggiu in southern Corsica may have raised this superb line of menhirs to mark a sanctuary or a place of assembly for their community. Erosion and aggressive invaders have together reduced it to a still impressive jumble of ruins.

Soul-statues of Corsica

For hundreds of years on the Mediterranean island of Corsica, a peaceable population of farmers and shepherds buried their dead in great stone chambers. Near the tombs they set up single standing stones called menhirs which, it was believed, contained the dead person's soul. These statues, 7 ft tall or more, were often just raised stones, roughly shaped.

About 1500 BC there came a dramatic change. What had been crudely shaped stones became distinct sculptures. Features were carved into the heads, and adornments such as tunics, swords and daggers were carved on the bodies.

More than 2,000 years ago the Greek philosopher Aristotle offered his own explanation for these enigmatic figures. He claimed that the Iberians (the name the Greeks gave to peoples who lived far to the west) set up obelisks around their tombs — one for each enemy the dead man had killed during his life.

Research by a young French archaeologist, Roger Grosjean, has extended Aristotle's explanation and cast new light on the mystery. Between the 14th and 12th centuries BC, the Mediterranean lands endured invasions by various bands of pirates whom the Egyptians called the Sea People. Among the pirates were the Philistines of the Bible and a tribe called the Shardana. In a bas-relief at the temple of Medinet Habu in Egypt, both these groups are shown being defeated by the fleet of the pharaoh, Rameses III.

From studying the bas-relief and from his excavations on Corsica, Grosjean concluded that the statues represented Shardana warriors. But it was not the roving Shardana themselves who erected them – for they burned their dead and did not put up monuments. Instead, speculated Grosjean, the statues must have been carved by the tomb-builders, the Corsicans, probably to depict invading chiefs killed in battle. Whether they were war trophies or memorials to a courageous enemy is still debatable.

While Egypt managed to beat off the invaders, the Corsican farmers had no chance in the long run. They had only stone-tipped arrows against the Shardana's bronze armour and weapons.

The Shardana overran the southern part of the island. The remnants of the defeated islanders fled north, where they put up a few more uncarved menhirs. Then, soon after 1000 BC, they vanished forever.

But some of their stones survive, thanks to their Shardana conquerors. The Shardana took over most of the fine megalithic sites in southern Corsica, tore down the statue-menhirs and built them into the walls with which they defended their villages.

In this way the statue-menhirs were preserved for 3,000 years. Now they are being brought to light by archaeologists to bear witness to an ancient tragedy.

ROBERT WERNICK

A masterpiece in stone, Filitosa IX looms over the site of Filitosa in the south-western corner of Corsica, where the greatest concentration of statues has been found. This statue was shaped by artists in the final phase of Corsican megalithic art, when it reached its highest pinnacle. While the neck and shoulders are crudely shaped, the facial features are realistically drawn. Like most of the Corsican statues, Filitosa IX is of granite, painstakingly chipped into shape with sharp stone tools.

Seen from the back, Filitosa VI wears the same battle armour as is shown being worn by Shardana warriors in an ancient Egyptian bas-relief at the temple of Medinet Habu. The helmet tapers to a point to protect the back of the neck, and padded straps protect the shoulder blades. Cattle horns were sometimes added to helmets.

Soul-statues of Corsica

The statue Filitosa IV has not suffered the fate of many others, which were broken up when the shrines of the island's megalithic people were overrun by invaders. Nearly 10 ft high, the figure carries a dagger on its right hip. Such metal daggers gave the invading Sea People a decisive advantage in battle over the natives of Corsica.

Shaded areas indicate Corsica's principal megalithic sites. Most of the 60 known statue-menhirs are concentrated in the coastal region of the south-west, particularly in the area of Filitosa. After the Shardana invasions, which spread successively over the southern regions, the natives fled north, and the last menhirs – which were never carved into statues – are to be found on the north-west coast of the island.

A general view of Filitosa today shows menhirs re-erected in the foreground, aligned in a protective cordon in front of the megalithic burial places. The original site was not fortified. It was simply a settlement on the sunny southern slope of a hill from which the inhabitants could watch over their sheep and goats in winter. In summer they drove their flocks up to mountain pastures by paths which can still be traced. But around 1500 BC this peaceful village life was upset by the invaders who landed in the south of the island. When the invaders – later called Torreans after the round stone towers or torri they built – conquered Filitosa they surrounded it with huge boulders and built the characteristic towers, some of which survive to this day in southern Corsica. In many of them, large numbers of stone arrowheads can be found – traces, perhaps, of the vain attacks which the megalithic natives made to recapture their lost homes.

Three of the Corsican statue-menhirs which were cut up and used to build the fortifications of Filitosa have here been removed from the walls and stand upright as they did originally. After a long struggle, the invaders drove the megalithic natives out of the south and conquered their main shrine at Filitosa. Here they found the statues of their own slain chieftains. Possibly, they thought that these enigmatic stones were directing spiritual forces against them. They broke up the statues and used them as building materials for their own walls. The invaders remained for only a few centuries and left Corsica in about 1000 BC.

The secrets of Stonehenge

*An air of mystery broods over Stonehenge. Learned
men from all fields of science, as well as spiritualists,
clairvoyants and cranks, have studied the remains
to try to uncover the secrets of its past. Was it a
temple of the sun? A royal palace? A magic shrine?
An observatory for studying the heavens?
Was it even a gigantic computer built centuries
before the Greeks mastered mathematics?
One day, perhaps, the answers to all the questions
will be known. Or will these colossal stones
guard their secret for eternity?*

Seen from a distance, the ring of grey stones called
Stonehenge appears tiny on the desolate and windy
Salisbury Plain in southern England. Chalk grassland
stretches as far as the eye can see, and Stonehenge
itself is the only interruption on the bleak and level
horizon. Closer to the monument, however, the huge
size of the upright stones, most of them more than 13 ft
high, makes a powerful impression. The rain, frost and
wind of centuries have worked strange hollows and
crevices at weak points in the sandstone, yet many of
the stones still stand where they were erected, and bear

*Stonehenge's circle of stones seems to spin giddily against
the sky; it was once known as the Dance of the Giants.
According to Geoffrey of Monmouth, a 12th-century chronicler, the stones were brought over from Ireland and set in
place 'not by force but by Merlin's art'.*

the marks of tools which shaped them 4,000 years ago.

Stonehenge seems to defy the forces of time and
nature, and also the attempts of those who seek to
understand its meaning. 'You may put a hundred
questions to these rough-hewn giants as they bend in
grim contemplation of their fallen companions; but
your curiosity falls dead in the vast sunny stillness that
enshrouds them . . .' wrote the novelist Henry James.

Stonehenge is unique among sites of prehistoric
standing stones, for it is the only monument whose
stones were artificially shaped and combined into an
architectural plan. The subtleties and refinements of
this plan are apparent only after a careful study of the
ruins. For example, the great stones or lintels which
were raised up to link the tops of the upright stones are
not merely straight-edged slabs of rock. Each was
carefully cut on the curve so that when they were
assembled they formed the outline of a circle. The

upright stones were shaped with a central bulge – like the columns of many classical Greek temples – apparently to allow for the effect of perspective, so that they would appear straight when seen from below: the innermost lintels were cut to a tapering shape for the same reason.

For what purpose were such efforts of manpower and ingenuity expended? Was Stonehenge a royal palace, a temple for magic and ritual, or a scientific observatory built for watching the sun, moon and stars in their courses?

Older than the Druids

In the 17th century, before the advent of scientific archaeology, historians imagined that Stonehenge had been built by the Druids, the white-robed Celtic priests of Britain and Gaul, of whom a little was known from the accounts of Roman writers. This is still the most widely held notion, but it does nothing to penetrate the mystery. For we now know that Stonehenge is at least 1,000 years older than the Druids.

But the 'Druid theory' is by no means the most far-fetched of the many explanations offered by archaeologists and historians for the existence of Stonehenge. Some of its earliest students, like the 17th-century architect Inigo Jones, for example, thought the carefully calculated design could only have been the work of Roman architects. A similar theory was put forward 50 years ago when the archaeologist Elliot Smith suggested that the designers were Egyptian or Phoenician.

Interest in such extravagant notions was powerfully stimulated by the discovery nearby of a number of prehistoric graves with bronze daggers and personal ornaments of sheet gold, bone, amber, faience (a fine glazed pottery) and polished stone.

The bluestones used in building Stonehenge II were apparently carried from the Prescelly Mountains in South Wales on sledges and rafts. Most of the 240-mile journey could have been by water, round the coast of South Wales, across the Bristol Channel and along the Bristol Avon. Some recent evidence suggests that the bluestones may have been transported not by man, but by glaciers during the Ice Age

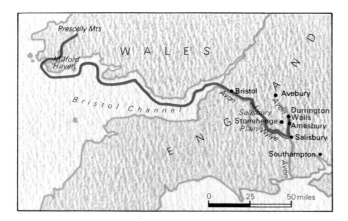

The most famous find of this type was described in 1808 by a well-known English antiquary, Sir Richard Colt Hoare, who set his labourers to work on a barrow, or prehistoric burial mound, within sight of Stonehenge. They found the skeleton of a tall, sturdy man, buried with an axe, several daggers and ceremonial equipment, which included a mace with a polished stone head and carved bone mounts. There were also a gold scabbard hook and two lozenge-shaped ornaments of sheet gold, intricately decorated with delicate lines, which may have been fastened to the dead man's clothing in some way.

The splendour of these 'golden burials', together with the unique quality of the Stonehenge architecture, suggested to Sir Richard and his contemporaries that the ancient Britons must have imported their skills from abroad. Some archaeologists suggested that the great wealth of these burials indicated that a small number of invading Bronze Age warriors from abroad had established themselves at Stonehenge, and directed the less skilled native population in the construction of the monument. One possible source proposed for these invaders was Mycenae, the great Homeric citadel on the Greek mainland. Some of the precious objects, such as the faience beads and amber discs bound with gold, pointed to trade with the Aegean and indirectly with Egypt. Moreover it was remarked that the stone gateways of Mycenae were

constructed with the same skilful use of peg-and-socket joints as at Stonehenge. Could the designer have been a wandering Odysseus from the Mediterranean?

A second possible source suggested for the Bronze Age invaders was Brittany, the region famous for its spectacular monuments of menhirs – standing stones – such as those at Carnac where thousands of huge stones are arranged in parallel lines. In this area, too, are concentrated single 'warrior' burials of great richness, although it has yet to be demonstrated that the Carnac stones were erected by these same Bronze Age people. The type of grave goods, especially bronze daggers, found in the Breton barrows is strikingly similar to those from the Stonehenge region.

However, the real explanation for the building of Stonehenge seems to lie not in any explosive force from outside but in the slowly developing prosperity of the region itself.

Trade with the Mediterranean?

A new date established by the carbon-14 dating method for Stonehenge (about 2750 BC) was a great shock to archaeologists. It became clear, for example, that the architecture of Stonehenge could not possibly have been inspired from the Aegean area, because it belonged to a time as much as four or five centuries before the Mycenaean period. On the other hand, the

The outer ring of the great temple, built of sarsen stones in about 1900 BC, was to make Stonehenge the most impressive megalithic monument in Europe. The peg-and-socket joints which secure the lintels are also used in carpentry.

The great wooden rotunda which stood at Durrington Walls, near Stonehenge, was the work of skilled carpenters who lived more than 4,000 years ago. It was 127 ft in diameter and contained 2,750 yds of wooden framework, which must have required felling at least 10 acres of woodland.

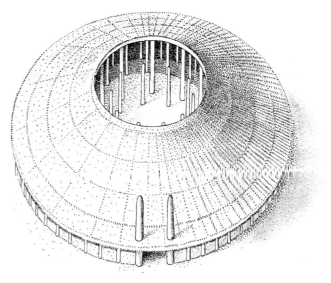

dates for two of the 'golden burial' barrows were much later than expected, so that exotic objects such as amber discs and faience beads could indeed have been traded or imported from the Mediterranean. It still seems possible that there were Breton warriors in the region of Stonehenge at least during part of the period of wealth and power concentrated there after about 1900 BC, and that they formed the kernel of an aristocracy which ruled there for at least 600 years.

But important as the immigrants were, Stonehenge cannot be ascribed to them alone. It does not stand in a cultural vacuum, nor was it as isolated in its own time as its lonely position on Salisbury Plain might suggest. There are more than 900 other stone circles to be found throughout the British Isles, although none of them is as elaborate in its structure as Stonehenge. These stone circles were built by New Stone Age and Bronze Age people who led a settled agricultural existence, mainly dependent on cattle and cereals such as wheat and barley. Their way of life was clearly prosperous enough to enable them to join together at certain times of the year to build monuments requiring considerable manpower.

Professor Gerald S. Hawkins, the American astronomer, claims that a computer has 'decoded' the mystery of Stonehenge: the monument was designed as an astronomical observatory. But given the present state of the monument, some of his controversial theories are difficult to verify.

The raising of the megaliths

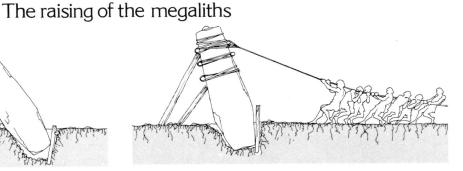

Deep pits with one sloping side were dug to house the great sarsen stones, some of which weighed as much as 45 tons. The stones were probably lowered into the pits with the aid of

ropes and rollers, then slowly raised by using a scaffold as the fulcrum of a rope-operated lever. In the last stage, ropes alone may have been used to straighten the stones.

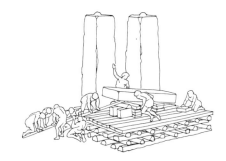

Once the uprights were in position, the 7-ton lintels were probably placed on a timber platform. As the stone was inched higher with levers, wedges and blocks, the platform

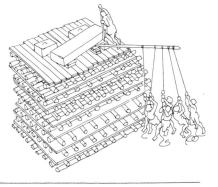

was built up from below. Finally, the lintel was slid into position on top of the uprights, which had pegs carved to fit exactly into the mortise sockets on the lintels.

One of these monuments, known as Durrington Walls, is only about 2 miles from Stonehenge. Here archaeologists uncovered evidence of two huge circular wooden buildings, one of them with a diameter of 127 ft, marked by concentric rings of post holes dug into the chalk. Certainly the people who erected these structures must have been skilled carpenters, for the larger of the two Durrington Walls buildings, dating to about 2500 BC, probably featured a sloping, cone-shaped roof, with a central courtyard left open to the sky. Such imposing buildings could have accommodated several hundred people if, as the excavations indicate, they were not used for everyday living but for communal gatherings or rituals.

The tradition of building these complex wooden structures may well have left its mark on Stonehenge. The technique by which the lintels of Stonehenge were fastened to the uprights and to each other, with joints of projecting pegs fitting into sockets, is appropriate to woodworking, as if the builders were imitating the wooden archways of the circular buildings.

A thousand years of building

Stonehenge was constructed in three different phases which cover almost 1,000 years of prehistoric time. The earliest phase, which archaeologists call Stonehenge I, probably dates from about 2750 BC. This phase includes one of the most mysterious features of Stonehenge, the Aubrey Holes, named after their 17th-century discoverer, the writer and antiquary John Aubrey.

These holes were dug soon after the bank and ditch which enclosed the whole site. They consisted of a ring of 56 shallow pits carefully spaced out just inside the line of the bank. They were filled in again almost immediately after being dug. Excavations showed that they had never contained stones or wooden posts, although in some cases the contents of the pits included cremated bones, frequently inserted after the holes had already been filled. Other features for which it is equally difficult to find an obvious explanation can also be assigned to the Stonehenge I phase. For example, the famous Heel Stone and several irregular lines of wooden posts were set outside the entrance to the north-east. In interpreting the posts, stones, pits and earthworks which date back to this time, it must be remembered that many of them have disappeared under the building phases and structures which followed. Archaeological work has helped to establish the position of many vanished features, but much still depends on guesswork. For example, no one has yet

Heavy stone hammers shaped the monoliths in Stonehenge's outer ring before they were raised into position. Several of the stones still bear the hammer marks. Some of the uprights are slightly convex at the top so that perspective would create the illusion that they were straight. The lintels were carefully shaped so that matched together they formed a circle.

The rays of the rising sun strike the Heel Stone at the summer solstice. The sun does not rise exactly on the centre-line of the stone but slightly to the left, then moves to the right during the day. When Stonehenge was built it would have risen further to the left, suggesting that the Heel Stone could not have been used for precise astronomical observation.

building of a long avenue of twin parallel banks and ditches, a processional way to the Hampshire Avon nearly 2 miles away. It seems likely that this was the route taken by at least 82 stones, each of which weighed more than 4 tons. These stones were brought to the site from the Prescelly Mountains in south-west Wales, where rocks of an identical composition, known as bluestone, are found. This journey must have involved transporting the bluestones by sledges and rafts for 240 miles, over half of which must have required manoeuvring the stones through the tidal waters of southern Wales and the Bristol Channel.

Sacred rocks of Wales

It is difficult to imagine both the extraordinary hazards of this operation and the motives which could have inspired it. But one clue is that axes and other implements fashioned from bluestone rock were traded widely throughout Britain, including the Stonehenge region, and it seems likely that some special or sacred value was attached to the material.

The western part of the double ring was never completed. There is no indication as to why the buil-

excavated at the centre of Stonehenge, or in the entire western half of the site.

The later stages of construction show engineering skill and architectural ambition of a much higher order than Stonehenge I. The stage known as Stonehenge II, dating from about 2000 BC, probably began with the

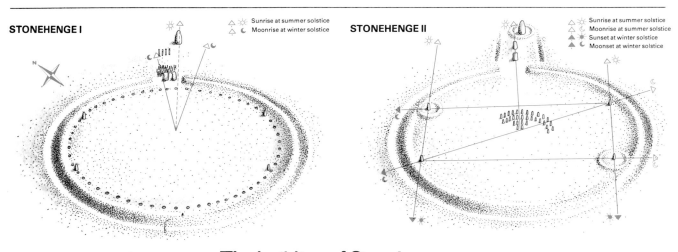

The building of Stonehenge

Stonehenge I *Building was begun in about 2750 BC. First a circular ditch was dug and rubble from the excavation was used to build a raised bank 2 yds high and 106 yds in diameter. Then a circle of 56 holes, known as the Aubrey Holes, was made just inside the bank. There is still no obvious explanation for the holes, which were filled almost as soon as they were dug. Two 'gateway' stones flanked the entry into the enclosure, and outside it the Heel Stone was raised on about*

the axis of sunrise at the summer solstice. Forty wooden posts marked the most northerly position of the moon at different winter solstices, a position which changes slowly over a cycle of 18·61 years. The four upright stones, known as the Station Stones, mark out a rectangle in which solar and lunar sight-lines intersect.
Stonehenge II *In about 2000 BC an avenue nearly 2 miles long was built to link the monument with the Hampshire*

Stonehenge has suffered a great deal of damage since it was first completed, nearly 4,000 years ago. Yet the monument's layout is still clearly visible. The great uprights and lintels of sarsen stones, which once formed a complete circle, can be seen, as well as the ditch and bank. The 56 Aubrey Holes, just inside the embankment, are now marked in concrete.

ders should have broken off their plans after all the extraordinary efforts required in transporting the bluestones from Wales. But it may have been because they had conceived the idea of erecting the final and even more impressive temple, known as Stonehenge III, which dates from about 1900 BC.

The practical engineering capabilities of the people who built Stonehenge III leave no doubt that they were far from being primitive savages. They selected at least 75 blocks of the tough sandstone which occurs naturally as loose boulders, known as sarsens, in the region around Avebury. Each sarsen stone was dragged by ropes on rollers or sledges to the site of Stonehenge nearly 20 miles to the south. Perhaps this was carried out when there was hard-packed snow or ice on the ground, and the stones were pulled along on sledges. Nevertheless, to shift the largest stone, perhaps 1,000 men would have been required to haul on the ropes. Then these immense blocks were pounded and knocked into shape with the use of dozens of small boulders of the same material.

Once the huge operation of transporting and shaping the stones was over, there was the equally difficult job of raising and positioning them with the lintels placed accurately on top of the uprights. The stability of the ring was dependent upon the delicate balance of each stone. Furthermore, the ground on which Stonehenge stands is not level, but slopes downwards for 18 in. across the ring towards the north-west. It is difficult to measure the top surface of the lintels with

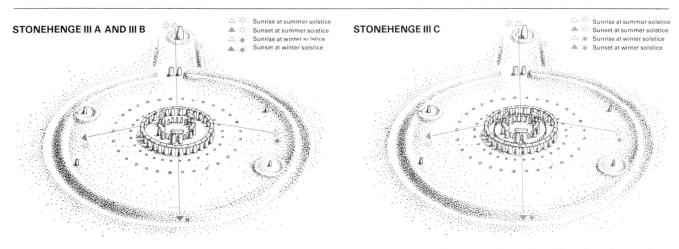

STONEHENGE III A AND III B

△ ☀ Sunrise at summer solstice
▲ ☀ Sunset at summer solstice
△ ❋ Sunrise at winter solstice
▲ ❋ Sunset at winter solstice

STONEHENGE III C

△ ☀ Sunrise at summer solstice
▲ ☀ Sunset at summer solstice
△ ❋ Sunrise at winter solstice
▲ ❋ Sunset at winter solstice

Avon. Inside the enclosure, work was begun on setting up a double circle of bluestones. The direction in which the sun rises at the summer solstice was marked much more clearly by eight stones which were erected at the entrance to the double circle and two more stones on the centre-line of the avenue. The four stones which marked the entrance to the monument were removed. Small circular ditches were dug round the Heel Stone and two of the Station Stones, perhaps to mark these vital astronomical observation points.

Stonehenge III A and III B *The third phase was started in about 1900 BC. To make way for the monumental circle of*

sarsen stones – huge sandstone boulders found near Avebury, 20 miles away – the bluestones were removed and new holes were dug for them in two concentric circles round the ring of sarsen stones. These new sites, however, were never used. Inside the ring, a horseshoe-shaped arrangement of trilithons – two uprights with a crossbar – was raised, probably with some bluestones in the centre. The entrance to the monument was once more marked by two upright stones.

Stonehenge III C *The final touches were made when the last bluestones were placed in a circle between the ring of sarsen stones and the horseshoe of trilithons.*

precision, but certainly it varies by less than 7 in. from one side of the ring to the other. This is a striking indication of the technical abilities of the builders.

Further minor modifications to the layout of the site, which included rearrangements of the bluestones of Stonehenge II, continued over a period of at least 500 years. During that time, Stonehenge maintained its importance as the most impressive megalithic monument in Europe.

But if archaeology has successfully established the dates of Stonehenge and the method by which it was built, it has never satisfactorily answered the most baffling question of all: what purpose did this gigantic landmark serve? Unfortunately Stonehenge, like many prehistoric monuments of its kind, seems to be free of the debris normally found on sites which were once inhabited. This debris, flint, broken pottery, remains of food, and so on, is normally a vital clue to the purpose and date of a site. Perhaps the very fact that it is missing at Stonehenge is evidence that stone circles were sacred places, set apart from day-to-day life and visited only on special occasions.

Important meeting places

In general, stone circles in the north of Britain surround graves more frequently than in the south, and these monuments probably mark the burial places of important chieftains or warriors. Some of the large rings like those at Avebury or Castlerigg, near Keswick in Cumbria, were almost certainly meeting places and important centres for the communal and religious life of prehistoric people. Other sites, like Callanish on the Isle of Lewis in the Outer Hebrides, may also have been simple observatories for astronomer-priests. There is clear evidence that stone circles served more than one function, and that some sites were rebuilt and reused over and over again for centuries.

In the past ten years great public interest has been aroused by theories which announced that Stonehenge was a complicated astronomical observatory and was perhaps even a kind of prehistoric 'computer'. But similar theories go back for many years to some of the first speculations about the motives for Stonehenge.

For example, the antiquary William Stukeley, whose celebrated book, *Stonehenge, a temple restored to the British Druids*, appeared in 1740, noted that the axis of the monument pointed to the midsummer sunrise. Some of the early theories took the form of fantasies like those of the Reverend Edward Duke who, in the 1840s, proposed that the monuments situated across the whole of Salisbury Plain were set out as a gigantic model of the solar system, in which Stonehenge represented the orbit of Saturn.

More scientific investigations of the astronomy of Stonehenge were attempted by Sir Norman Lockyer in 1901 and by an astronomer at Boston University, Gerald S. Hawkins, in 1963. The publication of Hawkins's book *Stonehenge Decoded* two years later, in which the author described how a computer had proved the existence of many significant astronomical alignments at Stonehenge, sparked off a lively controversy.

Astronomers such as Hawkins and Sir Fred Hoyle have produced some startling theories. They confirmed that several important positions on the site, including the Heel Stone, seemed to be very rough indicators of the midsummer solstice, when the sun appears to rise in its most northerly position before starting back south on its seasonal journey. The same sight-lines reversed in the opposite direction could have been used to observe the midwinter solstice, when the sun appears to set furthest to the south. These two key points in the year would have been of obvious practical use in establishing a simple calendar for regulating the harvests and times of festivals.

The structure of Stonehenge also seems to include alignments of important lunar risings and settings. Scientific curiosity or religious motives, or perhaps a mixture of both, could explain the systematic study of the moon's motions carried out at Stonehenge. The builders' interest in the moon may well have arisen when it became obvious that the moon does not follow the simple yearly movements of the sun.

As well as its own monthly pattern of risings and settings, the moon follows an additional cycle lasting 18·61 years. About 40 post holes arranged in six rows near the entrance to the monument coincide in a remarkable way with the most northerly position reached by the moon during this cycle. Since six rows are present, it is possible that these posts represent six lunar cycles, or more than a century of careful observations of the moon's movements. If this is true, it represents a remarkable achievement for observers who apparently had no form of writing and had to pass down their knowledge by word of mouth.

The prediction of eclipses

More elaborate theories took the lunar argument a stage further to suggest that attempts were made to predict eclipses by regular observations of the sun and moon. One of Hawkins's most ingenious ideas was that the number of the Aubrey Holes corresponds to a 56-year cycle which could have been useful for eclipse prediction. So in Hawkins's theory the Aubrey Holes became a kind of 'computer' with movable markers for keeping track of the repeating pattern of eclipses. Unfortunately, despite this attractive explanation for the mysterious Aubrey Holes, other numbers than 56 would have been more obvious and useful for detecting eclipses. No features exist on the site today which can be interpreted as convincing evidence that eclipses were ever observed or predicted at Stonehenge.

The use of the stone circle as an observatory is already apparent in Stonehenge I, the oldest part of the site. The later stages of the building, though far more elaborate than the oldest ring, do not seem to have represented any advance in astronomical science. The builders of Stonehenge II clearly marked the midsummer sunrise alignment by four pairs of stones at the entrance to the double ring. This preoccupation with astronomy continues in the third and final phase, since 30 uprights of the main ring and the 19 bluestones at the centre coincide with solar and lunar cycles.

Very few of the major sight-lines of the first two periods were blocked by the imposing architecture of the final temple. But Stonehenge III was not in any sense an accurate or sensitive observing instrument, in the way that the first phase of the monument had been. The intriguing possibility exists, therefore, that over the 1,000-year history of the monument there was actually a decline in the level of astronomical investigation – a decline from the systematic and practical layout of Stonehenge I to the monumental and symbolic architecture of Stonehenge III.

But these are no more than possibilities, for the limitations of the archaeological evidence raise countless questions to which there can be no final answer. However, most researchers would recognise that Stonehenge's builders possessed architectural skills of a surprisingly high order, while many others have tried to fill the gaps in the evidence with ingenious and often wildly imaginative theories. Some think that a class of astronomer-priests controlled the monument, using it to make improbably precise observations of the moon. Others have made highly accurate measurements of the dimensions of Stonehenge, convinced that its builders must have used some standard unit. Suggestions for such a unit have ranged from the megalithic yard to the Roman foot, the English foot, the Egyptian cubit and the Pyramid inch.

Yet the final explanations remain as elusive as ever, for the monument preserves an air of mystery which has resisted inquiry and guesswork for centuries. While Stonehenge was almost certainly an observatory and a temple, it may also have served other purposes which still belong to the realm of the unknown.

EVAN HADINGHAM

Ghostly in the dawn light, the stone circle of Stonehenge still poses many questions. Perhaps modern science will one day be able to explain why this ancient monument was built.

The giants of Easter Island

It was called 'the navel of the world' or 'the eye turned towards the sky', this volcanic speck lost in the vastness of the Pacific Ocean. Yet its inhabitants, cut off in one of the loneliest spots on earth, managed to create a complex and prosperous society, and peopled their island with a race of stone giants so big that even engineers still marvel. Modern research has shown how the islanders could have built and moved colossal statues weighing up to 90 tons. The mystery is...why?

'In Easter Island the past is the present, it is impossible to escape from it; the inhabitants of today are less real than the men who have gone; the shadows of the departed builders still possess the land. Voluntarily or involuntarily the sojourner must hold commune with those old workers; for the whole air vibrates with a vast purpose and energy which has been and is no more. What was it? Why was it?' Since these words were written by the Englishwoman Katherine Routledge, who explored Easter Island in 1914–15, much has

been revealed about the nature and origins of the island's unique culture, yet it remains in many ways a fascinating enigma.

One of the most isolated spots in the Pacific, tiny Easter Island is separated from the rest of the Polynesian chain, of which it forms the easternmost part, by vast tracts of ocean. It lies more than 1,000 miles east of Pitcairn Island (where the mutineers of the *Bounty* found refuge) and 2,300 miles west of the coast of Chile, to which it has belonged since 1888. The island owes its roughly triangular shape to the three volcanoes – Rano Kau, Maunga Terevaka and Katiki – which form its three corners. Its interior, dotted with numerous satellite cones, consists of rolling grass-covered volcanic soil interspersed with lava flows. There is evidence that lush vegetation and considerable timber may once have flourished on the island, but today its plant and animal life are sparse.

It is the brooding appearance of Easter Island's statues that gives them such an air of mystery. They seem like sentinels, standing guard over the horizon. The likeliest reasons for their creation – religious fervor, ancestral pride or even the boredom of island life – have often been overlooked in the past in favour of more fanciful theories.

There are few trees and no running streams, although there are crater lakes in which rushes grow in abundance. No lagoons surround the rocky coast, and indeed there is none of the soft, languorous air that characterises the more tropical Pacific islands. Because it lies near the northern edge of the southern temperate zone, Easter Island has distinct seasons and a pleasantly moderate climate, with an average temperature of about 72°F and an average yearly rainfall of about 50 inches.

Easter Island was called by its ancient inhabitants *te pito o te henua*, 'the navel of the world', an apt name for such a remote, dramatic spot. It is a place of surging breakers, precipitous cliffs, towering volcanoes and open, windswept slopes. Dominating the landscape are the island's famous statues.

Gullivers in a Lilliputian land

These massive, stylised figures of buff-coloured volcanic stone, known as *moai*, are both majestic and disturbing. Their heads are immense, their expressions brooding and disdainful, their ears grotesquely elongated, their chins jutting and powerful. Their arms hang rigidly at the sides of their legless trunks; their hands extend stiffly across their protuberant bellies. So far some 1,000 of them have been found, many weighing 20 tons and standing 12 to 15 ft tall. Of the finished statues which once stood on the island's numerous outdoor *ahu* (altars), the largest is some 32 ft tall and weighs an astonishing 90 tons. Unfinished statues more than twice the size of this colossus have also been found.

What captures the imagination even more than the forbidding magnificence of these stone giants is the fact that they exist at all in such an unlikely spot. What are these great Gullivers doing in this Lilliputian land,

The rocky islet of Motu Nui, off Easter Island's south-western tip, was a focus for the curious Bird-Man ritual, in which swimmers braved sharks and dangerous currents to search for the eggs of the sooty tern. The sponsor of the man who brought back the first egg became Bird-Man for a year.

a mere 45 square miles in extent? What happened to the men who carved them? How were the statues moved from their quarries and raised on their stone altars, and where is the timber that must have been used to accomplish this task? Above all, why are there so many statues, why are they so large and what was the purpose they served?

The first European to visit the island, a Dutch explorer named Jacob Roggeveen (who sighted it on Easter Sunday of 1722 and named it in commemoration of the day), made no attempt to answer these questions. Unable to believe that the great figures he saw along the coast could have been carved from the living rock, he assumed that they were clay construc-

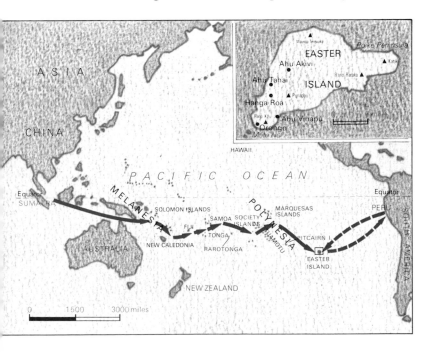

The Polynesians were magnificent navigators. From their original homeland in south-east Asia they moved gradually eastward, reaching Hawaii, New Zealand and Easter Island sometime near the beginning of the Christian era. There is a disputed theory of additional contact with Peru.

tions filled with stones. The islanders he found inhabited thatched huts and eked out a meagre living from the sparsely vegetated soil. Roggeveen described them as being heavily tattooed, their earlobes pierced and stretched to touch their shoulders.

During the remainder of the 18th century, European visitors were rare. In 1770 the Spaniard Felipe Gonzalez visited Easter Island, took possession of it in the name of King Carlos III of Spain and then apparently forgot it. Four years later the great English explorer Captain James Cook visited the island, and in 1786 the French admiral Jean François La Pérouse landed there, but their stops were also brief and their explorations relatively superficial.

What these 18th-century explorers found was a scattered population (now estimated to have numbered 3,000 to 4,000), apparently much reduced and demoralised by years of internal strife – a people living in a state of near anarchy amid the wreckage of their once high culture. Cannibalism was common, perhaps as an out-growth of earlier population pressures and food shortages. The island's various kinship groups were constantly at war with one another, and at some time during this period most of the great statues were deliberately toppled from their stone *ahu* and many of these altars themselves dismantled. A few statues remained standing during the visits of the 18th-century explorers, but by the mid-19th century all had been brought down.

Taken for slaves

The Easter Islanders were easy prey for the 19th-century exploiters who inevitably followed the explorers. In 1805 the American schooner *Nancy*, out of New London, Connecticut, carried away 22 islanders as slaves. Other depredations followed, culminating in

In 1960 the seven moai *below, each of which weighs 16 tons, were restored to their original positions on Ahu Akivi near Easter Island's west coast. Although this group is now the island's most celebrated, it was by no means the most ambitious. Ahu Tongariki, which was completely destroyed by a devastating tidal wave in 1960, once held 15 large statues.*

Children playing on a moai *give some indication of the scale of these giants, roughly marked out on the slopes of the Rano Raraku volcano. They are so enormous that some scholars have wondered whether the unfinished statues, the largest of which are 65 ft long, were ever intended to be moved.*

a series of raids by Peruvian slavers between 1859 and 1862. During one massive raid in December 1862, the Peruvians rounded up some 1,000 islanders and shipped them to islands off Peru to dig guano, seabird droppings used as a fertilizer. Many of those taken were high-ranking islanders whose special knowledge and skills disappeared with them. Some 100 survivors were eventually released for repatriation, but only 15 of these reached the island alive – bringing with them the scourge of smallpox, which further reduced the island's population.

By 1877 only 111 native Easter Islanders were left, living in miserable poverty, the days of their greatness a dim memory. Shortly thereafter, when missionaries and Chilean colonists arrived, they found a world in ruin, one to which the keys seemed irretrievably lost.

But from this unhappy period also dates the beginning of the European obsession with the Easter Island mystery – an obsession that has created its own extravagant theories but has also led to extensive, painstaking research, notably the work of the American W. J. Thomson (1886), Katherine Routledge of England (1914–15), Alfred Métraux of France and Henri Lavachery of Belgium (1934–5), the German missionary Sebastian Englert (1935–9), the Norwegian Thor Heyerdahl (1955–6) and the American anthropologist William Mulloy of the University of

Discovered in a bay near Easter Island's oldest dated altar, Ahu Tahai, this head of red volcanic stone is thought to be far more ancient than any of the classic, stylised moai. *Its rounded, naturalistic features are similar to those found in certain* tikis *made by the Marquesas Islanders.*

Wyoming, the most recent student of the island's ancient civilisation.

Thanks to the work of these and other dedicated researchers, many of the island's treasures have been uncovered and catalogued, and a number of the giant *moai* – to the world the island's most compelling symbol – have been restored to their original positions on the outdoor altars.

Although impressive stone statues have been found on other Polynesian islands, the *moai* of Easter Island are by far the largest and most numerous, and their distinctive style is duplicated nowhere else. Most of them were hewn out of a close-grained volcanic tuff from the slopes of the satellite volcano Rano Raraku on the eastern part of the island. An extraordinary site, Rano Raraku contains about 300 statues in every stage from bare outline to near completion, and thus it serves as a fascinating museum of the island sculptors' highly stylised and systematic techniques. Scattered around the site are stone picks and adzes, apparently discarded in haste; their abandonment suggests that this vast natural workshop was suddenly deserted.

On and around the slopes of Rano Raraku are about 100 finished, standing *moai*, partly buried in the soil; there may well be other statues still entombed in the rubble. These upright *moai* are a fascinating group and may represent the last phase of Easter Island carving. Like some of the statues formerly erected on *ahu*, a number of them have bodies marked with intricate tattoo-like symbols, but not one bears the cylindrical red stone *pukao*, or topknot, which sometimes adorned the heads of upright *moai*. The statues in this group are often called the Blind Giants because their eye sockets have not yet been carved – a detail which may have been added only after the *moai* were raised on altars, enabling the figures to 'see'.

Fallen giants

There are more than 300 finished *moai* on the island which were apparently overturned during the period of prolonged civil strife that began sometime in the 16th or 17th centuries. These are of classic stylisation; the carving of their eye sockets is complete, and some of them bore topknots of red scoria, a stone from the small volcano of Punapau in the southwest.

The *ahu*, or altars, on which these *moai* once stood are found mainly near the shores of the island. These sacred platforms – which, like the statues, are thought to have been erected by members of individual kinship groups – are related to other east Polynesian monuments known as *marae*. But on Easter Island they are remarkably numerous; at least 300 have been discov-

ered so far. Many are in an even greater state of ruin than the toppled *moai* themselves.

Though the *ahu* were built in several styles, the typical form was a narrow, elongated masonry platform with lateral wings – sometimes 200 yds long and more than 20 ft high – which varied in breadth from about 6 to 15 ft. The platform walls were of large unmortared stones and the interiors were filled with rubble. Paved ramps descended from the inland side of the altars toward plazas on which worshippers may have assembled, and some platforms had elevated central sections on which were set pedestals for the *moai* (although it is thought that many *ahu* actually predate the classic statues themselves).

Like Inca stonework

The finest *ahu* masonry work yet discovered is at Ahu Tahira in a place known as Vinapu on the south-west coast. The huge, unmortared basalt blocks that face its platform, no two alike, are so smoothly pecked and precisely fitted that it would be difficult to pass a knife blade between them. The stonework here bears a strong resemblance to Inca masonry, although earlier, prototypical examples of it suggest that it was independently developed on Easter Island.

The *moai* and their altars, however, are far from being the island's sole treasures. There are many other architectural monuments of impressive design, such as the priests' houses, or *hare paenga*, built of masonry blocks and shaped like overturned canoes; masonry-

Partly buried in the slope below the quarry at Rano Raraku, this statue, now badly eroded, is essentially complete except for the carving of its eye sockets. It was probably set upright in the ground in this temporary excavation to await transportation to an altar elsewhere on the island.

lined caves; and the ceremonial centre of Orongo. There is a large, naturalistic statue from the Rano Raraku quarry, thought to represent a singer or chanter in an island ceremony, which was executed in a style totally unlike that of the *moai*. There are many small stone statues in a variety of forms, often found in caves; stone petroglyphs in high relief; and carved wooden statuettes known as *moai kavakava*, some of which may represent *akuaku*, or malevolent spirits.

Perhaps the most enigmatic of Easter Island's treasures are the inscribed wooden tablets and chest ornaments known collectively as 'talking boards'. Once numerous, they were apparently used by the later Easter Islanders for firewood and canoe-building materials; only 26 of them remain in existence. All are covered with minute, beautifully incised characters, largely derived from human and animal forms.

It is thought these tablets were once used in religious ceremonies by the *maori ko hau rongorongo*, or 'masters of the art of recitation' – men specially trained in writing and reciting the sacred inscriptions. Thomas Barthel, a German ethnologist who has studied the tablets intensively, has concluded that their language is of Polynesian origin. A satisfactory translation of the ideographic script is difficult, however, because so few examples of it survive; the task of reconstructing it is rather like attempting a complete re-creation of English literature on the basis of a few pages torn at random from the great classics.

Vision of a new homeland

Who were these men who fashioned the *moai*, the *ahu* and the 'talking boards', and where did they come from originally? Ever since Roggeveen chanced upon the island in 1722, scholars and the merely curious have been seeking answers to these questions, sometimes offering fantastic theories. Easter Island was the Lost Continent . . . it was formerly inhabited by beings from outer space . . . it was once mysteriously joined to ancient Egypt. Contemporary scholars, however, are almost unanimously agreed that the people who settled the islands and carved its *moai* were Polynesians.

According to the islanders' own legends of the coming of man to 'the navel of the world', a great chief or *ariki henua* (supreme religious leader) called Hotu Matu'a was forced to leave his homeland in the archipelago of Hiva after being defeated in battle. (Another version has it that he and his people were made homeless when the land of Hiva disappeared beneath the sea.) Several accounts agree that Hiva was situated toward the setting sun and its climate was hot.

Placing the red stone headpiece on top of the ahu moai *must have been more difficult than setting up the statues themselves. These stones may have been roughly rounded before they were moved from the quarry, and then shaped once they had arrived at the* ahu. *The largest of them must have been secured in place before the statue was raised.*

Whatever impelled his departure, the legend goes on to say that Hotu Matu'a – or one of his associates – had a vision of a new homeland somewhere in the direction of the rising sun, and seven young men were sent out to find it; hence the discovery of Easter Island.

The strange cult of the Bird-Man

The Easter Island village of Orongo was the centre of a religious ritual which was probably unique in Polynesia.

Orongo lies at the southernmost point of the island, between the crater of the volcano Rano Kau and a cliff that descends over 800 ft to the sea. Just off the shore are three islets called Motu Nui, Motu Iti and Motu Kaokao.

Once a year, in September, representatives of the tribes would gather in Orongo together with young men chosen for their athletic prowess. Each athlete was sponsored by an individual warrior. The young men swam across the shark-infested sea to Motu Nui where the *manutara* bird (sooty tern) nested. It was a race to see who could find the first *manutara* egg of the season. The winner took the egg back to his sponsor who was then declared *tangata manu* or Bird-Man for that year. The Bird-Man had important ceremonial functions and was held in great veneration.

These rites seem to have been established fairly late in Easter Island's history. As the islanders became isolated from the mainstream of Polynesian religions, the god Makemake, who was believed to be incarnated in seabirds, took over from traditional deities. The earliest-known date for the Bird-Man cult is the 15th century. The latest is 1867.

When Hotu Matu'a himself came to the island with his entourage, he brought many kinds of plants, trees and animals, but not all survived. Later, when the Polynesian chief felt death approaching, he divided the island among his children – and this presumably accounts for the origin of the 10 or 12 kinship groups eventually established on Easter Island.

This tradition lends weight to the theory that the Polynesians, master navigators that they were, became Easter Island's first inhabitants. For a long time, however, the controversy about the islanders' origins simply reflected the age-old dispute about the origins of the Oceanic peoples in general. Most specialists in the field tended to reject the notion that the islanders, and perhaps other Polynesians, originated in South America. But in 1947 Thor Heyerdahl, in his famed *Kon-Tiki* expedition, demonstrated that it is possible to reach Polynesia's Tuamotu archipelago from Peru on a simple raft – and Tuamotu is even farther from the coast of South America than Easter Island. Eight years later, while conducting research on Easter Island, Heyerdahl sought additional evidence to support his theory

The numerous moai *that dot the grassy slopes below Rano Raraku seem like blind guardians at the entrance to some mysterious shrine. In all, some 300 statues in varying stages of completion have been found in and around this great quarry, which is the island's most spectacular monument.*

reasonable to assume that the structure was not built by brand-new arrivals; indeed, the island may have been inhabited as early as the 1st century AD.

Recent carbon-14 datings present a picture of the ancient Polynesians' gradual eastward movement which is incomplete but nonetheless impressive. People from south-east Asia were in New Guinea some 26,000 years ago, in the Solomon Islands 5,000 years ago and in New Caledonia and Fiji 3,000 years ago. By about 500 BC they had arrived at Tonga and soon afterward they reached Samoa, spreading from there to the Marquesas and the Society Islands, which they probably reached near the beginning of the Christian era. From there they scattered toward the points of the Polynesian triangle – Hawaii, New Zealand and Easter Island. This outline suggests the gradual eastward movement of a culture that originated in south-east Asia and later developed its distinctive oceanic forms through adaptation to new environments in the scattered Pacific islands.

An obsession with building

Were the first Easter Islanders – the settlers who came sometime before AD 690 – the followers of Hotu Matu'a, as the legends suggest? Did their descendants produce the great statues? The best evidence now indicates that the answer is yes. The whole spectacular *moai-ahu* complex seems to reflect a remarkable obsession with religious building peculiar to the island – but one based on essentially Polynesian ideas. Moreover, the island's culture demonstrates a clear

The one statue yet found in the Rano Raraku quarry that in no way resembles the classic moai *is the figure above, known as* tuku turi. *This full figure of a bearded, kneeling man – discovered by a member of the Heyerdahl expedition – has been compared to the statues of other South Pacific islands.*

of a link between Polynesia and the New World.

Heyerdahl's hypothesis rests on a number of assumptions, many drawn from Inca legends as reported by the Spanish *conquistadores* of Peru, others from the study of Pacific currents, the analysis of blood groups and botanical evidence. He also pointed to the strong resemblance between the workmanship of the famous Ahu Tahira at Vinapu and Inca masonry in Peru.

Most students of the area disagree with Heyerdahl's conclusions. No American Indian languages appear in Polynesia, nor do any crafts resembling New World metalwork, textiles or ceramics. But many cultural traits which can be traced westwards to Indonesia do appear on Easter Island, as elsewhere in Polynesia.

Today, it is generally agreed that the island was first settled by voyagers who came from the west sometime before AD 690, the earliest reliable radiocarbon date yet found there. Further, since the source of this date is the first construction phase at Ahu Tahai, a large monument fashioned in distinctively local style, it is

The unmortared masonry walls of Ahu Tahira at Vinapu are the most perfectly made on the island. Although the altar is in ruins today, some of its beautifully cut and fitted stone facing remains in place. Despite the resemblance to Inca stonework, it appears to be of local origin.

continuity of conception and style from its simple beginnings to its final, tragic disintegration in the prolonged upheaval of more recent times.

It is characteristic of the various Polynesian colonies, isolated from one another in the vastness of the Pacific, that each developed in its own way, and that the outlying areas – Hawaii, New Zealand and Easter Island – developed the most distinctive local cultures. On Easter Island, the abundance of volcanic rock suitable for carving and the developing scarcity of timber – plus such probable social factors as strong competition among kinship groups and intense religious fervor – led to the flowering of a unique tradition of sculpture in stone.

As has been indicated, Easter Island craftsmen presumably began building altars well before AD 690, and there is evidence suggesting that prototypical, naturalistic statues may have been placed on them by that time. The classically stylised *moai*, however, appear to be a somewhat later development, and the red scoria topknots still more recent. The earliest dated *ahu* known to have served as an altar for a classic *moai* was built about AD 1110–1205, although statues of the same type may have been made somewhat earlier. The period of classical statue-building was to continue

at least another 450 years, until about AD 1650.

There exists on Easter Island a controversial oral tradition which concerns the division of the islanders into two main groups. According to this tradition, during the period of *moai-ahu* building the island was ruled by a class-based theocracy in which the dominant group was called the Hanau Eepe, a name incorrectly translated as 'long-ears' but actually meaning 'heavy-set people'. The lower classes were called the Hanau Momoko (slender people), and the tradition relates that they descended from Hotu Matu'a, whereas the Hanau Eepe had arrived – possibly quite accidentally, since they are thought to have brought no women with them – in a later migration.

End of the oppressors

In any case, the usual story is that one day the Hanau Eepe ordered the Hanau Momoko to gather and remove all the millions of stones that littered the island's fields. Oppressed beyond endurance, the Hanau Momoko not only refused but rose in revolt, forcing their erstwhile masters to flee to the slopes of the volcano Poike. Here the Hanau Eepe dug a long fortification trench (traces of it still remain) and filled

Overlooking the crater of Rano Kau and not far from Orongo, the Bird-Man village, there is a closely spaced series of rock engravings. It is thought that they were carved by generations of worshippers who wanted to win favour with Makemake, the Bird-God, or give him thanks.

Hidden in corners on the volcano of Rano Raraku are hollows where embryonic statues lie. One of them can just be made out behind this worn profile and shows the technique used by the sculptors. The outline was chipped out using a stone chisel, and then the surplus rock was removed, leaving the rib of rock down the back until last.

it with fuel, which they planned to ignite if necessary to repulse any frontal attack. But they were betrayed by a spy and attacked from behind by the Hanau Momoko, who threw the enemy into their own flaming pit. In the end, only one Hanau Eepe was spared; there are contemporary islanders who claim descent from him.

It is reasonable to suppose that such a civil war must have been caused by factors far more complex than a squabble over stones. Indeed, it is likely that the Hanau Momoko were the victims of an economy of ever-growing scarcity brought on by overcrowding, depletion of the island's limited agricultural resources, and the increasingly intolerable burden of religious building and associated ceremonial activities. If such was the case, it would help to explain the sudden cessation of work in the quarries of Rano Raraku, the vindictive destruction of the *ahu* and the great statues,

and the apparent abandonment of the cult associated with them.

What, in fact, was that cult, and what was the significance of the *moai*? Most scholars now agree that the great statues do not represent gods but were made as images of great chiefs or spiritual leaders, ancestor-figures who were believed to be imbued with a super-natural power, known as *mana*, which protected their descendants in the living communities. The significance of the red stone topknots which adorned some of the figures is not known. They may represent long hair pulled into a knot or some kind of ritual headgear, or they may have been intended simply for decoration.

Interrupted efforts

The standing *moai* found embedded in the soil around Rano Raraku have been interpreted by some scholars as a special group set there deliberately to commemorate deified heroes. But, in fact, archaeological examination has revealed that these embedded statues are fixed in improvised holes, that the buried portions of their bodies are sculptured in detail and that their bases are flat – all of which suggest that they were awaiting transportation to *ahu*, an arduous task which

The man who made the 'talking boards' speak

For 140 years after Easter Island was discovered by the outside world, some of its most remarkable treasures remained unnoticed. These treasures were the 'talking boards' – wooden tablets like the one pictured on the right – each covered with the characters of an unknown language. The first European to notice the boards was a French missionary, Brother Eugène Eyraud. When he spotted them in the 1860s, he found that the islanders had been using these irreplaceable keys to their history for firewood. With their leaders kidnapped or killed by slavers from South America, they had nobody to decipher the script.

Scholars were keenly interested in Brother Eyraud's find, for the boards were the first examples of a written native language that had been found anywhere in the South Sea islands. But by the time the salvage campaign got underway only a pitifully small number were left: just 21 tablets, and a handful of other artefacts with inscriptions.

As the years passed, linguists puzzled over the boards. At first, some dismissed the marks as cloth-printing designs – pretty but meaningless. Others tried to link them with the picture-writing of a tribe of Panamanian Indians, with the rock paintings of Australian aborigines, with Egyptian hieroglyphics, even with 4,000-year-old inscriptions in the Indus Valley in India and Pakistan. None found the answer.

Then in 1953, a German scholar, Thomas Barthel, took up the challenge. He reasoned that since the script contained about 120 symbols combined into more than 1,000 signs – far more than would be needed for an alphabetic or syllabic system – each sign must stand for a complete word or idea. But he still needed some key to get him started. He found it by following a clue from the previous century: the story of an early Easter Island investigator, the French Bishop Tepano Jaussen. The bishop was known to have found on Tahiti an Easter Islander who had been trained in his youth as a professional chanter – a rongorongo man.

The story went that the man, Metoro Tauara, had been able to chant songs from four of the boards the bishop had collected. The bishop had noted each song in Polynesian and then found, to his dismay, that Metoro's translations made no sense at all.

Barthel suspected that Metoro had guessed at some of the symbols, rather as a choirboy will guess at the words in a complicated piece of church music, but that he did know at least some of the island script. So he tracked Jaussen's notebook from Tahiti to France, Belgium and Italy, discovering it finally in a monastery near Rome. 'Those lines of Polynesian syllables in Jaussen's shaky hand,' he wrote later, 'became my Rosetta Stone ... I'll never forget the moment when the first textual fragments began to make sense.'

By 1960, Barthel had begun publishing his translations – showing the boards to contain mostly prayers to gods, instructions to priests, and accounts of island mythology. But there are too few boards to be absolutely sure, and some of Barthel's translations have been rejected by other experts.

Nevertheless, Barthel believes that there is enough evidence to show that the writing was developed by the Polynesians who reached Easter Island some 2,000 years ago.

The inscribed tablets, or 'talking boards', of Easter Island are covered with minute ideographs which turn back and upside down at the end of each line, like furrows in a ploughed field. That such an isolated culture developed a script of its own is an astonishing accomplishment.

---

was destined never to be completed.

Individual statues have also been found lying along ancient roads on many parts of the island. According to William Mulloy, who has been studying Easter Island intensively since 1955, many of these figures were simply abandoned – some during the period of civil strife, others after they were damaged or broken in transit. At any rate, construction seems to have halted about AD 1650, the most recent radiocarbon date recorded for a building site.

This much seems reasonably clear, but other questions remain. How long did it take the island sculptors to carve one of these giants, and how were the statues transported and raised? The most convincing estimate of the time required to carve a large statue was made by archaeologist Arne Skjölsvold of the Heyerdahl expedition. His careful experiments and observations led him to conclude that a statue 16 ft long could be carved in about a year – provided the work was done by the maximum number of sculptors who could conveniently collaborate on a single project.

The more difficult question – how the *moai* were transported and raised – has given rise to some fantastic notions. Vanished armies of slaves hauled them to their altars; or perhaps volcanic eruptions threw the statues onto their pedestals, right end up. One island tradition relates that the statues were full of that supernatural power called *mana* and simply walked to their appointed places; another, more down-to-earth story says that vast carpets of sweet potatoes and crushed yams were laid on the slopes and the statues were slid along them. In fact, the study of Rano Raraku itself demonstrates that some system of cables, presumably made of strong cordage, must have been used to restrain the *moai* as they were eased down the slope to prepared pits; a number of bollards, holes and grooves are still visible in the rock at the top of the crater that furnished the quarry.

Reading the patterns of the waves

The Polynesians were master navigators who tracked their way across huge expanses of ocean without any of the complex aids, such as the Greek astrolabe or the sextant, compass and chronometer, which Europeans found essential.

As late as 1837 a British ship set sail for Raratonga, in the Pacific, from an island less than 150 miles away, but even with the help of a chart, a compass and a telescope failed to find it. Yet centuries before, the Polynesians crossed thousands of miles of ocean without getting lost.

How did they do it?

Like all navigators they used the stars as fixed points of reference. They understood the significance of stationary clouds, the presence of birds and flotsam as indications of nearby land. But most extraordinary of all, they had learned how to read and interpret the changing patterns created by ocean waves.

A stone thrown into a pond will set up a series of ripples. Any object, like a rock or even a mooring post, which breaks the surface, will affect the pattern of the ripples. Pond or Pacific Ocean, the same principle applies. Islands and atolls have the same effect as rocks and posts. The Polynesians observed that when waves hit an island, some are reflected back in the direction from which they have come while others are deflected at angles round the island and continue their passage in a modified form.

The art of reading the waves was taught to Polynesian boys with the aid of the mattang, *a web of interlocking sticks which demonstrated all the basic patterns that waves can form when they are deflected by land.*

The adult navigator gauged these wave patterns entirely by his sense of touch. He would crouch in the bow of his canoe and literally feel every motion of the vessel.

In this way the original colonisers of Easter Island might have 'felt' the presence of what was to be their new homeland before actually sighting it.

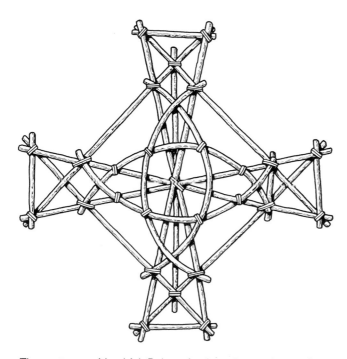

The mattang *with which Polynesian boys learned to navigate over the trackless wastes of the Pacific Ocean by studying the motion of the waves deflected from islands.*

It is revealing to look at the problem in terms of other Polynesian cultures. The Marquesas Islanders, for example, used stretchers and inclined planes to place rocks weighing up to 10 tons on their sanctuaries, and the Maori of New Zealand managed to haul large pieces of canoe timber, heavier than some of the *moai*, over long distances. Yet such achievements pale when one considers that Paro, the largest Easter Island *moai* known to have been erected on an *ahu*, was 32 ft tall and weighed 90 tons without its topknot, which alone weighed nearly 12 tons.

Moving the monsters

How could the islanders have moved such monsters? Part of the answer may lie in the fact that Easter Island's population in its heyday was probably far larger than has usually been estimated – perhaps as large as 20,000 – and the land far more abundant than it is today. But even given the necessary men and materials, just how was the task accomplished?

The most recent hypothesis has been put forward by William Mulloy, using as an example the gigantic Paro statue, which was found toppled and broken nearly 4 miles from Rano Raraku. Mulloy suggests that it was transported prone and head first on a Y-shaped, curved bottom sledge, probably made from a tree fork, of a type he believes the prehistoric islanders were familiar with. He further suggests that the protruding belly and jutting chin of the typical *moai* were not arbitrary stylisations but were dictated by the use of this sledge system.

Once lashed to its sledge, the statue was pulled by ropes in a series of rocking movements along a prepared road covered with reeds or grass. Mechanical advantage may have been provided by a bipod, placed transversely across the statue's neck and inclined slightly forward at the base, with a rope passed between the neck and the bipod juncture. When this rope was pulled, the statue's head would rise, then the figure would move forward with a rocking motion – a movement that may have given rise to the idea of 'walking' statues in the island legends. The bipod could then be repositioned and the process repeated. Mulloy has estimated that by this means the islanders could have moved Paro at a rate of just under 1,000 feet per day, reaching the *ahu* in a little under a month. But once there, how was the *moai* raised on its altar?

One widespread theory grew out of an experiment suggested by Mulloy during the 1955–6 Heyerdahl expedition, of which he was a member. A dozen islanders were challenged to replace a 25-ton statue on its altar, but were given no instructions on how to proceed. They accomplished the task in 18 days by building a masonry platform under the *moai's* belly while levering up the statue with two 16-foot-long tree trunks. But since the statue was badly scarred during the raising process, Mulloy concluded that in the past the *moai* had probably been protected by some kind of wooden armature. He has also suggested that the red

stone topknots were lashed to the heads of the statues designed to wear them, so that *moai* and topknot could be raised as a unit.

In 1960 Mulloy, his colleague Gonzalo Figueroa and a team of islanders raised seven 16-ton statues on Ahu Akivi near the island's west coast. The first took more than a month to set upright; the last, with the benefit of experience, less than a week.

Mulloy has calculated that the carving, transportation and raising of Paro involved something in the region of 23,000 man-days – and Paro is only one of hundreds of great *moai*. The American anthropologist's work and that of other scholars has provided plausible explanations for many of the age-old enigmas of Easter Island, yet intriguing questions remain.

What compelled the islanders to produce such a wealth of religious art and architecture on such a colossal scale? Exactly what were the seeds of this magnificent culture's destruction – class warfare, in-

The recently restored ceremonial centre at Tahai on the island's west coast has three great ahu: *Ko te Riku, Vai Uri and Tahai. The* moai *in the background weighs more than 20 tons. Besides the* ahu, *this centre has other structures, including a paved ramp used for hauling canoes ashore.*

tense competition among kin groups, overpopulation and depletion of resources or a combination of the three? Above all, in a world in which it is taken for granted that great civilisations usually develop through intensive cultural interchange among many groups, how did such an astonishing culture evolve on the most remote inhabited island in the Pacific?

We can only speculate and wonder. The entire truth about Easter Island's past may remain shrouded in mystery for a long time to come, perhaps forever.

CHARLES LEBARON

Cities of mystery

Teotihuacán, city of the gods

A thousand years before the Aztecs, Teotihuacán was the religious capital of Mexico. Its streets were crowded with pilgrims. Its art and buildings glittered in the sun. This was where even the mighty Aztecs felt a sense of awe, calling it 'the place of those who have the road of the Gods'. Yet it crumbled, suddenly and inexplicably. Its streets emptied, its temples fell, its people fled. Who were they? Where did they come from? Where did they go, and why? Even today, nobody knows. The people of Teotihuacán, like gods themselves, left only mystery in their wake.

Some 1,400 years ago, at a time when in western Europe uncouth barbarian tribes such as the Saxons were beginning to attract the attention of Christian missionaries, there flourished on the other side of the Atlantic a brilliant and gifted civilisation that was able to create a city of perhaps 150,000 people.

Yet in less than a thousand years, when the Aztecs overran the region, Teotihuacán had been reduced to a collection of awe-inspiring ruins, its precisely patterned streets and plazas empty, its palaces deserted, its magnificent pyramids crumbling. The Aztecs, how-

ever, were in no doubt about the city's importance. The name they reverently bestowed on it means, according to the American scholar Thelma Sullivan, 'the place of those who have the road of the Gods'. At its peak, during the 5th century AD, Teotihuacán was the spiritual metropolis of Mexico, capital of an extensive empire and a remarkable feat of urban planning – its 8 sq. miles laid out according to a specific grid plan.

Much is known about the civilisations that succeeded Teotihuacán. Yet, despite a century of modern research, it is still not certain who built the city, who lived there, why they suddenly vanished or where they went. Even their language is unknown.

All that stands today is just a fraction of the magnificence that was Teotihuacán. Nine-tenths of the city is still buried, and in fact there is more than one Teotihuacán to be unearthed, because over the long history of the city buildings were periodically rebuilt,

Seen from the Pyramid of the Sun, the ruins of Teotihuacán stretch away to the horizon. Though still nine-tenths buried, the basic structure of the sacred city is clearly evident. It had a population of some 150,000, and was built according to a remarkably precise urban plan.

109

possibly every 100 years or so. Excavations to date have shown three of four separate levels, each superimposed on the preceding one.

The site was an excellent choice. The plateau on which the city stands is more than 7,500 ft high, and is on the natural route linking the Valley of Mexico and the Valley of Puebla, which to the east joins the tropical lowlands along the Gulf of Mexico where Veracruz is situated today.

Teotihuacán overlooked a fertile valley, with streams giving plenty of water; and the volcanic environment provided ample supplies of obsidian, a volcanic glass which was a raw material of prime importance in the making of instruments, utensils and weapons. Tools or weapons edged with obsidian were so sharp that a man could shave with them.

The plateau was inhabited by Indians who cultivated the soil. They lived in wattle-and-daub huts in villages of 100 to 300 people, sometimes more. It was, no doubt, with the participation of some of these local villagers that the founders of Teotihuacán began building what was to become the most impressive ceremonial centre in all pre-Columbian Mexico.

The amazingly high record of accomplishment,

seemingly from the moment Teotihuacán appeared, suggests that it did not rise up out of a completely barren past. Another culture had blossomed before it – that of the Olmecs, whose civilisation rose and fell between the 13th and 1st centuries BC. They were a race of master builders, as well as sculptors of colossal heads and of figurines in the hardest and most beautiful jades. The Olmec site of La Venta, with its mounds set around quadrangles and its ceremonial area laid out along a central north-south axis, set a pattern for all future Middle American cities.

Legends of the Aztecs

Although Teotihuacán seems to have emerged from the local population of the valleys of Teotihuacán and Mexico – the city's cultural antecedents and

The heavy religious style of this coloured terracotta mask, dating from the Xolalpan period (AD 400–600), is typical of the sculpture found in Teotihuacán. The stylised butterfly shape of the nose plate signifies the performing of a ritual act, leading to the conclusion that the mask may have belonged to one of the religious centre's priests.

Teotihuacán's zone of influence covered Mexico's central plateau area, part of the Gulf coast and the land of the earlier Olmecs. To the south, it may have extended as far as the site of Kaminaljuyú, some 700 miles away in Guatemala. Kaminaljuyú is thought to be an outpost of Teotihuacán, created perhaps during the 5th century AD.

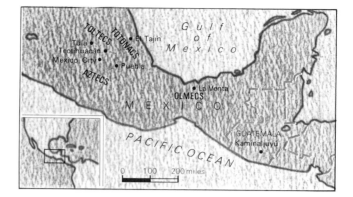

connections are clearly with the local peoples who preceded the builders – this, however, gives no clue to their ethnic origin. A Frenchman named Désiré Charnay first uncovered a small part of the city of the gods in 1880 and, like many others after him, took it to be a Toltec city. However, further studies showed that the history of the Toltecs had begun in the second half of the 10th century AD, when Teotihuacán was already in ruins; and the Toltecs had their capital further north at Tollan, now the town of Tula in the state of Hidalgo.

The Toltec theory, however, should not be entirely discounted, since the Aztecs in their legendary epics and chronicles used the general name of Toltec to refer to the ancient race whose religious tradition – and part of whose learning – they claimed to retain. Moreover,

they appear to have thought that Teotihuacán was the Toltec capital. For the Aztecs, the word Toltec came to mean 'great craftsmen', and no description could be more fitting for the prodigious architects of Teotihuacán or for those people of the City of the Gods who created over the many centuries burial masks and ceramics of a standard that was unparalleled in the classical Mexican era.

But perhaps a deeper meaning should be sought in the term 'great craftsmen'. For according to one in-

---

The sacred ball game

The favourite game of the peoples of Middle America before the Spanish conquest was a curious, and violent, cross between soccer, volleyball and the Spanish game of pelota. But it was much more than just a game – it also had religious significance and was a vital part of important community rituals involving sacrifice and death.

The ball game, as it is known now, seems to have been first played by the Olmecs. By 400 BC it was already popular among the other peoples of Middle America, and it spread over the centuries to the inhabitants of Teotihuacán, and to the Toltecs, the Mayas and the Aztecs. In Aztec times, the game was known as tlachtli, and the central precinct of Tenochtitlán (now Mexico City) contained several massive I-shaped courts with stone rings and exaggerated end pieces where the game was played.

It was in Teotihuacán, however, that the game appears to have evolved most uniquely. For there, according to scholarly interpretations of a single fresco and a number of mysterious stone post assemblages, it differed from other versions in at least three important ways. First, sticks were used, swung perhaps as they are in field or ice hockey today. Second, the game was played in what appears to be a relatively informal area; and, third, the vertical stone posts may have functioned as special Teotihuacán goal posts.

Nonetheless, it is the Aztec version of the game that is best known today, because more of their ball courts have survived and because Aztec and Spanish historians have left detailed accounts of their games.

Winners who chased fans

In the game, two teams faced each other over a line drawn across the centre of the court between two giant side walls. Their aim was to knock a heavy rubber ball into their opponents' end of the court in much the same way as volleyball players do today. The difference was that these players were allowed to bounce the ball off the walls, and to hit it only with their hips, knees or elbows. Teams could also win a game outright by knocking the ball through either of two stone rings that jutted out from midpoint

of each side wall. The rings were sometimes 20 ft or more above the court and only just big enough for the ball, so goals were uncommon. But a player who scored was allowed to confiscate the clothes and possessions of any spectators he and his friends could catch.

The players wore padded knee-caps, leather aprons and face-masks to protect themselves from the flying ball. They also wore gloves to protect their hands from the stony ground when they fell. Injuries were common, and sometimes fatal.

The game was so popular that goods of all kinds were wagered on the result. Some were ruined by it. The Indian chronicler Ixtlilxochitl tells of one game in the late 15th century when the Aztec emperor Axayacatl played against the ruler of the neighbouring city of Xochimilco. Axayacatl bet the market-place of Mexico City against one of the ruler's gardens, and lost. But the next day, Aztec soldiers appeared at the palace of Xochimilco and 'while they saluted him and made him presents they threw a garland of flowers about his neck with a thong hidden in it, and so killed him'.

Losers who lost their lives

Wherever the ball game was played, it had, besides its popular appeal, enormous ritual importance. Ball courts were always laid out east-west or north-south, and each part of the game had its own significance. The court represented the heavens, the stone rings symbolised sunset and sunrise or the equinoxes; and the movement of the ball represented the path of the sun, moon or stars depending on the beliefs of the area. Among the Mayas, where the ball game was known as *pok-ta-pok*, some matches even ended with the ritual sacrifice of the losing team.

Among the Aztecs, the game was also used for divination – as when Montezuma played against the lord of the nearby city of Texcoco to test the truth of a prophecy that strangers would come to rule in Tenochtitlán. The legend records that Montezuma won the first few games in the series of matches but was finally defeated – and it was not long afterwards that Hernán Cortés landed to begin his conquest of Mexico.

Teotihuacán, city of priests and temples

Long before the Aztecs came to dominate central Mexico, Teotihuacán was a magnificent abandoned ruin, the capital of a civilisation that lasted nearly 1,000 years, but declined and vanished in the 8th century AD. As shown in the imaginative drawing below, based on the work of anthropologist René Millon of the University of Rochester, the city was laid out in a precise grid pattern extending from either side of its main thoroughfare, the north-south Avenue of the Dead [1]. This processional route runs from the Plaza of the Moon [2] south to the Citadel [3], the religious centre of the city. The Citadel's platform surrounds an enclosure containing the temple of Quetzalcoatl, the Feathered Serpent [4]. Towering over the Avenue of the Dead and the city itself are the Pyramids of the Sun [5] and the Moon [6]. The city's leaders lived in numerous palatial housing complexes spotted along the avenue. One such complex is shown situated to the east of the avenue [7] and another to the northwest [8]. This last was one of the most beautiful of the priestly palaces, Quetzalpalalotl, the Palace of the Butterfly-Bird. Many of the city's housing complexes were large and contained a number of rooms, all opening out onto patios. Some were built, like the pyramids, of a red volcanic rock which was mined locally. Although Teotihuacán's priests and leaders lived along the avenue, elsewhere in the city the population's living quarters formed a unique kind of mosaic, with high-status barrios, or housing clusters, alternating directly with those of middle and lower status. At its largest, Teotihuacán covered an area of approximately 8 sq. miles, and by AD 600 it held a population of perhaps 150,000 to 200,000.

terpretation of Aztec writing, the City of the Gods was built to mark the Fifth Sun, or fifth renewal of the world. This sun, said the Aztecs, rose in Teotihuacán to climb to the centre of the universe. The founders of the City of the Gods were considered for long after the city's destruction as the founders of a new era, spiritually recognised as the era of motion. This at least is the view put forward in a bold, brilliant and concise interpretation of Aztec mythology which has been advanced in recent years by Laurette Séjourné, a Mexican archaeologist of French origin.

A celestial signpost

Certainly its prodigious architecture, prolific art and unparalleled manufacturing industry suggest that it was indeed the thriving hub of a confident, pioneering society. And its most dominant building, the Pyramid of the Sun, stands in the centre like a celestial signpost to a new world.

A few scholars consider that a priesthood or theocracy governed Teotihuacán and that these rulers might have come from some other land, probably to the east and possibly on the Gulf coast. For instance,

the Mexican Jiménez Moreno and the Frenchman Jacques Soustelle favour the Totonacs, a people who still existed in the north of Veracruz, near El Tajín, when the Spaniards landed there. But the identity of the inspired people who made Teotihuacán the spiritual centre of ancient Mexico is still unknown.

The city was constructed to a vast geometrical pattern on a grid plan based on two huge avenues which crossed each other at right-angles. The main road was the so-called Avenue of the Dead, running north-south for more than a mile, and reaching a width of 140 ft in places. The avenue's name was given to it by the Aztecs, who believed it was lined with tombs. But the pyramid-shaped platforms along its length are now believed to have had flat tops on each of which stood a temple.

The avenue is interrupted for a short distance south of the Pyramid of the Sun by a number of rectangular spaces, sometimes with an altar or temple in the centre. According to a recent theory, one section of the avenue could have been used for the ritual ball game which was played throughout Middle America. Experts were puzzled by the absence of any evidence of this sacred game in Teotihuacán until the discovery of a fresco and some strange goal posts provided proof that a variation of the game, peculiar to that part of Middle America, was practised there.

To the east of the Avenue of the Dead is the Pyramid of the Sun. It has been calculated that the pyramid, which was apparently completed in the 1st century AD, took at least 50 years to build, with a work force of thousands. About 1 million cu. yds of material were used. Faced with a local red volcanic rock, it soars 216 ft above ground and is about 720 by 760 ft at its base. The belief that the pyramid was built to represent the centre of the universe is associated with its similarity to a number-sign sacred to the ancient Indians – the *quincunx*. This consisted of four points set at the corners of a square or rectangle, with a fifth point in the centre, much like the number five on dice. The central point denoted the centre or heart of life – the vital point in man where opposing forces met and became unified. The pyramid, with its lofty apex standing central to the four corners of its base, could be seen as a translation of the *quincunx* into three-dimensional terms on a monumental scale.

The serpent god

Nearby, at the north end of the Avenue of the Dead, is the Pyramid of the Moon, which is smaller but similar. At the other end of the avenue is the third major monument of the city – the Citadel, a sunken plaza

The huge Avenue of the Dead, with the Pyramid of the Moon at one end and the Pyramid of the Sun to the left, is divided to the south by a series of broad staircases. More than 100 smaller religious buildings also lined the avenue. It was named by the Aztecs, who mistakenly believed that these structures were sepulchres.

surrounded by platform temples, which was undoubtedly a place of worship and perhaps a training centre for the priests of Teotihuacán.

Rising up out of the centre of this ceremonial square is the Temple of Quetzalcóatl, the Feathered Serpent, an Indian god so named because he had the feathers of the quetzal bird and the body of a snake. Only the temple's spectacular base remains, a six-stepped pyramid with large powerfully styled heads sculpted in relief around its walls and ramps.

The heads are those of Quetzalcóatl and another idol, the god of rain. In general the plumed serpent appears much less frequently in Teotihuacán sculpture than the rain god, whose saucer eyes surrounded by rings signify a depth of vision capable of cutting through appearances. Although it could be concluded that he was more widely worshipped, it is generally thought that he was simply more popular. In a dry land the rain god would have attracted the hopes and devotion of a peasant mass whose crops depended on water. Peasants formed the bulk of the population and so provided the greatest number of pilgrims.

A union of heaven and earth

Laurette Séjourné has suggested that the whole city may have been built to the glory of Quetzalcóatl, starting a new world with a closer alliance between heaven and earth. According to writings in Nahuatl, the language of the Aztecs, the bird, *quetzal*, symbolised heaven and spiritual energy, and the serpent, *coatl*, denoted earth and material forces.

Quetzalcóatl stands as a giant symbol representing the creation of the universe, expressing the alliance of heaven and earth and the union of spirit with matter. Laurette Séjourné suggests that the hidden meaning of the cult of the plumed serpent is that it implies a double nature in man. It awakens in him a consciousness of his double nature and it guides him on the way to becoming a 'solar being'.

Laurette Séjourné considers it probable that the buildings surrounding the Temple of Quetzalcóatl were not simply the homes of priests but clerical colleges and religious schools – in short, a training centre for initiates. She imagines that there might have been a ceremony where at the appointed time the new priests would ascend the Avenue of the Dead in stages marked out by the various temples, and proceed to a ritual mounting of the steep steps leading to the Pyramid of the Sun, which they would then enter.

It is believed possible that the worship of Quetzalcóatl belonged primarily to the priestly class, who built Teotihuacán. There are strong reasons for thinking, as the Aztecs did when they named it, that Teotihuacán was built by and for men who believed that they knew their precise role in the cosmos, their origin and their heavenly destiny – a city where an initiated élite of men worked diligently to follow the 'road of the Gods'.

The ceremonial area of Teotihuacán appears to be divided into two sections joined by the axis of the Avenue of the Dead. At the top is the 'celestial' section where the two pyramids stand, and below the 'earthly' section containing the Citadel, which encircles the temple of Quetzalcóatl.

All the buildings, including the palace and the dwelling houses of the city, conform to the east-west orientation of the Pyramid of the Sun, which represents the axis followed by the sun as it sets – or, as the ancient Indians believed, travelled down into the world of darkness – to rise again and resume its ascent heavenwards.

Whatever the religious theories, there is ample evidence to show that the city was a hive of industry. On each side of the Avenue of the Dead, grid-shaped rows of residences were built, many with lanes about 8 ft wide around the four outer walls. These were probably the homes of Teotihuacán's noble élite. Beyond them,

This mask from Teotihuacán is made of green stone encrusted with turquoise and red shells. A necklace of pink shell beads hangs from the earlobes. Masks of this type are believed to have been used in funerals. They were probably placed over the face of the dead before cremation. The Aztecs later made masks in a similar style.

stretching out of and around the city, were huge communal dwellings, where perhaps the city's artisans and labourers were housed.

All these living complexes, no matter how palatial, consisted of a number of interior patios surrounded by columns. Rooms were windowless, for the sake of coolness, and connected by a network of internal corridors. They opened out onto the patios for light and ventilation, and were arranged around a large central courtyard open to the sky. Interior walls, covered in smooth dazzling white stucco, which reflected light from the courtyard, were often beautifully painted with scenes of ritual processions of gods and various mythological symbols and stores.

In the centre of the courtyard, rainwater, which poured in from sloping pavements and slightly sloping roofs of the building, entered underground drains that carried excess water away from the houses. Polished stone plugs could be used to block the drains at will to hold supplies.

In one of the city's dwelling complexes, known as Tlamimilolpan, no fewer than 175 rooms have been found, arranged around 21 patios and five courtyards. One palace, called Zacuala, has been unearthed over an area of more than 4,000 sq. yds. It has an imposing entrance, a private temple and a main quadrangle surrounded by porticos and 12 other patios.

In excavating the dwellings the archaeologists often came upon circular pits about a yard in diameter and

The ancient god of fire had the face of an old man; he lived in the navel of the world and is one of Teotihuacán's noted deities. Here he is doubled up in a crouching position supporting a brassero, or incense-burner. This work in stone is typical of the Xolalpan, or the Teotihuacán III, period dating to about AD 400–600.

the same in depth, dug into the soil of the patios or the floors of the rooms. These are graves, where bones have been found, sometimes half-charred, sometimes cleaned, and sometimes arranged in an order that does not form the skeleton. It seems that at Teotihuacán the dead were often burned, then wrapped in shrouds with ritual offerings of pottery objects. Some of the most beautiful vases have been found in the graves, though the quality of the offerings varied according to the rank of the deceased.

Masks that defy time

As well as being master builders, the people of Teotihuacán were expert potters and sculptors, though they had only stone tools. Their skill is shown most spectacularly in the burial masks they made relatively early in their history. These were huge, powerful creations, with oval eyes and broad faces, modelled in clay or carved in basalt, obsidian, ophite or onyx. They appear to have an interior life of their own as they contemplate eternity. Even ancient Egypt produced

the surrounding areas. The growth of an extensive city and its effects on the surrounding region have fascinated a school of American archaeologists, and for the last dozen years or so Professor René Millon of Rochester University has been sending study teams to Teotihuacán. They collected a million pieces of broken pottery and fragments of obsidian, and then analysed, compared and classified them according to the sector in which they were found.

According to Millon, Teotihuacán already covered some 7 sq. miles by the year AD 150 and had 50,000 inhabitants. From then on the area of the city did not increase significantly, but the population did.

A city of potters

The maximum surface area of 8 sq. miles was then reached around the beginning of the 5th century AD, when the city was at its prime, and the 100,000 or so inhabitants already made up a very dense population pattern. Two centuries later, Professor Millon suggests, the city was densely populated, housing between 125,000 and 200,000 people. In his view, Teotihuacán was not only the religious capital, the holy city to which vast pilgrimages were made from regions in the east, south and centre, sometimes covering great distances, it was also a powerful city where an enormous quantity of pottery was produced – vases, braziers and every kind of ceramic, marked by purity and variety of form, and by a sometimes austere grace. Figurines were produced by the tens of thousands, in moulds, and the hallmark of the city is a tripod-style vase with three slab-like legs and a cover often painted with scenes similar to those that can be seen on the walls of its many buildings.

Such industry in Teotihuacán gave rise to extensive trade throughout Middle America. Professor Millon

This six-tiered pyramid forms a monumental base for the temple of Quetzalcóatl, the Feathered Serpent god, and is noteworthy for its impressive sculpture. The head of the rain god, who has wide rims round his eyes, alternates with the head of Quetzalcóatl. The temple stands in the Citadel, Teotihuacán's religious centre.

nothing better able to convey timeless serenity.

At the same time as fulfilling its function as decoration, the classical art of Teotihuacán constantly gives evidence of a desire to express a set of beliefs about the creation of the universe. Unfortunately, the present inability of scholars to decipher the hieroglyphic code means that there is only a limited understanding of the hundreds of frescoes discovered in the City of the Gods. But the extraordinary energy of their design is clearly evident.

There is no doubt that construction of the ceremonial centre, which occupied three centuries, called for the recruitment of a huge permanent body of manpower, and may have led to rural depopulation in

From an almost square base of 720 by 760 ft, the steps of the Pyramid of the Sun rise at a sharp angle to a height of 216 ft. The facing of dressed stone emphasises the structure's clean lines. A temple once stood on its summit. The pyramid was probably built in the 1st century AD. Experts have estimated that it would have taken thousands of men 50 years to build.

117

Time and Teotihuacán

Many archaeologists today agree that the rise, development and fall of Teotihuacán must have taken place between the year 200 BC and the 8th century AD, a period which covers most of the so-called classical era of pre-Columbian Mexico. The valley over which Teotihuacán presided was rich and fertile. And at its height, this first of all American cities was even larger than Caesar's Rome, and it had a population to match its size.

About 200 BC the valley seems to have contained a cluster of villages – and it was out of these that the precisely planned city later grew. By AD 200 it had more than 50,000 inhabitants. It swelled from then until its extraordinary peak in the 5th and 6th centuries, when its population was at least 75,000, probably about 125,000 and possibly more than 200,000. Then Teotihuacán collapsed, suddenly and mysteriously, its magnificent buildings scorched by a fire that raged through it in about AD 750, roughly eight centuries before the Spanish explorer Hernán Cortés landed in Mexico.

Archaeologists have identified six phases in the rise and fall of Teotihuacán. The earliest, known as the Patlachique, or pre-Teotihuacán I, phase, lasted from 150 BC to AD 1. Then came the Tzacualli age, also known as Teotihuacán I, from AD 1–150; the Miccaotli, or Teotihuacán II, period (AD 150–200); the Tlamimilolpa, or Teotihuacán II-III, phase (AD 200–400); the Xolalpan, or Teotihuacán III, phase (AD 400–600); and the Metepec, or Teotihuacán IV, phase during the city's decline and eventual fall between AD 600 and 750.

These six phases have been deduced by scholars from variations of style found in architecture, pottery and sculpture at the site; from successive increases in the city's size discovered during excavations; and from evidence of decay and disrepair in the years before the city was finally abandoned by its remaining inhabitants during the 8th century AD.

A Teotihuacán
tripod vase

But the wealth of buildings and artefacts that have been unearthed at the city have confused the patient archaeologists, for much of it points to different and sometimes apparently contradictory conclusions.

Recently, even the timing of the city's six phases of development has been thrown into some doubt by new research using the carbon-14 dating method. This research involved an attempt to determine precise dates for ashes and pieces of wood from a building called Quetzalpapalotl, a palace that was used by the city's priests. The results of the tests have subsequently led some experts to suggest that the whole chronology of the city should be pushed further back into the past by several hundred years. In the city of mystery, it seems, even time itself is still an enigma.

even attributes to the City of the Gods a kind of monopoly in the working and trading of obsidian, a volcanic rock resembling green or black glass, which was to the Middle American peoples what iron and steel are to us. In the course of his study and analysis of the site, he identified an astonishingly large number of workshops where this volcanic material was processed into a variety of articles.

Thus a more concrete picture begins to emerge of a large population of farmers and masons, potters and modellers of figurines, craftsmen in obsidian, weavers and specialists in feather-work, in polishing fine stones and in cutting jewels.

Such a concentration of population brings problems of food supply. The American researchers do not believe that the crops harvested from the valley would have been sufficient after the 4th century AD to provide nourishment for such a large city, despite the likely development of improved methods of agriculture and irrigation in the area. It therefore would have been imperative for Teotihuacán to call on the area under its influence for food as well as the raw materials needed by the craftsmen.

Excavations have revealed that the influence of Teotihuacán penetrated to some extent all over the central plateau region, to several points along the Gulf coast, into ancient Olmec country and as far as Guatemala. There, on a site at Kaminaljuyú, pyramids were made in the image of the temples of the City of the Gods. This has given rise to the theory that there was a sort of Teotihuacán empire. But, despite its prestige, the influence of its religious and artistic standards and regular trade between the various areas, it can never have been firmly established, though it may have lasted for several centuries.

The glory departs

The question of the end of Teotihuacán is still bogged down in a tangle of largely incompatible theories.

How was it possible that a prestigious holy city with a civilising influence and a population in the 7th century AD that American experts estimate to have been 150,000, if not 200,000, should have found itself in the following century a languishing town, largely deserted, with the principal monuments of its ceremonial centre already in ruins? Some trace has been found of large-scale fires, many of which appear to have been methodically prepared. But it has proved difficult to date and interpret these conflagrations.

It is the belief of some archaeologists that Teotihuacán was invaded and destroyed by nomadic warrior tribes from the north. If indeed such an invasion took place, they argue, then the City of the Gods would have been ill-prepared to resist, for its citizens seemed to lack the ferocity that became commonplace among later Middle American cultures.

Yet there is evidence to indicate that the people of Teotihuacán did practise human sacrifice. And if the city had few formal fortifications, it did have a number of natural ones. Large segments of Teotihuacán, for example, were surrounded by walls and other areas shielded by imposing platforms. Even the city's housing complexes, which contained few exterior doors, and its monumental religious structures could have served as 'instant' fortresses in case of attack. In addition, there are indications that the military played an increasingly important role in Teotihuacán as the city approached its mysterious end. Nor is this so very surprising. For in any highly stratified society, some scholars argue, the need for a dominating force is likely to become increasingly urgent as the years pass.

The city in decline

Nonetheless, some of those who believe in an invasion of the city place the event at the beginning of the 7th century AD. Others place it much earlier, around the beginning of the 6th century, a time generally agreed to have been the peak period of Teotihuacán's development. The Swiss writer Henri Stierlin, for example, believes he can demonstrate that the barbarian invasion must have produced a massive migration of the natives towards the Kaminaljuyú 'colony', some 700 miles south-east of Teotihuacán, from the early 6th century.

Nevertheless, the majority of specialists identify the first signs of the fall of the Teotihuacán civilisation as occurring only during the 7th century. If the decline was not brought about by invasion, another possibility is that a new aristocratic class could have arisen to compete with the priests and distort their theocratic rules. They could have created a form of government that was severe and oppressive – suited to their own ends of power and personal enrichment. This would have led in the long run to general disorder, and upset the existing equilibrium, eventually causing the city to disintegrate. Quarrels and rivalry within the priestly class would have arisen, and the population would have become more and more difficult to feed adequately, especially when harvests were poor.

These and other conjectures await progress in our very incomplete knowledge and understanding of the pre-Columbian past. Only one thing seems certain – that from the beginning of the 8th century what continued to exist of Teotihuacán lived on in obscurity. The city was partially destroyed, deprived of its priestly élite and its religious substance, and abandoned by most of its people. Today, as the purest source of civilisation in ancient Mexico, it remains a challenge to archaeologists and a wonder to all who visit the City of the Gods.

OLIVIER DE MAGNY

Long after its fall, Teotihuacán continued to influence Middle American civilisation. Found about a mile from the Avenue of the Dead, this statuette is Toltec and post-dates the city's demise by several hundred years. Nonetheless, it is a reworking of a basic Teotihuacán fertility figure.

The lost empire of the Indus Valley

*Superb examples of town planning, with drainage
systems that rival those of today . . .
neatly aligned streets that form a modern grid
plan . . . these were the cities of
Harappa and Mohenjo-Daro, which flourished
in the Indus Valley 4,500 years ago.
The people who built these cities also
built an empire. But their social organisation,
religion and customs all remain a mystery . . .
a mystery that will last until their strange
picture writing is deciphered.*

In the Victorian Age, the introduction of a railway system was a symbol of progress – a way of taking a country at a single bound into the modern age. Ironically, it was the building of India's railway system, in the 19th century, that unlocked the secrets of her remote past, pushing back the origins of her civilisation by almost 2,000 years.

Two engineers, the brothers John and William Brunton, were having difficulty laying tracks for the East Indian Railway on the sandy alluvial soil of the Indus Valley, and in 1856 John, as he later wrote, was 'much exercised in my mind how we were to get ballast

---

There is little to catch the eye in the stark alleyways of the cities of the Indus Valley civilisation. And yet their very bareness tells a great deal about the respect for order and planning shown by the men who lived in them 4,000 years ago.

for the line of the railway'. Then he heard that not far from the line was an ancient ruined city called Brahminabad. He visited the city, found it had been built of hard, well-burnt bricks and came away 'convinced that here was a grand quarry for the ballast I wanted'. And that is what Brahminabad became.

In the north, brother William's section of the line ran near another ancient ruined city, a collection of mounds from which bricks had been taken to build the modern village of Harappa on the same site. William Brunton duly followed his brother's example and plundered prehistoric Harappa for ballast. Thus, 93 miles or 163,680 yds of good ballast were obtained at little expense.

Along with the bricks, the workmen dug up small quantities of artefacts, including engraved soapstone seals. One of these aroused the interest of General Sir Alexander Cunningham, an archaeologist as well as a soldier, who visited Harappa in 1856. The seal was engraved with the figure of a bull and various signs in an unfamiliar script. The general realised it was an important discovery, but he was unable to have the area excavated until 1872 when he was Director-General of the Indian Archaeological Survey. News of his discovery was not published until 1875, nearly 20 years after the event, and then it passed unnoticed.

Until 1920, all the specialists agreed that the origins of Indian civilisation should be placed within a few hundred years of Alexander the Great's expedition to the sub-continent in 327 BC. The oldest-known example in India of a human settlement being consolidated into a city were the massive dry-stone walls of Rajag-riha, which scholars dated to the 6th century BC.

However, early in the 20th century Sir John Marshall, Director-General of Archaeology in India, compared General Cunningham's seal with other ancient seals from Harappa. Their features suggested that the Harappan civilisation was older than had been thought, and in 1920 Marshall sent one of his Indian archaeologists, Rai Bahadur Daya Ram Sahni, to begin excavating the mounds at Harappa. The Indian made discoveries that supported an assertion by Marshall that before Alexander's invasion 'a well-developed and flourishing civilisation had existed in India for at least 1,000 years'. Despite the boldness of Marshall's statement, for there were then no known structures older than the walls of Rajagriha, he had underestimated by more than 1,000 years.

In 1922, another of Marshall's Indian archaeologists began to excavate some great mounds at a place known as Mohenjo-Daro ('Mound of the Dead'), about 350 miles south of Harappa. The excavations at these two sites continued for several seasons, and eventually revealed remains of two ancient cities so similar that they obviously belonged to the same civilisation – one not mentioned in Indian tradition.

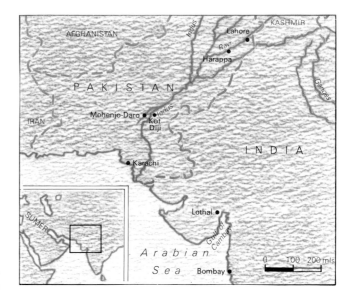

The influence of the Indus Valley civilisation extended from the borders of Iran to the plain of the River Ganges and from the lowest foothills in Kashmir to the port of Lothal on the Gulf of Cambay. Most of the cities, including Harappa and Mohenjo-Daro, were along the Indus and its tributaries.

This civilisation now appears to have been established by 2500 BC and to have come to an end by about 1500 BC. Its two major cities, however, apparently suffered a different fate. Though evidence suggests that their complex urban systems and impressive social and economic foundations emerged suddenly, the cities seem to have been abandoned before the end of the civilisation itself, perhaps as early as 2000 BC. Unfortunately, the circumstances of their decline remain an enigma to archaeologists.

The civilisation is known as the Indus after the river which gave it life and perhaps caused its downfall, or as the Harappan civilisation after the first urban site to be discovered. At its most developed, however, the culture extended much further than the Indus Valley, and covered an area far greater than the contemporary states of Mesopotamia or the kingdom of Egypt.

For more than 50 years, careful excavation of this civilisation has been a continuing source of many riddles. It is like a gigantic jigsaw puzzle in which each new element, far from giving a clue to the whole, serves only to obscure it a little more by making way for new interpretations, each as uncertain as the last. The puzzles concern the nature and function of the buildings excavated, the script, and the economic, social and religious organisation of the society. There

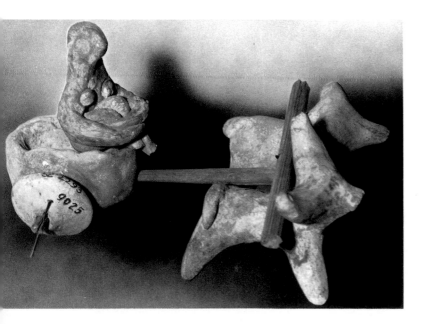

Tiny terracotta models of everyday objects, such as this cart pulled by bullocks, seem to have been very popular at Mohenjo-Daro. Probably children's toys, they make it possible to reconstruct scenes of daily life at the time. Carts like this one are still used in the Indus Valley today.

is also the question of how such a well-organised civilisation rose so suddenly and fell so mysteriously.

Harappa and Mohenjo-Daro, which both cover hundreds of acres, are the two most important known urban centres of the Indus civilisation. In addition there are about another 100 known sites which either belonged to the same culture or were strongly influenced by it. Few of these cover more than 24 acres. Most are situated in Pakistan, though some have been found in India. A glance at the map will indicate the vastness of the area of the so-called Indus Empire.

Most of the sites so far uncovered show a similar general pattern of development, and it is that similarity which indicates the unity of the Indus civilisation. This development has not been well documented at Mohenjo-Daro since the lower levels of the site are buried deep within the water-logged silts of the valley and have not yet been excavated. But at Kot Diji, across the Indus river from Mohenjo-Daro, a complete sequence of evolution has been unearthed.

The first town planners

The layout of Indus settlements is regular, with streets crossing one another at right-angles. The plan of the buildings and their materials are severely functional with little ornamentation. The larger cities and towns seem to have been divided into districts, each principally housing workers of a particular trade.

This leads to the conclusion that the cities were conceived almost in their entirety before they were built. There was no room for fussy additions or whims, and scrupulous care was taken over matters of hygiene and utility. In short, the Indus cities are the first manifestation of town planning.

Harappa is situated close to the old course of the Ravi, a tributary of the Indus, and Mohenjo-Daro is on the bank of the old Indus river bed. The layout and orientation of the two cities are similar. In both cases the city has a high rectangular hillock to the west, and a lower, broader mound, less regular in shape, to the east. This eastern section would have been where the bulk of the people lived.

The higher western mounds seem to have been the administrative and religious centres – though little is known of the form that religion or government took. Some curious buildings have been found at Mohenjo-Daro, undoubtedly the most spectacular being the Great Bath and the Granary. The Bath is a sort of rectangular 20×40 ft pool which is remarkable for its filling-and-emptying system, and also for the meticulous jointing of the bricks. The bricks of the bottom and sides of the pool were set on edge in gypsum

All the evidence points to small statues like this as having been images of mother-goddesses who watched over the hearth. This one wears a short skirt held up by a wide belt – and an astonishing head-dress. Oil or incense may have been burned in the containers at each side of the head.

mortar and covered with a layer of bitumen, which in turn was covered with more bricks. This ensured that the Bath was watertight. A series of small washing-rooms, each with a narrow entrance set to one side and a carefully made floor connected to a drain, surround the Bath. Given the small size of the Bath compared to the population of so large a city as Mohenjo-Daro, archaeologists have concluded that only a small number of people had access to this area. The Great Bath, it would appear, had more to do with ritual and cleanliness of the spirit rather than that of the body.

The cities of the Indus do not seem to have had any monuments obviously dedicated to worship, although archaeologists think that one particular building in Mohenjo-Daro may have been a temple. The Granary in all probability acted as a store or public treasury where the revenues from a tax paid in kind by the peasants was kept. It has been suggested that the large number of labourers directly employed by the govern-ment may have been paid for their work with grain.

The masters of Harappa and Mohenjo-Daro would have been able to look out from the relative peace of the citadel at their subjects going about their business on the plain and in the low-lying town. Behind the citadel walls they were protected from invasions and to a lesser extent from the caprices of the river, often prone to flooding. The impression given by these citadels is not one of a democratic and egalitarian society. They suggest the presence of a military and religious ruling power, similar to that of almost all primary civilisations.

It is at Mohenjo-Daro that much can be learned about the nature of the lower city. Where once there was nothing but a field of ruins, today whole districts have been opened up by excavation. The city rose up on a four-sided mound situated about 220 yds east of the citadel. A number of hypotheses have been put forward to explain the purpose of the land between the two mounds, but none of them is entirely satisfactory. The most likely supposition is that the course of the Indus at that time passed close by instead of some distance away as it does today, and that the solid embankment discovered on the side of the town facing the citadel formed the bank of a canal or a branch of the river which provided water access to the city.

Whether they are large or small, whether they housed rich or poor, the dwellings of Mohenjo-Daro all look alike in their orderly rows. Most of them had a courtyard round which were grouped the kitchen, living-rooms and sometimes a bath-room. Every house was connected to main drainage.

It is thought that Mohenjo-Daro at its peak must have housed some 40,000 inhabitants, a substantial number for an era and a place in which the principal sources of wealth were agricultural land and domestic animals. But the city itself was a commercial metropolis serving an extensive territory.

More astonishing than its extent is the grid-plan: a fabric of streets about 10 yds wide running from north to south and from east to west formed rectangular blocks of roughly equal size, about 400×300 yds. From this it is an easy step, if not strictly correct in a scientific sense, to imagine the inhabitants of Mohenjo-Daro measuring distances by blocks in the modern American manner.

In contrast to American cities, however – and more akin to cities in the Middle East and Asia – was the custom of having blind walls facing out onto the main streets. All the doors thus open on interior lanes – some up to 3 yards wide – leading into the centre of the blocks. In this way each individual household was shielded from inquisitive eyes and dusty main streets, busy during the day with creaking bullock carts and raucous merchants hawking their goods.

Impressive as its size and regularity may be, Mohenjo-Daro possessed another, equally admirable attribute: it had a complex sanitary and sewage system. For the people of Mohenjo-Daro developed both public and private hygiene to a remarkable degree, one unparalleled in pre-classical times and still unmatched in many parts of the world today. Most private dwellings, for example, both large and small, were equipped with a special kind of trash chute that was built into one of the outside walls and passed

This part of the residential quarter of Mohenjo-Daro is laid out to a rigid north-south, east-west plan of streets, outlining blocks of approximately 400×300 yds. Narrow alleys led into these blocks, giving access to the houses. The system has been taken to indicate an authoritarian form of government which dictated the overall plan and strict alignment.

This figure with a commanding air may be a representation of a priest-king who watched over the fate of Mohenjo-Daro. He is wearing what appears to be a ceremonial robe, decorated with a three-leaved design which may have had some religious significance.

streets and what might have been an eating hall in Mohenjo-Daro – adds to the impression of monotony.

The same basic layout was strictly followed in later reconstructions, except in the latest phases when craftsmen's equipment, previously found only in the outlying parts of the town, began to encroach on public streets. This suggests that during most of the course of the Indus civilisation craftsmen appear to have lived and worked in their own areas, and that this was not just a tacit agreement but an explicit ruling by an authoritarian power.

The overall plan of the town gives little indication of the character of the Harappans, which can more easily be glimpsed in the small detail of everyday objects such as pottery, toys and weights, or even those seals engraved with mysterious inscriptions.

Terracotta was the material most often used for these objects, and in the pottery it is covered on the outside with a beautiful polished red material and painted with a variety of decorative motifs in black, ranging from abstract geometric designs to stylised figurative patterns. Plants and animals appear in abundance, but humans are rarely shown. The large number of pottery vessels found indicates the existence of an organised industry, though the work was done by hand, with the potter bent over his wheel.

Model housewives

The city's inhabitants take on bodies and facial expressions through the numerous clay figurines, toys and ritual objects that have been found. Many of them show women, either goddesses or dancers, adorned with jewels and with the hair carefully styled. But there are also figures of simple housewives and mothers going about their daily tasks.

In contrast to the women, who nearly all wear loin-cloths, the men are often shown naked. Add to these figures tiny models of carts and domestic animals – which often have jointed, movable heads and are thought to have been pulled along by the children of the Harappans – and it is possible to reconstruct simple scenes of the daily life of the time.

The seals which first aroused interest in the sites have since been found in such great numbers that it seems possible that every family in the community had its own. They are square and generally engraved with an animal motif and an inscription, which appears to read from right to left.

It has so far proved impossible to decipher these inscriptions. About 400 characters have been listed, but in the absence of other written documents, linguists are a long way from knowing what kind of

through to the street. These chutes allowed householders to slide debris into small individual gutters outside, and these gutters in turn were connected to a covered central sewer system.

At intervals along the central system there were sumps, or drainage pits, designed to collect the heaviest waste so that it would not obstruct the main passageways. In addition, wells were liberally placed throughout the city, some directly accessible from the streets and therefore public, some constructed as part of individual houses and thus reserved for private use.

What was life like in Mohenjo-Daro and the other cities? It was undoubtedly austere, tending towards trade and labour rather than festivals, the arts and the sweet life. All the houses were alike in their basic plan. The only difference between the home of the rich merchant and that of the poor craftsman was in their size and in a few technical refinements. The overall impression is one of perfect coherence – a coherence amounting to uniformity. The miles of uninterrupted brickwork would have been featureless, and the absence of any kind of meeting place – apart from the

messages were conveyed in this pictographic writing.

There have been several attempts to decode it, and one of these produced some surprising results. It was carried out by a group of Finnish linguists who suggested that the Indus inscriptions should be read like riddles or puns. They suggested that the signs themselves – showing fish, humans in different poses and so on – did not refer to the things they represented but to the sounds used to describe them. It is rather as though, in English, the pronoun 'I' were to be represented by the drawing of an eye. However, a decisive ruling on this theory will not be possible until some bilingual document is found.

The full functions of the seals will not be known until the writing on them is deciphered. But one purpose for which they were used was as stamps on various commodities used in trade. It is likely, therefore, that they were evidence of ownership, in the same way as the brand on a steer shows who owns it.

In many ways the cities of the Indus remain mysterious, and the supply of certainties about the Harappan culture is almost as thin as the supply of theories is inexhaustible. There are several theories as to how the civilisation ended, and it is likely that there were several contributory causes. It has been suggested that a spectacular rise in the waters of the Indus (such as still occurs today) finally overcame the energy of the people who had previously been determined to keep

Among the ruins excavated in the citadel of Mohenjo-Daro are two remarkable buildings. One is the Great Bath, a pool which may have been used for ritual ablutions. It is in relatively good condition, unlike the other building which stands beside it to the west (shown in the foreground in the photograph below and in a reconstruction, right). This was the Granary; only a little of its substructure has survived. It covered about 50×25 yds and was made up of 27 massive blocks of brickwork resting on a foundation. There was also a wooden superstructure. This Granary, which looked very like a fortress, could be quickly enlarged. In a barter economy it was equivalent to the central bank to which each man brought his tribute of grain. The grain was preserved by the circulation of air.

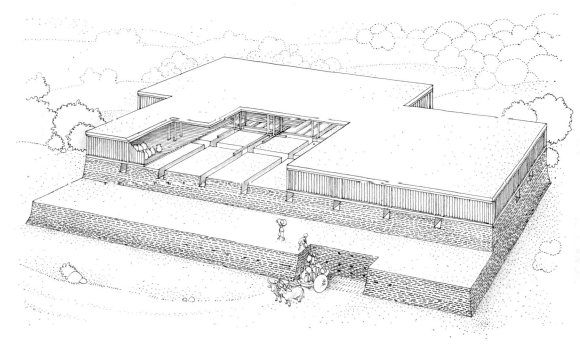

the river under control. On the other hand, it has been suggested that an Aryan invasion, occurring around 1500 BC, was responsible for the decline. Neither of these two arguments has completely convinced archaeologists working on the Harappan culture. It seems that both explanations are too simple to account for the eclipse of such a well-organised society; moreover, there is evidence of a general decline over a period of 500 years before the arrival of the Aryans. Some have suggested that the abandonment of the two major cities was directly related to an internal breakdown of the political and economic institutions that long distinguished the society.

The vision of what this civilisation was like in its prime remains fragmentary. It is strange to reflect that so little is known about a culture so dominated by a meticulous sense of rationality and order. It was a preoccupation no doubt imposed by the rigours of the climate and the flow of the river, but possibly also as a consequence of developing commercial change.

There is a great deal of evidence to show that trade was vigorous and wide-ranging. Seals from the Indus Valley have been found at Sumer. Lothal, at the head of the Gulf of Cambay in India, was a busy commercial centre with extensive trade relations with the inland areas of central India. The largest brick structure known to have been built by the Harappans, the so-called wharf at Lothal measuring about 230 × 40 yds, suggests that this site in addition also an Harappan seaport.

The Harappans also had a remarkable system of weights and measures. Large numbers of weights have been found at Harappa, Mohenjo-Daro and other sites. Carefully made from a variety of stones, they range from weights so large that they had to be lifted by a rope or a metal ring to others so tiny that they may have been used by jewellers. They are usually in the shape of a cube, though flattened spheres, cylinders, cones and barrel shapes have been found.

The scales with which these weights were used are rare, because they were made of wood, which has perished over the centuries. Scale pans of metal or pottery are more frequently found.

The bull is one of several animals which appear frequently in Indus Valley art and seems to have had both social and religious significance. This bull, for instance, may have been the emblem of a family group and an object of worship, an ancestor of the bull Nandi, mount of the Hindu god Shiva.

Among the many questions that must be left to the skill and good luck of future archaeologists is the significance of a statue found in Mohenjo-Daro. Some say it represents a priest-king. If so, was he recruited from the merchant aristocracy? Did he rule an empire, or was the Indus civilisation made up of a federation of self-governing cities? And what religion did this great person serve?

There is an intriguing clue to be found in the seals. Some of these depict a horned figure, sitting with crossed legs, who is thought to be an early form of the many-armed Hindu god Shiva. It seems, then, that the cities of the Indus Valley may have created gods, just as, from the evidence of the seals, they appear to have invented a form of writing.

The fact that it is impossible, in our present state of knowledge, to be more definite should not cause too much disappointment. It is thanks to such enigmas that archaeology becomes a living science, a challenging science, which does not simply follow a fixed set of rules that lead to inevitable conclusions, but one in which imagination, inspired guesswork – and luck – still have their part to play.

ROBERT DAVREU

The Indus Valley excavations have revealed such an impressive number of soapstone seals that it is presumed these must have had some everyday use such as business stamps. A number of them probably had religious significance, however – as was probably the case with the one on the right. It is one of many showing an animal which is as mysterious as the writing above it. This beast has been nicknamed the 'unicorn', though its single horn in profile may mask another.

The civilisation which was nurtured by the waters of the River Indus flourished only at the cost of a constant struggle against its floods. One of many theories put forward to explain the premature, though lingering, decline of its twin cities, Harappa and Mohenjo-Daro, is that the river burst its banks once too often, perhaps changed course and swept away the protective walls of the urban centres it had originally helped bring to life.

The silent stones of Tiahuanaco

When the winds of the Andes howl through Tiahuanaco's deserted buildings, it is easy to believe in the Indian legend that the city was built by a race of giants. It was already a majestic ruin when the Incas arrived there in the 15th century, and they knew nothing about its vanished inhabitants. We know little more today. It has been discovered, though, that five cities flourished and died at Tiahuanaco, each rising on the site of the one that came before. Only the last still speaks to men – through ruins as colossal as they are mysterious.

On a bleak plateau, nearly 13,000 ft high, in the Andes are the remnants of a brilliant long-forgotten civilisation. The city of Tiahuanaco, devastated by earthquakes and partly demolished, stands in the midst of a windswept desolation near the Bolivian shore of Lake Titicaca. Its stones bear witness to a colossal style of building, square and rigid, which expresses itself in mathematically ordered and forbidding walls. Imposing stone steps lead up to monumental gateways, each cut from a single block of stone. They are gateways which today open on to emptiness. Huge statues stare vacantly out from crumbled terraces and look as though they are holding up the sky. The temples and palaces are sadly deserted. The priests who once officiated there are forgotten.

Tiahuanaco has been repeatedly ravaged by man as well as the elements, at least from the time of the Spanish conquest. It has been pillaged by treasure-seekers, and it was used as a quarry. Its stones and sculptures were ruthlessly removed to be used in building or decorating new structures. Today, the city is nothing but a collection of gigantic ruins, perpetuating strange images of men fashioned by some unknown creator, jealously guarding the secrets of an ancient people whose history is not known.

Who founded it? Who lived there, and ruled there, and when? Was it the political, administrative and cultural headquarters of some powerful state which won for itself an empire in the continent of South

On a scale fit for giants or gods, a stairway at Kalasasaya, near Tiahuanaco's Gateway of the Sun, is impressively outlined against the sky. The heavy monolithic blocks seem to have been carved by superhuman hands. High stone steps, worn perhaps by the tread of pilgrims, lead to an inner court.

131

America? Or was it a sanctuary, visited during holy festivals by bands of pilgrims bearing gifts? Or was it perhaps the city of the gods of the Andes, where strange soothsayers ministered, wearing head-dresses with representations of felines and birds of prey?

Unlike some of the other vanished pre-Columbian cultures, the people of Tiahuanaco seem to have left no written records. Grooves on the statues could be some form of picture writing, but as yet no one knows how to decipher them. Indian legends refer to 'sacred tablets' in gold, copper or silver engraved with symbolic signs which are supposed to be hidden on one of Lake Titicaca's sacred islands. Everything about this dead town smacks more of myth and legend than it does of reality.

In the 16th century, adventurers owing allegiance to Charles I of Spain, who had set out in search of a fabulous treasure, reached the already-abandoned city. All they found were the last echoes of a past about to sink into oblivion.

From the Indians who lived in the area – and brought sacrifices to the feet of the giant, geometric stone statues – they learned that the Incas had been there a hundred years or more before them and had

For centuries giant statues have stood guard over the ceremonial terraces of long-dead Tiahuanaco. The great stone known as The Friar is carved with indecipherable symbols and is thought to represent a god or a high priest. It is a silent witness to an unknown civilisation established some 2,200 years ago, whose disappearance baffles archaeologists.

At an altitude of more than 12,500 ft, Lake Titicaca is the highest navigable lake in the world. The largest of its scattered islands is the Island of the Sun, whose hills are stepped by ancient crop-growing terraces. Tales of ancient palaces being seen in the lake led scientists to explore its depths. They found high walls and paved paths beneath its waters.

According to folklore, the waters of Lake Titicaca once lapped the walls of Tiahuanaco, which now lie in ruins some 25 miles away. The lake covers an area of 3,200 sq. miles, and its level varies considerably with the seasons.

According to folklore, the waters of Lake Titicaca once lapped the walls of Tiahuanaco, which now lie in ruins some 25 miles away. The lake covers an area of 3,200 sq. miles, and its level varies considerably with the seasons.

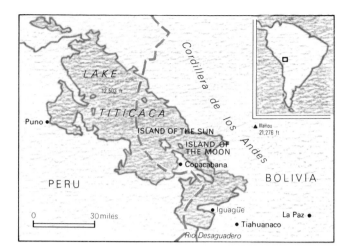

found the mysterious city already destroyed and apparently deserted from a very long time beforehand. When asked about the origins of the city, the Indians could only reply by telling of a tradition that 'Tiahuanaco was built in a single night, after the flood, by unknown giants. But they disregarded a prophecy of the coming of the sun and were annihilated by its rays, and their palaces were reduced to ashes . . .'

The Spaniards who related the story reckoned that the remains of Tiahuanaco 'were more the work of demons than of men'. But they had to be content with transcribing the legendary beliefs that had been handed down through generations of Indians. The ambiguous phrases of the legend succeeded only in adding to the curiosity of the early historians, instead of enlightening them.

Numerous theories have been put forward on the subject of Tiahuanaco and its origins. Some people

have credited the city with a fabulously ancient history. It has even been called the cradle of American man. Serious authors have described it as the capital of an empire which may have equalled that of the Incas. Others have seen it as the capital of Atlantis, or as a city of Venus, built millions of years ago by cosmonauts wearing space suits.

For hundreds of years there seemed to be no solution to this pre-Columbian puzzle. Tiahuanaco inspired an abundance of fantasy. Few other archaeological sites have produced so many crazy conjectures. And in spite of archaeological research carried out since the end of the 19th century, most of the problems have remained unsolved.

In 1892 the German scholars Max Uhle and Alphons Stübel published the first scientific description of Tiahuanaco's ruins, based on the latter's observations. Two years later Uhle visited the site and subsequently undertook the study of the Tiahuanaco culture in relation to the other great cultures of the Andean area. In this way Uhle was able to trace, mainly through the remains of pottery, the widespread influence of the Tiahuanaco style, which spread as far as the coastal areas and for several centuries co-existed with many of the purely local styles.

Further excavations were organised in 1903 by a French scientific expedition under the leadership of Count Créqui de Montfort. These excavations were fairly limited, but they did bring to light a kind of small temple, built half underground, the walls of which were dotted with heads carved in blood-red sandstone, each held in place by a stone spike.

In 1932 an archaeological team under the American Wendell C. Bennett found within the temple ruins Tiahuanaco's largest idol – a giant nearly 24 ft high, which was buried 10 ft below the surface. Another idol, only 8 ft tall and also carved of red sandstone but in a completely different style, was lying beside it, resting against its side.

The archaic, almost smiling face of the second statue contrasts with the austerity of Tiahuanaco's great geometric statues, which are thought to be of later date. This statue could possibly be connected with one

133

of the most curious legends heard and handed down by the first Spaniards in the area. This is the story of Viracocha, the bearded white god who created the Andean world. He is said to have appeared in Tiahuanaco after a flood which was supposed to have lasted 60 nights and engulfed cities in its path.

This smaller idol has saucer-shaped eyes beneath the thick dash of his eyebrows, which are joined together so that they lend a T-shape to the nose. He has a kind of thick moustache which encircles a thick-lipped mouth to join a sharply pointed beard. The original natives of America were almost beardless, so it is easy to see why scholars have been perplexed by this image.

A close study of the small idol, however, has led some archaeologists to suggest a more plausible explanation. Were the apparent moustache and beard really a *nariguera* – a gold face ornament worn by the priests of the time? The *nariguera* was worn through the nose and hung over the lower part of the face. But even if the face was decorated with a *nariguera*, the mystery of the 'white' god still remains to be solved.

A stone head resembling those still attached to the inner walls of the small temple was also found buried on the terrace at the foot of the second statue. These stone heads call to mind the bloody cult of head-hunting. Another indication of the cult comes in the head-shaped ritual vases excavated at Tiahuanaco. Actual human heads have been found – in a curiously shrunken condition – attached by a small plait of human hair to the belts of mummies in ancient Peruvian tombs.

It is also apparent that there were cruel sacrifices in the temple. Severed human skulls polished like ivory were found there. They appear to have been used as cups for a sour brew made from fermented corn, which

A jumbled heap of stones, looking as if they were hurled to the ground by some great natural catastrophe, is all that remains of Puma Puncu, one of the city's largest buildings. Was it a palace or a temple? Whatever its purpose, it was massive: some stones are 26 ft long and 16 ft wide.

is believed to have been the favourite libation to the gods and the drink of their servants.

Despite such fascinating discoveries, the problem of dating the strange dead city remained. The investigator who suggested that Tiahuanaco was the cradle of all the American pre-Columbian civilisations estimated its age to be 14,000 years. It was not until 1958, however, that further scientific research threw new light on the mysterious city.

Starting in that year, excavations planned on a grand scale and carried out by the Bolivian archaeologist Carlos Ponce Sanginés marked a stage in the faithful restoration – as faithful as it is possible to be – of the principal monuments of this civilisation, and in the reconstruction of the lost history of Tiahuanaco.

Five hundred shafts were sunk into the ground, cutting through many archaeological layers, and aerial photographs were taken.

The first problem was to establish some acceptable limits to the city's existence, even if precise dates were not possible.

Wendell Bennett's excavations in the 1930's had disposed of the idea of a single Tiahuanaco epoch. Instead, the American archaeologist had proposed three different cultural phases for Tiahuanaco – periods which he called Early, Classic and Decadent. To these Ponce Sanginés added two additional and even earlier periods, suggesting a 1,400-year chronology lasting from about 200 BC to AD 1200.

The Bolivian scholar related his two earliest phases to an Andean Upper Formative period, put Bennett's Early and Classic categories in a Regional Development era, and finally equated the Decadent phase with what he called Expansive Tiahuanaco. Ponce Sanginés demonstrated that Tiahuanaco's temples were actually constructed during the third phase, Bennett's Early period, with only slight additions made during the so-called Classic period immediately following.

A study of the various archaeological strata has indeed revealed traces of five cities, one often overlapping the other. Very little is known about the five different cities, except that they lie buried in tangled confusion and that the architects who designed and built them were men of genius.

Majestic-looking monuments of colossal dimensions were built, as stoneworkers became increasingly proficient. The art of monumental statuary reached a peak of perfection as sculptors covered the great stone figures with strange tight symbols in the manner of a tapestry. Huge monolithic gateways were erected, like the famous Gateway of the Sun, which was carved from a single block of volcanic andesite and stands today, damaged by lightning and yawning into emptiness, as the most remarkable example of the imposing heights reached at Tiahuanaco.

In the search for the true meaning of the remains of Tiahuanaco, the most prudent archaeologists took careful account of local tradition, relating it to their scientific research. For often the golden thread of legend leads to completely unexpected findings.

Such a discovery, based on legend, was confirmed in 1967 by a scientific expedition authorised by the Bolivian government. Scholars had been intrigued by the account of a flood which the Indians related to chroniclers of the Spanish conquest, and by the Indians' lively insistence that the legend was true. Moreover, it seemed to tie in with stories, recounted with equal obstinacy by the fishermen of Lake Titicaca, which told of sunken palaces whose roofs they could touch when the lake waters were low during the long dry spells that come to the Andean plateau.

However, for a long time scientists were sceptical about tales told by Indian divers who claimed to have seen the ruins on the floor of the lake.

The Indians say that this stone face depicts Viracocha, the legendary god who arose from the sacred lake of Titicaca. The idol stands by the church porch in modern Tiahuanaco – a village built from stones torn from the temples and palaces. Remains of the old city were also used for buildings in La Paz.

This temple, excavated by a French expedition led by Count Créqui de Montfort in 1903, was reconstructed by Bolivian archaeologists in 1964. Open-air ceremonies are believed to have been held in the sunken patio, around three carved slabs of red sandstone that stand in its centre.

Speculation persisted until frogmen, braving the dangers of a plunge at high altitude, descended into the depths of the lake, laden with heavy equipment and oxygen apparatus. They discovered high walls, coated in mud and slime and eaten away by the brackish waters.

During this expedition the frogmen made a second discovery, which was even more remarkable and posed an entirely new puzzle. Not far from the shore, they made out a number of embankments and paved paths and a sort of giant puzzle composed of blocks cut finely and set with great precision in the lake bed. They counted about 30 of these parallel formations, connected by a crescent-shaped base.

Was this a chequerboard of wharves reserved for vessels of state which carried important men to the sacred islands in the lake dedicated to worship of the Sun and the Moon? Or did funeral boats pull in here, carrying the mummies of dignitaries to some necropolis long-since drowned by the waters of the lake? Archaeologists, who had seen nothing like this elsewhere, are still seeking answers to these questions.

According to one widespread theory, Tiahuanaco was a holy city of the high plateau, built up gradually by generations of pilgrims who came in procession from the most distant provinces at times ordained by a religious calendar now lost.

Since it is obvious that the city's large public buildings could hold thousands of people at one time, it might then be reasonable to suppose that they came as pilgrims, with their arms full of gifts and offerings. If so, they would have left behind a variety of objects, bearing witness to the different cultures from which they sprang. Yet archaeologists have found no convincing evidence of such variety. All the objects found and studied up to now, whether utilitarian or ceremonial, point exclusively to styles proved to be typical of the Tiahuanaco culture. So any theory which proposes large numbers of outsiders flocking into the city breaks down before this lack of evidence.

For a long time, other researchers believed that Tiahuanaco was purely a religious centre, of vast size and high reputation, inhabited only by a small group of grand priests who were the sorcerers, magicians, soothsayers and prophets of a dominating, idol-

Parts of Tiahuanaco have been painstakingly restored by Bolivian archaeologists. This example of their work is one of the remarkable stairways at Kalasasaya. The stairs are made of huge blocks of stone embedded in the ground.

worshipping religion. The generous size of the stone monuments, whose ruins alone now cover more than 50 acres, seem to contrast with the almost total absence of dwelling places.

Now that the city has been photographed from above, an altogether different notion presents itself. It appears that the civic and cultural centres of Tiahuanaco were surrounded by suburbs which must have been inhabited by a population that probably included craftsmen such as potters, weavers and goldsmiths, animal breeders and farmers.

There is no mystery about the reason why these suburbs had previously passed unnoticed. It was because the houses were not built of stone, like the magnificent buildings that can still be seen today, but of bricks made of mud and dried in the sun. They were built without mortar and once the city was deserted, they crumbled to dust. Over the centuries, what had been bricks became indistinguishable from the soil of the same colour.

This discovery meant that Tiahuanaco could be classified not only as a holy town but also as a large working and residential centre with an active permanent population. The fact remains, however, that the soil could hardly be called rich, and so far little trace has been found on the stony, forbidding plateau of any large-scale agriculture.

To some observers it seems unlikely that a large population could have survived in the arduous mountain climate with minimal means of subsistence. However, during the 1,000 years or more that Tiahuanaco flourished, there is no doubt that potatoes and corn

Strange heads carved from red sandstone have been found mounted on the walls of the temple, but their significance remains a mystery. Excavations have revealed dozens of the carvings, which are between 2½ and 14 in. high and adorn the walls in no apparent order.

were grown, as they still are today by local Indians. Then, as now, fish were abundant in the chill waters of Lake Titicaca.

The most troublesome question remains that of the actual building of this strange city in the heart of a high, windy plateau. There are no rocks or quarries to be seen nearby. So what was the source of the materials used to build the city's imposing public buildings? By what means were the colossal stones transported to Tiahuanaco?

Soon after the Spaniards discovered the city, a Jesuit wrote that 'the great stones one sees at Tiahuanaco were carried through the air to the sound of a trumpet' by some being endowed with – to say the least – exceptional gifts. There must have been people even then who were not satisfied with an explanation that invoked the use of magic.

Scientific examination showed that the stone used in the buildings and monuments of Tiahuanaco consists of volcanic tuff, limestone, red sandstone, basalt and andesite. Comparisons were made with rock samples taken from the Bolivian and the Peruvian mountains around Lake Titicaca. As a result, archaeologists were able to locate the quarries which provided the stone, at sites between 60 and 200 miles from the city. Consequently, the experts have had to face the possibility that blocks of stone weighing up to 100 tons each –

some even more – were transported considerable distances over ground that is for the most part uneven.

The archaeologists also found the outlines of the old roads, built long before the Spaniards came. These roads, which are paved with pebbles, radiate out in every direction to link the metropolis of Tiahuanaco with neighbouring towns. Several of these roads are still used by peasants going to market in the modern village of Tiahuanaco, which stands close to the ruins.

Moving huge stones

Assuming that these and similar roads connected Tiahuanaco with its quarries, the best engineers of today still ask themselves whether even they could cut and move huge masses of rock such as those used to build the city. The giant blocks look almost as though a die were used to cut them – a task achieved with none of the resources of modern technology. It is certain, too, that the mysterious builders did not have the use of animals in harness, and that iron and the wheel were unknown to them.

Illustrations showing how huge individual stones or giant statues were transported are totally absent, and this is clearly a serious obstacle to reconstructing the techniques used by builders of Tiahuanaco. But it appears the great distances did not constitute an insurmountable problem for them. Perhaps their secret lay in the size of the work force.

Probably there were bodies of specialists who were entrusted with everything concerned with public works. Some would have been in charge of calculating the number of men needed to transport the stones, taking into account the nature of the land. Others would have had the job of working out the right quality of rope for towing the blocks – twisted vegetable fibres or leather thongs made from llama skin – and the length and thickness required in each case.

For the heaviest stones, scientists have surmised that the ground would have had to be terraced, with ramps coated with wet clay up which the colossal blocks of stone could be hauled. Lighter pieces could have been carried by men using a stretcher-like contraption made from two wooden poles linked by cross-pieces padded with solid fabric or skin.

However, in some places there are natural obstacles which completely rule out land transportation – for example, in the case of the andesite blocks, which came from Copacabana, on a peninsula in Lake Titicaca. For these blocks there must have been some kind of alternative transport, using the lake. Many months were spent looking for the key to this mystery before it was discovered by pure chance at Iguagüe, 14 miles from Tiahuanaco on the edge of the lake.

This enigmatic figure, said to represent the creator god Viracocha, is carved on the central lintel of Tiahuanaco's Gateway of the Sun. It wears a head-dress decorated with shrunken heads and brandishes 'condor' sceptres.

There, columns identical to those in the ruins of the city are still lying in a sort of long, wide trench with one of the ancient pre-Columbian roads leading into it.

Because the level of Lake Titicaca varies considerably from season to season, this landing place is sometimes under water and sometimes uncovered. The columns must have been towed down to the shore near Copacabana and loaded on to boats – probably large rafts made from lakeside rushes – then floated across the lake in the wet season, when the waters of the lake were at their highest. At the trench, they must have been recovered a few months later, in the dry season when the water level was down and the trench dried out. From there they would have been hauled over land to the city in the customary way.

Bolivian scientists went on to do experiments which proved their assumptions to be right. First, they conducted a trial of this ingenious system of water transport, using a raft and a small block of stone. Then they experimented with land transport, using a rock weighing more than half a ton, which was dragged by six Indian soldiers with the help of ropes. Both experiments were conclusive in every respect.

A good number of the mysteries have still to be unravelled. Little is known of the inhabitants of Tiahuanaco, despite the patient research undertaken by scholars, and many questions remain unanswered.

Will we ever discover who these people, lost in the mists of age-old oblivion, really were? Will it ever be known when and why this city, with some of its buildings apparently unfinished, was abandoned forever? Was it as a result of murderous wars fought for possession of the rare productive areas of land, leading to the destruction of the city and the flight of the people to more hospitable lands? Was it a war of religion between rival castes, which could be just as lethal? Did some appalling geological upheaval wreck the city? Did some drastic change of climate create a hostile environment for agriculture? Did famine or an epidemic annihilate the population?

The giant gods that keep constant watch over the city have lost their voice. Will the archaeologists eventually be able to speak in their place?

SIMONE WAISBARD

The gigantic Gateway of the Sun, hewn from a single block of andesite, is Tiahuanaco's best-known monument. The carvings which decorate the lintel are thought to include Viracocha (opposite). They are typical of the Tiahuanaco style, and the motifs are also found on painted vases and fabrics. Some students have proposed that the symbols may represent a calendar – the oldest in the world – but so far these mysterious symbols have defied all efforts to decode them.

The world's first cities

Biblical Jericho, excavated to reveal walls 9,000 years old . . . Çatal Hüyük, a Turkish settlement almost as old . . . Lepenski Vir, an Old Stone Age site on the Danube . . . These three finds have shattered the belief that the world's first cities originated 5,000 years ago in Sumeria, when recorded history began. But, beneath the mysterious mounds scattered throughout the Near East, even older cities may exist, built even further back in the mists of prehistory.

If it were possible to view the recent history of our planet from space, the development of cities and towns would appear as a strange, fungus-like growth which, in a relatively short span of time, radiated to large parts of the earth's surface, swallowing up fields, forests, mountains and deserts. So rapid has been the spread of this phenomenon that it might have seemed that the expanding tapestry of towns would eventually devour the entire planet. Some prophets of doom have visions of a single city covering the world, and see humanity on the infernal road that leads from the megalopolis to the necropolis. Overcrowding, with its

Beneath this mound beside an oasis on the outskirts of modern Jericho lies the world's earliest-known city. This first Jericho is 9,000 years old – three times as old as Rome. Its walls were found 50 ft down, under the rubble of later cities.

attendant slums, traffic jams, pollution of the atmosphere and unacceptable levels of noise, makes the relentless march of the cities one of the great problems of our time.

How did it all begin? Where, when and why did our nomadic ancestors cease their wanderings, build their first permanent homes and so give birth to what has come to be regarded as synonymous with civilisation – the city?

Until recently, it was thought that the first cities were built by the Sumerians 5,000 years ago in the eastern segment of the Fertile Crescent – the area of the Middle East which lies between the rivers Tigris and Euphrates and which became known as Babylonia. In Ur, Uruk, Eridu, Lagash, Nippur and other wealthy cities of the land of Sumer, civilisation was said to have begun. Before that, there was just the void of prehistory, time without written record.

The fallen walls of Jericho

Archaeologists have long searched for the remains of biblical Jericho. The story of how the city fell to the Israelites is told in the 6th chapter of the Book of Joshua:

Now Jericho was straitly shut up because of the children of Israel: none went out, and none came in.

And the Lord said unto Joshua, See, I have given into thine hand Jericho, and the king thereof, and the mighty men of valour.

And ye shall compass the city, all ye men of war, and go round about the city once. Thus shalt thou do six days.

And seven priests shall bear before the ark seven trumpets of rams' horns: and the seventh day ye shall compass the city seven times, and the priests shall blow with the trumpets

And it shall come to pass, that when they make a long blast with the ram's horn, and when ye hear the sound of the trumpet, all the people shall shout with a great shout; and the wall of the city shall fall down flat . . .

And it came to pass at the seventh time, when the priests blew with the trumpets, Joshua said unto the people, Shout; for the Lord hath given you the city . . .

So the people shouted when the priests blew with the trumpets: and it came to pass, when the people heard the sound of the trumpet, and the people shouted with a great shout, that the wall fell down flat, so that the people went up into the city, every man straight before him, and they took the city.

A century of excavation by archaeologists has failed to uncover the fallen walls of the biblical city of Jericho, and it is now believed that their remains must have been eroded away in the distant past.

However, while searching for Joshua's Jericho in the 1950s, the British archaeologist Dr Kathleen Kenyon discovered a succession of ruins, one on top of the other. At the bottom, she found the oldest city in the world.

After the Sumerian centres of civilisation appeared, time could be measured and accounted for as a steady march of progress, from the first written word to the computer print-out.

Recently, however, many new discoveries have been made about the extent and complexity of the societies that existed in the time before recorded history. The most distant past of the human species becomes more crowded year by year. And views about where and when the first cities appeared are undergoing radical revision.

Added to this is some disagreement as to exactly what constitutes a city. There have been many attempts at definition, but none of them has been entirely satisfactory. Nevertheless, archaeologists have established a number of characteristics which, it is generally agreed, mark true urbanisation. They include permanence of settlement; specialisation of skills and functions among the inhabitants who, to some extent, need to draw on the surrounding regions for their food supplies; the development of a characteristic style of building; the erection of communal or public buildings, which presupposes appreciable resources and a work force; and the attainment of a certain size. All of these factors do not need to exist at once for a community to be regarded as urban.

The great advance in prehistoric research began just after the Second World War. In the case of carbon-14 dating techniques, which enable scientists to date ancient sites with remarkable accuracy, it was a by-product of nuclear research. There is now a wide range of scientific techniques available to archaeological research, both at excavation sites and in laboratories and computer centres. Great progress has been made in tracing mankind's history further and further back.

To understand the latest discoveries it is necessary to go back to the beginnings of mankind. The time of the creation is no longer considered to be the night preceding Sunday October 23, 4004 BC, as Archbishop Ussher claimed in 1650 – though that belief remained more or less unquestioned until the 19th century. Modern man, the sub-species *Homo sapiens sapiens*, has been the only form of man on earth for the past 30,000 years or so. But the discovery of man-like types, *Homo habilis* and the evolutionary 'dead end' *Australopithecus*, clearly indicates that humanity really had its origins 4 or 5 million years ago in the savannahs of East Africa. And that is where the oldest-known example of the crucial invention – the pebble tool – has been found.

Old Stone Age hunters were nomads. But it is now known that by about 30,000 BC they showed a preference for a more stable existence. They lived in small groups in caves, or on the plains in camps consisting of

The discovery of prehistoric settlements at Jericho in 1953, Çatal Hüyük in 1961 and Lepenski Vir in 1965 destroyed the belief that the world's first cities were built in Babylonia by the Sumerians 5,000 years ago. City life is now known to have begun at least 4,000 years earlier.

huts and other crude shelters. The oldest-known habitations, consisting of round huts 20 ft in diameter or 25-ft-long oval shelters, were made from animal skins and branches. Remnants of these have been found at mammoth-hunting camps such as Dolní Vestonice in Czechoslovakia.

All communities are born out of a need – for security, for companionship, for trade – but a community cannot survive without a supply of food. The critical change which enabled the nomadic hunter-gatherers to become city-dwellers was the development of a means of producing food, instead of relying on the luck of the hunt. This came around 8000 BC, at the end of the last great ice age, with the arrival of the 'New Stone Age Revolution'. This revolution, so rich in consequences for the whole future history of mankind, consisted of the cultivation of a few edible plants and the domestication of a handful of animals. It led to the transformation of hunters into farmers and of wanderers into settlers.

Agriculture called for many hands and required even more organisation than hunting. It demanded a more settled existence, with crops to be tended, herds to be fed and cared for, a surplus to be stored. And so the first permanent communities were formed. Land development had begun.

Exactly how long this transformation took is not known, but it was gradual, extending over perhaps thousands of years. One of the first areas in which this revolution took place was in the Middle East, though not in the great alluvial valleys, as was believed until recent years, but in the hilly areas around the edge of the Fertile Crescent. It was there that the nomads found the wild plants that were to become their first cereal crops.

In the foothills of Iran, Iraq, Israel, Jordan and Syria, archaeologists have found traces of the earliest settlements to be based on the cultivation of wheat and barley and the domestication of goats and sheep. They have discovered the remains of villages with the first grain silos and bakers' ovens – Jarmo and Zawi Chemi in Iraq, Ras Shamra in Syria, and others. And it is here that ruins of what can be called the world's earliest towns have been brought to light. Although the people who built them left no written records behind them it is possible to begin to see what these settlements were like in their original form.

The Jericho highway, which links Jerusalem and Amman, winds its way languidly across the mountains of Judaea in the middle of glistening mineral country. After the highway passes the site of the Good Samaritan Inn, it begins the long descent towards the valley of the Jordan, dotted at intervals with signs showing the

altitude – in reverse, for here it is measured in feet below sea level rather than above. In the heart of the low, scorching plain, where the river coils and meanders before losing itself in the Dead Sea, which can be seen shining in the distance, is Jericho. It rises up like a mirage, an oasis, a balmy Garden of Eden to welcome the traveller after the desert crossing. At more than 800 ft below sea level, it is the lowest urban settlement on earth. It is also the site of the oldest city that has been discovered to date.

In the Bible, Jericho is referred to as the 'city of palm trees'. It owes its existence to the fresh waters of the Ain es Sultan spring, or Fountain of Elisha, which is now channelled towards a concrete reservoir a mile to the north of the modern city. The spring flows at the foot of a curious oval hill, the colour of dried clay. This is Tell es Sultan, a dusty mound which has been marched over by generations of invaders, broken up by steady erosion, and dug into by archaeologists. It rises more than 60 ft above the plain, brooding and mysterious. It is now known that a city existed here about 9,000 years ago – 4,000 years before the Sumerian cities. This, it is believed, is the site of the original walled city of Jericho.

The biblical account of Jericho comes from the Book of Joshua. Moses died before the crossing of the Jordan, so he was not with his people when they

Among the spectacular finds made at Tell es Sultan, site of ancient Jericho, are some imposing fortifications. They include this massive stone tower which has a central stairway. Jericho was an ancient city even in the time of Joshua – at least 5,500 years old.

entered the Promised Land. It was his successor, Joshua, who led the people of Israel out of the desert and across the river. They besieged the first Canaanite city that lay on their route to the west – Jericho. After seven days its mighty walls crumbled at the shout of the Israelites, the population was put to the sword, the city was burned to the ground, and the spot was placed under a curse.

Around the end of the 19th century, the story in the Book of Joshua prompted a group of archaeologists to search for remains of the biblical Jericho. Today, after a century of excavation, no trace has yet been found of the walls destroyed by Joshua; erosion must have reduced them to dust. But excavations led by the British archaeologist Dr Kathleen Kenyon between 1952 and 1958 at Tell es Sultan did reveal some quite different walls from those they had hoped to find. Carbon-14 dating indicated that they were built as long ago as 7000 BC. The people of Israel fought their famous battle some time between 1400 and 1250 BC, at the end of the Bronze Age. So it appears that Joshua conquered and destroyed a city that was already at least 5,500 years old.

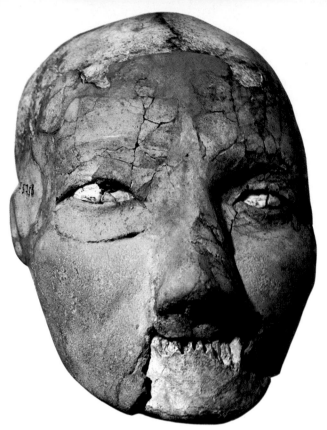

A portrait of one of the first city-dwellers, found at Jericho on a site believed to be 9,000 years old. It consists of a skull covered by a layer of clay, with the eye sockets inlaid with shells. The 'sculpture' was probably connected with a form of ancestor-worship practised in the city.

The discovery of a city dating from the New Stone Age upset established chronology and promised to revolutionise the theory that cities originated in Sumer.

Like Troy, but consisting of more layers, the site at Tell es Sultan is entirely made up of the ruins of cities superimposed on each other. The most recent of these dates from the Iron Age, which began around 1500 BC. The successive levels have been cut through by trenches in a grid pattern, and the various layers indicate that the settlement experienced more than 6,000 years of almost uninterrupted occupation by hundreds of generations of men.

From the edge of one of these vertical cuts it is possible to see the original city's walls – which are up to 20 ft high – rising up from the bottom of the dark trench more than 50 ft below. It is a startling vision, which seems to track the past back to the point where city living began.

Since the excavations at Tell es Sultan in the 1950s, other prehistoric cities have been discovered. First, a prosperous settlement dating from 6250 BC was un-

The first-known public works are the walls of the original city of Jericho, built about 7000 BC. They consist of well-cut, mortarless stones, are about 6 ft thick at the base and rise to at least 20 ft. No trace has been found of the much later walls which, in the Bible, fell at the shout of the Israelites.

covered in 1961 in Turkey, at the south end of the Anatolian plateau, by another British archaeologist, James Mellaart of the British Institute of Archaeology at Ankara. This was Çatal Hüyük, a major archaeological discovery.

Then in Europe, in 1965, Lepenski Vir was brought to light on the right bank of the Danube in Yugoslavia. This was a site dating back to before 5000 BC. The discovery was made by a team of Yugoslavian archaeologists under the direction of Professor Dragoslav Srejovic.

Archaeologists do not yet know enough to fit these discoveries into their exact place in the general story of the evolution of New Stone Age culture. But both have already contributed to a new view of the origin of cities.

In particular, Çatal Hüyük, although only partially excavated, has been the source of an abundance of rich archaeological material. Mellaart has written that it 'shines like a supernova among the rather dim galaxy of contemporary peasant cultures'. Çatal Hüyük's evolution as a city continued without interruption from 6250 BC to 5400 BC, when it was abandoned.

Jericho remains the oldest city in the world according to current archaeological knowledge, but there will undoubtedly be new discoveries in the future. It is quite possible that even older cities still lie buried beneath some of the innumerable mounds that are scattered throughout the Near East.

What were Jericho, Çatal Hüyük and Lepenski Vir like when they were in their prime? Most important, in what respect were they cities rather than simple village settlements?

At first, it is difficult to see a clear link between these three totally different sites that could define them as being part of the same evolutionary phenomenon. Jericho is an oasis in a valley at the northern end of the Dead Sea. Çatal Hüyük stands at an altitude of more than 3,000 ft, in the centre of a fertile wheat-

---

The Great Red Bull, one of the most striking frescoes at the prehistoric city of Çatal Hüyük, dates from about 6000 BC. The painting measures roughly 15 by 5 ft and shows the bull surrounded by armed hunters. It was undoubtedly the chief decoration in a sanctuary, and probably symbolised a god.

Its discovery has also provided information unobtainable from the site at Jericho, which consisted of nothing much more than the walls and a few bones. At Çatal Hüyük there is evidence of a true urban community with a well-developed economy and an intense religious and artistic life.

Lepenski Vir, on the other hand, is the work of hunters and fishermen of a pure Old Stone Age tradition scarcely touched by the New Stone Age. It is an example of the transitional form of settlement that was built after the early encampments, but before houses took on a permanent form. Lepenski Vir, coming into existence as it did before the New Stone Age Revolution, shows that urban existence had its beginnings in the Old Stone Age.

So far neither of these newly found prehistoric settlements has supplanted Jericho as the oldest city in the world. But it is important not to be too definite –

producing plain by the edge of the Çarsamba Çay river. Lepenski Vir is situated in a small enclosed valley, shaped like a horseshoe, near the Danube, in a forest area between the Balkan and Carpathian mountains, in the middle of the Iron Gate gorge. The only thing they appear to have in common is the presence of water, and this was an indispensable condition of their existence. But surely it is possible to establish some other connection, however subtle, between these three earliest-known urban settlements that indicates some general trend in the slow but inexorable development of urban living?

Their physical appearance throws little light on the question. They are all modest in size. Lepenski Vir is no bigger than a hamlet, covering an area little more than 185 yds long and 55 yds wide. It could hardly have had more than 200 or 300 inhabitants. The mound of Tell es Sultan, where Jericho once stood, is

about 284 yds long and 175 yds wide. It has been estimated that around 7000 BC the city must have covered about 10 acres and had between 2,000 and 3,000 inhabitants.

It is difficult to calculate the original size of Çatal Hüyük, since only a fraction of the huge mound – it is some 492 yds long – has so far been excavated. But it seems likely that this extensive and comparatively densely populated centre had between 6,000 and 10,000 inhabitants.

When compared with the Sumerian cities, which covered hundreds of acres each, and housed scores of thousands of inhabitants, these New Stone Age centres appear as undoubtedly small. However, they show great diversity of architectural styles and building techniques.

The first occupants of the Jericho site were a race of hunters of the Natufian culture, men of the pre-ceramic period of the New Stone Age of about 8000 BC. Later occupants lived in circular houses made from curved mud bricks which had dried in the sun. Kathleen Kenyon has called this style the 'hog-

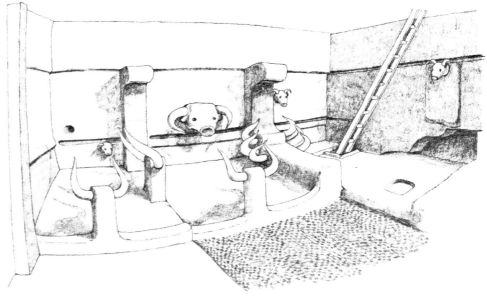

The Temple of the Bull God at Çatal Hüyük – a reconstruction based on discoveries made at the site. A large bull's head is flanked by two rams' heads, with a third mounted on another wall. The heads consist of skulls covered with clay and inset with real horns. On the floor, three pillars and a low bench of mud bricks bristle with cores from bulls' horns. The 40 shrines uncovered among the rectangular, terraced houses of the city are filled with paintings, sculptures and horns of animals. Heads of bulls were mounted on walls facing in any direction, but paintings of them are found only on walls facing the mountains which rise above the city. The ladder leads down from an opening in the roof – the only access.

146

backed-brick silhouette'. This spontaneous style of architecture originated in the old leaf or reed huts of the nomads – then developed into a more ordered form of building. Then inhabitants dating from around 6500 BC built rectangular houses which were clearly of a more advanced style of construction. Dried mud bricks were still used, but they were made in a flat shape, impressed with thumb prints to key the mortar. Floors and walls were covered with hard lime-plaster.

In these two strata of the excavations, the houses, whether round or rectangular, are all very small and built close together, with the door as the only opening. But the most outstanding feature is that the dwellings of both these early periods are clustered in the shelter of walled fortifications.

At Çatal Hüyük, the townscape is entirely different. There are no high surrounding walls guarding the city. As stone was not readily available, and sun-dried bricks were unsuitable for defensive walls, the inhabitants developed a novel way of protecting themselves: their houses had no doors, and were joined to one another. The only means of gaining entry was through an opening in the roof. The design was apparently successful, because there is no evidence that in the more than 2,000 years of its history Çatal Hüyük was ever sacked.

It was a city without streets, the people moving about on flat terrace roofs, which were joined to one another by wooden ladders. The houses were all rectangular in shape and remarkably well adapted to the needs of their occupants. They were built of rectangular clay bricks joined with mortar and assembled on a wooden framework. The houses varied in size and consisted of a main room – about 20 by 13 ft – and smaller secondary rooms used either for storage or as granaries with silos of dried earth. The main room was adorned with finely built fittings – fireplace, ovens, benches and raised sleeping platforms which seem to be prototypes of the sofa.

Well kept and newly plastered every year – it is possible to date the superimposed layers of plaster – these houses of Çatal Hüyük bear eloquent witness to the advanced level of building development reached on the Anatolian plateau.

Lepenski Vir has totally different characteristics. Its houses, built apart from one another, are curious forerunners of the modern detached home. The houses were all identical in plan and proportions. They were tent shaped and consisted of skins stretched across wooden uprights and extending to the ground. These houses were an extension of the hut form, but with the addition of various types of stone – limestone, sandstone and porphyry – which was quarried nearby.

The central rectangular stone-hearth was surrounded by sculptures and sacrificial altars which were fixed into the floor. Perfect insulation was provided by a meticulous coating of lime mortar applied to the floor.

At Lepenski Vir, there are really only four buildings of any size, which may have been temples of some kind. But both Jericho and Çatal Hüyük show evidence of public buildings which differ from the dwellings. The walls of Jericho – the first public work – were built of small, well-cut stones, without mortar, and are about 6 ft thick at the base. The original height of the walls is not known, but the parts that are still visible in the trenches at Tell es Sultan reach a height of 12 ft, and more than 20 ft in some places.

An enormous ditch, 21 ft wide and 8 ft deep, was cut into the rock round the outside of the walls. In the centre of the city is a high stone tower, which looks like a medieval castle keep. No one knows whether it was the people of the 'curved bricks' who put up these imposing fortifications, nor is it known how or exactly why they were erected.

At Çatal Hüyük, the city itself formed its own defences, for it had a continuous line of house walls facing outwards. Of the 139 living-rooms so far unearthed inside the city, James Mellaart has identified about 40 as being shrines or cult rooms. Many of these are larger than the other buildings, but the distinctive feature which made him decide that they were more

This statuette found at the site of Çatal Hüyük may have played a part in the fertility rites that were practised there. It represents a mother-goddess giving birth to a child on a leopard throne. The carving indicates the importance of agriculture and women in the society of the city.

Çatal Hüyük, a beehive city 8,000 years old

The strange, streetless city of Çatal Hüyük in southern Turkey marked a revolution in prehistoric building. The mud-brick dwellings, built more than 8,000 years ago, were clustered together like the cells of a beehive. They were lit by small windows built high in the walls and their only entrance was on the roof. The reconstruction of this remarkable city follows the painstaking work of the British archaeologist James Mellaart, who discovered Çatal Hüyük and excavated the site from 1961 to 1965.

The houses of Çatal Hüyük were all very much alike with main rooms [1] measuring about 20 ft by 13 ft. The roof [2] was constructed from bundles of reeds covered by a thick layer of mud and resting on two heavy beams and numerous joists. A ladder dropped through the entrance and visitors stepped down into the room below. The kitchen took up almost one-third of the living space. Along the walls were elevated platforms where the occupants sat and slept—large platforms for women and children, smaller ones for men.

Beneath these platforms the people of Çatal Hüyük buried skeletons of their dead [3]. The bodies were first left out in the open to be stripped clean by vultures before being laid to rest inside the mud houses.

Some of the buildings of Çatal Hüyük were religious sanctuaries [4, 16] where ceremonies almost certainly took place. They were impressively ornamented with wall-paintings and plaster relief [9, 10, 11, 15]. Such decorations, in dwellings as well as shrines, helped bring light within to supplement stone lamps placed in wall niches. Some purely decorative motifs are reflected today in the geometric patterns of Anatolian carpets [4]. Mellaart found on the walls many symbols of fertility. These took the form of a woman giving birth [13], of breasts or of a male god often associated with the bull [6, 7, 8, 14]. Other sanctuaries were adorned with vultures and were clearly linked with burial ceremonies [5, 12]. None had altars or sacrificial tables.

The people of Çatal Hüyük were most likely farmers or cattle herders who needed to live close to the broad plain stretching to the north of the city. There was no local stone to build with and the crude mud bricks were unsuitable for fortification. But the streetless city offered only a high and continuous wall to a would-be attacker.

In the event of an assault, the people simply took away their ladders and retreated into their houses. Capture then would be possible only by a long, difficult and costly house-by-house conquest—a daunting prospect for any attacker. The defences were probably effective, for no trace has been found at Çatal Hüyük of any plunder or massacre during its nearly 1,000 years of existence as an occupied city.

0 1 2 3 4 5   10 yards

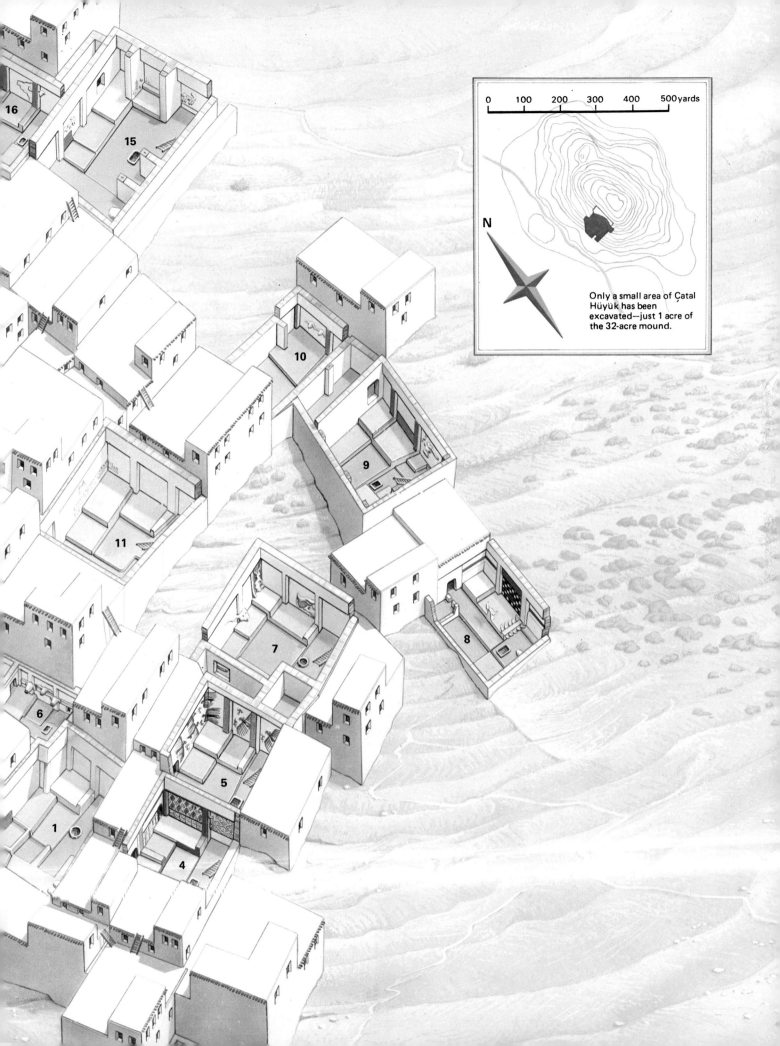

Only a small area of Çatal Hüyük has been excavated—just 1 acre of the 32-acre mound.

than ordinary houses is their interior decoration. It is richer and more elaborate than that of the simple dwellings, indicating an obvious ritual significance. Mellaart notes that 'The Neolithic [New Stone Age] city of Çatal Hüyük has yielded among many other splendours a unique sequence of sanctuaries and shrines, decorated with wall-paintings, reliefs in plaster, animal heads . . . and containing cult statues, which give us a vivid picture of Neolithic man's concern with religion and beliefs'.

Excavations of several building levels revealed one shrine to every two houses. It is possible that Çatal Hüyük may have been a holy city; or that the district which has been excavated was the area of the city occupied by priests and priestesses. In any case, the presence of both the walls and the shrines would seem to indicate that communities of some importance existed there and that these communities were already organised into groups of specialists.

On examining the remains and analysing the various elements which made up these primitive cities, researchers could see actual town plans emerging before them in surprisingly clear outline. It became evident to them that over a period of time the people in these cities had erected buildings of an increasingly sophisticated nature, and that there must have been social developments which ran parallel to the architectural developments. It is clear, then, that these early cities were much more than simple centres of habitation.

A bas-relief from Çatal Hüyük depicting a mother-goddess giving birth. It is believed that women outnumbered men in the city and that it was they who did the agricultural work. The face, hands and feet of the goddess were ritually broken when the sanctuary was abandoned.

The layout of Çatal Hüyük shows that it was definitely a planned city. In contrast to the other New Stone Age centres of population in the Near East, nothing was left to chance. James Mellaart stresses that 'Orderliness and planning prevail everywhere; in the size of bricks, the standard plan of houses and shrines, the heights of panels, doorways, hearths and ovens and to a great extent in the size of rooms. Hand and foot seem to have been the standards of measurement . . .'

The city itself emerges as an ordered architectural complex. According to Mellaart, it will eventually be possible 'to trace the plans of the successive building levels down to the original master-plan which the conservative builders of Çatal Hüyük continued to follow through numerous centuries'.

The appearance of a plan of this type marks the culmination of a process of cultural evolution. Such planning – but on a different scale – is evident at Lepenski Vir, which was also built to a precise design. It was constructed according to a series of constant mathematical proportions, and presents a pattern of streets which could be said to anticipate the Roman grid system.

On one level, at the central crossroads where the two main streets meet, was a square, on which stood the 'great house'. Around this square, other houses were strictly aligned in terraces, all facing west towards the Danube. This arrangement was designed to prevent the dominant east wind from striking the fronts of the houses where the openings were situated and to divert the wind along the walls at the sides. 'As far as we know it is the first demonstration of architectural aerodynamics,' writes the site's discoverer, Dragoslav Srejovic.

But most remarkable of all is the unique trapezoid plan of the houses, four-sided but with only two of the sides parallel. It seems to have been inspired by the shape of the valley; and the trapezoid design of the city fits exactly into the valley's contours. It is a fine example of the pursuit of harmony by the integration of habitat and location.

A simple comparison of these earliest New Stone Age cities immediately establishes the variety present in the urban environment from its very beginnings. Whether based on the form of a circle, a rectangle or a trapezoid, these are three completely individual towns. The first citizens – Palestinians, Anatolians and Danubians – succeeded in creating environments which have shown themselves to be the sources of original cultures.

Not only were the cities a deliberate, reasoned attempt to adapt to the surrounding environment, they were also an attempt to order people's relationships with one another. So what can be deduced about the inhabitants of these three cities? Certainly their life expectancy was short – 30 to 40 years at the most – but their health was generally good, at least in the case of Çatal Hüyük, although evidence of malaria, pneumonia and arthritis has been found. In all three

cities, the dead were buried underneath the houses, though in Jericho, bodies were interred outside the city from about 4000 BC.

Women seem to have held a dominant position in these societies, where fertility rites were practised and a mother-goddess was the principal deity.

Professor Srejovic notes that Lepenski Vir was a rigorously formal world, in which the strict traditions that governed both architecture and sculpture suggest that the people who built this place lived in a society in which the individual was subservient to the group, and depended entirely on the community for his livelihood. The architecture, he said, reflected the city's 'basic values, its aims and aspirations, and the instincts of the members of the community to identify themselves with these aims and regulate their behaviour accordingly'. It must have been a rigid collectivist system, which is not surprising considering the discipline necessary to maintain the economy which governed the city's day-to-day life.

In Çatal Hüyük, there is evidence of a more complex social life. According to James Mellaart, 'an ordered pattern of society is evident from the stereotyped house plans, from the standard features and equip-

Carving of a fish-god found at Lepenski Vir, the primitive site excavated on the banks of the Danube in 1965. Its inhabitants were Old Stone Age hunters and fishermen. The sculpture, carved from a piece of coarse-grained sandstone rounded by the river, is astonishingly modern in style.

ment, and a strong conservatism is shown by the frequent rebuildings on the same plan, the strict architectural layout and the very few changes that can be observed in the culture over a period of some eight hundred years'. Mellaart notes that some degree of social inequality is suggested by the varying sizes of buildings and differences in possessions and burial gifts, though the gap between rich and poor does not seem to have been a glaring one.

However, more research is required in order to progress much further with portraits of these first urban communities. One factor links all three: the alliance of tradition with innovation. Old Stone Age customs survived alongside new elements, such as a division of labour, which bear witness to a way of life that already had become complex at this crucial moment when urban society was crystallising.

What comes out of the countless finds at these sites as the most outstanding factor of all is that the standard of living, both material and spiritual, was high in relation to that of non-urban communities of the time.

The spectacular development of New Stone Age civilisation at Çatal Hüyük seems to have been based on the organised production and storage of food.

The inhabitants of Çatal Hüyük and Jericho appear more like the men of the land than men of the city. It would be more correct to refer to them as peasant-citizens, in so far as their lives were still governed by the crops they harvested. In small fields, which extended right around the city, they grew barley, wheat, peas, vetch and lentils.

It was the women who cultivated the crops, using stone tools, and they also looked after the cattle – in fact, most of the work in the fields was done by the women. The men went out hunting with their recently domesticated dogs, which shows that they had not yet become capable of producing all their own food. Even at Çatal Hüyük, where excavations have proved that at least 14 varieties of edible plants were cultivated, the New Stone Age citizen remained a great hunter, and the hunt continued to play an important part in the food supply. At that time the Anatolian plain had a rich diversity of wildlife. Ancient man probably hunted deer, aurochs, wild boars, leopards, wolves, bears, weasels, foxes, ibexes and birds.

The development of agriculture encouraged population growth and hence the growth of the urban settlement. The increase in population in turn stimulated more agriculture. However, the rise of the city was not due to agriculture alone. It may have set the stage for the rise of Jericho and Çatal Hüyük, and provided much of the food needed for the inhabitants' day-to-day existence, but the real reason for the growth and prosperity of the cities must be sought elsewhere.

A number of domestic items found in these cities indicate that people were beginning to look for the comforts that city living could provide. The quality and refinement of the countless day-to-day objects discovered at Çatal Hüyük seems to suggest a certain degree of luxury linked to the new urban way of life. These finds also reveal the existence of a thriving craft industry, although these people were not innovators in their use of wood and basketwork, nor in the fact that they carved bones and stone implements. But their woodwork and bone carving reached new levels, and their stonecraft marked the peak of the New Stone Age arts of cutting and polishing.

Of greater importance was the appearance of new techniques. The people of Çatal Hüyük made pottery and wove wool. The finds at the site include the earliest articles of clothing ever discovered in a preserved condition.

Weapons and jewellery buried in the sepulchres, as well as statuettes and mirrors of obsidian, indicate that the inhabitants of Çatal Hüyük achieved a certain level of technology and utilized both copper and lead. Mel-laart stresses that 'the variety of arts and crafts practised at Çatal Hüyük ... is nearly as great as that of developed civilisations of the Early Bronze Age. Only the arts of book-keeping or writing and music are not represented among the finds.'

Although the workshops where these things were made have not yet been unearthed their existence cannot be disputed, and the presence of such a specialised craft industry and high standard of living cannot be explained merely as 'fall-out' from the New Stone Age Revolution. Some new element is needed to account for all this. Everything seems to indicate that this new element was the growth of trade.

A budding and already fruitful commerce was certainly established at both Jericho and Çatal Hüyük. Its existence can be reconstructed from several finds that provide the first clues – in particular, shells and minerals. The flow of trade was organised around the stonework industry which was inherited directly from the Old Stone Age. Raw materials and finished products began to be transported along routes which can now be traced.

Jericho was built round a spring, but the development of the oasis was brought about by intensive trade. Salt from the Dead Sea and minerals dug from its shores were conveyed by way of Jericho, which was also a convenient stage on the journey between southern Palestine and Anatolia, between the nomads' posts in the desert and the Mediterranean, forming a kind of crossroads.

Çatal Hüyük traded with areas to its south. This is known from the presence on the site of Mediterranean shells such as whelks, cowries, cockle shells, cardiums and tooth shells. In their search for raw materials, the craftsmen scoured the neighbouring mountains, but soon moved further and further afield. Apart from timber, the raw materials that these craftsmen used included flint, limestone, alabaster, marble, greenstone, rock crystal, carnelian, chalcedony, jasper and many other minerals.

The then active volcanoes that can be seen from Çatal Hüyük, such as Hasan Dag, were a source of obsidian, a volcanic rock which looks like dark glass. It was much prized and very widely used for cutting utensils and weapons. From about 6000 BC, the city traded with people in places as far apart as Cyprus and Palestine. This network of exchange and trade lay behind the new urban prosperity.

All this recent research has revolutionised our image of the age which produced the first cities on earth. But who continued the process they began? Even now, little is known of the maturing process which, over a period of 4,000 or 5,000 years, raised the earliest urban communities from the level described to that of the remarkable city-states of Sumer, with their complex organisation rivalling that of the cities of today. This is the intriguing missing link that still awaits discovery.

MAY VEBER

A reconstruction of Lepenski Vir (right) as it is believed to have looked 7,000 years ago. This Old Stone Age settlement, situated in a game forest on the banks of the Danube, was a kind of primitive blueprint for the New Stone Age cities that followed. Even though the economy was limited at that stage to hunting, fishing and plant-gathering, Lepenski Vir was not only one of the earliest fixed centres of habitation but also one of the first examples of town planning.

The houses, consisting of skins stretched over wooden uprights, vary in size, but are identical in plan and proportion and are laid out in a strictly ordered pattern. In this way they foreshadow the repetitive architecture of our own day. Each of the houses has a central fireplace built of stone blocks, and a sacrificial altar.

Near the altars are sculptured figures whose heads have pronounced fish-like features (below). Other animals depicted on sculptures were the stag and the dog. The remains of these and of fish have been dug up near the altars, indicating that they were sacrificed. According to Professor Dragoslav Srejovic, whose team discovered the city, the fish and the stag were sacred animals which probably played a part in myths about the origins of the world.

The last refuge
of the Incas

*Shooting, pillaging and burning, the 16th-century
adventurers known as the* conquistadores *ravaged
the mountain empire of the Incas. They melted down
the Incas' treasure, executed leaders and enslaved the
people in an orgy of avarice and destruction. But
the last of the Inca rulers escaped deep into the
Andes mountains to a city as impressive as
any the Spaniards had conquered. And when this fugitive
emperor died, he took the secret of his
hiding place to the grave. It is
still to be identified.*

They had been seen in the Pacific, approaching in great floating houses, hurling bolts of fire with the speed of lightning and the sound of thunder. Fair-skinned and bearded, just as the prophecy said, the gods of antiquity had returned. The news quickly spread to the far corners of the Incas' Andean realm.

The Spanish *conquistador* Francisco Pizarro and his band of 180 soldiers – the men who had been mistaken for gods – arrived in Peru in the wake of a struggle for leadership that had weakened the once-mighty Inca empire. Around 1527 a virulent epidemic – possibly

The Urubamba, legendary river of the sun, thunders through the Andes, the almost vertical sides of its canyon swathed in mist. A narrow road which crosses the rushing water on a tiny bridge snakes up a 2,000-ft precipice. It leads to the abandoned Inca city of Machu Picchu.

European in origin and introduced to the Americas by the *conquistadores* – had swept Peru, claiming the lives of both the emperor, Huayna Capac Inca, and his probable successor, Ninan Cuyachi. In the confusion that ensued Huayna Capac's son Huascar had become ruler at the capital of Cuzco while another son, Atahualpa, had remained in command of the imperial army in the northern city of Quito.

After a few years of outward tranquility, during which each brother maneuvered to wrest full imperial authority from the other, civil war erupted. Atahualpa won, but he was not destined to enjoy his triumph for long. Late in 1532 Pizarro and his troops moved inland from the coast and in a bold gesture on November 16 seized Atahualpa in the midst of his vast army at Cajamarca. Intimidated by the Spaniards' horses and fire power, the natives put up no resistance.

To secure his release, Atahualpa offered to pay

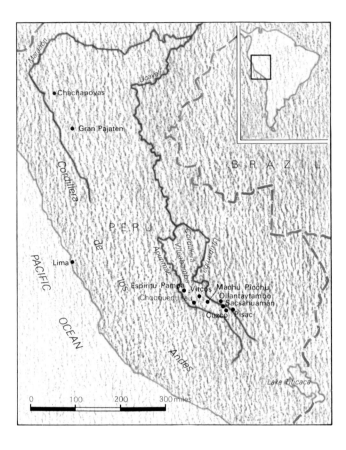

When their empire fell, the Incas retreated into the Andean cordillera, which is well suited to guerrilla warfare with its high passes, narrow river gorges and steep tracks hidden in dense jungle. Their last stronghold was the city of Vilcabamba, hidden in the Vilcabamba mountains, somewhere between the valleys of the Urubamba and Apurimac rivers.

Pizarro the most fabulous ransom in recorded history. Indicating a point roughly 8 feet up the wall of the room in which he was being held, the Inca promised his captor that he would fill the chamber to that height with various objects of gold – jewellery, jars and pots, tiles and plaques. He also pledged to fill another room twice over with silver.

When this priceless treasure had been amassed, Pizarro had it melted down and, after reserving a portion for the king, distributed it among his men. He then accused Atahualpa of plotting against him and had the hapless Inca ruler garrotted, rightly guessing that the local population still supported Huascar and would therefore accept, if not condone, Atahualpa's assassination. Pizarro now appointed Huascar's brother Manco as successor to the slain emperor.

Over the next two years relations between Manco Inca and the *conquistadores* deteriorated steadily, and by late 1535 they had become almost intolerable from the puppet emperor's point of view. Far from being the promised gods of ancient legend, these white men were proving to be ruthless tyrants capable of committing any outrage in their singleminded pursuit of New

World gold. Emboldened by the support of Manco's numerous rivals, the Spaniards stripped the imperial palace of its gold fittings and looted the gold-bedecked mummies in the imperial mausoleum. Next they desecrated Cuzco's temples, melting down gold vessels in the sanctuaries and gold statues on the altars.

What little sovereignty Manco initially enjoyed was soon largely eroded and he became subjected to daily insults and harassment. Juan and Gonzalo Pizarro, nominally in command of Cuzco in their brother Francisco's absence, pressed Manco to reveal the whereabouts of new caches of treasure. Dismayed and frightened, Manco attempted to flee the capital, only to be overtaken and imprisoned.

The Inca's escape

Realizing that outright resistance to the *conquistadores* and their numerous Indian allies would be futile, Manco feigned tolerance of the new order – and plotted revenge, In April 1536 he asked Hernando Pizarro, a third brother of Francisco's, for permission to journey to the Yucay valley to make obeisance to the ancient gods. Manco promised to bring back a life-sized gold statue of Huayna Capac. Gold-lust apparently clouded Pizarro's judgment at this point, for he permitted the Inca to depart over the strenuous objections not only of his own lieutenants but also of his Indian allies.

Within days Manco had assembled an army 100,000 strong, as men from all parts of the Inca realm abandoned their homes and farms to join him. Thus began the long resistance to the Spaniards, a struggle led first by Manco and later by his sons that was to last 36 years, from 1536 to 1572.

From his headquarters at Calca, Manco now laid siege to Cuzco. He set fire to large sections of the Spanish-held capital but was unable to reclaim it. By the summer of 1536 the discouraged Inca and his troops had withdrawn to Ollantaytambo in the valley of the Urubamba river, the juncture of the Andes and the Amazon basin. Shortly thereafter the Inca's army successfully repulsed a Spanish assault on Ollantaytambo, but the incident left Manco determined to find a truly invulnerable and inaccessible refuge. He therefore moved his base of operations once again, this time to Vitcos in the Vilcabamba river valley.

Pursued there by a Spanish force under Rodrigo Orgóñez, an energetic and ambitious young *conquistador*, Manco was forced to flee again. The Spaniards who paused to loot Vitcos presumably passed up their chance to take the rebellious Inca alive, for while they sacked the city Manco beat a hasty and disorderly retreat further up the valley of the Vilcabamba.

The murder of Pizarro

The spoils of Vitcos included some 20,000 prisoners and 50,000 head of llamas and alpacas, a loss which threatened to curtail Manco's guerrilla war before it

THE LAST REFUGE OF THE INCAS

began. Manco's losses at Vitcos also lulled the invaders into a false sense of security: 'We are no longer concerned about any war that the Inca could wage,' wrote a *conquistador* at the time. After the Spaniards returned to Cuzco in July 1537, Manco and the remnants of his army seemed to disappear into the mountains.

From his remote redoubt in the upper Vilcabamba, Manco was to direct a brilliant resistance campaign against the invaders. Then, one day in 1541, heartening news reached Vitcos, to which the Inca had returned. Informers from the new Spanish capital of Lima visited Manco in his retreat and informed him that the Spaniards, in their insatiable hunger for gold and empire, had taken to killing one another – and that the Inca's archenemy, Francisco Pizarro, had been murdered. A group of disaffected soldiers had burst into Pizarro's palace on a Sunday morning and hacked him to death with their swords.

Some of the renegades were taken prisoner and executed. But seven of them managed to escape into the mountains, where they were welcomed as fugitives by Manco. During the years they stayed there they helped to train his soldiers in Spanish fighting techniques. Manco himself learned to ride a horse and fire an arquebus.

But in the deep silence of the mountains, time weighed heavily on the Spaniards. When, in their fastness, they heard reports that Spain had sent out a

viceroy, and that he had clashed with the supporters of the surviving Pizarro brothers, the fugitives saw their chance: by killing Manco they could win themselves pardons for Francisco Pizarro's murder and so return to Cuzco and civilisation. They invited the Inca to join them in a game of quoits, one of the emperor's favourite pastimes. While Manco was taking his turn, the Spaniards fell on him with their daggers.

With the Inca murdered, the Spaniards dashed to their horses and spurred them down the path to Cuzco. But they took a wrong turn and were caught by a detachment of Manco's soldiers. Some of the assassins died under the spear; others perished when the building to which they had fled was set alight.

After the death of Manco in 1544, resistance to the Spanish was led by his son Sayri Tupac. Some years later Sayri Tupac accepted the offer of a pardon from the Spanish crown, left Vilcabamba and made his way to Lima. Early in 1558 the royal party entered the city, the first and only time that a native ruler would set foot in the Spanish capital of Peru. Sayri Tupac then

The Spanish conquistadores *thought that these stone ramparts at the fortress of Sacsahuaman were the work of the devil. Three massive walls, each more than 400 yds long, make up the fortress, which is on a hill above the Inca capital of Cuzco at an altitude of more than 12,000 ft.*

The fortress of Ollantaytambo guards the mouth of the Urubamba canyon. It straddled the Inca route from Cuzco to Machu Picchu and the citadels farther downstream. After the Inca Manco failed to retake Cuzco, he withdrew here before moving deeper into the Andes.

journeyed on to Cuzco, where a Christian ceremony formalised his marriage to his sister Cusi Huarcay. Incestuous liaisons of this sort were the rule rather than the exception among members of the imperial family, but this particular union, presided over by the bishop of Cuzco in that city's cathedral, required a special dispensation from the Pope.

Two years later Sayri Tupac died on his estate in the Yucay valley, his death so unexpected and mysterious that many suspected foul play.

Back in Vilcabamba, a second son of Manco's, Titu Cusi, succeeded to the Inca throne. Eleven years later he was cut down by disease and the succession passed to Tupac Amaru, yet another of Manco's sons. This last emperor of the Incas became a staunch defender of the crusade against the *conquistadores* which his father had launched three decades earlier.

A university of idolatry

In March 1572 the new viceroy of Peru, Francisco de Toledo, sent an emissary to Vilcabamba with a letter for Tupac Amaru. Toledo's envoy was fated never to reach Vilcabamba, however. Inca soldiers intercepted him en route and executed him, a gesture that enraged the viceroy and prompted him to launch a final assault on the Inca's citadel – which, according to a Spanish missionary, was a veritable 'university of idolatry'. Sorcerers and soothsayers – 'masters of abomination' – were supposed to officiate there, joined in their secret rites by the Virgins of the Sun, who worshipped before a fabulous golden disc.

On the morning of June 24, 1572, the Spaniards forced the gates of Vilcabamba, but they found only the smoking ruins of a deserted town. Tupac Amaru and the last of his followers had fled into the dense vegetation of the Amazon jungle. But some Indians informed on him and he was taken prisoner. Weak with exhaustion, he was led back to Cuzco with a golden chain about his neck. There he was beheaded before a huge crowd of prostrate Indians, who wept for days over his death.

None of the maps of the Spanish colonial era showed the location of either Vitcos or Vilcabamba, and in time the knowledge of their exact whereabouts was lost. The search for the last refuge of the Incas has intrigued scholars and adventurers ever since, particularly since local rumour had it that the last ruler had buried his treasure there.

As early as 1768 a theory was put forward that the Incas' last hideout, the legendary city of Vilcabamba, was in fact the ruins at Choqquequirau, which is situated in a steep range near the Apurimac river. The lure of Inca gold proved a durable one indeed, and so it was that when the young American scholar Hiram

158

Bingham passed through the Apurimac region in 1909, the prefect of the province urged him to visit Choqquequirau, insisting that it was the remains of the lost city of the Incas.

Bingham's small group set off on a perilous march along paths cut into the side of a chasm which led into the depths of the Apurimac gorge. They crossed a dizzying bridge of lianas spanning the tumultous mountain torrent, and there before them were the jungle-infested ruins of Choqquequirau.

There were palaces hanging over precipices, a ceremonial square and ransacked temples. Many Peruvian researchers were prepared to accept Choqquequirau as Manco's Vilcabamba, but their conviction was not shared by the famed Lima historian Don Carlos Romero – or, ultimately, by Bingham.

According to Bingham's reckoning, moreover, the location of Choqquequirau did not correspond with the rare descriptions of the city of Vilcabamba left by 16th-century writers. He returned to the United States but became obsessed by the idea of exploring the area behind the mountains where, he believed, the last centre of Inca resistance must lie. He re-read contemporary accounts and also those of more recent explorers. So infectious was his enthusiasm that he had no difficulty in organising a scientific expedition, and in 1911 he returned to Peru.

From Cuzco, he followed the route Manco had

Not so long ago the only way to cross the Apurimac river was by means of a fragile hanging bridge made of creepers, slung like a hammock from the sides of the canyon. This bridge led to Choqquequirau, the mysterious 'cradle of gold', one site proposed as the lost city of the Incas.

Machu Picchu was rediscovered in 1911 by the American explorer Hiram Bingham. Set 7,000 ft up in the Andes, in a saddle of the hills above the Urubamba, it was thought originally to have been the last refuge of the Inca Manco. Modern researchers, however, are divided over the questions of when it was built and what purpose it served.

taken when eluding Pizarro – but here Bingham had a considerable advantage. The colossal granite barrier presented by the Urubamba canyon, previously impassable, had been opened up by the use of dynamite to form a trail.

Slowly, the expedition made its way along the trail. One night they left the road and camped at the river's edge. A man named Melchor Arteaga, who lived in a hut by the river, was intrigued by the presence of the group and approached their camp. They questioned him, and for a few coins he gave away the secret so jealously guarded from generation to generation by all the Indians of the sacred valley of the Urubamba river. He offered to guide Bingham to some ruins which lay in the hollow of a peak towering more than 2,000 ft above the Urubamba.

The next morning, Bingham, with Arteaga in the lead, set out across the river, then through the jungle to the base of the precipitous slope. After a strenuous climb, he came upon 'a great flight of beautifully constructed stone-faced terraces, perhaps a hundred of them, each hundreds of feet long and 10 ft high'. Bingham, who had seen similar flights of steps before, was unexcited until his guide led him along one of the

159

widest terraces into the forest. 'Suddenly,' he wrote, 'I found myself confronted with the walls of ruined houses built of the finest quality of Inca stonework. It was hard to see them for they were partly covered with trees and moss, the growth of centuries, but in the dense shadow, hiding in bamboo thickets and tangled vines, appeared here and there walls of white granite ashlars [square-hewn stones] carefully cut and exquisitely fitted together.'

The site that Bingham had found was called Machu Picchu. Discovery followed upon discovery: first, a cave lined with the finest cut stone which Bingham guessed had been a royal mausoleum; above it, a semicircular building whose outer wall 'followed the natural curvature of the rock and was keyed to it by one of the finest examples of masonry I had ever seen. Furthermore it was tied into another beautiful wall, made of very carefully matched ashlars of pure white granite, especially selected for its fine grain. Clearly, it was the work of a master artist'.

To Bingham, his discovery seemed like an unbelievable dream: 'Dimly, I began to realise that this wall and its adjoining semicircular temple over the cave

This gate of honour in Machu Picchu stands at the end of a 625-mile-long imperial road. Like all Inca roads it was paved and had post houses at intervals. Inside the city there was a system of paved streets, often cut into steps because of the city's sloping site. Decorations or torches may have hung from the jutting stone above the gateway.

The massive wall of the Temple of the Three Windows, one of the most important sacred places in Machu Picchu, looks out over the peaks of the Andes. The three windows are unique in pre-Columbian architecture and commemorate a mythical cavern where the founders of the Inca dynasty appeared.

This ancient Peruvian city in the sky appeared as fascinating and disturbing as ever. But still Bingham was uncertain whether he had really found Vilcabamba, the abominable 'university of idolatry' and final refuge for the Incas.

He set out again to explore the entire region as far as the edge of the tropical forest, looking for some clue which would clinch the matter. But he gave up after reaching and partly exploring a site called Espíritu Pampa, or Plain of the Spirits.

Had Bingham known of and trusted fully the accounts left by the early Spanish chroniclers of the conquest of Peru, he might have succeeded in identifying Vilcabamba. For these early accounts – some of which have only come to light since Bingham's initial findings – state that the Spanish troops dispatched to Vilcabamba in 1572 by the viceroy Francisco de Toledo could not possibly have reached Machu Picchu. Toledo's troops had crossed the Urubamba river at the bridge of Chuquichaca and set out along the gorge of a tributary, the Vilcabamba, on a route that would have taken them past and away from Machu Picchu.

Moreover, there is no archaeological evidence that foreign soldiers ever reached the dramatic citadel discovered by Bingham, though Spanish soldiers certainly occupied the city of Vilcabamba. All this suggests that Machu Picchu was never visited by the Spaniards and thus cannot be the lost city of the Incas.

were as fine as the finest stonework in the world . . . It fairly took my breath away. What could this place be?'

Bingham went on to discover not just a few structures but a whole city, so well preserved that only the reed and straw roofs needed to be replaced and it would come to life again. But he was tortured by a nagging doubt – had he really discovered Vilcabamba or was it some other Inca citadel?

Perhaps, Bingham speculated, Machu Picchu had been constructed during the reign of Pachacuti Inca, who ruled during the first half of the 15th century and who was, by some estimates, 'the greatest man that the Aboriginal Race of America has produced'. In Pachacuti's time Machu Picchu might have served as a military garrison, protecting the northern flank of Cuzco from the hostile Indians who inhabited the upper Amazon basin. Or perhaps it had been used in the following century as a sanctuary for the Virgins of the Sun, to shield them from the *conquistadores*' lust. The burial caves on the mountain contained an unusually large proportion of female skeletons, and the valuables buried with them indicated that they had been persons of importance.

In 1915 Hiram Bingham returned to Machu Picchu.

This carved stone at Machu Picchu was sacred in the Incas' sun cult. Each year at the winter solstice in June, when the sun was at its lowest point in the sky, the high priest symbolically bound the sun god Inti to the stone with a golden chain to make sure that he returned for the Southern Hemisphere summer. The prism-shaped pillar was also used as a sundial.

The question of the mysterious last refuge of the Incas came up again suddenly in 1964, after the discovery of archaeological remains different from any ever seen in the Andes. A group of farmers who had set out in search of arable land in the north of Peru came across some unknown ruins which they named Gran Pajatén.

This new lost city is perched on a crescent-shaped cliff about 9,500 ft above sea level, overlooking chasms which resound with the thunder of many waterfalls. Its architecture is unusual in that the buildings, both temples and palaces, are round, like giant drums on circular bases. Paved paths, short flights of steps and small squares, each with a raised stone in the centre, give access from one to the other.

An aerial survey showed that there were many ruins at Gran Pajatén. At least 3,000 have already been recorded, scattered over seven hills and linked by a roadway – in some places more than 4 yds wide – which crosses Gran Pajatén and disappears far into the forest. Did this route link the Chachapoyas and

Vilcabamba regions, more than 600 miles apart? How does this place fit into the odyssey of the last Incas?

Titu Cusi related that his father, Manco, at one time left Vitcos because some chiefs in the Chachapoyas region had advised him there was a good fort at Rabantu where he could defend himself from his enemies. Rabantu was the capital of the fierce Chachapoyas, whom the Incas could never subdue and whom they had to accept as restless allies. Nevertheless, Manco was tempted by this offer and set out for the northern fortress. But he soon abandoned his desperate exodus.

Since the beginning of the century, when Bingham's discovery revived the search for the lost city of the Incas, several other civil and military expeditions have been formed with the same object in mind. In 1964–5 Gene Savoy, another American, took up where Bingham left off.

Savoy identified Vilcabamba with the ruins discovered by Bingham at Espíritu Pampa, basing his assumptions on several pieces of evidence. First, he had investigated some ruins in the forest nearby which

The ruins of Pisac, perched on the edge of a dizzying cliff in the Urubamba valley near Cuzco, are outstandingly beautiful. The city had forts, huge palace halls, shrines, even a hanging garden. According to legend, a local chief's daughter was turned to stone on the mountain, and still haunts the area.

included blocks of stone arranged in the manner of the Incas. There were also fountains served by an ingenious system of pipes and drains ending in gargoyles from which the water issued – very similar to ones in Cuzco.

Second, he had observed that the walls of the monuments at Espíritu Pampa were coated with 'red ceramic-like stucco or terracotta'. He had also unearthed a considerable number of roofing tiles – many of a type previously unknown in the Americas – made in the European manner, but covered with a clay peculiar to Inca ceramics and decorated with characteristic Inca motifs of serpents and birds.

These finds could tie in with a report by the Spanish Friar Martín de Murúa that 'Manco had a house built in Vilcabamba with two storeys, covered in tiles. The entire mansion, with its doors made of highly perfumed cedar, was decorated in different varieties of painting and well worth seeing'.

Finally, Savoy saw a horseshoe identical to those used by the *conquistadores*. It is probable that he would have found many other relics of those times if Espíritu Pampa had not been plundered by the Machiguengas Indians, the same tribe that had prevented Bingham

The horseshoe-shaped Tower of the Sun was used in Machu Picchu's religious ceremonies. Its stones are cut with perfect precision and assembled without mortar. Each slightly sloping course is shallower than the one beneath it. Niches in the walls probably held effigies of the gods. Behind the tower an opening leads to the mausoleum shown at left, above.

Gran Pajatén, in north-eastern Peru, could have been one of Manco's hiding places. The city, rediscovered in 1964, was a centre of the Chachapoyas' pre-Inca kingdom. High in the mountain forests, it boasts extraordinary bas-reliefs showing worshippers of an Andean condor-god dancing stiffly, their faces ringed with stone feathers.

from going any further in his research. Savoy saw in the huts of the Machiguengas great ears of corn made of gold, which they claimed to have found in large numbers in the ruins, along with cloaks embroidered with condors in gold, bronze tools and ceramics.

Did Savoy too readily identify Espíritu Pampa with Vilcabamba? Subsequent discoveries have led many researchers to doubt his conclusions.

Recently, for example, one of Gene Savoy's guides discovered another lost city with an area of just over a square mile. The entrance to this town is cut out of a single block of stone and, instead of being trapezoid-shaped in the Inca tradition, this one, strangely, is in the form of a half-moon. This could have been an attempt to build an arch, indicating the presence of

Ancient buildings found in the tropical forests of the Vilcabamba region are more roughly made than those in most Inca cities. Crude shelters such as this one, now green with lichen and moss, were probably built in haste by Inca refugees who fled to the jungle to escape the Spaniards.

Spanish influence. The Indians who live in the valley call these ruins Hatun Vilcabamba, which means Great, or High, Vilcabamba.

Another set of ruins was suggested as the site of Vilcabamba when a Peruvian army brigade, crossing the area between the Apurimac and Urubamba rivers some time ago, had an unusual experience. They were forbidden access to a group of imposing ruins by hostile Indians of the Paucapuris tribe, who kept guard over all the entrances by road and river. The Indians claimed to be the legitimate heirs of the Incas and, since the fall of the empire, guardians of Vilcabamba. According to them, the Inca treasures lay at the bottom of a lake which only they could approach.

Choqquequirau, Machu Picchu, Gran Pajatén, Espíritu Pampa . . . any of these might be the lost city of

Vilcabamba, though Peruvian archaeologists are not prepared to make a pronouncement. Their caution is understandable, for there are still half a dozen or so splendid ruins which have not yet been studied. If anybody knows the truth about the last sanctuary of the Incas, he is keeping the secret to himself, as the Indians did so many centuries ago.

SIMONE WAISBARD

Defended by forts and guarded by lookout posts, the hilltops and ravines of the Vilcabamba region kept the Inca Manco and his sons safe for 36 years. But after the last of them died, the forts were abandoned, the access tracks became overgrown, and the knowledge of their last capital, the city of Vilcabamba, slowly faded from the memory of man.

Secrets
of the
pyramids

The men who built the Tower of Babel

*Soaring in platforms towards the sky,
bold in their design, capped with
temples, the towering structures known
as ziggurats were the crowning glory
of the city-states that emerged in Mesopotamia
5,000 years ago. Eclipsing them all was
Babylon's ziggurat – renowned as the Tower
of Babel. But their function remains
a mystery. Were they royal tombs, astronomers'
observatories . . . or gigantic stepping stones
for the gods to come down to earth?*

The world's first great civilisations blossomed five millennia ago in the rich, alluvial plains of Mesopotamia, the present borderland between Iraq and Iran. In this fertile strip between the Tigris and Euphrates rivers and in the hilly flanks to the east, there came and went over the centuries after about 3500 BC a succession of inventive, often fierce and contentious people – Sumerians and Elamites, Assyrians and Babylonians, Kassites and Persians.

The bustling cities these people built in the narrow plain are now no more than 'tells' – mounds of mud-

An aerial view of the site of the Tower of Babel in Babylon – all that remains of this prodigious monument. The outline of its huge, square base, consisting of earth embankments overgrown with vegetation and surrounded by hollows and palm trees, can still be clearly seen.

brick buildings, artefacts and debris, rising above the surrounding flatlands. Some of the spectacular temple-monuments they erected to their gods – the soaring brick-built ziggurats – still tower over the ruined cities. The ziggurats were pyramid-like towers, consisting of a series of platforms each decreasing in size as they climbed, some nearly 300 ft towards the sky. At the top stood temples into which the gods were believed to step on their way to an earthly dwelling place; a second temple was at the pyramid's base.

The prolific city-states of Mesopotamia left some 30 known ziggurats dating to between 3000 and 500 BC. To the men of their day they were as impressive as the great pyramids of Egypt, but today most of them are mere rubble. The most remarkable of all can no longer be seen – the ziggurat of Etemenanki, thought to be the biblical Tower of Babel.

All that remains of this huge building that stood

beside the Euphrates in Babylon, the magnificent capital of Nebuchadrezzar II (605–562 BC), is the outline of its vast square base.

The ruined state of the ziggurats today makes them particularly difficult to study. No monuments have been more exposed to destruction. Their bricks were often pilfered for house-building, and they were constantly menaced by erosion and in danger of crumbling to dust. Most of the great cities of Mesopotamia had at least one ziggurat, built to honour the particular gods its citizens worshipped. There is evidence of no fewer than three at Ashur, the old capital of the ferocious Assyrians which stood beside the Tigris in northern Iraq until it was sacked by the Chaldeans from the south in 614 BC. Much still remains of the huge ziggurat built at Ur, a major city first of the Sumerians and later of the Chaldeans. And there are ziggurats still standing at Birs Nimrud near Babylon and Aqarquf not far from Baghdad.

The ziggurats appear not to have been the brainchild of one particular builder, but to represent the culmination of an evolution about which little is known. Some light has been thrown on their possible origins by excavations at Warka. This site, lying near the desert border of southern Iraq, is ancient Uruk – the Erech of the Bible – which was the capital of several Sumerian dynasties.

There, within a vast perimeter, stood some spectacular examples of sacred architecture. One temple,

called the White Temple because of the lime coating its walls, was probably dedicated to Anu, god of the sky, the supreme master, comparable to the Greek god Zeus. It was built around 3000 BC, on a platform or pedestal about 40 ft high. It is relatively small and does not appear to have been designed to receive the faithful, but was rather a welcoming sanctuary for Anu when he came to earth. Archaeologists believe that Uruk's White Temple mound may have been a prototype of the later ziggurats which were built higher and higher, one level upon the other.

Like all Mesopotamian buildings, the ziggurats were built of brick. Palm trees grew in abundance, but their timber was poor and unusable for building; and in the immense alluvial plains of Mesopotamia there is no stone – although an inferior kind is found in the northern part of the country.

The bulk of each ziggurat was made up of crude bricks of moulded clay mixed with chopped straw and left to dry in the sun. Baked bricks were used for the framework, joined together with bitumen mortar. The procedure is described in the Book of Genesis, chapter 11, in the account of the Tower of Babel: 'And they said one to another, Go to, let us make brick, and burn them thoroughly. And they had brick for stone, and slime had they for mortar.'

The Bible's 'slime' was in fact bitumen – a substance imported from the Iranian plateau and widely used throughout Mesopotamia. It was used not only as a binding material in buildings but also for various coat-

The Tower of Babel has inspired artists down the ages. This painting, by the Flemish master Peter Bruegel the Elder (1525–69), was inspired by the story in the Book of Genesis. It shows a stage of construction before the Lord caused the builders to speak in a babble of tongues, so that they could not work together and finish the tower.

170

All that remains of the mighty city of Babylon is a huge shapeless mass of brick rubble. The band across the middle of the site is the processional way, which ran past the famed Hanging Gardens. The square block with a central courtyard in the left foreground is a reconstructed temple.

and 1934, noted that the main architectural lines of the structure had been built with slight curves to avoid the impression of weakness that would have been given if they had been completely straight, and to correct the optical illusion of a bend in the middle. The Greeks have been admired for their application of this principle – to the columns of the Parthenon in Athens in particular – but we now know it was brilliantly used by the Mesopotamians 2,000 years earlier.

No effort was spared to add to the splendours of the ziggurats; bright colours may have been painted on the exterior walls. Woolley established that the lower levels of the ziggurat at Ur were coloured black and the upper level red, and possibly this represented the contrast between darkness and light.

The remains of the Assyrian ziggurat discovered at Khorsabad, near ancient Nineveh in northern Iraq, showed successive levels of white, black, rose, blue, vermillion, silver and gold. The walls were decorated with carved veneers, painted panels and statues. The sanctuary on top glittered. It was built between 717 and 707 BC during the reign of Sargon II.

ing purposes, such as waterproofing the boats that sailed on the Tigris and the Euphrates.

The low-lying marshes of the Tigris and the Euphrates provided an abundant supply of tall rushes, which were used in rather strange ways in building. In the ziggurat at Aqarquf, the capital of the invading Kassites in the 14th and 13th centuries BC, reed mattresses were placed on every eighth or ninth layer of bricks – in the same way the Romans inserted courses of bricks between layers of concrete. Often these reeds were plaited into thick ropes and set into the thickness of a wall to strengthen a joint.

Architects of many skills

The Sumerians and their successors were artists who used all their skills to break up the monotony of the huge wall surfaces of the ziggurats. They built majestic sloping ramps, oblique stairways linking each stage to the one above, and decorative buttresses dividing the walls into sections.

The great English archaeologist Sir Leonard Woolley, who excavated the ziggurat at Ur between 1922

Mesopotamia was the land of the ziggurat builders. These massive buildings once towered over the ancient cities grouped in the alluvial plains of the Tigris and the Euphrates, now in southern Iraq. There were also ziggurats in the land of Elam, which was outside Mesopotamia, in what is now Iran.

Ancient Babylon and the Tower of Babel

A colossus with feet of clay—that was ancient Babylon, a city which, after some 1,500 years of splendour, fell into decline in the 4th century BC and was claimed by the clay from which it had been built. Only the writings of biblical times and modern excavations have enabled archaeologists to reconstruct a plan of the city, in the centre of which rose Etemenanki, celebrated as the Tower of Babel.

Babylon was the most splendid and impressive city of its time. The outer wall [1] is estimated to have been 10 miles in circumference. Within the shelter of this wall, King Nebuchadrezzar II (605-562 BC) had a vast palace [2]. The city's inner wall [3] was up to 90 ft high, with towers along its length. On one side of the city ran the Euphrates [4], which has changed its course since ancient times, but was once an important natural line of defence. A citadel [5] formed part of the wall, and plunder and trophies from successful wars were stored there. A new town [6], built on the other bank of the Euphrates, was linked to the city itself by a large bridge [7], supported on piers of baked brick and asphalt faced with stone. The building of this bridge across a river as deep and swift-flowing as the Euphrates is evidence of considerable engineering skill.

Nebuchadrezzar had another splendid palace inside the city [8]. His throne room there was 150 ft by 45 ft. Beside this palace were the Hanging Gardens [9], one of the Seven Wonders of the Ancient World. The gardens were irrigated by water raised from the Euphrates. Babylon was studded with temples. The district reserved for Marduk, the supreme god, was a sacred enclosure [10] and covered an immense area. A 72-ft-wide processional route [11] led to the temple. On either side of the route, brick lions glazed in blue looked down from a high wall. Marduk even had a palace on earth [12]. Soaring over the whole religious complex was the Tower of Babel [13]. This seven-storey monument was 295 ft high, but all that remains is the outline of its base in the ground.

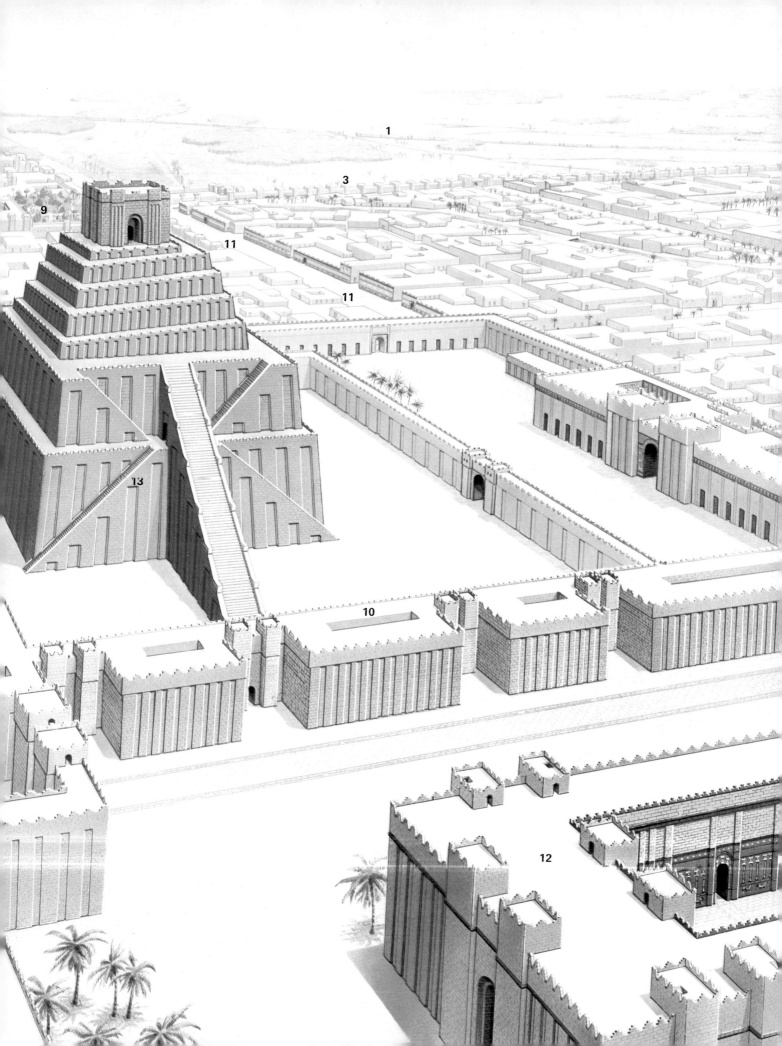

In the swampy deltas of the Tigris and the Euphrates the 'reed people' still continue a way of life which has scarcely changed since the days when the ziggurats were built. The reed huts on the islands and the boats which link them with the outside world have a timeless aspect.

There is an inscription by Nebuchadrezzar II in which he declares that he built Etemenanki, now popularly identified as the Tower of Babel, at Babylon 'with baked brick enamelled in brilliant blue'. And Ashurbanipal (688–627 BC), last of the great Assyrian kings, stated that when he destroyed the ziggurat at Susa he knocked down 'horns that were worked in glittering copper', apparently symbols for the city's deity set into enamel tiles. It is possible, too, that the terraces were planted with flowers and trees in the same style as the Hanging Gardens of Babylon.

The ziggurat at Ur, the Sumerian capital for several centuries, is the best preserved and the most spectacular ziggurat, thanks to skilled restoration work. Ur, in the south of Iraq, is the Ur of the Chaldees mentioned in Genesis as Abraham's native land. Woolley found there beautiful treasures of Sumerian art and royal graves containing bodies of sacrificed retainers.

The dominating bulk of the ziggurat of Ur can be seen from afar. Although the entire upper part has disappeared, it remains an impressive monument through the vastness of its conception and the power and balance of its construction. It has a surprising

unity, despite the fact that it was built in several stages. It goes back to the very early days of ziggurat building at about 3000 BC, but was rebuilt possibly in the year 2100 BC and then raised higher during the vigorous reign of Nebuchadrezzar II. This ziggurat was built to the moon-god Nanna, who was particularly honoured at Ur, and whose sanctuary stood at its base. The high tower by which the god descended to earth and the temple where he dwelt were always linked to each other in this way.

The ziggurat at Birs Nimrud, also built by Nebuchadrezzar, was sacred to Nabu, the god of writing, who was the son of Marduk, the god of nearby Babylon. Travellers who saw this ziggurat in ancient times often thought it was the Tower of Babel. It measured 270 ft to a side at the base, and its remains are imposing. Bricks of the upper stages were melted into glazed blocks by a fire which partly destroyed the ziggurat and which may have been caused by spontaneous combustion of bitumen and straw.

The builders used some ingenious devices to prevent the rains from eroding the crude bricks – interior drainage systems in particular. These have been found in the ziggurat at Ur. Nebuchadrezzar II noted at one time that the Birs Nimrud ziggurat was crumbling because 'its water pipes had become useless'. Whatever precautions were taken, most of the ziggurats must have deteriorated and been rebuilt many times over the centuries.

The largest surviving ziggurat has been discovered

This bronze model was found at Susa, the ancient capital of
Elam. It was made in the 12th century BC and is believed to
represent a ceremony of worship at sunrise. Two naked men
are washing between two symbolic ziggurats.

not in Mesopotamia but at Tchoga Zanbil in the
ancient land of Elam, in what today is western Iran. In
spite of its individual character, this country was in
regular contact with Mesopotamia, and the ziggurat,
about 18 miles from the site of Susa, the ancient capital
of Elam, is evidence of this contact.

The ziggurat was built somewhere around 1250 BC
by a king of Elam whose name is constantly repeated
on the bricks: Untash-Napirisha. It had five levels and
was more than 170 ft high. The shrine at its summit
was dedicated to an Elamite god known as In-
shushinak. Apparently pilgrims had access to the first
level, while the rest of the structure was reserved for
the priests. Digging at the site revealed evidence of
little-known rites; within the thick walls of the construction there were arrangements of rooms which at
some stage had been carefully walled up.

The size of this ziggurat indicates that Untash-
Napirisha was a powerful king, but almost nothing is
known about him. A statue of his wife, Napirasu, was
found some time ago on the site at Susa, and is now in
the Louvre Museum in Paris. It is made of cast bronze
with a chiselled finish, weighs 1¾ tons and is technically

This statuette of a man carrying a sacrificial offering dates
from 2000 BC and was found at Susa. Made of an alloy of gold
and silver, it is just over 2 in. high. The man is taking a small
animal, a kid or ibex, to his god and has his right hand raised
to ask approval of his offering.

The tower of the ziggurat of Tchoga Zanbil, built in the 12th century BC, measures nearly 350 ft along each side and is more than 160 ft high. It originally had five storeys.

and artistically of a quality which makes it one of the masterpieces of the ancient Middle East.

It is a tragedy that among the ruined ziggurats that have survived to the present day, nothing remains above ground of the most illustrious and probably the biggest of all, Babylon's Etemenanki.

The biblical account of the famous tower, attributing it to the descendants of Noah, is well known:

And they said, Go to, let us build us a city and a tower, whose top may reach unto heaven; and let us make us a name, lest we be scattered abroad upon the face of the whole earth.
And the Lord came down to see the city and the tower, which the children of men builded. And the Lord said, Behold, the people is one, and they have all one language; and this they begin to do: and now nothing will be restrained from them, which they imagined to do. Go to, let us go down, and there confound their language, that they may not understand one another's speech.
So the Lord scattered them abroad from thence upon the face of all the earth: and they left off to build the city.
Therefore is the name of it called Babel; because the Lord did there confound the language of all the earth: and from thence did the Lord scatter them abroad upon the face of all the earth.

The biblical interpretation of the name is fanciful. The Bible connects Babel with the Hebrew verb *Bâlal*, 'to confuse', whereas it really comes from *Bâb-ili*, which in Babylonian means 'Gate of God'.

Etemenanki, 'the foundation house of heaven and earth', was built and rebuilt a number of times, lastly and most splendidly by King Nebuchadrezzar II.

An earlier Babylonian kingdom came to a dramatic end in 689 BC when the Assyrian ruler Sennacherib sacked and destroyed the city, including its temple tower. But the kings of the new Babylonian dynasty, which began with Nabopolassar (625–605 BC), set about restoring it. There is an account of this reconstruction in an inscription in which Nabopolassar declares that 'gold, silver and precious stones from the mountain and from the sea were liberally set into its foundations . . . Oils and perfumes were mixed into the bricks . . . I made a likeness of my royal person carrying the brick basket, and I carried it into the foundations. I bowed my head before Marduk. I took off my robe, the sign of my royal rank, and carried bricks and clay upon my head. I had my eldest son Nebuchadrezzar, who is so dear to my heart, carry clay and offerings of wine and oil . . .'

The continuation of the work is indicated in another inscription attributed to Nebuchadrezzar: 'As for Etemenanki, Nabopolassar . . . had set its foundations and built it to 30 cubits [about 45 ft], but he had not built the summit. I set about doing this. With pure hands I cut great cedars from the splendid forest of Lebanon and used them in the building. I made the tall gates to the enclosure a work of splendour, dazzling as the day itself, and I put them in place.'

Reliefs on the buildings show kings and members of the royal family taking part in the construction, bearing on their heads baskets filled with building materials and carrying tools and architects' instruments.

Honouring the gods

The riches displayed in Babylon in honour of the gods were dazzling. Beside the Tower of Babel stood the great temple of Marduk, which was the centre of the city's religious life. There the god sat on his throne and, according to Herodotus, the complete sacred gold sculpture weighed no less than 800 talents, the equivalent of 22 tons.

Another inscription lists the places of worship in the interior of the enclosure at Babylon. It lists '53 temples of the great gods, 55 chapels to Marduk, 300 chapels for the earthly deities, 600 for the heavenly deities'. Added to this were nearly 400 altars to the gods.

The work force required to complete such numerous and often gigantic structures must have been considerable. When Nebuchadrezzar set the Babylonians rebuilding the Tower of Babel after it had been destroyed by the Assyrians, they were forced, as an inscription records, to call on 'the various peoples of the Empire, from north to south, from the mountains and the coasts'.

A quarter century after Nebuchadrezzar's death, Babylon became a Persian province. After the Persian king Xerxes crushed a rebellion there in 478 BC, Etemenanki was allowed to fall into neglect. It is probable that the inhabitants of the nearby town of Al Hillah eventually took bricks from the crumbling

The façade of the ziggurat of Ur, which according to Genesis was the city from which Abraham came. The building was reconstructed about 2100 BC, when the city was at its most splendid. Majestic ramps and stairways link the storeys.

mound to use in the construction of their own houses.

Nonetheless, the Greek historian Herodotus, visiting the city about 460 BC, still found much to admire. 'It has a solid central tower, one furlong [220 yds] square, with a second erected on top of it and then a third, and so on up to eight. All eight towers can be climbed by a spiral way running round the outside, and about half way up there are seats for those who make the ascent to rest on.' This ziggurat had seven terraces – in writing of eight towers, Herodotus must have counted either the earth platform at the base or the sanctuary at the top.

His brief description is amplified by a precious tablet said to be from Esagila, the temple of Marduk at the base of the tower, which gives the dimensions of the huge ziggurat as 295 ft on each side at the base with a height also of 295 ft. Archaeologists found that the base actually measured 300 ft, so it appears that the measurements given on the tablet are very nearly exact.

The substantial dimensions of the Tower of Babel considerably exceeded those of other known ziggurats. The larger size was justified, for the monument belonged to Marduk, originally the local god of Babylon, who later became a national god as a result of Babylon's long pre-eminence over the other cities of Mesopotamia. The powerful gods of the sky, Anu, and the earth, Enlil, were dispossessed in favour of Marduk's supreme power, and his rule was said to extend over the whole universe. He was god of the world and of the nation, and as such not only protector of armies – the warrior who led men to victory – but also the merciful sovereign, bestower of life and health and protector of the riches of the earth.

At the summit of the Tower of Babel, Herodotus wrote, 'stands a great temple with a fine large couch in it, richly covered, and a golden table beside it. The shrine contains no image and no one spends the night there except (if we may believe the Chaldeans who are the priests of Baal) a Babylonian woman, all alone, whoever it may be that the god has chosen. The Chaldeans also say – though I do not believe them – that the god enters the temple in person and takes his rest upon the bed.'

The symbolic marriage rites of Marduk, supreme god of the city, with a priestess substituting for Sar-

The ziggurat at Aqarquf is an extraordinary sight. Every side of the tower looks as if it has been pared away, yet it still stands nearly 200 ft high. It was built by the Kassites, invaders from the mountains to the north-east. The ruins of a vast sacred complex lie beside the monument.

A pair of Sumerian worshippers. These gypsum statues date from about 2500 BC. The artist has expressed the anxiety that the worshippers must have felt in the presence of the god. Their bodies seem petrified and their eyes are huge with awe.

them. They worshipped a sun god and a moon god, and they deified the planets, especially Venus.

Some writers have supported another theory, based on the accounts of Strabo, who asserted that the Tower of Babel was the tomb, or rather the cenotaph, of the great god Marduk. The archaeologists have not been able to verify this, because the ziggurat has been totally destroyed. It may have been a symbolic burial site with a mock tomb.

It was later thought that the ziggurats, like the Egyptian pyramids, might have concealed tombs and secret chambers. The early pioneers of archaeology in Mesopotamia even considered destroying the ziggurats in order to resolve the question.

One of them was Fulgence Fresnel, head of an expedition sent to Babylon by the French government in the middle of the last century. His interest centred on the impressive ruins of the ziggurat at Birs Nimrud, just south of Babylon, the one frequently mistaken for the Tower of Babel. Fresnel wrote in a letter to the French Minister for Foreign Affairs: 'With regard to the Birs Nimrud monument located to the west of the Euphrates, which is usually identified with the Tower of Babel, Colonel Rawlinson [an English consul and orientalist] told me he believed the only easy way of getting to it would be to mine so that the explosion would split the tower in two and open up the centre for us. If I should succeed later on in establishing friendly enough relations with the Arabs who rule the desert where Birs Nimrud is situated to be able to attempt an operation of this kind, would you, Mr Minister, permit me to carry it out?'

The French government gave its consent, but fortunately Fresnel's time was completely taken up with his research in Babylon. The climate, and exhaustion brought on by the exploration, proved too much for him, and he died before he could carry out his plan.

Today, it is generally agreed that the ziggurats were built as majestic pedestals which enabled the gods to come down among their followers and bestow blessings upon them. Although these gods were heavenly beings, they were not confined to the heavens but were constantly involved in worldly affairs. They were always shown with human features and were considered to have the same needs and the same passions as men.

It is easy to understand how, in a world exposed to floods on the one hand and a merciless, scorching sun on the other, the people and their priests would constantly feel the need to call on their gods for help. It was their desire to bring the gods down to earth that inspired one of the most impressive eras of monumental building in man's history.

HENRI-PAUL EYDOUX

panitum, his divine wife, however, probably took place in the shrine at the base of the ziggurat. The ceremony concluded the new year festivities, known as the *akitu*, which were conducted in an atmosphere of extraordinary solemnity. The tradition of the holy marriage was to encourage fertility in men and nature.

A century after Herodotus' visit, Alexander the Great arrived in 331 BC and conceived the notion of rebuilding the ruin. But he was forced to give up such an enormous task. Indeed, the Greek geographer Strabo reports that the initial clearing of the land alone took 10,000 men two months to complete.

The arrival of the Greek conqueror marked the end of Mesopotamia's great civilisations, and for centuries the purpose of the crumbling ziggurats remained shrouded in mystery. Ancient writers put forward a number of theories about the massive structures. The Greek historian Diodorus Siculus, who lived in the 1st century BC and travelled widely, saw them as astronomical observatories. It is certainly possible that priests used the ziggurats as observatories, for the Mesopotamians had a wide knowledge of astronomy, based on complex calculations. The worship of heavenly bodies was of great cultural importance to

In this 15th-century painting, the construction of the Tower of Babel is shown in a purely imaginary way. Illustrating a ducal book of hours, this quaint view actually records medieval building techniques.

Pyramids in the Americas

Ochre-coloured when they catch the rays of the sun, they rise in their thousands out of the tropical forests and scrub of Middle America. Some are gigantic, others modest in size; some narrow, others huge and bulky. These 'barbaric curiosities', as they were called at the time of the Spanish conquest, are the pyramids of pre-Columbian America, many of them raised by the Mayas, a people whose dazzling civilisation began a mysterious collapse around AD 900.

Many of the pyramids have been cleared of the enclosing vegetation and carefully reconstructed. But many more are simply vaguely conical hillocks or mounds buried beneath the thick shroud of the jungle, where they lie lost and forgotten, their stones corroded and dislodged. Staggering numbers of pyramids are believed to exist in the region. It has been suggested that Mexico alone harbours some 100,000 pyramids which have not yet been uncovered.

The only thing the pre-Columbian pyramids have in common with their Egyptian counterparts is their name, and even that is not really correct. Truncated pyramids would be a more accurate description, for they do not have an apex. Whereas the pyramids of Egypt were built as tombs for the pharaohs, those of pre-Columbian America – with such notable exceptions as the pyramid at Palenque – were solely built as gigantic bases for miniscule temples. Like the Mesopotamians with their ziggurats, the inhabitants of Middle America placed their temples at the top of pyramids so that they would be nearer to their gods.

These pyramids have steps fit into them, up which the priests, and those intended for sacrifice, ascended to the temple. Other worshippers had to stare up at the ceremonies from ground level. These enormous stair-cases are steep, like tall ladders reaching up towards an accessible heaven.

The pyramids of Middle America reveal not only a remarkable continuity of religious thought, but also the social structures of the civilisations that produced them. It was the lower classes – the peasants from the cornfields – who did the actual building.

The main purpose of the pyramids was to enable the high priests to meet the gods of the people. The fervour of the people was reflected in the almost absolute power of the priestly aristocracy.

There must have been a period of about 2,000 years in Middle America when the building of pyramids was a virtual obsession. Among the oldest was a circular one at Cuicuilco, south of the present-day capital of Mexico. It was built before 300 BC, when the Mayan culture had yet to reach its full vigour. The most recent are the *teocallis*, or temples, where, much later, the Aztecs practised the horrifying butchery that Cortés and his fellow *conquistadores* tried to destroy.

The Spaniards, in their zeal to spread the faith, took to building Christian temples on top of the pyramids. The Nuestra Señora de los Remedios, for example, stands on top of the great pyramid of Cholula. This, the largest pyramid the world has known, is even larger than the Great Pyramid of Cheops in Egypt.

MAY VEBER

Rising out of the jungle in the land of the Totonacs, in what is now the Veracruz area, is the Pyramid of the Niches at El Tajín. It stood more than 80 ft high on its square base, and each side measured some 118 ft. The pyramid takes its name from a unique feature: its seven levels were decorated by 365 square niches – one for every day of the year.

Who were the mysterious Indians who built El Tajín around the 5th century AD? Were they the Totonacs, referred to by the Aztecs as 'the people of the warm lands', or some other race who may have come from the central plateau? Perhaps the answer lies beneath the vegetation, where other pyramids are still buried.

Towering above the thick and stiflingly humid jungle of Petén in Guatemala, Tikal is the largest of the Mayan centres. Most of its sharply pointed pyramids were built over earlier structures in the 7th and 8th centuries AD. They are the tallest pyramids in the Americas, with their temple rooftops reaching as high as 230 ft. The palaces and the pyramids were centred around great squares. Standing out against the horizon, the vertical lines of these buildings seem to be the defiant response of a mystic race to the hostility of the expansive jungle around them, and are a reminder of the centuries of Mayan domination in this region.

Pyramids in the Americas

The Temple of the Giant Jaguar is one of the best-preserved buildings in Tikal. Strange as it may seem, the colossal pyramids of the Mayas evolved from the design of the simple peasant hut, with wooden walls and thatched roof. In temple architecture the base of the building eventually rose higher and higher, until it formed a pyramid, acting as a pedestal for the sanctuary. Early temples were made of wood, but later the Mayas used stone. The pyramid is disproportionately large for the tiny rooms which form the temple at the summit. Sacrifice was an essential part of Mayan religion. Domestic animals and agricultural produce were the usual offerings, but later Mayan sites also show evidence that human sacrifice was practised.

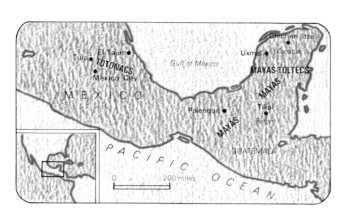

The pyramids of Middle America are scattered over an area of nearly 350,000 sq. miles – about twice the area of ancient Egypt. Only a few have been uncovered. It has been estimated that in Mexico alone there are 100,000 still hidden in the rich jungle. Outside this area, but also in the Americas, there were more primitive pyramid-type structures, mainly in Peru (the Pyramids of the Sun and Moon at Moche) and in the United States (mounds in the Mississippi and Ohio river valleys).

The pyramid of El Castillo, seen here from the colonnade of the Temple of the Warriors, is the greatest architectural achievement of Chichén Itzá, when the former Mayan capital was ruled by the fierce Toltecs. El Castillo means 'the castle', but is in fact a temple. Its four symmetrical staircases, together with the step leading to the temple on top, have a total of 365 steps, the number of days in the year; for these people were obsessed by time. Built to a square plan, it is 78 ft high, and is made up of two superimposed pyramids. In the Americas, pyramids were constantly embellished and enlarged, and were built successively one on top of another, so that some of them consist of up to seven superimposed structures, one over the other.

The eastern staircase of the Pyramid of the Magician at Uxmal in Mexico consists of 89 steps, without landings or ramps. The angle of inclination is almost the same as that of the pyramid of Chephren in Egypt. Some researchers studying the steepness of the pre-Columbian staircases have suggested that they were designed in this way to make it easier for the priests to dispose of the bodies of the victims they sacrificed at the summit.

Pyramids in the Americas

This is how the teocallis, or temples, must have appeared to the conquistador Cortés and his men in 1519 as they moved inland. They were the sinister 'houses with steps' where the priests of Montezuma's empire committed 'Indian idolatries', sacrificing humans to their bloodthirsty gods. The Spaniards were horror-struck. They climbed the stairs and threw down the blood-smeared idols, erecting Christian crosses in their places. This pyramid, Santa Cecilia, near the city of Mexico, has recently been restored and is an almost perfect example of an Aztec pyramid. Its height would have enabled the sacrificial rituals to be watched from afar by a large crowd of spectators. Usually the sacrifices were dedicated to Huitzilopochtli, the cruel and vindictive god of war and the sun.

In the heart of Tula, first capital of the Toltec people, stands a pyramid dedicated to the incarnation of the planet Venus, Quetzalcóatl, the feathered serpent, in one of his many guises. Four basalt pillars can be seen carved in the shape of warriors with feathered head-dresses, and behind them stand four square pillars. These columns supported a roof that has long since disappeared.

When Hernán Cortés led a band of Spanish conquistadores into the Yucatán in the early 1520s he passed within 30 miles of the great Mayan temple-city of Palenque. Once a sprawling metropolis that encompassed hundreds of temples, Palenque had been precipitately and inexplicably abandoned centuries before the conquest – and neither Cortés nor his Indian guides were aware of the ghost city's existence. In 1949, when the Mexican archaeologist Alberto Ruz Lhuillier was studying the Temple of the Inscriptions at the crown of this 7th-century pyramid, he noticed that one of the flagstones in the floor had handholds concealed by stone stoppers. He unplugged them, and lifting up the stone discovered a rubble-choked stairway which led 65 ft down to a triangular slab. Ruz found that the stone could be pivoted. 'I found myself in a spacious crypt which seemed to be cut into ice, for the walls were covered with a glittering layer of limestone. There were countless stalactites hanging like a curtain from the vault, and big stalagmites rising up like huge candles in a church . . .' He had discovered the tomb of the great king, Pacal, who ruled Palenque from AD 615 to 683. Pacal's remains lay beneath the 20-ft-high roof of a vaulted secret chamber. His corpse was wearing the jade face mask and numerous amulets and bracelets in which he had been buried almost 1,300 years earlier. The pyramid at Palenque was the first in Middle America found to have a royal tomb like those of ancient Egypt.

The corbel-vaulted staircase which connects Palenque's Temple of the Inscriptions to Pacal's burial chamber was filled with tons of stones and earth after the tomb was closed. So successful were the efforts of Mayan labourers to prevent intruders from disturbing their departed ruler's eternal slumber that it took Mexican archaeologists four seasons of patient work to clear away the rubble.

Pyramids in the Americas

A masterpiece of classic Mayan sculpture, this stucco head was one of two found at the foot of Pacal's sarcophagus. 'The artist,' says the Mexican archaeologist Alberto Ruz Lhuillier, 'has not only tried to reproduce the features of his model as faithfully as possible, but he has also expressed the spirit, the austerity and the interior strength of the priestly class.'

Covering the sarcophagus buried within the Temple of the Inscriptions at Palenque was a 5-ton tombstone. The beautiful reliefs cut in the fine, hard limestone slab are well preserved, despite the extreme humidity in the crypt. The elaborate carving, according to one interpretation, shows Pacal himself falling at the moment of death into the jaws of an underworld monster. The discovery of this remarkable tomb bore out the words, 120 years earlier, of Mexican dictator General Antonio López de Santa Anna, who described the pyramids at Palenque as worthy of comparison with those erected by Egypt's pharaohs.

Inside the pyramids
of the pharaohs

*For more than 40 centuries, the skyline of the
Nile Valley has been dominated by the man-made
mountains of the pyramids. Intended as eternal
monuments to the god-kings of Egypt, and as
everlasting sanctuaries for their bodies,
the pyramids, like the Sphinx, retain their enigma.
For how did the ancient Egyptians raise such majestic
hills without the wheel? And why did they build
on so superhuman a scale? Can royal vanity alone
explain the feat? Or is some other, secret motive
still buried beneath the desert?*

The pyramids of Egypt, rising majestically above the
desert sands of the Nile Valley, continue to amaze and
confound mankind more than 40 centuries after their
construction. Monuments to the technological skills
and the spiritual aspirations of ancient man, they pose
questions about how and why they were built that are
still only partly answered.

The fascination of the pyramids is legendary. They
figure in *The Arabian Nights*, in the tale of al-Mamun,
caliph of Baghdad and son of Harun al Rashid, who is
said to have ordered the opening of the tomb of the

Pharaoh Cheops and to have found there a golden
statue embellished with precious stones. Arab authors
declared that the whole of ancient Egyptian knowledge was inscribed inside the pyramids. Men of the
Middle Ages looked at the three Great Pyramids of
Giza and believed that they saw the grain silos built
by Joseph in anticipation of the seven years of famine
– a story graphically represented in a cupola of the
Basilica of St Mark in Venice.

It was only in the 19th century that European
scholars began systematic studies of these giant royal
tombs, which were enduring expressions of religious
faith. For the Egyptians believed in an after-life in
which humans continued to live if their human bodies
were preserved and provided for – and the safe-
keeping of the body of a king, who was both mortal and
divine, was of paramount importance.

The French writer Chateaubriand defined the func-

*Under the blaze of 20th-century floodlights and against the
ageless background of the desert night, the pharaohs' monuments loom like mountainous beacons marking Egypt's past.
Here the Great Sphinx stands guard over the pyramid of
Chephren, one of the three pyramids at Giza.*

The pharaohs of the Old Kingdom (2686–2181 BC) chose the west bank of the Nile in Lower Egypt for their tombs. During the New Kingdom (1567–1085 BC), the pharaohs tried to protect their resting places from tomb robbers by having secret chambers cut into the rock of the Valley of the Kings.

tion of the pyramids when he wrote, 'It is not from a sense of obscurity that man has erected such a sepulchre, but from his instinct of immortality. The sepulchre is not a boundary marking the end of a day; it is the entrance to a life without end. It is a type of door built on the edge of eternity.'

A wealth of theories has been advanced to explain the pyramidal form of the royal tombs. They may have been solar monuments, since worship of the sun, the symbol of the falcon-headed god Ra, was an integral part of the ancient religion. The centre of this cult was Heliopolis, a Greek name meaning Sun City, where the priests of Ra proclaimed the sun kings and pledged that, at death, a king would rejoin Ra. The Pyramid Texts – hieroglyphs carved in stone columns in the pyramid of the Pharaoh Unas – were discovered in 1881, and consistently refer to the concept of a divine stairway or ladder to the heavens. The very shape of the Great Pyramids could be taken to suggest the rays of the sun falling from the sky.

The typical pyramid was the centrepiece of a complex of funeral structures. At its base stood the high temple, sacred to the king, which was linked by a causeway to a low temple or sanctuary of welcome. The whole complex followed strict religious rules for ensuring the ruler's passage into immortality.

The crux of this ritual was the belief that when a man died, he went to an after-life that was so similar to life on earth that he would need his earthly body and his

The man who cracked a code in stone

In August 1799 an unknown soldier of Napoleon's army in Egypt uncovered a smooth black lump of basalt while digging a trench at a fort near the town of Rosetta. Within months it became clear that this was probably the most important single find in Egyptian archaeology. For on the cracked stone, 3 ft 9 in. by 2 ft 4½ in., were 14 lines of hieroglyphics (from two Greek words meaning 'sacred carvings'), 32 lines of the common demotic script based on them, and 54 lines of Greek. And scholars quickly established that the inscriptions were translations of one another, so providing a key to the baffling hieroglyphics used in the time of the pharaohs.

The Greek was soon translated as a decree by priests at Memphis in 196 BC, praising the pharaoh, Ptolemy V Epiphanes (205–180 BC), for benefits conferred on them. But for more than 20 years, the rest of the stone stumped the best minds of the day.

As it often does, the hour produced the man: an extraordinary French linguist named Jean-François Champollion. By the age of 11, in 1801, Champollion had mastered Latin, Greek and Hebrew; and at that age too, he was first shown the hieroglyphics in the collection of the scientist Jean-Baptiste Fourier. 'Can anyone read them?' he asked. Fourier shook his head. The young Champollion replied with absolute conviction: 'I am going to do it, when I am big.'

Within two more years, Champollion had learned Arabic, Syrian, Chaldean and, finally, Coptic – the Greek-based language of early Egyptian Christians – and at 18, on his first try at the Rosetta Stone, he found the correct values for a whole row of the elaborate hieroglyphic script.

In the next ten years, the English physicist Thomas Young deduced that royal names were inscribed in oval frames known as cartouches, and he intuitively guessed the right translation of 76 out of 221 groups of characters. But the central secrets of the language still eluded him – and every other scholar throughout Europe.

Meanwhile Champollion, who became a professor at Grenoble University at the age of 19, painstakingly groped towards the real solution – that some signs were alphabetic, some phonetic, and some simply represented ideas. In 1822 he published the paper that made him famous, *Letter to M. Dacier in regard to the alphabet of the phonetic hieroglyphics*, which for the first time gave the basis of a successful decoding method. The most vivid clues to the story of the ancient Egyptians were at last at the archaeologists' finger tips.

The massive pyramids of Giza stand on the fringe of the desert. In the foreground are the monument to Mycerinus and three smaller pyramids for members of the royal family. Behind them soars the 447-ft-high pyramid of Chephren, and in the background to the right is the Great Pyramid of Cheops.

worldly goods. This was why the Egyptians perfected the art of embalming, to preserve the body – and the personality – for all eternity. Mummification was a long and costly process in which the internal organs which would hasten decay were removed and the body was dried out – first by soaking it in a salt solution, and then by dusting it with natron, a carbonate of soda. It was wrapped in bandages, soaked in oils, and finally placed in a shaped and painted coffin.

Magical rites at the funeral ceremonies ensured that the mummy enjoyed perpetual life in the underworld, existing on the food and drink which were brought to the tomb. Many rich Egyptians would set aside a part of their wealth to maintain a priest, one of whose duties was to re-stock the tomb regularly.

The pyramids, the earthly guarantees of their occupants' places in immortality, began and reached their greatest magnificence in the golden age of the Old Kingdom (c. 2686–2181 BC) The first great royal sepulchre of pyramidal design – and one of the world's oldest existing stone monuments – was built at Saqqara near Memphis during the reign of Zoser, an early king of the Third Dynasty (c. 2686–2613 BC). Known as

the Step Pyramid, it marks the emergence of Egyptian architecture from its wood and brick beginnings into monumental stone construction.

The Step Pyramid was the creation of Imhotep, a brilliant artist and the first architect to leave his name in history. Imhotep was chief minister to the king – later revered as a patron of the arts and sciences, especially medicine – to whom ritual homage was paid.

In an inscription found near the Step Pyramid, Imhotep's titles and duties were recorded. 'The Chancellor of the King of Lower Egypt, first after the King of Upper Egypt, Administrator of the Great Palace, Hereditary nobleman, High Priest of Heliopolis, Builder, Sculptor and Maker of Vases in Chief.' He was eventually deified in Egyptian tradition, and it was the discovery of this inscription by archaeologists that

How the pyramids of Egypt were built

The pyramid group at Giza is the only one of the Seven Wonders of the Ancient World which still survives. Cheops' Great Pyramid is the gigantic tomb of a king who had been blessed with the powers of a god. It covers an area of 13 acres, originally rose 481 ft above the ground and was built of 6½ million tons of stone.

The only entrance [1] is on the north side. Two provisional tombs were built for the king in case he died before the work was completed. One is deep in the underlying rock [2], the other in the heart of the pyramid [3]. The final burial chamber was built 138 ft above ground level [4]. It is reached through a great gallery [5], 153 ft long and 26 ft high lying at the end of narrow corridors in which it is possible to walk only by bending double. The entrance to the tomb is a narrow passageway, easy to block [6]. The burial chamber itself measures only about 17 ft by 34 ft and is 19 ft high. The ceiling consists of nine blocks, weighing 400 tons. To spread the load of this enormous weight, five supporting compartments [7] were built.

The sarcophagus, or stone coffin, of the king was placed directly on a tiled floor [8]. In this vault the mummy of Cheops was placed 45 centuries ago. It was adorned with a gold mask overlaid with precious necklaces and jewels. Food, weapons and sumptuous furniture were placed around it. The ancient Egyptians believed that the dead king should be able to continue to observe the acts of everyday life.

When the funeral procession was over, all exits from the burial chamber were blocked by heavy stones, and the priests left through a shaft [9], which in turn was blocked. Despite all these precautions, the burial chamber suffered the same fate as most of the royal tombs in Egypt: it was stripped of its treasures.

Around the pyramid were built a great number of monuments: the funeral temple [10], where the survival rites of Cheops were celebrated; three small pyramids covering the burial places of members of the royal family and high officials [11]; and additional low, rectangular tombs, known as *mastabas,* for nobles and priests [12, 13]. In a nearby pit [14] was buried a boat to carry the pharaoh through the after-life.

Chephren, successor to Cheops, had a pyramid built for himself, nearly as high but not as large. It is shown on the left in the course of being built. The enormous blocks were put into place in horizontal tiers. Many hypotheses have been put forward as to how they were raised. The most plausible was that ramps were fitted [15] up which slaves and workers hauled the stones on rollers or sledges. Chephren's funeral temple [16] is connected to the Sphinx by a monumental roadway [17].

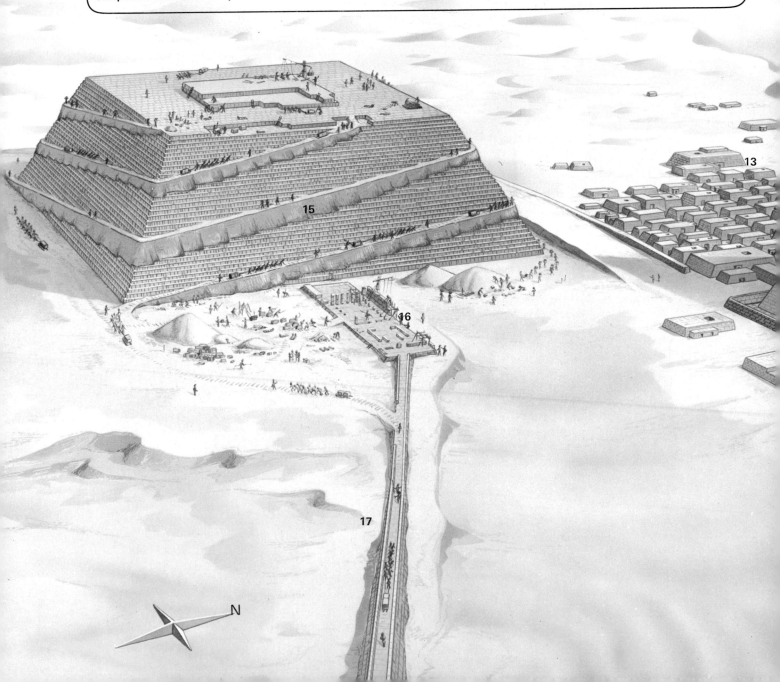

This long, dark corridor with its polished and precisely fitted limestone walls is one of the architectural wonders of the Old Kingdom. Called the Grand Gallery, it runs deep inside the pyramid of Cheops to a high step. Beyond the step, a narrow passage leads to the burial chamber of the pharaoh.

labyrinth of rooms and corridors. The king's chamber, hollowed out below ground level at the bottom of a shaft, was covered with granite slabs and sealed, after the funeral ceremonies, with a cylindrical plug weighing 3 tons. Recent excavations of this chamber reveal that, for all the precautions against violation of the tomb, plunderers over the centuries have looted the king's riches, leaving only a few human remains.

In his after-life, the pharaoh was expected to continue the rituals and routines of his mortal life. So in addition to Zoser's burial chamber, the pyramidal complex was built over subterranean apartments which he would occupy after death. Here were duplicated the structures and decorations of his earthly palace - false doors and simulated windows, sculptures and inscribed slabs telling stories of the king's life and walls tiled in blue faience, glazed earthenware. Some 40,000 stone vessels for use in the next world were stored in side galleries.

The Step Pyramid ushered in the age of monuments, and Imhotep's plan for the construction of the royal tomb was elaborated on by his successors, ending with the Great Pyramids of Cheops, Chephren and Mycerinus at Giza. But before these giant structures came the three pyramids of King Seneferu, founder of the Fourth Dynasty (c. 2613–2494 BC). Tradition portrays him as a liberal ruler and a conqueror whose expeditions into Libya and Nubia increased the wealth of his kingdom and added large numbers of captives to

Professional mourners played a major part in the funeral rites of ancient Egypt. Here a group is shown calling on the sky to bear witness to their grief. The fresco was found in one of the most beautiful tombs in the necropolis at Thebes – the tomb of Ramose, who was the vizier, or chief official, of Amenophis IV (1379–1362 BC), a ruler also known as Akhenaton.

gave the modern world its first clue that Imhotep was man as well as myth.

Zoser's monument is not a pyramid in the strict sense: it is formed by six graduated or stepped tiers rising to a height of around 200 ft.

In spite of its visual coherence and grandeur, the structure is the result of at least five different designs. The changes were made while the pyramid was being built – possibly at the demand of the king who wanted a successively grander monument. And Imhotep's attempts to fulfil his pharaoh's wishes are plainly visible, somehow humanising the huge tomb.

While all pyramids were built to house the remains of kings, the Step Pyramid also contains members of the pharaoh's immediate family, though not in the royal burial chamber; and it has an underground

the labour force. There are different theories about why he built three pyramids, but it seems likely that they were vast 'public works projects' to employ peasants and prisoners of war.

The first, at Maidum, was called the 'false pyramid' by the Arabs because of its unusual shape (see page 199), sheer walls rising from a large mound. The recent theory of Kurt Mendelssohn suggests that the Maidum pyramid was abandoned before completion when its structural weaknesses – caused by the miscalculations of an over-ambitious builder – led to a spectacular collapse of its outer casing. Today it stands impressively isolated upon the mound formed by its own debris.

Similar construction methods were employed in the so-called Bent Pyramid built for Seneferu at Dahshur. This pyramid, also known as the Southern Pyramid, slopes upwards at an angle of 54° from the base, then changes abruptly to a 42° incline. There have been many explanations for this double incline, but today it is generally agreed that Seneferu's architect was forced to change his plans to prevent the weight of the structure from causing the sides to buckle, like those of the

Maidum pyramid. Nevertheless, it rises to more than 320 ft, and its limestone casing is remarkably well preserved.

Not far from the Bent Pyramid stands the Northern Pyramid of Seneferu which was the first to be conceived as a true pyramid. The failings of earlier buildings were taken into account, and this structure rises gently from its huge base area at a 43° 36' angle to its summit of some 328 ft. The Northern Pyramid brought to a climax the period of invention and experimentation, and the way was clear for the Great Pyramids of Giza, which together were the first of the Seven Wonders of the Ancient World – and the only wonder which has survived.

The greatest of the pyramids was built for King Khufu, or Cheops in Greek, the son and successor to

King Zoser's stepped pyramid was built at Saqqara in about 2620 BC and marks a major turning point in the history of Egyptian architecture – the transition from the age of wood and brick to the age of stone. The columns on the right are part of the Step Pyramid's funeral-temple complex.

The unusual shape of King Seneferu's so-called Bent Pyramid at Dahshur may be due to the fact that its architect lowered the slope during construction to prevent the walls from buckling, as apparently had happened at Maidum.

Seneferu. Though very little is known about Cheops (*c.* 2545–2520 BC), his burial monument, a few miles from Cairo, is 750 ft square at its base, covering just over 13 acres, and so perfectly laid out that the sides vary in length by only 7 in. The angle of inclination is 51° 52′.

But the orientation of this massive structure is perhaps the most amazing fact about the Great Pyramid. For its sides run almost exactly from north to south and east to west. The deviation – within 5 arc minutes from true north – is so slight as to make it seem impossible that the alignment happened by chance. Some theorists believe that the builders of this most impressive of ancient monuments used the star Alpha Draconis, which was nearest to the north celestial pole when the pyramid was built, as a guide by which to achieve the amazingly precise orientation.

Given this remarkable alignment, it has been claimed that the Great Pyramid was not only a tomb, but also a sundial, a calendar, and an astronomical observatory. For at its original height of 481 ft, the pyramid would cast a shadow 268 ft long in mid-winter, diminishing almost to zero in spring, and could thus be used to mark the hours of the day, the seasons, and the exact length of the years.

Mystical mathematics

That so massive yet precise a structure could have been built by the ancients has naturally aroused endless speculation, and the theories advanced by the scholars and the curious could – and do – fill volumes. In the absence of hard evidence, some interpreters tended to find mystical revelations in the measurements of the pyramid of Cheops. The royal sarcophagus, or granite coffin, was supposed to be a standard unit of volume (though why this standard should be the equivalent of $1\frac{1}{4}$ tons of water and sealed up in a man-made mountain is not clear).

The founders of the cult of 'pyramidology' were the Scottish astronomer Charles Piazzi Smythe and the London publisher John Taylor, who evolved the theory that the Great Pyramid had been built under divine guidance; that it incorporated such cosmic wisdom as the true value of *pi* (the ratio of the circumference of a circle to its diameter), the mass and circumference of the earth, and the distance of the earth from the sun. They spoke of 'sacred cubits' and 'pyramidal inches' (said to equal the 500 millionth part of the polar diameter of the earth).

Another theory holds that the pyramid's base can be measured in units that add up to 100 times the number of days in the year. And one author claimed to have calculated the great dates in history, including the declaration of war in 1914, from the measurements of the pyramid (though similar calculations which predicted a miracle akin to the Second Coming of Christ in 1881, and the end of the world in 1953, proved to be without foundation).

Sir Flinders Petrie, the man who made the first

accurate measurements of the pyramid in 1880–2, was sceptical about men who arrived at spectacular mystical results by applying very small units of measurement to a very large structure. He said: 'It is useless to state the real truth of the matter, as it has no effect on those who are subject to this type of hallucination.'

The astonishing building which still has such power over men's minds contains three vaults which were prepared successively for the burial of Cheops, perhaps so that a sepulchre would be ready in case the ruler died before completion. The first was hollowed out of rock below ground level; the second was located in the lower level of the pyramid itself; and the third chamber was built in the middle of the structure 137 ft above ground level.

The sarcophagus was built into the third chamber during construction, but its lid has disappeared, and today the chamber stands bare of the opulent trappings of royal burial.

Though the pyramid itself has been extensively explored, its approaches may still produce surprises. For instance, in 1954, during continuing excavations of the pyramid's perimeter, a sealed pit was discovered. In it was found an intact cedar boat, about 140 ft long and almost 16 ft wide, which has since been restored. Closely resembling the vessels which sailed the Nile in the 3rd millennium BC, it may have been a 'solar boat'

to take the king and his retinue on his voyage to immortality.

The second stone giant of Giza, the pyramid of Chephren, stands at a slightly higher level than the pyramid of Cheops, and seems to be the taller though it was originally 10 ft lower, or 471 ft. Today it stands 447 ft 6 in. high – 2 ft 6 in. lower than the present Cheops structure's 450 ft. Its interior is less complex, with two burial chambers and two entrances, but the second chamber was desecrated nearly 1,000 years ago by Arab marauders who left inscriptions as evidence of their presence.

The interior simplicity of Chephren's pyramid perplexed the scientists, and beginning in 1966, a radiograph – a technique similar to X-ray – was made of the structure and revealed that it is, in fact, a solid mass with a burial chamber in its base. This austerity contrasts sharply with the splendour of Chephren's nearby funeral temple and with the guardian Sphinx.

The smallest of the Giza group is the pyramid of

After the coffin had been carried down into the tomb and the chamber had been sealed, the ceremonies ended with a huge funeral feast in honour of the dead person. This relief from the tomb of the vizier Ramose at Thebes shows guests at a funeral banquet, holding bouquets of lotus flowers.

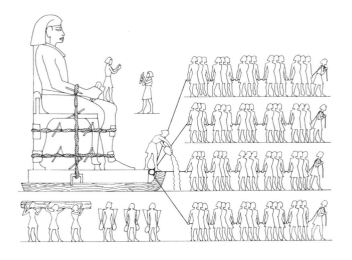

This bas-relief from the tomb of a nobleman named Djehutihotep, at El-Bersheh, illustrates the way the ancient Egyptians transported their giant loads. It shows a statue of Djehutihotep, which must have weighed about 60 tons, being hauled along on an enormous sledge by 64 men. Another worker is helping to make the sledge slide more easily by pouring water on the ground in its path. Space limitations must have restricted the artist, because such a load would certainly have required many more men.

In a pyramid-builder's toolbox

Egypt's giant stone monuments were put together almost entirely using only these primitive wood, stone and copper tools. The heads of mauls, or hammers, used by the stonemasons were made of diorite, a very hard rock. Chipping tools, drills and cutting edges were made of flint. Copper was

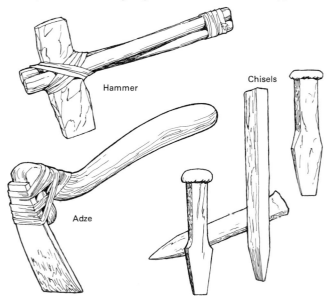

Hammer

Chisels

Adze

the only metal the ancient Egyptians knew at that time, apart from gold. The main tools used on the pyramids were the chisel (the classic cutting tool still used today), the adze and the saw, which was often used with an abrasive of moistened grains of quartz. For quarrying, wooden wedges were hammered into slots in the stone, then soaked until the wood swelled and cracked the rock. Stonemasons chipped the stone into shape with chisels and hammers before it was dragged into place on the pyramid.

Mycerinus, which is barely one-tenth the mass of its two neighbours. The blocks used in its construction are heavier and less well-hewn, indicating that it may have been hurriedly finished. Its funeral chambers, deep in the rock under the pyramid, were explored by the English archaeologist Colonel Richard Howard-Vyse in 1837–8. The basalt sarcophagus, which – unlike the plain sarcophagi of Cheops and Chephren – was finely decorated, was lost when the ship transporting it to England was wrecked off the Spanish coast.

After Mycerinus, his successor Shepseskaf abandoned the Giza site, and had his own funeral monument, which was not a pyramid but looked like a giant sarcophagus, built in the southern necropolis of Saqqara.

The time of the pyramids coincided with the peak period of political and economic order in the Old Kingdom. The stability of society was built around the centralised authority of the monarch, who maintained his control by asserting his divinity. In their man-dwarfing proportions, the pyramids symbolised the distance between ordinary men and their god-king.

This Golden Age lasted about five centuries, and was followed by a period of uncertainty and unrest when the absolute power of the pharaohs was successfully challenged by the nobility. It was a time of religious as well as political change, and nothing like the Great Pyramids, those grandiose architectural expressions of earthly as well as unearthly power, was attempted again until the next period of political stability, in the Twelfth Dynasty (c. 1991–1786 BC).

The physical mass of the pyramids is astonishing. The pyramid of Cheops was built from about 2,300,000 blocks weighing a total of 6,500,000 tons, and the weight was even greater before the blocks were hewn and dressed. Napoleon, during the Egyptian campaigns, calculated that the materials of the Great Pyramids would form a wall 10 ft high and 2 ft wide around France. But the excavation and transportation of such great weights seem to have posed few problems for the ancients.

How the work was begun

The first essential for such an enormous structure was an absolutely level base, and it is believed that the Egyptians established this by using a primitive but highly effective spirit level: cutting channels in the rock, filling them with water, then inserting rods and marking off the waterline. The surface of the rock was then cut down to the waterline, and the site was ready to be laid out. The fact that the pyramids are almost exactly square indicates that the designers had some geometric knowledge, and it is thought they achieved their right-angles either by measuring the diagonals across the square, or by using the '3-4-5' method of drawing a right-angled triangle later elaborated by the Greek mathematician Pythagoras.

Quarrymen worked at three widely separated spots to provide the stone for the pyramid of Cheops. The coarse desert sandstone of the Giza region itself provided the central core. The gleaming limestone casing was quarried at Tura, 30 miles south of Cairo. And the granite that lined the inner galleries and the burial chamber was hewn from rock at Aswan, 600 miles away at the first cataract of the Nile.

There, the quarrymen hewed the massive blocks from the rock by chipping them away with hardened copper chisels, or by inserting wedges of wood and then soaking them in water so that the expansion of the wood caused the rock to split away. Then the blocks were roughly hewn into shape using mallets of dolorite, a stone which is harder than granite. Transportation of these colossal chunks of stone, averaging $2\frac{1}{2}$ tons and some weighing 15 tons, was the next problem. It was solved by floating the stones up the Nile on huge barges during the flood season.

Unloading and hauling the stones to the work site was almost as difficult. It was accomplished by dragging the blocks on wooden sledges resting on rollers up the great stone causeway which was built from the banks of the Nile, half a mile away.

Thousands of masons, quarrymen and stone cutters laboured on the Giza site for more than 30 years to build the mighty tomb for their pharaoh, Cheops, and

The 'false pyramid' at Maidum is believed to have been built during the reign of Seneferu (c. 2570–2545 BC). Five of its eight planned steps have vanished, possibly because of errors in design which, it has been proposed, caused the monument to collapse and the pyramid left uncompleted.

Chephren, builder of the second pyramid at Giza around 2500 BC, is protected in this sculpture by the wings of the falcon-god Horus, his personal deity. The ancient Egyptians believed that the pharaohs represented the gods on earth.

they worked with such remarkable precision that, as Petrie reported, 'neither needle nor hair' could be inserted at the joints of the limestone casing blocks.

How the master builders of Cheops raised these perfectly cut blocks into position with no mechanical aids other than the lever, the roller, and the inclined plane (it is thought that the wheel was unknown in Egypt for another 800 years) is still a matter for vigorous debate among archaeologists. But the most commonly accepted view is that an enormous supply ramp was built, and gangs hauled the stones to the lip of the ramp before sliding them into place on a bed of liquid mortar. As the pyramid rose, the ramp was lengthened – for the slope always had to remain the same. Remains of such ramps have been found at the pyramids of Maidum and Lisht, south of Dahshur.

Another suggestion is that the ramp, instead of stretching out from the base of the pyramid, wound its way up the side like a spiral staircase. But whichever method was employed, when the core was complete, the ramp was dismantled as the masons worked their way down from the top, placing the fine limestone casing blocks in position as they went.

Further confusion arises because the Greek historian Herodotus, who lived in the 5th century BC, recorded that the Egyptians had hoisting machines made out of short planks of wood. No trace of anything

One of the most important funeral ceremonies in ancient Egypt was the Opening of the Mouth, which was supposed to revive the life-force of the dead person. Here a priest (right), holding a ritual adze, prepares to open the mouth of King Tutankhamun, shown with the traits of the god Osiris.

like these wooden hoisting machines has been found in Egyptian art, architecture or literature. But it is known that the builders did have cables made out of twisted reeds, and the Egyptians have used since prehistoric times a system of counterbalanced levers – the 'shadouf' – to draw water. It is just possible that an elaborate version of this system could have been used in lifting, especially as the pyramid blocks decrease in size from the bottom to the top of the structure.

When Cheops died, his builders completed their labours by springing the traps which it was hoped would preserve his body for all time. His coffin was put into a granite sarcophagus, so made that when the heavy stone lid was slid into place, stone bolts dropped into recesses in the trough and secured it. Further obstacles were designed to keep out tomb robbers. On their way out, the workmen knocked away props that allowed three huge stones to fall, blocking the vestibule; and the removal of more props in the Grand Gallery allowed three great granite plugs to slide into the Ascending Passage and seal it. The entrance door itself was cunningly designed to swing so imperceptibly into place that the Caliph al-Mamun could not find it when he raided the Great Pyramid in the 9th century.

These scientists, who accompanied Napoleon to Egypt in 1798, found only the head of the Sphinx standing above the encroaching sand. The face, long thought to be that of a woman, is now known to be that of the Pharaoh Chephren.

Still enigmatic and beautiful despite the erosion of the centuries, the Sphinx of Giza gazes at the setting sun. Carved out of a limestone hillock, this lion with the face of a man stands nearly 66 ft tall and sprawls 240 ft along the ground beside the sacred royal tombs it guards.

Instead, he had to bore his way straight into the stone.

The building of the pyramids obviously required a vast labour force, but it seems unlikely that the builder kings impoverished the nation by forcing Egyptians to work in the stone gangs.

Rather it seems that though prisoners of war did some of the heavy work and maintenance jobs, most of the ordinary labourers were peasants, who worked during the flood periods when farming was impossible anyway. There is little evidence that they were coerced into working on the great tombs.

The labourers were probably paid in food – because money did not yet exist – and were organised in squads with such heartening names as 'Vigorous Gang' and 'Enduring Gang'. Although the classical picture of legions of slaves being lashed with whips is probably wrong, paintings do show foremen carrying yard-long rods which were no mere symbols of office. A later architect, Nekhebu, boasts on his tomb that he never struck a workman hard enough to knock him down.

Barracks for the workers

Herodotus gave traditional figures for the pyramid work force of Cheops: 100,000 men replaced every three months for a period of 20 years. It is impossible to prove or disprove these figures, though they are probably wildly exaggerated. Petrie found to the west of the pyramid of Chephren the barracks for a permanent work crew, and estimated their number at no more than 4,000, augmented by an unknown number of peasants during the flood season.

The Greek historian Diodorus Siculus, a contemporary of Julius Caesar, wrote: 'It is agreed that these works surpass anything in Egypt, not only for their great mass and their prodigious costs, but also for the beauty of their construction. The workers who have made the pyramids so incomparable are much more worthy of praise than the kings responsible for the expenditure. For the former gave memorable proof of their genius and skills, while the kings merely provided wealth gained through inheritance or extortion.'

The Roman author Pliny the Elder (AD 23–79) was an even more severe critic, calling the pyramids 'vain and foolish ostentations of the fortunes of kings'.

Vain and foolish? Perhaps – but the Egyptians who worked on the pyramids came to serve their god-king, and the work helped to unify once-independent tribes. And though the pharaohs may not have achieved the physical immortality they craved, their monuments at least will live forever.

CHRISTOPHER ANGELL

Vanished peoples, forgotten places

When the Sahara was green

One word can conjure up images of sand and heat, with men and beasts dying of thirst. That word is Sahara. But the world's greatest desert was once a bountiful land where rain fell, streams flowed and grass and trees flourished. Elephants, antelopes and many other animals roamed at will. Men lived there too, raising cattle, harvesting grain and producing vivid works of art that show what life was like when the Sahara was green.

As far back as man's written knowledge extends, the Sahara has always been feared as a strange, inhuman and mysterious land. It gripped the imaginations of the classical authors of Greece and Rome. The first to mention it was Herodotus about 430 BC, when he described it as a desert with high dunes and vast waterless regions, dotted with hillocks of salt, and inhabited by peoples with strange and exotic customs.

Today, more than 2,000 years later, the picture is not radically different. The world's largest desert, the Sahara extends for 3·3 million sq. miles – an area

This dramatic Saharan rock painting was made about 5,500 years ago at Takededoumatine in the Tassili N'Ajjer. It shows a busy camp scene in the life of the pastoral people of the cattle period. Calves are tethered in front of the oval-shaped huts, while a herd of long-horned cattle returns from pasture.

almost as large as the United States of America. Great tracts of it are still little known, difficult of access, and seared by violent extremes of climate. The outlook for its 2 million scattered inhabitants is not encouraging. Continuing drought and the need to dig ever-deeper wells have lowered the level of the water table dramatically; and over-grazing to support a population increase among the desert tribes has allowed the Sahara to encroach still further on the few fertile areas.

Even the resources of modern technology are largely powerless to reverse the trend. Some attempts at reclamation have been made, but grandiose plans to run a canal from the Mediterranean to the Qattara Depression or divert the courses of some Central African rivers proved to be of doubtful value and prohibitively expensive.

Yet the Sahara is not the endless sea of sand of popular belief. Only a quarter of its surface is covered by the vast oceans of continuous sand called ergs, in which steep-sided dunes sometimes soar to 750 ft. The rest is made up of gravelly deserts called regs, boulder-strewn plains known as hamadas, a few oases and the mountain massifs which reach considerable heights. At the Sahara's highest point, Emi Koussi, the Tibesti mountains reach 11,204 ft. This and other ancient ranges, the Aïr and the Hoggar, are studded with volcanoes which covered the plateaux with outpourings of lava in comparatively recent times. Vulcanologists believe that volcanic activity could be renewed.

Nor has the Sahara always been the barren, inhospitable land that Herodotus described. There is abundant evidence, both archaeological and geological, that once it was a green and fertile country in which a Negroid race of people hunted or tended a large variety of land and aquatic animals such as elephants, hippopotamuses, fish, molluscs, buffaloes and the ex-

tinct wild oxen from which all European breeds of domestic cattle are believed to be descended.

The most vivid and dramatic evidence of life in the Sahara's thousands of years of prehistory lies in the magnificent cave and rock paintings which have been found throughout the region, but especially at Tassili N'Ajjer. There is a greater abundance of prehistoric rock paintings in the Sahara than in any other area of the world; and these paintings provide us today with the earliest-known expression of Negroid art.

The death of the Sahara

Why did the Sahara die? What has caused it to become today the perfectly preserved skeleton of a once-fertile and thriving country? The answer, scientists now believe, lies in the history of monsoon rains that bring moisture from West and Central Africa into the Sahara. The flourishing of late prehistoric cultures in the Sahara was originally made possible when the monsoon rains expanded far northwards – as we know they did from the evidence of the area's former lakes and stream-fed marsh regions. Conditions began to be more moist around 10,000 BC and were substantially wetter for most of the time between 7000 and 2000 BC. The lakes reached their maximum extent about

---

The Sahara – from the Arab word for desert – stretches for 3,000 miles across the whole of northern Africa, from the Atlantic to the Red Sea, averaging nearly 1,000 miles from north to south. About a quarter of the area is the 'sea of sand' of popular imagination. The rest is made up of barren mountains, gravel wastes and arid, rocky plains.

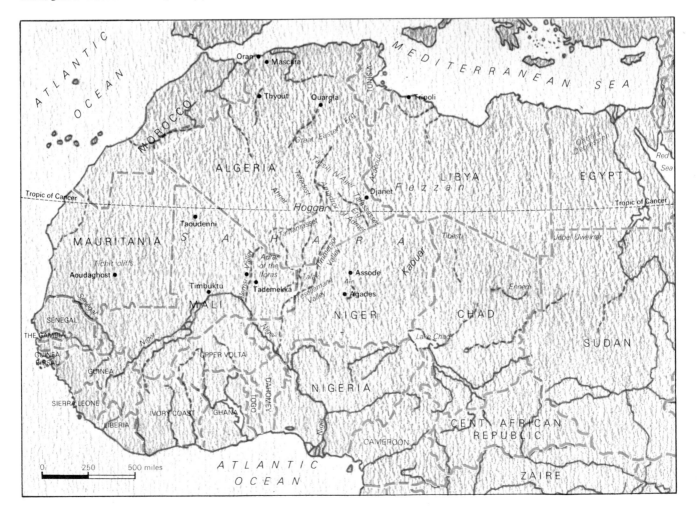

3500 BC. For unknown reasons, however, monsoon rains began to diminish over the Sahara and an irreversible imbalance between rainfall and rate of evaporation eventually took place. Quite simply, moisture was soaked up by the sun faster than it fell from the clouds.

Despite a few minor phases of wetter climate about 750 BC and again about AD 500 the lakes began to dwindle and the Sahara reverted to desert. Mediterranean plants retreated and tropical species replaced them in the valleys and gradually invaded the plateaux. Man, too, contributed to his own downfall, for the increasing number of domestic animals destroyed the plant life as they grazed – a pernicious process which can still be seen in the Sahara today. Mountain woodlands opened up to allow flocks and herds to pass through; whole areas were burned off and reduced to grazing land. Century by century the vegetation degenerated, going from savannah to steppe, from steppe to desert, leaving only the paintings and the artefacts that strew the Sahara's surface as evidence that man once thrived there.

The sands of the Sahara were formed by the peculiar nature of its water system. The relief map of the desert and aerial photographs show a highly complex pattern of ancient watercourses and powerful rivers which shaped and eroded the mountains. However, all these streams and rivers ran not into the sea, but into inland basins. When a normal river drains towards the sea, it carries with it the alluvial material which it scours out of its path. In the Sahara, however, this debris was deposited in the inland basins, gradually filling them. The slopes of the stream beds were reduced, and the currents flowed less strongly.

The weakened currents could no longer carry away the alluvial deposits, and instead they were dropped wherever the slopes of the watercourses became less steep, forming obstacles which blocked the streams. The water was forced to find different outlets, and spread to form marshes on either side. In the fierce sun, the water evaporated and the marshes began to dry out. This is how the streams and rivers of the prehistoric Sahara died. Salt deposits which are still worked at places such as Amadror, Teghaza and Taoudenni are simply the remains of old inland basins

The surface of the Sahara is strewn in places with milling and grinding stones from the New Stone Age. Their presence gave rise to a belief that the inhabitants had practised agriculture on a large scale. Now, however, biologists and scientists who study fossil pollens believe that the stones were used solely to grind wild, grain-like grasses.

A typical valley of the central Sahara. Leaving the mountains it winds its way across a reg, a wide stretch of gravel and small stones where alluvial deposits have accumulated over the centuries. In the background can be seen peaks of the southern Tefedest mountains, part of the Hoggar massif.

Paintings like this one, from Tin-n-Tazarift in the Tassili N'Ajjer mountains, have given rise to the theory that beings from another planet visited the Sahara more than 7,000 years ago. This is pure fantasy. The 'space helmets' are probably nothing more than skull caps decorated with feathers. The confrontation of armed men suggests a tribal war, possibly over the ownership of animals.

from which water has evaporated, leaving grains of sodium chloride which were dissolved out of the rocks.

Some very large streams, such as the Timmersoï-Assakarï, collect waters from the southern slopes of the mountain masses and flow towards the River Niger. This has allowed them to continue normally for much longer than the others. But of the vast lakes of the past, only Lake Chad remains – and it has been reduced to 15,000 sq. miles, compared with the 200,000 sq. miles it once covered. The drying up of the streams and rivers left the ancient alluvial deposits bared, and the wind carried them from the heights to the low ground until eventually particles of quartz accumulated in vast quantities, giving birth to the ergs and their dunes. The regs, or deserts of gravel, on the other hand, have been formed in two ways – by the debris laid down when rivers overflowed, and by the erosion of the old sandstone massifs.

Journeys into the past

The evidence of the Sahara's past, and the discovery of the remarkable rock paintings, only began to be assembled after European penetration of the desert began in the 19th century. It was pioneered by three British explorers, Dixon Denham, Hugh Clapperton and Walter Oudney, who crossed the barren wastes and discovered Lake Chad in 1822. Four years later, Major Alexander Gordon Laing, a Scotsman, crossed the Sahara and became the first European to reach the fabled city of Timbuktu (Tombouctou), where he was murdered. In 1828 the Frenchman René Caillié, disguised as an Arab, started from Timbuktu on the first Saharan journey by a European from south to north. He finally reached Morocco after facing torrid heat, sand-laden whirlwinds, exhausting stretches on foot, and a near-fatal shortage in his water reserves. Caillié faced, too, the torment of the mirage. This phenomenon, which has always plagued desert travellers, occurs

208

when layers of air expanding on contact with the superheated ground refract the light and cause illusions. In Caillié's case, it was the classic illusion of a huge lake, fringed by rustling trees.

After Caillié's epic trek, the French played an increasing part in the penetration of the Sahara. In 1830 France occupied Algiers and a slow southwards advance followed. There were surveys for projected trans-Sahara railways, expeditions to establish French claims to territory, and military campaigns to subdue the native tribes. All this colonial activity led to the production of the earliest definitive maps of the area – the first of them by the German explorer-scientist Heinrich Barth, who left Tripoli in 1850 and did not return until 1855. He crossed the Fezzan region, the Tassili N'Ajjer and Aïr massifs, and the Kaouar, venturing as far east as Chad and as far west as Timbuktu. His map gave the first true idea of the contours of the Sahara and showed the high mountains – dotted with ancient olives and cypresses – and the dead valleys running from them.

Barth, though perhaps he did not fully realise it, also laid the foundations for archaeological research in the Sahara when he studied rock engravings in the Aïr and Fezzan which represented oxen and were similar to work discovered earlier, in 1847, at two small oases called Thyout and Moghar Tahatania in the southern Oran district of Algeria. Barth assumed that people who herded cattle must once have lived in the region, and pointed out that the camel did not appear once in these engravings. His theory that the camel did not reach the Sahara until later proved to be correct, and it was on his division of the desert's history into the camel period and the pre-camel period that later work was built up.

The next step into the desert's unknown past came at the turn of the century when a French geologist, G. B. M. Flamand, carried out comparative studies of the cave engravings of southern Oran in Algeria. He concluded that there had been a division into a camel era and a pre-camel era, as Barth had deduced. But he went further and separated out various technical characteristics such as the type of line used, whether it was chipped or smooth, the degree of patina, the style and details of clothing and weapons on the human figures depicted. He also noted that the oldest wild animal shown was the buffalo, which did not appear in the later engravings.

Clues from the animals

This extinct animal did not appear, either, in the engravings of the Ahnet mountains which the French scientist Théodore Monod studied. But the large number of domesticated cattle in these pictures led him to suggest a cattle period more recent than the buffalo period of southern Oran. More recent engravings, Monod thought, were part of the camel period, into which drawings of the domesticated horse also fitted. But later, when the importance of the horse and

the peoples who introduced it was realised, a horse period was inserted between the cattle and camel periods of the desert's history.

This classification, based on zoology, was founded on the appearance, one after the other, of domestic animals which came to replace wild fauna such as the buffalo. The present camel period started around 2,000 years ago – the camel in Africa was first mentioned in texts in 46 BC – and the animal probably spread on a fairly wide scale after the beginning of the Christian era.

The archaeological evidence of the Sahara's past

This olive tree is one of the few reminders of how the Sahara looked before it became a desert. Some surviving specimens, clinging to life in mountain valleys where a little moisture collects, could be thousands of years old.

This is the world's earliest-known painting of the cultivation of a date-palm tree. It goes back to 1,000 years before the birth of Christ. Note how the labourers are pruning the branches of the tree with their billhooks.

was added to by the discoveries of Fernand Foureau, a French geologist who had travelled throughout the Great Eastern Erg and joined a trans-Saharan expedition from Ouargla oasis to Chad. For he was one of the first to report the existence of the stone tools that littered the Central Sahara. He assembled collections of these relics which formed the basis of much research into the prehistory of the Sahara. From Foureau's time on, curiosity about the desert's past gathered momentum, and in 1933–4 discoveries were made of Old Stone Age tools together with the bones of animal species which had long ago vanished from the region. Then New Stone Age deposits in the dunes of the Tesellamane Valley in Niger were found, confirming that land animals such as elephants and antelopes coexisted there at the same time as water animals, and that humans were hunting, fishing and rearing livestock at that time. Several human skeletons were found among the remains of foodstuffs.

Savage beauty of the rocks

At the same time came the discoveries of engravings in the Hoggar, the Fezzan, the Tibesti, and the Kaouar, which confirmed the existence of the animals that had been identified from the food remains. Scientific interest in the Sahara became intense in 1956 after a French expedition to the numerous galleries of paintings in the Tassili N'Ajjer. This fragmented sandstone plateau stretches in an arc in the north-east of the Hoggar and has been carved by water into a grand, savage beauty. The highest parts have been eroded into shapes that resemble ruined castles or crumbling cathedrals, and high spires and mushroom-capped pillars make the tortured scenery similar to that found in the Utah and Arizona deserts. The sandstone blocks are strangely worn at the base, and deep cavities, creating shelters, have gradually formed. These were easily adapted for human habitation, and in them were found thousands of often magnificent paintings. Some of the subjects are shown on an enormous scale, with figures up to 26 ft tall. Not all date from the same period – the rule that graffiti attracts more graffiti means that all the peoples who have followed one another through the centuries in the Tassili N'Ajjer have each left their own colourful mark.

The oldest layers of paintings were probably made by a Negroid ethnic group, with a somewhat crude

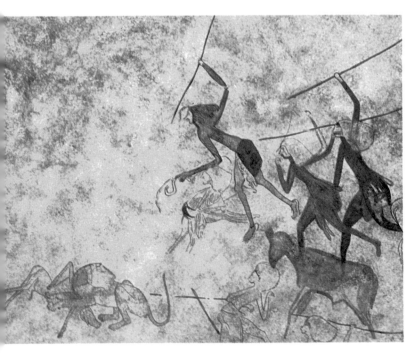

Hunters armed with spears race to attack a lion which has seized one of their sheep. This scene, from the days when Stone Age men grazed their flocks where only desert now exists, is painted on a wall at Iheren in the Tassili N'Ajjer.

210

How – and why – the desert is still dying

The evidence of the plundering of the Sahara's meagre resources even up to the present day is shown most clearly in the dramatic fall in the region's precious water reserves. In a land composed of impervious crystalline rock, like the mountains of the Central Sahara – the Hoggar, the Aïr, and the Adrar of the Iforas – water cannot be stored, and the water supply depends entirely on rainfall. So it is easy to understand why there are fluctuations in the water table – but the seriousness of the situation goes far beyond merely seasonal changes.

In the Aïr, for instance, where the first observations by Europeans go back 125 years, it is known that wells of the balance-beam type were once used in cultivated areas. This way of drawing water is intended for the irrigation of gardens and small plots, and works only if the water table is not more than about 16 ft below the ground. Today, though, not one well of this type exists. They have all been replaced by wells from which the water has to be raised by draught animals, because it is now 80 ft down. So in these cases, where accurate monitoring has

been possible, the water table has dropped by more than 60 ft.

In a classic example of a vicious circle, shortage of water has meant that more wells had to be dug, then deepened, to save the flocks and herds. This inevitably reduced the level of the water table, while ongoing soil erosion also played a major role in drying out the land still further. The Aïr, for instance, which was at one time considered the Switzerland of Africa because of its temperate climate, was once criss-crossed by valleys filled with palm trees. Yet today, only one-third of the palms in existence at the beginning of the century still remain.

Once, too, there were small villages in the mountain massifs – Assode, with more than 3,000 inhabitants, Ti-n-Taghoda, Anisamane and others. All of them now lie in ruins and cannot be brought back to life, for the wells which fed them have long since dried up.

In the face of this systematic depredation of the basic essential of life, modern attempts to reclaim fertile land from the desert have proved ineffective, and the Sahara is still inexorably dying.

---

drawing technique and using a multitude of styles and colours. The human silhouettes are static with podgy limbs, and the legs are usually short in relation to the arms. The women often have very prominent navels, and their breasts – which are always small and conical – are placed one above the other. The head is characteristic of this period – drawn as a round symbol without any sense organs, though these are sometimes replaced by geometrical designs. Body decorations in the form of scars or painting can also be seen, and several of the figures have masks which are similar to those still worn today by villagers in Upper Volta – strongly suggesting that these ancient painters were Negroid. The considerable number of styles, sometimes superimposed on a single wall, shows that the people must have lived in the region for several thousand years, and the presence of buffaloes among the wildlife shown indicates that the paintings probably go back to at least 6000 BC, since at about that date these animals vanished forever from the Sahara region.

Link with South Africa

Many of the women shown in silhouette in the Tassili N'Ajjer and other Sahara galleries have prominent buttocks, and this has given rise to an intriguing theory. For this condition, called steatopygy, is common among the women of the Bushmen, a small brown-skinned people of southern Africa who are now reduced to a population of 40,000–50,000 living in the Kalahari desert. On the basis of the Sahara paintings, steatopygous statuettes from Old Stone Age Europe and certain other data, it has been suggested

that the ancestors of the Bushmen founded a single stream of culture which covered all Africa and the southern part of western Europe. This has not been established, but the link with similar people depicted in the galleries of the Tassili N'Ajjer is dramatic.

Certainly it is now known that Africa was the birthplace of mankind, and the remains of an early form of man – a species of the genus *Homo*, possibly as much as 1·5 million years old – have been unearthed in the north of Chad. Extremely primitive artefacts called worked pebbles have also been found in various places in the Sahara, showing that the area was inhabited from the very dawn of man's existence.

During the earlier part of the Old Stone Age, the region was relatively densely populated with men who

This chariot was painted about 3,000 years ago on the wall of a rock shelter at Tin-n-Anneuin, in Algeria near the Libyan border. Chariots were used in battle and hunting. This one is unusual in having two shafts rather than one.

Death and survival in the Sahara

In a few high, basin-shaped valleys of the Sahara region there is living evidence of the days when the desert was green. Two amphibians – a toad and a frog, both common in Europe – are found in these valleys which are fed with water from permanent springs. So, too, are several species of fish, including a catfish, the Nile perch and some varieties of mullet. Crocodiles, too, were still there as recently as 1924, when the last known specimen was shot.

The fish have taken refuge in the canyons which run down from the highest parts of the Tassili N'Ajjer. But, paradoxically, the biggest threat to them lies in the rains which so infrequently replenish their habitats. For when the rivers rush in flood, the fish are often swept out of their ponds and carried down the valleys to broad, shallow lakes, sometimes more than half a mile across. But these lakes are short-lived in the fierce sun, and when they evaporate, thousands of fish are left to die.

Other kinds of animals have managed to adapt and stay alive in the Sahara. Many of them – small rodents, small carnivores, reptiles and invertebrates – spend a large part of their lives sheltering from the sun in burrows, for at a depth of only 20 in. underground there is hardly any variation between day and night-time temperatures. The jerboa, or desert rat, is one of the most successful desert dwellers. In addition to its burrowing abilities, its kangaroo-like hopping run on two large hind legs reduces the area of contact with the hot sand. It can also live its life without ever drinking, breaking down the dry plant material which it eats to manufacture its own water.

Contrary to the widespread belief, the best-known animal of the Sahara, the one-humped Arabian camel, does not store water in its body. But it has evolved the ability to use water with great economy, for the camel excretes as little as 2 pints of urine a day and does not start to sweat until its body temperature reaches 40°C (105°F), while its concentration of body fat all in one place – the hump – means that the rest of the body acts as a radiator to dispel heat. Like the desert antelope, the camel has widely splayed toes, an adaptation to walking on sand. Many other desert creatures, such as hares, have large ears, which help them to detect danger and dispel excess heat by radiation.

Plants, too, are constantly battling against drought in the Sahara. They protect themselves by spreading their roots out in all directions to extract the maximum amount of moisture from the soil; or they have on their leaves a thin layer of salt which absorbs as much moisture as possible from the air, and allows them, in some cases, to survive on the night-time dew.

On the heights of the Tassili N'Ajjer, the Hoggar, and the Aïr, trees such as cypresses and olives still survive. Today, these trees can no longer reproduce themselves in their arid environment. But they defy the passage of time and are living evidence of the days when trees covered the slopes of the mountains. Some of them, with huge, thick trunks, could be as much as 4,000 years old, with roots reaching 25 ft down. Many plants simply evade the drought, in an astonishing adaptation to the desert. Primrose seeds, for instance, are carried by wind under stones and stay dormant, perhaps for years, until the rains come.

---

worked with hand-axes, and thousands of these artefacts have been found in the narrow passages between the dunes of the great ergs. No trace remains of these men in the heart of the desert, but now, thanks to several jawbones excavated at Ternifine, near Mascara in Algeria, it is known that they were a variety of *Homo erectus*, who first appeared in Africa as early as a million years ago.

The area was less heavily populated in the period that followed, corresponding with the expansion of the great lakes – and until about 5,000 years ago Lake Chad still covered a considerable area. Rivers such as the Tilemsi, the Tafassasset, the Timmersoï and the Tamanrasset ran regularly, keeping the region moist and encouraging the growth of a luxuriant carpet of vegetation. The peaks of the Hoggar, the Tassili N'Ajjer and the Tibesti enjoyed a Mediterranean climate, and analyses of ancient pollens have shown that the Aleppo pine grew there, together with cypresses, cedars, ash trees, evergreen oaks, nettle trees, walnuts, alders, myrtle, limes and olives.

About this time, New Stone Age man began to take possession of the Sahara. Negroid peoples from the south advanced beyond the Tropic of Cancer, and from 4000 BC onwards they were replaced by herdsmen from the east, moving along the valleys and driving before them large flocks of goats and sheep and herds of cattle.

It is from this period that we can deduce the most evocative picture of what life was like when the Sahara was green, for the pastoralists achieved a mastery of rock art, and with naturalistic and lively style they

handed down to posterity pictures of their everyday life – what may be called the first strip cartoons.

They show herds being led to pasture, and camp scenes with calves tethered as they still are today by herdsmen in the Sudan. They show hemispherical grass huts, with pottery objects standing on the ground inside them, and the leather water bottles which were carried by their pack oxen. Other vivid scenes show women doing their hair or joining in wild dances in a hand-clapping circle. Some of them appear to be naked or wearing nothing but a tiny loincloth, while others are dressed in elaborate clothes with stoles of animal skins or feathers over their shoulders, and puffed-out trousers tied at the ankle. They have hair styles which are often exceedingly complex, resembling the modern bouffant style.

The men, for their part, join in hunting elephants and the other wild game which was abundant at the time. War was also an important part of the men's activities, to judge from some frescoes showing groups armed with bows confronting one another over ownership of a herd. Some of them wear only a brief loincloth and cap, like that worn today by a tribe of the Sudanese steppes, the Fulani. Others, who appear to be dignitaries, are dressed in wide, stately cloaks and wear decorated skull caps, sometimes with feathers on top. Armed, uniformed troops, grouped in soldierly style under the command of a chief, bear witness to an advanced hierarchical structure.

The social life of the people in the Tassili N'Ajjer during the cattle period can also be glimpsed in the rock paintings. In a representation of an encampment, with all the huts shown one beneath the other, the first is unoccupied and each of the remainder has a woman and her children sitting before the door. This arrangement would appear to show a polygamous society, with the first hut being reserved for the lord of the enclosure. The women would doubtless take turns to join him at night, and each of the other huts is for one of them and her children – exactly what happens today among the Fulani of the steppes.

Other scenes relate to the rules of pastoral life, such as the ritual throat-cutting of sheep and cattle in front of the flock or herd; the ceremony to remove magic spells from sick animals; and the annual sacrificial purification of the herd.

Despite the investigations that have been carried out in the Tassili N'Ajjer, no skeletons have been found in the shelters, and not a single funeral monument which could relate to the cattle-herding people has been found near the paintings. It is not known what they did with their dead, though a mummified child wrapped in an animal skin has been dug up in a shelter in the Acacous, a region near the Tassili N'Ajjer. But this is the only example of its kind. However, further south, in the Talak, a clay plain north-west of the Aïr which the herdsmen also inhabited, the dead were thrown out on to a pile of camp refuse. Others were buried in a doubled-up position, piled more than 6 ft deep in a cemetery containing several hundred bodies.

The skill of the cattle-period people allowed them to depict on their shelter walls most of the wild animals around them, such as elephants, rhinoceroses, hip-

This graceful gazelle was carved about 8,000 years ago on a rock wall at Tin-n-Terirt, in the Tassili N'Ajjer mountains. It is one of the earliest-known examples of Saharan rock art.

A ceremony to ward off illness is being conducted in this painting which was made about 5,000 years ago at Ouan Derbaouen in the Tassili N'Ajjer. In the middle of the picture, an ox is about to pass through a U-shaped gate made of palm fronds. This ancient custom was still being carried out a few decades ago by nomadic Fulani people in central Niger. It suggests a link between the traditions of the cattle-period pastoralists of the Tassili N'Ajjer and those of the Fulani shepherds who are their distant descendants.

popotamuses, a whole range of antelopes, wild asses, aardvarks, lions and ostriches. With the help of this invaluable bestiary, it is possible to reconstruct the environment the animals needed in order to survive.

The hippopotamus, shown being hunted from canoes, indicates the existence of living rivers. And for a huge beast such as the elephant – which eats an average of 450 lbs of forage a day – to have lived on the Tassili N'Ajjer and the surrounding area, there must have been a dense cover of vegetation. This must have existed, too, to satisfy the appetites of a large number of domesticated animals, whose existence can be assumed from the many painted pastoral scenes.

The cattle were of two kinds, the African breed, with long, lyre-shaped horns, and the short-horned breed with thick, arc-shaped horns. There was also a variety with down-turned horns, but this was probably an artificial deformation practised on short-horned cattle. The humped zebu type of cattle never appeared, and it cannot have been introduced into Africa from India before recorded history began.

There is a wide variety of colour and pattern in the coats of the animals, and the cows' udders are well

developed – both characteristics which point to an advanced stage of domestication. As far as can be judged from the paintings, the cattle seem to have been in excellent physical condition, and their graceful outlines are a further indication of very good pasture. Goats and sheep do not seem to have occupied an overwhelming place in the affairs of the pastoral people, but domesticated dogs are shown.

These pastoralists who lived near the shelters left quantities of food refuse mixed with ashes from the hearth, shards of pottery, millstones and other stones for crushing grain, and the decomposed excreta of domestic animals, for which the shelters also served as stables. They lived mainly on meat from their flocks and herds – few bones of wild animals have been found. No fish remains have been found in the Tassili N'Ajjer deposits; yet fishing was carried on in the rivers running at the foot of the plateau. Catfish bones have been recovered from a deposit at Djanet and from the Erg of Admer nearby. Fishing-net weights – egg-shaped, with a groove running round the middle – have been collected from the centre of the erg.

Carbon-14 dating of charcoal shows that these pastoralists must have occupied the Sahara between 6000 and 2000 BC. Amid the ashes, all sorts of small articles have been recovered which throw light on the customs of these people. There are small discs cut by the women from the shells of ostrich eggs for stringing into necklaces – often found near the hearthstones where the meals were cooked. Flints for boring holes have also been found, and several bone awls suggest that the

A detail from the great painted wall of the Iheren rock shelter in the Tassili N'Ajjer. The picture shows a graceful interweaving of giraffes, antelopes, buffaloes, oryx, ostriches, and two partly effaced elephants, all painted in a remarkably naturalistic style. A profusion of animals probably lived in the now arid desert land between 4,000 and 8,000 years ago.

women spent their time mending skin clothing while the cooking pot was on the fire. They owned pearls and triangular pendants, and small drop ear-rings of ochre-coloured shale, while the men ornamented their arms with bracelets of the same shale.

The tools of the artists

This ochrous shale, plentiful in certain parts of the Tassili N'Ajjer, has a varying iron-oxide content. It provided the painters with a range of shades – from light to dark red, yellow, and other ochres which were greenish and even bluish. They had no black, for the area was deficient in manganese oxide; but white, in the form of kaolin, or china clay, was frequently used. Shale palettes with the remains of ochre on them have been found, as well as small stone pans for thinning colours, and little millstones and grinders for crushing ochres to powder. Studies of the paintings have established that the subject was sometimes sketched in first with a sharp flint, and that the painters used brushes, clear marks of which can be seen in places.

Another aspect of the artistic ability of these cattle-period people came to light with the discovery among the cooking refuse of a beautiful small sculpture. It showed some member of a cattle family, lying in a crouching position. A few statuettes of this sort had already been picked up on the surface of the Tassili N'Ajjer and in the surrounding districts, but no one knew where they had come from. This find in the cattle-period refuse showed that they were the work of

the pastoralists, and scores of these statuettes have now been found. Most represent types of cattle, but some show hares, and animal heads inset with sacred stones. They are produced with economy of line. The same people also made tools and polished stone bowls.

The large number of milling and grinding stones on the sites of New Stone Age cattle-period dwellings, together with thousands of fragments of broken pottery, for a long time led to the belief that these people were agriculturalists. Now, however, scientists are less certain. No cultivated plant species has appeared among the ancient pollens which have been analysed, and entomologists studying insects which feed on plants cultivated in the oases of the Sahara have concluded that they do not belong to the local insect population but must have been imported, comparatively recently, with the plants they feed on.

Botanists and entomologists now propose that the milling and grinding stones found in the Sahara were used to crush the seeds of wild, grain-like grasses. These are still eaten in great quantities by the nomads of the outlying regions to the south. In Mauritania, on the other hand, villages which developed later – about

This large solar disc, carried aloft on bulls' heads, is similar to Egyptian representations of the sun god Ra of Heliopolis, though in Egyptian paintings the image of the sun is replaced by that of the pharaoh. This detail is from a Saharan cattle-period painting made about 5,500 years ago at Tissoukai in the Tassili N'Ajjer massif of Algeria.

The extinct buffalo gives its name to the oldest period of Saharan engravings. This particular sandstone engraving, found at Oued Mathendous in Libya, is about 8,000 years old.

south of the Tropic of Cancer was wetter, and remained wet longer than the northern area. Certainly there is a great dearth of aquatic animal fossils in the geological strata north of the Hoggar.

Dwelling sites are more compactly grouped, too, in the south, whether one looks at the north of the Timbuktu area or at the cliffs of Tichit-Oualata in Mauritania. Travellers who cross the vast depressions in the desert – called 'djoufs' on the old maps – can pick up flint arrowheads from the ground for mile after mile of their journey. Moreover, the Tichit includes more than 100 New Stone Age villages built of stone, which was unusual at that time. Thus it becomes increasingly evident that the Sahara was relatively well populated, especially during a period between 6,000 and 5,000 years ago – long after the original primitive inhabitants were painting their buffaloes and curious 'round head' people.

These discoveries of tools, bones, engravings and paintings, supplemented by modern research and analytical techniques, make it possible to form a less sketchy, though far from complete, picture of what the Sahara's past must have been. They bear witness to the slow and gradual deterioration of the environment,

The great god of Sefar, painted on a rock wall in the Tassili N'Ajjer about 7,500 years ago. The scene probably illustrates a fertility cult: the god is surrounded by women raising their arms to him in supplication. The painting is from the 'round head' period, the earliest-known expression of Negroid art.

the time when metals made their appearance – may have been familiar with agriculture.

The ancient fishermen

South of the Tassili N'Ajjer, on both sides of the Aïr massif, the wide valleys of the Tafassasset and of the Timmersoï, now only desiccated rivers, abound in the remains of dwelling sites occupied by herdsmen who supplemented their food supplies by fishing. Piles of kitchen refuse alongside these ancient rivers contain remains of cattle, together with the bones of antelopes, the teeth of warthogs and porcupines, and fragments of hippopotamus incisor teeth. Fishbones, freshwater mussel shells and crocodile bones are also found frequently, especially along the banks of the Timmersoï, whose springs rose in the highest mountains of the Aïr and ran west, not east.

The very large number of bone harpoons, together with weights from fishing nets, show that fishing was already practised by the seining technique – in which the ends of the net are brought together and the net is drawn ashore. It is probable that the part of the Sahara

reflected in the disappearance from the Tassili N'Ajjer paintings some 4,000 years ago of hippopotamuses, rhinoceroses and giraffes to join the extinct wild buffaloes in the steadily lengthening list of the Sahara's vanishing species.

Enter the horsemen

Within another 2,000 years, the herds and flocks of the cattle-period peoples had probably moved south, pushed by the need to find new grazing grounds, and had been replaced by a horse-owning, chariot-driving people who moved into the Central Sahara. No further trace of the herdsmen remains in the Tassili N'Ajjer shelters. The newcomers' style of painting and engraving is so different from that of their predecessors that it is impossible to imagine any cultural contact between them, still less any racial mix.

By 1000 BC, new people from the north, speaking Hamitic languages, were well established in the Sahara region. The Berbers who dominate the area today are their direct descendants. Though this was the chariot-and-horse period, these peoples also raised cattle and goats; and though their animals destroyed the pasture to a lesser extent than the animals of the cattle herders, the vegetation still did not regenerate fast enough. Waterholes became rarer, and by 2,000 years ago the creation of the desert was an accomplished fact. Those awesome expanses of sand called ergs had been formed and the rains had become completely irregular, leaving the water-eroded rocks of the desert as tortured evidence of the power they once had.

The first Arab travellers – who moved into the Sahara from AD 642 to the mid-11th century – told of trials they had to endure as they roamed the desert on their dromedaries. It was a tale of exhausting, waterless days as they trekked from one oasis to the next, and of the torments of heat and sandstorms. They also reported how unsafe the tracks were, because of the organised bands of robbers who pillaged the caravans and held them to ransom.

The fact is that the Moors, the Tuaregs and the Tedas who then inhabited the Sahara had reached the limit of survival. If a period of drought deprived them of the supply of milk from their animals, then it became a necessity of life for them to go and rob caravans, neighbouring tribes, people living in the oases, and the agriculturalists on the southern fringe of the Sahara.

Slavery increased enormously, and the most profitable item of merchandise for the caravanners became the unfortunate black man from West Africa, upon whom the Arabs preyed remorselessly.

From time to time, cruel famines were suffered by the small towns which had grown up on the southern fringe of the desert, towns like Tademekka, Agades, Timbuktu, Aoudaghost and Assode, all founded before or around AD 1000. Not one century passed without these straggling towns being the scenes of appalling warfare. Their populations were decimated.

These stark rocks stand out of the arid desert at Tassili N'Ajjer, but they owe their weird shapes to water. Their shapes were created by thousands of years of rain and flood in ancient wet periods of the Sahara.

Timbuktu and Agades suffered such slaughter that for several years they were uninhabited; other towns, such as Tademekka and Aoudaghost, and the villages of the Tichit cliffs, never recovered. The direct cause may have been warfare, but the deeper reason was the interminable droughts, which led the Zenet tribes to push the blacks back beyond Senegal, destroying the ancient kingdom of Ghana and Aoudaghost.

The terrible blood-letting which stained the sands of the desert went on for century after century, and even in the 20th century, with its sophisticated technological and scientific development, the process of drought and famine which began thousands of years ago still goes on. In 1913, after several years of inadequate rainfall accompanied by plagues of locusts which caused enormous damage, famine struck the region which lies along the southern fringe of the Sahara.

It is estimated that more than 1 million people died, and children, women and old people were the first victims. Tuaregs from the Hoggar, who had gone to Niger to renew their stocks of millet but had found none, hurled themselves upon the camps of their brethren in the Sudan area and pillaged them. Murder, even fratricide, served to heighten the horror of the vengeful Sahara.

And yet, gradually, life began again and the flocks and herds were slowly built up, despite semi-famines in 1924–5 and 1935–6. Then, in 1972–4, a fresh disaster struck. In less than two years the vast herds that the Fulani and Tuaregs had patiently re-established were reduced by 90%. Exhausted, reduced to skeletons, the animals came to the dried-up wells and died there, filling the air with such a stench that it was unbreathable. The vultures were so gorged that they had difficulty in waddling from one decaying carcase to the next.

Women huddled in the scant shade of the few trees. They had projecting ribs and flaccid breasts, against which they held dull-eyed children with stomachs swollen by vitamin deficiency, and limbs so frail that they were only wrinkled skin stretched over brittle bone. Men turned on one another and committed murder to seize the property and food of their fellows. An influenza epidemic added to the nightmare as it carried off thousands of children. No statistics are available on the true number of victims, but they are certainly numbered in the hundreds of thousands, and only a massive inflow of international aid prevented a catastrophe on the scale of the 1913 famine.

Algeria, too, has suffered from disastrous droughts throughout its history – the worst in 1867–8 which brought the deaths of 300,000 people at a time when the total population was only 2½ million. More recently, in 1944–5, over-stocking led to the deaths of 7 million sheep out of a total livestock population of 10 million. In 1930, 100 deaths were recorded in a single month in the Hoggar, officially from broncho-pneumonia – but in fact from malnutrition. More than 300 people died in the Tassili N'Ajjer in 1969 for the same reason.

Yet these recurrent catastrophes have always followed periods of relative prosperity during which men forgot, or deliberately ignored, the errors of the past and the laws governing the balance of nature.

The nomadic herdsmen of the Sahara throughout the ages have practised an ungoverned and heedless way of raising stock which has virtually no relation to the systematic use of pasture. They have always sought

---

The sandstone mountains of the Terarart, near Djanet in the Tassili N'Ajjer, were a favourite place for prehistoric engravers, who left a number of their works there. In the distance are the dunes of the great sand mass of the Erg of Admer.

A land of violent extremes

The Sahara is not the perpetual oven of baking sand of popular belief; it has a typical continental climate of alternating hot and cold seasons, with transitional phases in between. Its high temperatures are consistently the world's greatest, ranging up to the 58°C (136·4°F) recorded at Al Aziziyah, Libya. But it has also dropped to −15°C (5°F) in the Tibesti mountains in mid-winter.

Snow sometimes falls on the Hoggar and at Tassili N'Ajjer, though it rarely lies longer than 48 hours; and hail storms are not unusual. There are periods of continuous rain, too, but the water often evaporates in the hot air before it reaches the ground.

Vast areas of the Sahara – some 770,000 sq. miles – receive no rain for years at a time; and in the eastern Sahara the sun bakes the land for 97% of the daylight hours. The relative humidity can fall to 2·5% – creating a dehydrating effect that is heightened by the strong winds which sweep mercilessly across the desert.

These dry, desiccating winds create and drive before them walls of dust and sand that blot out the sun entirely. They blow across the desert for up to 70 days of the year, often for days on end.

From March onwards the temperature begins to rise, reaching a peak in June and July, with typical highs of over 50°C (123°F) in the shade. The nights are generally cool, and the extremes of temperature over 24 hours cause the rocks to expand and contract, especially in summer, so that some travellers have reported that the desert night is full of the sound of rocks groaning and falling.

But the most striking effect occurs on the slopes of the high dunes in the ergs. As a result of the alternating expansion and contraction in the grains, very large masses of sand become detached and then slip, forming avalanches that produce a prolonged, low rumbling sound.

Desert Arabs, poetic and credulous by nature, attribute this sound to Raoul, the drummer of death and the genie of the ergs. They can never hear the rumbling of the sand without an inward shudder of fear . . . yet another example of the many romantic mysteries which rule the lives of those who live in the Sahara.

to increase the number of horned animals they possess, for reasons of social prestige, rather than concentrating on finding good meat-producing stock.

They did not stop to consider whether the pasture could survive, and the result was over-grazing, which brought first an obvious deterioration in the vegetation, and then a critical imbalance between the number of mouths to be fed and the area available to produce the food. For lack of foresight and a 'live for today' attitude have always been the characteristic of nomad peoples. Once the crisis has passed and the drought has taken its heavy toll, the areas afflicted are quickly repopulated. In the past, this may have been a social necessity in order to maintain the tribe's ability to resist its pillaging neighbours – a kind of self-defence – but its long-term effects are akin to mass suicide.

Yet today a large increase in the population is taking place, as it is among many other developing peoples. A census taken at the beginning of the century showed the Tuareg tribes of the Aïr as consisting of some 15,000 people. In the 1965 census they numbered 45,000, in spite of the droughts which have afflicted them this century. Flocks and herds showed a similar increase – while in the same period the plant resources were reduced by half. In these figures can be read the unchanging history of the Sahara.

The discoveries in the last few decades of the mineral wealth that lies beneath their feet do not seem likely to benefit the people who battle to survive in the Sahara. Major finds of oil, gas and iron-ore reserves have been made in Algeria and Libya, and a long list of valuable metals has been discovered in the mountains. But the inaccessibility of these metals appears to have delayed their exploitation until the world's other resources begin to seem exhausted. In any case, such economic development as has taken place has not changed the traditional character of the Sahara – it brings modern technology and improved communications, but gives limited opportunity for local work.

High wages in the oil fields attract labour, but jobs are relatively few, and they disrupt the traditional life of the desert. The age-old products of the Sahara – salt, animal skins, wool and fruit – have a dwindling market, and only dates have commercial importance today.

The Sahara is still dying. The oven-hot ergs and the barren regs are enveloping and submerging more and more of the fertile land needed for even the hardy desert tribes to survive. Do their growing numbers simply mean more people facing an early death? These peoples continue to practise the self-destructive habits of their predecessors as they plunder the dwindling vegetation and sink ever-deeper wells.

In the Sahara today, as it has always been, man's greatest enemy is himself.

HENRI LHOTE

The skeleton of a camel which has died from thirst and exhaustion lies in the centre of a seemingly endless reg, one of the many stony plains of the deserts. All trace of the animal will soon vanish – dried out by the sun and eroded by sand.

The Scythians, fierce horsemen of the steppes

*Among the mounted nomads of the Russian plains
one shadowy tribe rode supreme for a time: the Scythians.
Barbarous even by the standards of their own epoch, they
strangled scores of their own people in
grim rituals. For centuries they were Europe's
chief guard against the Mongol hordes of the East.
In the end, these brutal warriors rode out
of history as they had entered it, without a word.
For they had no writing. All they left were
footnotes in Greek history – and some of the
finest gold art in the world.*

'What men! They are real Scythians!' Napoleon is said to have exclaimed at the sight of a thundering charge by Cossack cavalry, as his tattered forces fought endless rearguard actions on the wintery retreat from Moscow. Thus nearly 2,000 years after their barbaric domination of central Russia had been ended, the magnificent Scythian warriors of the Pontic steppes lived on – as a byword for ferocity and daring.

Looming on horseback 8 ft above the ground, screaming maniacally, capable of unleashing repetitive and deadly flights of triple-edged arrows, they must

This 2-in. gold plaque, from the 4th century BC, helps confirm the account of the Greek historian Herodotus of the Scythians' rite of brotherhood. 'They pour into a great cup wine mingled with the blood of the parties to the oath,' he wrote. 'They dip their weapons into it and then drink.'

have seemed the very embodiment of horror to those who had to stand and fight them. Nor were such fears unwarranted, for Scythian warriors regularly beheaded their enemies and sometimes even skinned them whole. If an enemy were known personally, his skull might receive special treatment: sawn through below the eyes, it would be cleaned and painstakingly fashioned into a richly appointed drinking vessel. Not surprisingly, Scythian ceremonies, especially royal funerals, were drenched in blood and are among the most grisly in human history

Yet these thundering, rapacious, illiterate horsemen were capable of remarkable accomplishments as well – of stunning military strategy and, even more mysteriously, of the creation of a dazzling array of exquisitely formed golden objects. Combs, breastplates, chalices, scabbards, helmets, rings – all either executed by Scythian metalsmiths or commissioned from Greek craftsmen – have been found in glittering profusion amid the carnage of royal gravesites.

Blood and gold, bestiality and beauty, myth and fact, these are the strands that bind the curious paradox of the lost Scythians. Where did they come from, scholars ask, and what was their life like 2,500 years ago? Why had they no coins, no written language? And at the heart of the mystery this question: what forces conspired to infuse these barbarous nomads with a deep and clearly delightful appreciation of beautifully crafted gold?

If paradox and mystery shroud the Scythians, however, the few facts we do possess concerning them are hardly less troublesome. Indeed, if it were not for two vastly dissimilar historical figures, we would probably know very little at all about the Scythians! The first of these giants is Herodotus of Halicarnassus, the 5th century BC Greek writer known as the father of history; the second is Peter the Great, Tsar of All the Russias at the beginning of the 18th century.

It was nearly 2,500 years ago, in the middle of the 5th century BC, that Herodotus, gathering information for his monumental history of the Greco-Persian Wars, journeyed to the frontier trading city of Olbia on the Black Sea. To the east of this burgeoning Greek outpost lay the Don river, to the west the Carpathian mountains and the Danube river, to the north the broad, sweeping girth of the Pontic steppes, terminated only hundreds of miles away by rough forest and intractable marshes. In the months that followed, Herodotus appears to have learned as much about the Scythians as the battles he came to chronicle. For as revealed in Book IV of his *Persian Wars* the barbarous aspects of Scythian life held a great fascination for Herodotus, and he took a certain pleasure in describing them, knowing that he would make his readers tremble even in the 5th century BC.

Having beheaded and skinned an enemy, for example, Herodotus reports that the Scythians sometimes made coats, capes and cushions out of the skins. It is unclear whether Herodotus actually saw – or perhaps even touched – such grisly artefacts, but he does describe them as being white and glossy. In their use of human skulls, Scythian warriors, if they were rich, might not only cut and clean but also bind a skull's exterior with rough cowhide and gild its interior for use as a drinking cup. Entertaining a guest, the warrior might then courteously offer his visitor a drink served in one of these skulls and provide as well a chillingly detailed explanation of the crime that had merited the punishment. Sometimes the victim might be a relative, perhaps one as close as a father or brother, who had been foolish enough to start a quarrel.

In battle Scythian warriors not only performed in a bloodthirsty manner, they *were* bloodthirsty, drinking the blood of the first enemy they killed. Each year, in fact, as the tribes gathered, it was considered a great disgrace not to have killed anyone since the previous festival. On the battlefield Scythians also believed in obtaining proof of their viciousness: they took scalps,

On the northern borders of Afghanistan, along the fringes of the Asian steppes, mounted tribesmen like these Turkmenian nomads carry on a traditional way of life which has survived almost unchanged for at least 25 centuries. The patterns of their life today are the same as those around which the Scythians built their culture on the plains of the Ukraine.

an act that Herodotus described in vivid detail. 'The Scythian soldier,' he wrote, 'scrapes the scalp clean of flesh and, softening it by rubbing it between the hands, uses it thenceforth as a napkin. The Scyth is proud of these scalps and hangs them from his bridle rein; the greater the number of such napkins that a man can show, the more highly is he esteemed among them. Many make themselves cloaks by sewing a quantity of these scalps together . . .'

All prisoners were not scalped. In honour of their god of war, Scythian warriors also performed sacrifices – one of each hundred prisoners was ceremoniously

The land of the Scythians covered roughly what is now the Ukraine and the Don country, from the Danube in the west to the Volga in the east. The plains beyond their eastern frontier were inhabited by other mounted peoples with very similar customs – among them the Sauromatae, or Sarmatians, and the Massagetae. The Persians called them all Scythians.

offered up. This the Scythians did by killing the prisoner, then slicing off his right hand and arm and tossing the severed limb into the air. 'Then the other victims are slain,' Herodotus wrote. 'Those who have offered the sacrifice depart, leaving the hands and arms where they may chance to have fallen, and the bodies, as well, separate.' Blood also bathed Scythian agreements and alliances, with the participants joining in the creation of a mixture of blood and wine. They might then dip arrows or javelins or swords in the potion and finish by drinking it down.

Despite his obvious fascination with Scythian barbarism, Herodotus provided a more mundane – and perhaps more important – view of the mysterious Scythian world. His portrait is hardly flattering, for it tells of a people with wild, cavernous eyes, long and undoubtedly filthy hair and weathered, leathery skin. It tells of men who rarely if ever bathed and women who used a kind of mashed herb paste to so so. It tells of hard, cruel men who had numerous wives, who relished strong, undiluted wine and the smoke of hashish. These men lived constantly in the saddle and were as wedded to the steppes as the horses they rode. 'Level, well-watered and abounding in pasture' is the way Herodotus described their domain.

This was the race that Darius the Great of Persia prepared to crush – and Herodotus has left us a remarkably graphic account of the Scythians' cunning scorched-earth triumph over Darius' powerful armies. By the end of the 6th century Darius' empire was truly vast. To the west it spread to the Balkans in Europe; to the south it bordered Libya, Tunisia and the sun-baked wastes of Ethiopia and the Sudan. To the east the empire covered the whole of southern Asia as far as the Punjab and the Indus Valley, ending at the Indian Ocean and the Arabian desert.

Darius' northern frontier, however, consisted of seas, icy mountains and deserts – the Caspian and Aral, the Caucasus, the Gobi. And it was this stretch of broken terrain that most worried Darius. For behind it roamed the shadowy but terrible Ashguzai horsemen – the Scythians. They had suddenly appeared from no-

---

Conical tents like these, known as yurts, are still the best protection the nomadic peoples have against the icy winds that sweep across the steppes in winter. These efficient shelters – made of felt and reed matting over a wooden framework – were probably known to the Scythians. Herodotus said they often set their tents on wagons for greater mobility.

where three or four generations earlier, sweeping down astride their tireless horses like an avalanche from the passes of the eastern Caucasus. They had ridden all over upper Asia, spreading terror, pillaging and slaughtering everyone who resisted until King Cyaxares of Media took advantage of a drinking bout and massacred their chiefs. But this did not put an end to the Scythian threat on the Persian frontier.

In the spring of 514 BC, Darius, hoping to end the Scythian menace and conquer the steppes from the west, crossed the Bosphorus at the head of a vast army and moved up through Thrace into Scythian territory. It would take a month or two to suppress these upstart horsemen, Darius reckoned.

What happened in fact was that the 700,000-man Persian force was very nearly consumed by the Scythians in what must be considered one of the most remarkable examples of tactical wizardry in military history. According to Herodotus, writing almost half a century later, Darius and his troops simply could not find the enemy army. Nonetheless, crops were burned and wells filled in as the Persian probing actions were teased forever forward in pursuit of an enemy who always vanished just over the horizon. And thus for months did the Scythians, helped by neighbouring tribes, toy with Darius, leading him in all directions between the Danube and the Volga without ever letting him take them or their herds by surprise. Finally, Darius challenged the courage of the phantoms he sought to destroy by sending on ahead a message in which he commanded the Scythians to fight or surrender. The succinct reply was: 'Go weep.' In the end, troops exhausted, supply lines perilously thin, the struggle to find food as torturous as fighting itself,

Influenced by the tastes of their Scythian trading partners, Greek artists abandoned traditional mythological subjects to depict, with the same skill, scenes from the daily life of the steppes. This scene is part of a gold pectoral, or breastplate, which is a masterpiece of Greco-Scythian art. It shows two men sewing a sheepskin to make a tunic.

Another remarkably realistic scene of daily life from the same gold breastplate, which was found at Tolstaya Mogila, a Scythian burial site on the Dnieper river, shows that history is not always about change. The scene depicts a young man milking a ewe into a pitcher, using a technique which is still common in the Caucasus today.

This beautifully moulded group of realistic figures adorns a golden comb discovered in a Scythian tomb at Solokha in the Ukraine. It shows a battle between peoples whom the Greeks would have called 'barbarians'. The comb was made by a Greek, and shows the horseman wearing a Greek helmet.

Darius withdrew, leaving the Scythians in total command of the steppes.

However, this story of a scorched-earth guerrilla war is not the only interesting point in Herodotus' account. A man of great curiosity, he was the first person to make a proper study of the customs of different races. To use his own words, he was not content with simply 'ensuring that the great deeds of men are not effaced by time'. He wanted to see the countries that had been the scenes of these great deeds and to observe the daily life of their inhabitants.

In one memorable passage in his *Persian Wars*, he comes perhaps closest to capturing the essence of the Scythians: 'Having neither cities nor forts,' he wrote, 'and carrying their dwellings wherever they go; accustomed, moreover, one and all, to shoot from horseback; and living not by crops but from their cattle, their wagons the only houses they possess, how can they fail of being unconquerable and unassailable?'

Not long afterwards another famous Greek, Hip-pocrates, the father of medicine, corroborated and expanded Herodotus' account with these words: 'The smallest of these wagons have four wheels, but some have six; they are covered in with felt, and they are constructed in the manner of houses, some having but a single apartment, and some three; they are proof against rain, snow and winds. The wagons are drawn by yokes of oxen . . .'

Not all of Herodotus' accounts seemed credible, however, and over the years doubts developed concerning most of them. For example, Herodotus told three conflicting stories about the origin of his all too mysterious – and perhaps fictional – Scythians. One story suggested that they came from Asia; a second, that they were descended from Targitaus, an offspring of Zeus' liaison with a daughter of the Borysthenes river (the Dnieper), and were thus a local people. The third, involving Scythes – son of Heracles and a half-woman, half-snake creature who lived in the Scythian woodlands – reinforced the idea of a local origin.

Herodotus' legend-tainted reports of the people who lived around the Scythians hurt his credibility even more. There were the promiscuous, luxury-loving Agathyrsid; the Neurians, who turned into wolves once a year; the Budini, who had bright red hair and were furious drinkers; and other people he called the Man-eaters for their peculiar habits.

Eventually almost all that Herodotus had written about the Scythians came to be doubted. 'Legend monger,' he was called by none other than the philosopher Aristotle. And so the already mysterious Scythians became and remained for more than 2,000 years uncertain figures in a world of myth and legend. And then, in 1715, the spell was broken by a gift of gold, from the owner of Siberian mines to Tsar Peter of Russia. Thus began the modern effort to explain the blood-and-gold paradox of the Scythians.

After that first shipment of Scythian gold, some 20 exquisite pieces in all, other discoveries followed, and other treasures reached Peter. Finally, when it became clear that dozens of gravesites, or kurgans, had been robbed in the search for gold, Peter ordered such looting stopped and commanded that all Scythian treasures be delivered to the crown. Nonetheless, the openings continued, especially after Peter's death in 1725; and with each, scholars came closer to a very exciting conclusion: Herodotus had been remarkably accurate in his descriptions of Scythian funerals. The father of history had been telling the truth after all.

Herodotus wrote in one account, 'When a king dies, they dig a great square pit, and, when it is ready, they take up the corpse, which has been previously slit open, cleaned out, and filled with various aromatic substances, crushed galingale [an aromatic plant], parsley seed, and anise; it is then sewn up again and the whole body coated over with wax.' Then the king's body was carried in a wagon from tribe to tribe until the funeral cortège reached the land of the Gerrhi, the most isolated of the Scythian tribes.

'Here the corpse is laid in the tomb on a mattress, with spears fixed in the ground on either side to support a roof of brush laid on wooden poles, while in other parts of the great square pit various members of the king's household are buried beside him: one of his concubines, his butler, his cook, his groom, his stew-

The detail below from a gold vase may depict a Scythian legend in which aspirants to the royal throne competed by demonstrating their prowess as warriors. Here, one of the less successful competitors, while trying to bend a massive bow, has wounded himself in the leg. A companion binds up the wound while the failed competitor grimaces with pain.

ard, and his chamberlain – all of them strangled. Horses are buried too, and gold cups (the Scythians do not use silver or bronze), and a selection of his other treasures ... This ceremony over, everybody with great enthusiasm sets about raising a mound of earth, each competing to make it as big as possible.'

In 1898, N. I. Veselovsky excavated kurgans at Ulski Aul, in the Krasnodor district north-east of the Black Sea. Under the 49-ft-high earthworks of one he found a wooden structure. 'All around,' he wrote 'wooden pickets had been planted, near which lay the skeletons of horses.' Two oxen and more than 360 horses were buried next to the kurgan. During the 20th century the discoveries continued, especially after the Second World War. And then in 1971, near Ordzhonikidze, on the Dnieper, a Russian archaeologist named B. N. Mozoloevskii found another variant of the scene described by Herodotus: the servants seemed to be leading their horses.

Comparing reports of kurgan excavation with the

The stag was a common emblem of the many peoples who occupied the steppes. This elaborately shaped plaque, dated about the 7th century BC, shows one reclining, with its head arched inquisitively. It was found in a burial mound of the Scythians at Kostromskaya Stanitsa in the Caucasus.

Greek historian's accounts, it seems that Herodotus may have been writing about the 'ideal' kurgan – if such a word may be used to describe what happened on the first anniversary of the burial. 'When a year is gone by,' Herodotus wrote, 'further ceremonies take place. Fifty of the late king's attendants are taken ... and are strangled, with fifty of the most beautiful horses.

'When they are dead, their bowels are taken out, and the cavity cleaned, filled full of chaff, and straightway sewn up again. This done, a number of posts are set into the ground, in sets of two pairs each; atop every pair of stakes half the rim of a wheel is placed to form an arch. Then strong stakes are run lengthwise through the bodies of the horses from tail to neck, and they are set on top of the rims so that the arch supports the shoulders of the horse, while the one behind holds up the belly and quarters, the legs dangling in mid-air. Each horse is given a bridle, which is stretched out in front of the horses and fastened to a peg.

'The fifty strangled youths are then mounted on the fifty horses. To effect this, a stake is passed through their bodies along the course of the spine to the neck, the lower end of which projects from the body and is fixed into a socket made in the stake that runs lengthwise down the horse. The fifty riders are thus ranged in a circle round the tomb and so left.'

The grisly remains of such a scene – created perhaps

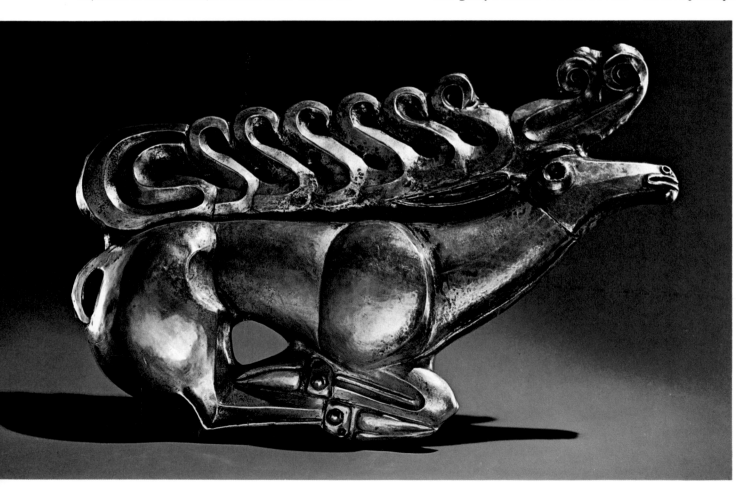

by the Scythians to protect their king after death or perhaps to frighten away potential graverobbers – maybe unearthed one day as more kurgans are opened. Yet even without such proof scholars no longer doubt Herodotus – at least in his reporting of funeral customs, the triumph over Darius and the Scythians' mode of life.

But what of other portions of his narrative – areas in which myth and fact blur even as they lead the reader on toward a better understanding of the Scythian paradox? The Scythians, for example, believed in the shaman who formed an important part of Scythian life. This unusual, significant figure, who has appeared in many cultures, was a unique sort of amalgam for the Scythians: part medicine man, part magician, part soothsayer and, perhaps most importantly, part ani-

This finely modelled figure of a bareback rider, less than 2 in. high, is the end-piece of a torque made in the 4th century BC. The torque, a collar made of twisted metal, was a favourite ornament of the Scythians. This one is made of gold wire sheathed in beaten gold decorated with enamel.

mal. In his healing and predicting rites, he used a variety of instruments – drums, sticks, bark strips, rattles, willow wands. And he also used drugs, as did all Scythian males, and probably relied on self-induced seizures and trances as well. Thus it is at least possible to speculate that the Scythian shaman might have served as a kind of artistic touchstone, or prime source, for the animal themes that so dominate Scythian art.

There are two perfectly good reasons for this. First,

229

The Scythians buried their chiefs with enormous ceremony. They built funeral barrows called kurgans, which rise like hills from the steppes. The one at Alexandropol in the Ukraine, shown here in a 19th-century engraving, is more than 100 yds across at the base and nearly 60 ft high. The barrows contained heaps of treasure and sometimes the remains of wives and servants – strangled and buried alongside their master.

the Scythians, like many early and primitive people, viewed their world in animistic terms. Surrounded by living things and natural phenomena that they could not comprehend, they quite naturally assigned special powers to them – especially the animals. Aspects of this transfer show up in the golden animal figures the Scythians created. Often such creatures are represented only in part by a claw or a head – or in a dead or contracted position. Most probably this was an attempt by the Scythians to control or extract their powers. Second, the shaman shared his prestigious position in society with only one other – the metal-smith. Both had unique powers, both worked with fire and both were participants in the special rituals and myths that made gold a sacred part of Scythian life. Though it came to the Scythians from distinctly earthly sources – the Caucasus, Ural and distant Altai ranges – the metal was very nearly worshipped by them. 'The Royal Scythians guard the sacred gold with the most

special care,' Herodotus wrote, 'and year by year offer great sacrifices in its honour.'

Gold also played a vital role in the myths of the Scythians. One such tale concerns the metal's origin. It came, the story goes, from the distant land of the Arimaspians, a fabled people who had a single eye and lived to the far north (which in Herodotus' time could be taken to mean Siberia). These people had seized the metal from the griffins that guarded it. No trace, of course, has been found of this one-eyed race except in the *Odyssey*, but griffins – great winged beasts – are a familiar motif in Greco-Scythian art.

Another myth that appears in Herodotus involves four golden objects: a plough, a yoke, a battle-axe and a drinking cup. These fell from the sky and three brothers rushed forward to pick them up. When the two older brothers approached them, however, the objects burst into flame. And so only Colaxais, the youngest, succeeded and thus became king. This myth, some scholars feel, explains the division of the Scythians into four tribes: the labourers, the farmers, the nomads and the royalty, who were also nomads but who exerted a tyrannical rule over the rest.

But are myths and shamans enough to explain the remarkable art of the Scythians – and their barbarity? Or is it possible that some further piece of evidence exists, a more complete account of life among the Scythians, perhaps one lost for thousands of years near the Black Sea? Extremely unlikely, most experts say, though they do admit that crucial discoveries could occur as additional kurgans are opened and explored. Or could the missing pieces in the Scythian paradox be already at hand – mundane bits of evidence scattered about on the table of known discovery? Possibly! For though the Scythians were infinitely barbarous, so too, though to a lesser degree, were most of the tribes round them. Perhaps then the Scythians simply reached the bloody heights they did because they had to – of necessity. After all, they occupied land that was the very epicenter of the invasion routes between East and West. In order to hold on, they may have been doing nothing more than trying to make every enemy death serve a dual purpose: to destroy an opponent *and* to serve as a warning to dozens of others. Perhaps the Scythians *had* to be barbarous to stay where they were. In equally practical terms, it may have been that aside from their animistic view of life, their use of drugs and the reverence with which they held gold, the Scythians created portable gold artefacts simply because they were nomads and thus had no walls or doors on which to draw or paint.

Speculation, of course; guesswork to be sure! Conclusions that most scholars would be forced to reject for lack of evidence even as they toyed with them. As a result, perhaps the most realistic thing that can be said about the Scythians is this: what we know about them, both good and bad, forms but a single, chilling chapter in human history. And yet it is one that states a very fundamental truth: most men are capable of being at least as creative as they are barbarous!

Whatever the answer to the riddle of the Scythians, their decline and ultimate disappearance was not mysterious. Like other tribes before them, and those that followed, they were driven from the steppes by a stronger, crueler people. These were the Sauromatae, who about 350 BC began crossing the Don.

Already weakened by a richer, more settled life, the Scythians scattered, some penetrating into Thrace (now Romania), others remaining in south Russia and mixing with the invaders. Those who refused to submit entrenched themselves in the Crimea and built a prosperous capital, Neapolis. Finally, in the year 106 BC, less than 400 years after their zenith, the last remnants of the Scythian tribes were destroyed by Mithradates the Great, king of Pontus, and the Scythians vanished into the pages of such ancient accounts as those of Herodotus.

MICHAEL AINSWORTH

'The Scythians are immensely rich,' wrote the Greek historian Herodotus. And, judging by the splendour of the funeral treasures found near the Dnieper river at Tolstaya Mogila, his description was accurate. This skeleton, found there in a kurgan, or funeral mound, is of a woman who was buried 2,400 years ago, decked in rings and bracelets. She wore a gold torque round her neck, her shroud glittered with 200 squares of beaten gold, and her veil was held by gold bands.

Zimbabwe, Africa's lost civilisation

A long-abandoned city of stone stands ruined and mysterious above the bush country of southern Rhodesia. It seems hauntingly out of place in a landscape whose only other known native architecture is the simple, timeless mud hut. European travellers who gazed at the impressive ruins of Zimbabwe a century ago thought they had discovered at last the legendary mines of King Solomon. But they were looking at what was probably the religious citadel of a powerful, forgotten black empire.

The time to see the fabled ruins of Zimbabwe is at the beginning of October when the trees and shrubs are in flower. Go alone if you can, or with an untalkative companion who is ready to share your wonder, for what lies before you are the mute stone-walled remains of a forgotten civilisation that will remind you of nothing you have ever seen before. So stark, so surprising is this silent city's sudden appearance that you might easily imagine Zimbabwe to be a mirage.

The name Zimbabwe translates from Shona – the Bantu language of the local Mashona people – as

either 'venerated houses' or 'stone houses'. It is applied by the Mashona to any of some 200 stone ruins, large and small, scattered throughout southern Rhodesia. Largest and most impressive, however, and consequently the ruins most consistently referred to as Zimbabwe, or Great Zimbabwe, are those located at the head of the long wide valley of the Mtilikwe river, not far from the road joining the Rhodesian capital of Salisbury with Johannesburg in South Africa. The valley's hills, kept verdant by prevailing south-easterly winds from the Indian Ocean, provide a magnificent setting. And in hollows near the water grow thickets of fever trees with green or yellow bark. Even the horizon adds to the panorama, for it is serrated by numerous *kopjes*, granite outcrops that appear at a distance to rise like ruined castles.

The first white man to describe Zimbabwe from personal experience and to tell the world of its marvels

What rituals were acted out within the great walled enclosure known as the Temple, which was part of the complex ruins at Zimbabwe? Centuries ago it was the heart of a great black trading empire, rich in gold. The 30-ft-high dry-stone walls are an impressive monument to its ancient builders.

233

was Karl Mauch, a German geologist, who wrote of his encounter: 'On the third of September 1871 we ascended this hill. It is about two miles long, fairly high with a bare top from which there is a magnificent view in all directions. At first my guide ventured gingerly on to the summit and then, one after another, walking like cats on hot bricks, we followed. Suddenly, in an easterly direction about five miles away, could be clearly seen a hill on which were great walls built apparently in European style.'

As Mauch approached, Great Zimbabwe revealed itself more clearly. It was a large, complex assemblage of roof-less stone structures, built with great skill of grey-granite blocks, some apparently in their natural rough state, others dressed, and all set together without any mortar save the *daga*, a mixture of gravel and clay, which often formed the rounded caps of walls.

Great Zimbabwe covers some 60 acres and includes three different structures. First, there is a majestic

fortress-like series of walls, labyrinthine passages, steps and corridors. Now popularly known as the Acropolis, these are not so much erected as wedded to a lofty *kopje*, so cunningly do they follow the natural curve of the rock. Second is a vast elliptical enclosure, the Temple, more than 100 yards long and about 70 yards wide. Standing on the plains some 250 ft below the Acropolis, the Temple has an impressive tower and walls more than 30 ft high and 20 ft thick. In between the Acropolis and Temple is a third site, one that contains what is left of numerous lesser buildings. These are known simply as the Valley Ruins.

Once within the city itself, Mauch found evidence of a rich and powerful population. Any clues as to who might have built these unique structures, when and for what purposes were not to be found. But one thing seemed certain: the builders could not be Africans, much less ancestors of the local Karangas, because the Karangas lived in modest mud huts and had few accomplishments that Mauch could equate with wealth or a noble past. Rather, Mauch was inclined to consider what he saw as the fulfillment of a belief widely held in Europe that eastern Africa was the site of King Solomon's mines or of the legendary kingdom of Prester John. Thrilled at his discovery, Mauch declared

At its height, the powerful Iron Age empire of Monomotapa spread across the whole of modern-day Rhodesia and large parts of Mozambique. The Africans used the Zambezi to reach the coast and trade their gold for Arab and Portuguese goods.

After Vasco da Gama visited Sofala, the Portuguese built this fort and tried in vain to find the Africans' gold.

234

himself 'on the threshold of my greatest achievement'.

Mauch, however, ran into enormous problems. He had come to Zimbabwe under the protective custody of Chief Mapunsure, leader of the Amangwa clan, a sub-group of the Karangas. Unfortunately, he soon learned that the Amangwas were on hostile terms with a neighbouring Karanga community and that both claimed ownership over the ruins. This political and territorial conflict made free movement within Zimbabwe all but impossible. In addition, Mauch had been deprived of virtually all his surveying instruments, his baggage having been conveniently lost by his bearers earlier in the expedition. The site itself was so overgrown that the general plan of the structures could not be seen or evaluated. Finally, Mauch contracted the tropical fever of which he eventually died.

Still, Mauch's written report, which was published in 1876, shortly after his death, went a long way towards stimulating new interest in long-lost cities and sent a parade of investigators, some amateur, some professional, to Great Zimbabwe and other stone ruins in Rhodesia. The unraveling of the mysteries of these ruins is a case history in archaeological detective work and in the particular difficulties associated with establishing a chronology for sub-Saharan Africa. The lack of written records, a climate and acid soil highly destructive to the physical evidence on which scientists base their findings and a long held presumption amongst white scholars that black Africans were incapable of producing such civilisations – all created enormous obstacles to finding the truth.

Probably the first news of Zimbabwe's splendours reached Europe in the Middle Ages by way of the Arabs. As early as the 10th century merchants from northern Africa, Persia and India frequented the city of Sofala, 250 miles east of Zimbabwe on the coast. Golden Sofala, as it was often called, was a centre for trade in ivory, leopard skins, iron and gold, which the natives from the interior exchanged for foreign-made beads, porcelain and finished tools such as knives and axes. Whether the Arabs actually reached Zimbabwe

---

The almost intact granite wall of the Temple clearly shows the artistry of the builders of Zimbabwe. It looks at first like a fortress, but the mortar-less wall of squared stone, without openings or means of scaling, has no apparent military function. More than likely, it was the principal residence of the emperor. It is now believed that the great wall was built to hide the secret life of the ruler – his harem, his banquets and his courts – from the public gaze.

or simply heard impressive reports of it from their African associates we do not know, but they passed on the word, embellishing their descriptions as they repeated them, whetting the appetites of Europeans as far away as Portugal and England.

As the Arabs often relied on their own folklore in interpreting imaginary wonders for others, they quite naturally linked Zimbabwe with the name of King Solomon, whose wealth was said to come in significant part from gold. The Europeans tended to accept such stories or to create still more fabulous descriptions based upon clues they found in the Bible. Another appealing notion was that Zimbabwe was the royal capital of Prester John, a legendary priest who was said to rule over an isolated Christian kingdom.

Following the Portuguese colonisation of the coast in the 16th century, explorers made repeated attempts to reach the region's most productive gold mines and thus the centres of native power in the interior. The 'heathens' there, it was said, had so much gold that they traded it without weighing it. According to one chronicler, they 'commonly gave 100 times more gold than they were paid for in exchange'.

Judging from their written records, the Portuguese never reached Zimbabwe and hence never had any

reason to refine their knowledge of the stone cities of which they had heard. So when the first white hunters and explorers did see Zimbabwe late in the 19th century, they fell into similar patterns of thinking without hesitation. Mauch, for example, remarked: 'I do not think that I am far wrong if I suppose that the ruin on the hill is a copy of Solomon's Temple on Mount Moriah and the building in the plain a copy of the palace [in Jerusalem] where the Queen of Sheba lived during her visit to Solomon.'

Theodore Bent, an English archaeologist who went to Zimbabwe in 1891, continued in the same vein. By now, the region was under commercial charter. As a result, Bent was engaged by the British South Africa Company, the Royal Geographical Society and the British Association for the Advancement of Science. His task: to make a serious study of the place. Unfortunately, archaeology was still an infant science and the techniques of digging and of scientific evaluation of data were primitive, even tinged with romantic misapprehensions. With the help of his wife, who took photographs and wrote an account of their trip, and R. M. W. Swan, who undertook the surveying, Bent reclaimed a good bit of Zimbabwe from the undergrowth. Unfortunately, Bent and his crew kept no formal records and paid little attention to the depth at which various artefacts were found, data which would have enabled later specialists to establish relative dates for the various buildings excavated.

The digging, which was shallow and spotty, proved a disappointment despite the discovery of several monoliths surmounted by sculpted soapstone birds of unique design. These evidently were part of the ornaments of the building where they were found. Bent thought they bore a resemblance to Phoenician stelae. In time the English abandoned excavation for the more intriguing study led by Swan, of astronomical measurement in orienting certain features of the buildings and in providing sight-lines for observing particular stars. Permitting himself great leaps of imagination, and having little real evidence, Swan concluded that the Temple had altars and wall openings positioned according to the movements of certain heavenly bodies. This remarkable alignment he attributed, smugly enough, to the influence of ancient architects from the Near East.

When all the work had been completed to their satisfaction, Bent summed up the findings: 'There is little room for doubt that the builders and workers of the Great Zimbabwe [belonged to] a northern race coming from Arabia ... closely akin to the Phoenician and Egyptian ... and eventually developing into the

The Acropolis, which was built on a natural rock spur, is now a ruin. The builders skillfully used the chaotic contours of the rocks, blending in with them the granite blocks they piled above. The door in the centre leads to the so-called secret passage. This is one of the oldest sections of the ruins at Great Zimbabwe and dates from the 11th century.

more civilised races of the ancient world.' Neither Bent nor Swan were ready to propose a specific date for Zimbabwe's creation as yet, but others, enlarging upon Swan's hypothesis, concluded that the stone structures were perhaps 3,000 years old. Pottery and other artefacts found about the site were identified – correctly – as being of local origin but were said to have no relevance to the ruins.

Meanwhile, Rhodesia was being overrun by treasure hunters looking for gold and other valuable artefacts. At first the British South Africa Company voiced no objection to this sort of freelance exploration, requiring only that it receive a share of the profits as the property owner. The site of Great Zimbabwe, like all the others in the region, came in for considerable disruption by diggers, and in 1902 the company appointed as the official curator of the ruins a British journalist named Richard Hall. Hall was thoroughly committed to the 'ancient peoples of the East' theory of Zimbabwe's origins. Not only was it believable, it also made good copy for the numerous books he was to write on the subject. It was also good for tourism, which was beginning to have some value to the Rhodesian government.

Hall was delegated to direct 'not scientific research but the preservation of the buildings', an assignment which he loosely interpreted as license to remove 'the filth and decadence of the Kaffir [Bantu] native occupation'. Unlike Bent and Swan, Hall dug down through several layers of deposits and thus added to the damage that would plague later archaeological investigations. Indeed, Hall's only positive contribution to Zimbabwe was that he ultimately forced responsible government officials to dismiss him for in-

competence and to send the first formally trained archaeologist to the site. The fortuitous choice for the new assignment was David Randall-MacIver, a Scottish Egyptologist, who was instructed to make a quick tour of Great Zimbabwe and of some other similar but lesser sites in Rhodesia and to prepare a report for the annual meeting of the British Association for the Advancement of Science.

It took MacIver little time to satisfy himself that Africans – most probably ancestors of the Mashona – had built Great Zimbabwe in successive stages and that most of the visible ruins were, far from being ancient, no older than the 14th or 15th century. He was not sure as to the purpose of the structures but, he declared, 'whether military or domestic, there is not a trace of Oriental or European style of any period whatever . . .' He also said that 'the character of the dwellings contained within the stone ruins, and forming an integral part of them, is unmistakably African' and 'the arts and manufactures exemplified by objects found within these dwellings are typically African . . .'

MacIver's conclusions, published in *Mediaeval Rhodesia*, divided opinion both inside and outside Rhodesia, with the majority of his professional peers giving him solid support and the local establishment taking angry exception. Most vocal of all his opponents

was his predecessor, Hall, who published a rebuttal called *Prehistoric Rhodesia* in 1909. To MacIver's hypothesis that Great Zimbabwe was the culmination of a gradual, progressive evolution of building styles, Hall answered that Great Zimbabwe could not be attributed to the Bantu because they 'were not a progressive people'. Instead, he wrote, their culture was inherently decadent owing to 'a sudden arrest of intelligence and mental development [that] befalls every member . . . at the age of puberty'.

Matters remained more or less at this impasse for a quarter century, with both sides reviving the debate from time to time but adding nothing to the meagre information at hand. Coincidentally Rhodesia's Public Works Department undertook an extensive rebuilding program to shore up some parts of the ruins, and in their well-intentioned effort actually redesigned some parts of the ancient structures. Then in 1929 the British Association for the Advancement of Science scheduled the ruins of Rhodesia as the main topic of their annual meeting and once again sought a competent archaeologist to prepare a report. Shortly thereafter, Gertrude Caton-Thompson was dispatched with instructions to undertake 'the examination of the Ruins of Zimbabwe or any monument or monuments of the same kind in Rhodesia, which seem likely to reveal the character, date, and source of the culture of the builders'. Caton-Thompson re-affirmed most of MacIver's findings, adding a number of significant details of her own. Zimbabwe's original foundation, she deduced, using an assortment of beads found at the bottom-most layer of occupation, was constructed somewhere around the 8th or 9th century AD. The earliest settlement of a significant size, she believed, probably dated to the 13th century. She did not set a date for the climactic years of Zimbabwe because of a lack of hard evidence, but she did identify it as somewhat earlier than the rock ruins of Dhlo-Dhlo, 100 miles to the west, which she fixed securely in the early 18th century based upon the discovery of Dutch and Chinese trade goods found at bedrock level.

Lest there be any ambiguity in her findings, she concluded her report with the declaration: 'Examination of all existing evidence . . . still can produce not one single item that is not in accordance with the claim of Bantu origin and mediaeval date. The interest in Zimbabwe and the allied ruins should,' she scolded traditionalists, 'to all educated people be enriched a hundredfold; it enriches, not impoverishes, our wonderment at their remarkable achievement: it cannot detract from their inherent majesty: for the mystery of Zimbabwe is the mystery which lies in the still pulsat-

Nothing at Zimbabwe is more mysterious than the conical tower in the Temple. For years, archaeologists and treasure hunters sought its entrance. But there is none. The tower is solid. There is no easy way of scaling its sides. Was it a watch tower, a religious symbol or just an ornament? Like much of Zimbabwe, this strange building has kept its secret.

ing heart of native Africa'. Though some of that mystery will doubtless remain forever, subsequent efforts not only by archaeologists but by other researchers using carbon-14 dating techniques have yielded a fairly rounded picture of Zimbabwe's past.

Its prime roots, it turns out, lie in the history of the migrations of the Bantu-speaking peoples. Their original home appears to have been somewhere in western Africa, probably in the area of the modern Nigerian-Cameroon border. Perhaps pressure from the north or some attraction to the south sent the first small waves of Bantu on their great migration sometime before the dawn of the Christian era. Over the centuries separate groups, probably no larger than extended families, moved slowly eastwards and southwards, absorbing technologies from indigenous peoples, transmitting their own in return and developing Bantu dialects as they went. The Bantuization of central and southern Africa took nearly 2,000 years and played a critical role in the advancement of sub-Saharan Africans from Stone Age to Iron Age. Ultimately, it led to the creation of powerful political units in areas such as Rhodesia. Though these entities, some relatively localised in their power, others large and wealthy enough to be called kingdoms, developed distinctive characteristics of their own, they all spoke dialects of the same basic language.

By the time Bantu-speaking peoples reached the area of Rhodesia their social structure was based on herding, crop cultivation, the mining and working of iron and other metals, the making of fired-clay pottery, and the construction of pole and *daga* shelters. Based on evidence found in deposits on the Acropolis, an Iron Age settlement was established at Great Zimbabwe in AD 320, give or take 150 years. Those who settled there, the Gokomere people, may have lived at the site as a permanent home or used it as a camp.

Another Bantu-speaking group, the so-called Leopard's Kopje people, were briefly in control from around AD 600 to perhaps AD 850, when the Shona began moving in. The main Shona group and the one most likely to have settled around the future Great Zimbabwe were the Karangas. They appear to have had all the technological expertise of their predecessors plus new, more sophisticated skills. Having migrated from central Africa, probably from iron-rich Katanga, they had an advanced knowledge of iron mining and metallurgy. As they swept down the eastern coast on their way to Great Zimbabwe, they came in contact with the Swahili Bantu and with Arab traders, and thus knew something of trade. Added to this were the superior skills of the Karangas in political organisation. As a result, in a short time they became the overlords of the indigenous Gokomere and Leopard's Kopje people. Not surprisingly, the Rhodesian plateau soon became a beehive of gold, copper and iron production, much used for trade with other Bantu peoples and with Arab merchants on the Indian Ocean. Great Zimbabwe itself does not appear to have produced any gold, the gold fields being well to

the northwest. But it does seem to have been a kind of provincial control or check point.

The Karangas prospered and by the beginning of the 14th century one of their chiefs had, as their oral history relates, risen above all other Karanga chiefs to become their king. By 1440 one of his successors, King Mutota of the Rozwi clan within the larger Karanga nation, had assembled an army. In the following ten years he and his men extended Karanga domination over almost all the Rhodesian plateau. In the process Mutota placed members of his Rozwi clan in many of the important seats of local power, thus assuring the Rozwi a future of orderly succession. Mutota was, in effect, the ruler of an empire, and he took the title of Mwene Mutapa ('master pillager' in the Shona language). Ultimately, Mwene Mutapa, or Monomotapa as the Portuguese wrote it, became the name of the Rozwi-Karanga empire, too.

Mutota had won his power by force. His son and successor, Matope, extended and held it largely through the constraints of the Karanga religious cult. The Karangas worshipped a supreme god, Mwari, creator of the world and everything living in it. A remote god, Mwari was inaccessible to the individual Karanga, except through the intercession of spirits of the ancestors of the ruling dynasties. Essential to calling upon these spirits, called the *mhondoro*, was the remembrance of their names, a task relegated to each community's chiefs and nobles. Thus, Mutota, Matope and other members of the Rozwi clan served a priestly role in addition to their political and economic functions. The stone birds found in the ruins of Great

The great outer wall of the Temple, over 800 ft in circumference, masks a web of inner walls which originally divided the whole area into several distinct enclosures. Each section had its own group of mud huts. Only the huts' bases and some walls remain now, forming a crumbling maze of passages and frustrating dead ends.

Zimbabwe, at first so puzzling, are now thought to have played some part in this religious process, perhaps serving as memorials to dead chieftains. Each bird, though basically similar to the others, bears unique marks; and these, some scholars speculate, could represent a kind of code that a non-literate priest might learn as a reminder of the ancestor with whom he was communicating.

Mwene Mutapa's court apparently moved about the empire as custom or circumstance required. Wherever he dwelled, however, his residence and those of his courtiers consisted of a number of pole and *daga* houses enclosed within a high wall; similar smaller communities were established by provincial chieftains.

It appears that the chiefs held themselves quite apart from their followers, remoteness re-affirming their special role. They were required as well, in their semi-divinity, to be in superior health, so isolation was a practical way of hiding infirmity and reducing the chances of infection. Once age or incurable illness took over, the chiefs were expected to commit suicide and thus clear the way for orderly succession. Nonetheless, they were paid homage when alive and after death – their subjects, for example, approaching them only on their stomachs as a gesture of obeisance.

Powerful as the Mwene Mutapa system may have been, it was nonetheless subject to upheaval relatively soon in its history. Matope died around 1480 and was succeeded by his son, Nyahuma. However, one of his father's Rozwi vassals, Changamire, had acquired suf-

ficient power from his provincial capital – at Great Zimbabwe – to dare to overthrow Nyahuma's rule. War was declared, Nyahuma was killed in battle in 1490, and Changamire became leader of the Rozwi clan and head of the empire.

A few years later Changamire was also killed and the line of succession returned to Mutota's descendants and their capital to the north on the Zambezi river. The new Mwene Mutapa was not successful in rebuilding the empire and the rival state remained separate under Changamire II, with Zimbabwe serving as its religious and political centre.

Though various details of these changes remain uncertain, several chronologies and theories enjoy the support of reputable Africanists. All seem to suggest the existence of four building periods at Great Zimbabwe. As the wealth and power of the kingdom grew, the sites of royal residence and of the worship of Mwari and the *mhondoro* came to be located at formal shrines, frequently situated on hilltops or at other locations favoured by nature. Thus, because of the beauty and lushness of its valley, Great Zimbabwe was probably created as a shrine town. As a result, the earliest of its stone structures probably dates from the third so-called Karanga phase of occupation, 1100 to 1450, the era preceding Mutota's consolidation of the Mwene Mutapa empire. The structures themselves were not the walls of covered palaces or temples, but simply enclosures for clusters of less permanent huts.

Early stonework, as evidenced in the lower portions of the Acropolis' south wall, was relatively crude. Stone blocks were used in their rough natural state, more or less as they were gathered in the local countryside.

Zimbabwe's greatest building phase, and the one which has provoked the greatest admiration among architects, followed the reign of Mutota. This final stage (1440–1833) shows a progressive evolution of artistic and technical skills that stretches to the beginning of the Changamire state. Stone walls are built of granite blocks chosen for uniform size (or dressed to achieve uniformity) and laid up in regular courses. Walls are battered, that is, they recede very gradually as they rise so that the tops are several feet narrower than the lower segments. The steps which carry traffic from one level to the next curve seductively inward as they rise, and the whole construction seems to spring from a single aesthetic source, as if one architect and a crew of expert workers had undertaken its construction. We know, however, that construction at Great Zimbabwe was traditionally a community responsibility with members contributing one day a month, or perhaps several weeks or even months of each year.

This strange soapstone bird perched on a pillar, or stela, is one of eight such carvings found at Great Zimbabwe. Scholars now feel that the birds could have been symbolic memorials to dead ancestors or chiefs. As such, Zimbabwe's priests might have used them to intercede on behalf of those who required the help of the gods.

One building which is generally assigned to the final phase, but about which very little is known, is the Conical Tower, which stands just inside the high outer wall of the Temple. Bent, the British archaeologist, attempted to dig around it – he worked just long enough to destroy valuable stratigraphic materials – and became convinced that it was solid. Gertrude Caton-Thompson, who followed some 40 years later, ran a trench under the tower to inspect it further, and others removed stones in search of interior openings. The tower, however, which resembles in profile certain grain bins of the area, has no interior space. It is solid. Scholars speculate it may have been a phallic symbol representing the chieftains' power.

Though the last phase occurred relatively recently, especially in archaeological terms, virtually all that remains of the smaller houses associated with it are piles of crumbled *daga* and other debris. Such goods as the houses must once have held have been largely destroyed or carried away.

The last people to inhabit Zimbabwe as a city, and a decadent one at that, probably were driven out some-

The ruins of the Acropolis at Zimbabwe look down at the great oval enclosure of the Temple in the plain below. With a few other ruins, they are all that remain of one of history's forgotten empires. Zimbabwe, built by a medieval black race, was a high point in the Iron Age civilisation which flourished in sub-Saharan Africa.

time around 1830 during the Zulu wars. The Amangwas and the other Karangas who subsequently laid claim to Great Zimbabwe did not actually live there, though they did on occasion celebrate ritual sacrifices, probably of cattle, to the god Mwari. Had the white men who came to Great Zimbabwe afterwards been open-minded enough to observe the evidence before them and to listen to the local lore, they would surely have found their answers sooner. And they would certainly have done so with less disruption of the place they themselves have come to venerate as one of the architectural triumphs of the world.

MITCHELL ADAMS

Splendour in the jungle at Angkor

For 400 years, the encroaching jungle hid a secret from the eyes of man. In the central plain of Cambodia stood the crumbling ruins of the civilisation of Angkor, the watery city-state where, for centuries, patient rice farmers, with the guidance of their god-kings, learned to control their hostile environment. They left their thanks, in the shape of scores of soaring sandstone tower-temples, and a mystery: why were these places abandoned?

It was little more than a century ago that Henri Mouhot first clapped eyes on the astonishing ruins of Angkor deep in the dense jungles of northern Cambodia. Mouhot, a French naturalist, had gone to Indochina in search of rare birds and insects, and like most Europeans of his day he looked upon the region as semi-barbaric – poor in history, poorer yet in technological skills. Yet there before him was incontrovertible proof of a brilliant ancient civilisation. Extending as far as the eye could see was a magnificent city with hundreds of daringly constructed towers, with the remnants of vast artificial waterways and broad, monumental highways. And everywhere there was sculpture, some of it in low relief, some colossal in size and free-standing, the work of thousands of artists.

'It is grander than anything left to us by Greece or Rome,' Mouhot recorded excitedly in his diary for January 1860 after gazing on the 200-ft-high temple-tomb of Angkor Wat outside the city walls. 'To obtain any idea of its splendour one must imagine the most beautiful creations of architecture transported into the depths of the forests in one of the more remote countries in the world.'

When local people were asked who had built these remarkable structures, they said variously that it was 'the work of Pra-Eun, the king of the angels', or it was 'the work of giants'. Others claimed that Angkor was created by the Leper King or that 'it made itself'. Mouhot concluded sadly that the names of the rulers,

Like guards, these giant stone statues flank the broad causeways which lead into the heart of the great capital city of Angkor Thom. They are supporting huge stone nagas – divine snakes and protective spirits of the Khmer empire – which form the balustrades.

243

the artists, even the race of people who had lived there 'seem destined to remain hidden among the chaos and ashes of the past'. Had Mouhot been able to pursue his curiosity at length, he might have been able to find at least some of the answers, but he died of tropical fever the year following his discovery; and the quest, which his reports inspired, passed to others.

In 1866 the French government, already an established presence in Indochina, began a systematic study of these fabulous ruins. An exploration commission began drawing up a list of principal monuments. Subsequent missions copied inscriptions written on Angkor buildings so scholars might translate them and, perhaps, learn something of Angkor's history. By 1885 they had worked up a chronology of the rulers and developed the outlines of a description of the civilisation that had produced the wondrous city.

The more the French learned, the more diligent was their pursuit of its inner mysteries, and in 1898 they decided to commit substantial funds to Angkor's physical preservation. Centuries of neglect had permitted the jungle to recapture many of the more significant structures, and unless efforts were made soon to free the buildings from the vegetal embrace of huge banyan and silk-cotton trees, they might be crushed to destruction. Gradually teams of labourers and archaeologists pushed back the jungle and exposed the acres of stone. Gradually the sun was permitted once again to illuminate the dark corners of ancient Angkor and to dispel some of its mystery.

This much they could document: Angkor had been constructed by a south-east Asian people known as the Khmers, and from this place they had flourished culturally, militarily and technologically for some 500 years. Still not completely answered, and perhaps destined to remain a matter of controversy, was the question of Angkor's sudden downfall and the disappearance of its people in the 15th century AD.

The history of the kingdom of Angkor began coincidentally with the dawning of the Christian era, when trade and other contacts between India and south-east

A dancing girl holding a lotus bud in each hand is one of many intricately carved figures that decorate the walls of Preah Khan, a temple dedicated to Jayavarman VII's father.

Asia started to evolve. Where loosely organised communities worshipping a variety of nature gods had existed, small states grew. Partly based on Indian civilisation, they took their spiritual inspiration from India too. Within a few years a state roughly corresponding to modern Cambodia, called Phnom, or Funan, meaning 'mountain', had been formed.

A legendary founder of Funan is memorialised in Cambodian and Khmer tales: a Brahman named Kaundinya was directed by a heavenly spirit to set sail eastward. After a difficult journey he came to shore along the Cambodian coast, where a beautiful young woman paddled out in her canoe to greet him. At first delighted at the prospect of so charming a hostess, Kaundinya was soon dismayed to find that she was Queen Willow Leaf, ruler of the country and daughter of a serpent deity, and hostile to his arrival. When she declared her intention to seize his ship and destroy him, he shot a magic arrow into her craft.

The queen instantly recognised that she was no match for the visitor and withdrew her threats after which the two made peace. Shortly after, they were married, so the legend goes; and from their union was born the ancestor of all Funan rulers and of later

At the height of its power, the ancient Khmer empire covered the whole of Democratic Kampuchea – formerly Cambodia – parts of southern Vietnam, Laos and Thailand. The natural centre of this enormous territory – an empire founded on the efficient cultivation of rice – was the plain of Angkor on the northern shore of the great lake Tonle Sap.

generations of Khmer rulers. In any case, the kingdom of Funan prospered for more than five centuries, developing an extraordinary network of irrigation and transportation canals that made the huge Mekong river valley fertile and the country rich with commerce.

Then, around AD 550, the Funan kingdom was overthrown – by the Kambujas, a mountain people living in what is now Laos but was then called Chenla. Seeing an opportunity to free themselves from Funan dominance – Funan defences had grown weak and a flood had ravaged the Mekong – they struck. Led by a king who was a rival descendant of the Funan royal line, the Kambujas, or Chenlas, first took over Funan and then its empire. Like the Funanese, they were

closely tied to Hindu tradition and they worshipped Hindu deities such as Vishnu, Brahma and most especially Siva, the god of destruction and creation. Their warlike course was brought to an end in the 8th century when a king from Java invaded and conquered the country and beheaded the Chenla ruler. Though the Javanese invaders withdrew, years passed before the Chenlas were able to regain any of their past might.

The first great Cambodian (Kambujan) leader – Jayavarman II – appeared in AD 802. And with Jayavarman was launched the brilliant Khmer empire and a royal dynasty that was to flourish for more than 600 years. Not only was Jayavarman (the name means 'protector of victory') a military genius, he was also an administrative one. And during his 48 years on the throne, he succeeded in melding his people into a unified state and keeping that state militarily strong and safe from invaders.

After declaring the Khmers independent from the hegemony of Java, the then dominant nation in south-

---

Strangled by the roots of a fig tree, the serene stone face of Buddha is still recognisable as it slowly disappears under the relentless attack of nature. The carving is at Ta Som, the temple north-east of Angkor Thom.

east Asia, Jayavarman II sought a new capital for the empire. He set up his government, after some experimentation, on the Phnom Kulen, or Mountain of Kulen, overlooking the plain of Angkor in Cambodia. There he brought an Indian 'skilled in magic science' to exorcise all foreign demons and to establish forever the protection of his city and empire by Siva, the all powerful divinity. To secure further his own position he had himself declared the god-king, the earthly incarnation of Siva and the link between mankind and the spirits. This cult, which was to provide the mantle of legitimacy for 30 Khmer kings, became the basis of social and political order in Cambodia and its growing dependencies. It also became the inspiration behind the feverish building that created the great urban complex on and above the plain of Angkor.

The capital of Phnom Kulen proved rather unsuitable for an administrative centre. Though it was well conceived as a defensive site, it stood too high above the fertile agricultural plain to enjoy easily the prosperity on which the country was based. Perhaps Jayavarman II had chosen it in deference to the common Buddhists' belief that gods and spirits make their dwelling place on mountaintops like that of the most holy Hindu mountain, the legendary Mt Meru.

In time Jayavarman recognised the error and moved his capital about 20 miles south-west to the fertile plain below. The region of Angkor was dotted with lakes and rivers, chief among them Tonle Sap, a 100-mile-long natural catch basin for the storing of seasonal flood waters. Fish and rice, then as now the two staples in the Khmers' diet, thrived there, and a generous supply of wood was easily accessible.

Jayavarman created a hereditary office of high priest to assist in the tasks of administration, and with the high priest he established a religious hierarchy to supervise every aspect of national life. The worship of the royal *lingam*, a phallic representation of the god-king and his creative power, became the centre of religious observance and ceremony. Jayavarman began the practice of constructing massive stone temples to house the royal *lingam* – a practice followed by his successors – thus giving rise to a distinctive Khmer type of religious edifice. Where previous kings had been content to erect relatively short-lived wood and brick structures on a more modest scale, the new Khmer kings demanded towering temples of sandstone whose design took inspiration from nothing less than the mountains of their ancestral homeland.

Jayavarman II's ambitions for building a capital were fractured repeatedly by wars with his neighbours, and it was not until his nephew Indravarman I took the throne in AD 877 that the Khmers built Hariharalaya, 15 miles south-east of the site that was to become Angkor Thom, the Great City.

In his 11-year reign Indravarman directed a survey of the nation's resources, drew up a plan for their intelligent management, and conscripted thousands of foreign artisans to design and execute extensive irrigation systems. To undertake the most arduous jobs, like

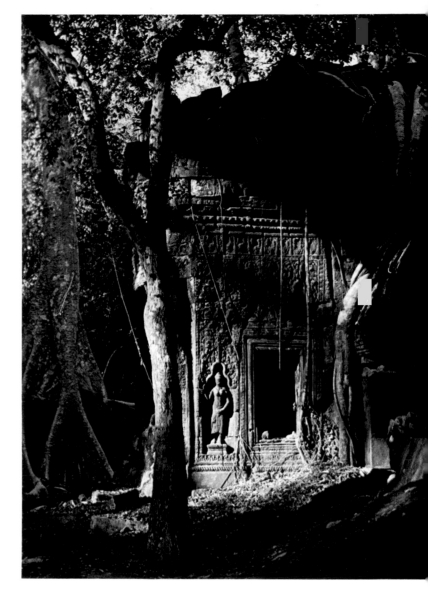

The monastery of Ta Prohm, built in 1186 by Jayavarman VII in memory of his mother, once covered more than 150 acres and housed more than 12,000 people. Now, silent and overgrown after centuries of disuse, its only inhabitants are birds and monkeys, and perhaps the spirits of a lost age.

building barays, raised water storage lakes, he used slave labour from throughout his empire.

Thanks to Indravarman's ambitious plans, Khmer farmers were subsequently able to draw water in the long winter-spring dry season as well as in the wet monsoon months of May through October, and they could rely on a degree of control of the Mekong river when it reached its annual flood stage. Three rice crops a year became a possibility, and fish were in such abundance as to feed everyone to their fill. In a land where the fertility of the soil and the bounty of the lakes and rivers were linked to the beneficence of the gods, the king's efforts in ensuring good harvests left

Angkor, a civilisation founded on water

Angkor Thom, the remarkable capital of the Khmer empire, was an almost perfect combination of religious faith and economic necessity. Seeing the need to control, store and distribute the waters of the monsoons so rice would flourish, the Khmer kings led the peasants in an ambitious building programme. They created great reservoirs and canals to feed the rice, and mighty temples to win the favour of the gods. This reconstruction shows how Angkor's monumental centre (a huge population lived in surrounding villages) looked at its height in the 12th century AD. Today, apart from the two barays, or reservoirs [1, 2], on either side of the city which are fed by rivers such as the Stung Siem Reap [3] from the nearby hills, the irrigation network of Angkor has dried up or become clogged with vegetation. The rice fields have been swallowed by the forest, but much of the architecture remains, showing the changing styles of the centuries. The master work of Khmer art is the temple-mountain, a symbol of Mt Meru, which in Hindu mythology dominates the universe. The temple-mountain usually consists of between one and five towers at the summit of a pyramid, with a staircase on each of the four sides. The Bakheng [4] was the first built on

this plan; it is on a natural hill and made of sandstone, unlike the Baksei Chamkrong [5], the Mebon [6] and the Pre Rup [7], all of which have brick towers standing on pyramids made of iron-oxide-rich rock. Later temples were more elaborate, with open galleries connecting different sanctuaries, as at the Ta Keo [8], the Phimeanakas [9] and the Baphuon [10]. The most magnificent temple is Angkor Wat [11], the triumph of Suryavarman II's reign (1113–50). The Bayon [12] shows a radical change in style. The principle of superimposed terraces circled by galleries is retained, but the distinct influence of Buddhism is seen in the appearance of towers with faces, an innovation of Jayavarman VII (about 1200). Although the general plan of Angkor Thom [13] remains classical and clear, the temples became more complex and their symbolism more confused. The temple of Neak Pean [14] has multiple basins, meant to be replicas of a miraculous spring in the Himalayas. In this period, before the decline of the Khmer empire following the death of Jayavarman VII in 1218, there was a remarkable surge of new building. The temples of Preah Khan [15], Banteay Kdei [16], Ta Prohm [17] and Ta Som [18] all date from this period.

0   500   1,000 yds

This statue, called the Leper King, damaged by time, may commemorate Yasovarman I, an early Khmer ruler who died of leprosy. It presides over the terrace at Angkor Thom where royal funerals once took place. Its walls are decorated with bas-reliefs of ceremonial parades, nagas and fishes.

no doubt that he was, as he said, the earthly manifestation of Siva.

Following traditional Hindu cosmology, the new city was conceived as a symbolic universe and regarded with all the reverence traditionally accorded a holy place. Forced to work in its behalf for part of every year throughout their lives, the Khmer people in all probability accepted the labour as part of their worshipful duty to Siva and the other gods.

Angkor Thom and the smaller provincial cities constructed elsewhere in the empire were arranged around one or more pyramid-temples in which were lodged the final remains of the great kings, or in some cases lesser aristocracy, and in which various cults

From a distance the temple of Bayon seems to be a chaotic mass of lifeless stone, without form. But closer inspection reveals a forest of faces – all the calm, enigmatic likeness of Buddha. His face is carved on each side of every pillar so that nothing escapes his gaze.

were celebrated. Inevitably, the structures built under Indravarman would later seem modest compared to those of his successors, each striving to dominate the rising skyline only to be outdone by the next.

However, a recitation of Indravarman's contributions to Angkor is impressive. A year after he came to the throne he ordered the excavation of a baray 5 miles long by a mile wide. Two years later he dedicated the temple of Preah Ko to his ancestors. In 881 he began the Bakong, the first great monument built entirely of masonry in Angkor and the beginning of the classical Khmer architectural style that was to reach its full development in the first half of the 12th century. Crowned by a single central tower, transected by axial staircases, the shrine houses a representation of the royal *lingam*. Ringing Bakong at lower levels are 12 smaller shrines and a number of secondary towers.

Indravarman's son and successor, Yasovarman I, was no less prolific. In honour of his father, he constructed a funerary temple in the middle of a lake. Then he went on to erect a stone pyramid to himself and a baray to the east of the royal city nearly 5 sq. miles in size. And so the work continued from generation to generation, this remarkable city growing outwards and upwards as the wealth and power of the empire grew. Eventually it sprawled over nearly 400 sq. miles, the city's vast population living in a series of villages and forts radiating out from the monuments.

In the 12th and 13th centuries, the kingdom of Angkor reached its peak under the reigns of two mighty kings: Suryavarman II, the 'protector of the sun' (1113–50) and Jayavarman VII (1181–c. 1219).

Suryavarman extended the power of Angkor from the China Sea to the Indian Ocean. His reign was marked by a brief but spectacular outburst of genius that gave birth to one of the most brilliant architectural creations in all Asia and what was to be the summit of Khmer artistry – the temple-tomb of Angkor Wat.

Angkor Wat mingles artistic vigour with ornamental delicacy and subtle architectural spacial arrangements to show the full flowering of Khmer art and power. Atop the structure are towers at each of the four corners and a fifth tower, 213 ft high, rises above the centre of the pyramid where the king's ashes may have been placed. All surfaces of the temple are covered with inch-deep reliefs, which delighted Mouhot.

He was especially enthusiastic about the scenes depicting the punishments of the infernal regions. 'While the elect, who are enjoying themselves in Paradise, are all fat and plump, the poor condemned beings are so lean that their bones show, and the expression of their faces is pitiful and full of a most comic seriousness. Some are being pounded in mortars, while others hold them by the feet and hands;

The Hindu influence is shown in this group of dancers which adorn the walls of the exquisite pink sandstone temple built at Banteay Srei by an early Brahman ruler.

Smiling Buddhas watch over the four corners of the earth from one of the gates of Angkor. Mahayana, or 'Great Vehicle', Buddhism – which became the dominant religion in the reign of Jayavarman VII – produced a new style in decoration.

Standing guard in one of the sanctuaries of the temple of Banteay Srei is this figure of Garuda – the bird which carries the god Vishnu in Hindu mythology.

some are being sawn asunder; others are led along, like buffaloes, with ropes through their noses.'

Mouhot thought the bas-reliefs exquisite. Examples of sculpture in the round were far less numerous but he found them nonetheless impressive. A magnificent 30-ft-wide causeway paved with huge blocks of sandstone and leading to the temple's main gate is lined with colossal likenesses of the *nagas*, the guardian spirits of Indian legend.

Remarkable as Angkor Wat is artistically, it has another distinction among temples that continues to puzzle scholars of Cambodian archaeology: the temple is situated so that its main gate faces west, a singular instance of such orientation among the temple-tombs of the Khmer empire.

Tradition was that all major ceremonial buildings faced east, west being the compass point associated with death, and it was long supposed that Suryavarman's break with custom was a subtle indication that he had some presentiment of the frailty of his enormous undertakings. Some recent studies, however, are tending toward an astronomical explanation. Scientists have argued forcibly that the placing and internal proportions of the temple all reflect an intimate awareness of the sun's movement throughout the year and are attempts to integrate the calendar, astronomy and religious mythology all in one.

With the passing of Suryavarman the Khmer empire entered a period of decline, for there was no direct heir. First to succeed was a cousin, perhaps the son of one of Suryavarman's uncles. Then, when the cousin died, an even more difficult struggle for the throne evolved. The claimants were the dead king's son, Jayavarman – the rightful heir who was later to become Jayavarman VII – and Yasovarman II, a close relative, perhaps even a brother. Finally, to avoid conflict, Jayavarman, a deeply religious man, went into exile. Yet the empire's troubles continued, first with the death of Yasovarman II in a civil uprising and then, in 1170, with a murderous invasion by the neighbouring Chams. Raping, pillaging, burning and killing wantonly, the Chams eventually seized control of Angkor. Though the Khmer armies drove them back, the damage had been done: the Cambodian people no longer believed in their government, king or religion.

Enter Jayavarman once again. Seeing his nation so demoralized, he finally took the throne to, as the chronicles put it, 'draw the earth out of the sea of misfortune into which it was plunged'. The task was enormous. Not only had the people lost faith but the many vassal states living uneasily under Khmer rule for so long had begun to have ambitions of their own during the period of unsettlement. Jayavarman VII, already in his fifties, showed himself to be not only a

One of the most beautiful of the Khmer temples, Banteay Srei, 'the fortress of women', was founded in 967 by the Brahman King Rajendravarman. It is elaborately ornamented with carvings and relief-figure sculpture illustrating Hindu mythology.

saviour, as he was soon dubbed, but also a man of steel.

After careful preparation he launched a merciless counterattack against the Chams, returning their brutal acts of war with retributions still more harsh. The rebellion was crushed, lesser principalities were intimidated and Angkor was once again supreme.

Khmer art and architecture also enjoyed a renaissance under this vigorous new king. At his direction the building of Angkor's magnificent royal city complex was resumed. An inscription recalls that 'the king wedded himself to this town . . . in order to beget the happiness of the universe'.

Marking out a section of the Angkor plain for his own as so many of his predecessors had done, he rebuilt Angkor Thom as his royal capital. To the original walls of the city he added 10 miles more. He also had constructed a number of imposing monuments, including the temples Ta Prohm, dedicated to

The mountain-temple of Bakheng, begun in 893 to the order of Yasovarman I, has 108 tower shrines, which stand for the heavens, the worlds and the moon. Bakheng was the centre of the capital and symbolic centre of the universe, representing Mt Meru, home of the gods in Indian mythology.

his mother, and Preah Khan, dedicated to his father. He was responsible for enlargements made on a number of earlier temples about the city, and the Terrace of the Elephants and the Terrace of the Leper King, both large ceremonial plazas near the palace. Jayavarman VII, who seems to have suffered from a form of urban developer's megalomania in his later years, also had constructed temples in all the major provincial cities of the empire in which the new cult of the Buddha king could be celebrated. And he ordered 102 hospitals and 121 hostelries built, the latter as way stations along the hundreds of miles of highways.

The most unusual of all the king's projects was, understandably, the temple dedicated to himself and to Buddha within Angkor Thom. Called the Bayon, it represented significant changes in architectural style and, unfortunately, in building techniques. Compared with the majestic Angkor Wat, this temple-mountain is cluttered and confusing in appearance, with 51 towers making its profile difficult to comprehend. Also unusual is the sculpture: huge smiling faces, representations of Jayavarman VII in the aspects of Buddha, cover all four sides of each tower as if to keep watch on the four corners of the earth.

The work of building the Bayon and all Jayavar-

man's other undertakings was carried on at an almost frantic pace in order that they would be completed before the elderly king died. Many fine old temples had to be torn down to make space and perhaps to provide the sandstone for newer construction as the quarries were rapidly running out of first-class stone. Workmanship tended to be shoddy, with the stone fitting less expertly than in earlier temples, a factor that has made the Bayon's conservation somewhat more difficult than some of the other temples.

Jayavarman VII died about 1219. An inscription on one of his buildings declares: 'The King suffers from the pains of his subjects more than from his own.' It was ironic that his extensive building plan, the most ambitious of any of the Khmer kings, was to sap the empire of its energy and hasten its decline.

From the 13th century onward, no Khmer king undertook a project anything like the scale of Jayavarman VII's enterprises. Many social and economic factors combined to weaken the empire, chief amongst them was the gradual migration of the Thais and the Vietnamese southward out of the Khmer sphere of control. But even in decline the Khmer empire was

magnificent. From all those centuries we have one dazzling glimpse of Khmer splendour. The curtain is momentarily lifted by a Chinese commercial envoy and traveller, Chou Ta-kuan, who arrived in the capital in 1296. During his long stay in the city, Chou Ta-kuan kept a record of his impressions and observations that give a priceless picture of life in Angkor 700 years ago. The careful Chinese observer wrote it all down in his *Notes on the Customs of Cambodia*.

At Angkor Thom, Chou Ta-kuan watched the daily procession of the people through the guarded entrances of the capital. Only dogs and criminals were denied admittance. He walked the city lanes, admiring the dwellings of princes which were built facing the rising sun and could easily be distinguished from the thatched houses of the peasants because of their round tiled roofs. He described the activities of servants who worked on the ground floors while their masters held meetings above.

Chou Ta-kuan had the rare experience of being admitted to the heart of the capital, where he saw the Bayon in its original condition. He described a gold tower flanked by more than 20 smaller towers and

The austere mass of sandstone of Angkor Wat is relieved and balanced by intricate carving. Above, the rays of the setting sun fall through a window to illuminate the temple. To the right, a carving from the walls of the Bayon in Angkor Thom illustrates the battle between the Khmers and the invading Chams, who captured Angkor in 1177.

hundreds of stone houses. He told of a gold bridge guarded by two gold lions at the eastern side of the complex – wonders which have long since vanished.

Chou Ta-kuan observed the king at first-hand, at royal audiences which he attended as a member of the ambassadorial party. He wrote: 'The king gives two audiences a day for the disposition of affairs of state . . . Dignitaries and common people alike come and sit on the floor of the council hall and wait for him. After a while, music is heard from far inside the palace, and men outside the hall begin to blow on sea-shell trumpets to welcome the king. Then two women of the royal household step forward and raise a curtain and the king is seen at the gold-framed window with the sacred sword in his hand. All those who have come to the audience clasp their hands together and bow down until their foreheads touch the earth . . . and so they remain until the trumpeting ceases. Then they are permitted to sit upright again and face the king. If he permits, they may come closer to him and as a mark of special dignity may be allowed to sit on a lion-skin that is near him. When he has transacted the day's business he turns about and the girls draw down the curtain

Long galleries, facing the four points of the compass, surround each of the terraces at Angkor Wat, linking the shrines, corner towers and stairways. The walls of the galleries are decorated with carvings depicting Hindu epics. Angkor Wat, the best-preserved monument of the Khmer civilisation, dates from the 12th century.

255

again. Then everyone leaves the royal presence.'

In addition to the impressive court ceremonies, Chou Ta-kuan described the king himself, a colourful portrait in contrast to the grey bas-reliefs. The king, he said, dressed in rich fabrics and wore either a gold diadem or garlands of jasmine and other flowers twined in his hair. He wore pounds of pearls and bracelets, anklets and rings of precious stones set in gold. The pomp and prosperity of Angkor clearly astonished the Chinese visitor, and he was there only during the kingdom's fading years.

Chou Ta-kuan also recorded something of the darker side of Khmer life. He saw close up the events of daily life when he lived with a Khmer family. He described what we would call an affluent society organised as a hierarchy. He did not envy the people at the bottom of the structure, whom he described as coarse, with sun-burnt complexions indicating their low status. Below these working people, who were farmers and craftsmen, were the slaves. These people,

Most of the monuments of Angkor depict only royal and religious scenes. But this carving, made to extol the care of Jayavarman VII for his subjects, also records many scenes of everyday life. It is part of a frieze on the Bayon and shows boating parties, people fishing and family life.

whom Chou Ta-kuan called 'a separate race', had no privileges and were completely subservient.

Chou Ta-kuan noted many of the details of city life. He wrote down everything he saw on his walks, and his descriptions of private life were particularly detailed. He wrote of a modest home: 'People of this class have a house but it lacks everything – table, bench, bowl or bucket. They have an earthenware stewpot for cooking rice and a cooking pot in which they make the sauce. They build their fire over three stones in the ground and use a coconut shell as a spoon.' The contrast between this humble dwelling and the palaces of the wealthy and the splendour of the temples of the gods did not escape him. Between the lines of Chou Ta-kuan's notes can be seen the last flourish of a fading empire, like the bright rays of a setting sun.

What else we know of ordinary life in Angkor comes from the reign of Jayavarman VII. Under his influence, the temple decorations, of which Bayon is a good example, became more than the records of the heroic and legendary acts of kings and gods. The day-to-day activities of his subjects were recorded in the bas-reliefs along with battle scenes celebrating the Khmers' victory over the Chams. On the walls of Bayon are friezes of fishing parties, the preparation of feasts, cock fights and a mother with her child. It is another of the ironies of Angkor's history that, while the grandeur represented by the temples has disappeared into the jungle, the everyday tasks pictured in these few sculptures are still performed in Cambodia today.

Night finally descended over Angkor two centuries later when, in 1431, the city fell to the Siamese. The end came in an all-out attack and a siege that lasted seven months. The Siamese returned home with as much loot as they could carry, planning to return the next year for more. But when they reappeared, they found the city deserted. Where more than a million people had once lived, there was no one. Where they went, history does not record.

In the centuries that followed, nature began to reclaim its territory. The huge reservoirs, the canals, the roadways and bridges all succumbed to the stealthy invasion of the jungle. And as farming became less and less productive without the administrative genius of the government to keep it going, even the population in the outlying districts thinned.

Today, 500 years after it was so mysteriously abandoned, Angkor faces yet another threat – the wanton man-made incursions of war. Even now it is not clear how these magnificent shrines survived the recent fighting that brought Cambodia under Communist control. Undoubtedly, they suffered damages, but whether slight or massive, easily reparable or disastrous, no official of what is now called Democratic Kampuchea has indicated. Nor has the new government spoken of the future, a future that clearly demands that Henri Mouhot's lost city be transformed once again into a treasure for all the world.

DAVID ROBERTS

The artificial lake of Sras Srang, above, is watched over by the nagas of Hindu mythology – divine snakes and spirits of the water – from the landing stage which was once used for the launching of royal boat processions.

Carvings made on the walls of the Bayon during the reign of King Jayavarman VII portray the daily life of the peasants. The scene below shows men at a cock fight – still a popular pastime in many parts of south-east Asia.

The Olmecs,
a race of precursors

Only a century ago, the Olmecs were entirely unknown, yet today they are regarded as the creators of the first civilisation of America, the precursors of the splendours that were to come with the cities of the Mayas. The intensive work of archaeologists has revealed little of their culture except that it influenced much of the Middle American world beginning in the 13th century BC and lasting until these mysterious people died obscurely 12 centuries later.

The Gulf of Mexico is unpromising territory for such precocious beginnings. Low-lying, swampy land, it was once covered in dense, advancing tropical jungle, periodically flooded by a network of rivers and streams. Yet it was there, on small islands rising from lagoons, that the Olmecs created the first sizeable ceremonial centres of Middle America.

Only four sites in the Mexican states of Veracruz and Tabasco have been explored – Laguna de los Cerros, San Lorenzo, Tres Zapotes and La Venta. In the surrounding forested plains are many rubber-bearing trees. From a later Indian name for rubber, *ollin*, the people who created this culture were given the name Olmec.

La Venta must have been the largest religious centre in Mexico at the height of the Olmec civilisation between 800 and 500 BC. Its architectural arrangement is remarkable, foreshadowing as it does the ceremonial town planning of pre-Columbian Mexico. There is a small stepped pyramid with a quadrangle in front of it, edged with basalt pillars, and nearby two parallel mounds forming the boundaries of the oldest sacred ball-game court in the Americas. The complex is completed by what looks like a large man-made model of a volcano, probably used as a burial ground.

Inside these enclosures, which must have been intended for religious ceremonies, carved stone slabs have been discovered, together with richly decorated altars and, most remarkable of all, the huge basalt heads which are perhaps the most striking works of Olmec art. The heads are curiously flattened in appearance and have thick, heavy lips with down-drawn corners, slit eyes and short broad noses, an unusual facial type which has puzzled anthropologists and led to much speculation.

The Olmecs were not only great sculptors, but also notable carvers of jade, from which they shaped statuettes, jewellery and axes. Towards the end of their history they seem to have interested themselves increasingly in mathematics and in the calendar. It is thought that they developed the system of writing numbers inherited by the Mayas.

But after reaching the high point of their achievement – and subsequently passing on this splendid legacy to the Mayas and other successors – the Olmec people seem to have collapsed and disappeared. The circumstances of that disappearance, if they were known, would no doubt transform our understanding of American prehistory. But the Olmecs have left no records save for their strange sculpture, calendrical inscriptions and the ruins of their buildings. Their end is as mysterious as were their origins in such inhospitable jungle territory.

HENRI STIERLIN

This green stone statue was venerated as an image of the Virgin and Child in the church of the Mexican village near which it was found. In fact it is an 8th century BC Olmec carving showing a male figure carrying one of the Olmec gods, probably the rain god. Often this Olmec god took the form of a half-human, half-jaguar figure. The markings on the face and limbs, together with the thick drooping lips and slit eyes, are characteristic features of Olmec sculpture. A male figure holding a child-like god is a common motif of Olmec art.

This basalt pillar, topped by a face straining towards the sky, is one of the enigmas of the Olmec world. What is this creature apparently lost in contemplation of the heavens? Is it a star worshipper? Or an astronomer? Is it a man, or could it be an animal? Some specialists have suggested, in fact, that it is a monkey.

This group of statuettes, made of jade and serpentine, was an Olmec ritual piece. It had been buried a few feet underground at La Venta. The figures are about 8 in. tall. They were originally closer together than they are here, but they were arranged in the same concentric pattern facing another statuette, one made of red stone. This central statuette has its back to a sort of palisade or fence made of six jade axe-like tools. Is it a priest addressing a congregation of worshippers, or a prisoner on the point of being executed? The meaning is still a mystery but the figures, carved towards the end of the Olmec era, were clearly arranged to make a scene charged with dramatic atmosphere.

The Olmecs, a race of precursors

Olmec civilisation flourished 3,200 years ago on the south
coast of the Gulf of Mexico, in the damp, swampy lowlands
of Veracruz and Tabasco. Wars and conquest spread its
influence far and wide. It reached the land of the Mayas to the
south-east and the country of the Zapotecs of Monte Albán
in the west. Eventually it spread across Central Mexico
leaving a cultural imprint to the land later occupied by the
ambitious builders of Teotihuacán and El Tajín.
Geographically and historically it was the crucible in which
was forged the mysterious civilisation of pre-Columbian
Middle America – an advanced civilisation which
archaeologists are only now beginning to discover.

Seated in an alcove hollowed out in the front of a basalt altar hewn from a single block of stone, a man wearing a sort of crown holds in his right hand a rope, which is round the wrist of a figure shown on the side panel of the altar. This figure is probably a prisoner who is to be sacrificed to the Olmec gods. This custom persisted until the time of the Aztecs, who carried out human sacrifice by cutting out the heart or by decapitation. The alcove may represent the open jaws of the jaguar god, whose eyes and canine teeth appear in the upper part of the altar. The crouching figure would then emerge from the mouth of the animal, which could be the Tepeyolohtli, or 'heart of the earth'. The symbolic meaning of this scene is probably now lost forever. The altar is from the principal Olmec site at La Venta.

The skill that Olmec artists brought to carving colossal works can also be seen in tiny figures like this statuette, known as the 'Weeping Child'. It is just under 5 in. high, and is made of jade, a favourite material of the Olmecs, who were the first pre-Columbian people to use it. The very broad nose, thick lips and down-turned mouth are typical of the Olmec facial type. The head, disproportionately large in relation to the rest of the body, is that of a baby – a subject which Olmec artists frequently depicted, sometimes with the features of a jaguar.

The Olmecs,
a race
of precursors

This stone slab, known as the King's Stele, comes from the Olmec religious centre of La Venta and is about 9 ft high. It shows several figures in bas-relief. Standing out amongst them is the form of a high dignitary who clasps in both hands a sort of crook – either a weapon or a symbol of authority – and wears an elaborate multi-tiered head-dress. The figures surrounding this warrior-king are vassals who have come to pay him homage in token of submission. The subjects of this stele, or upright stone slab, can be related to those found later on the Mayan steles of the pre-classical period at Kaminaljuyú, Guatemala, and those of the classical period at Copán, Honduras. The association of such steles with nearby temples was a feature that was continued by other pre-Columbian civilisations. The practice of dating steles, which is characteristic of Mayan civilisation, seems to have started with the Olmecs who had developed their own calendar and astronomy at least 2,500 years ago.

The Olmecs, a race of precursors

This colossal head, which is almost 9 ft high, was carved from a single block of basalt weighing about 18 tons. Today at least 14 of these strange, disapproving heads are known. The largest is more than 10 ft high and weighs 30 tons. Blocks like this must have been carried on rafts by river from the quarries, the closest of which were some 60 miles away. This implies the existence of a powerful and efficient social organisation. These colossal heads were never attached to statues and generally are believed to be portraits of Olmec leaders, although some archaeologists have argued that they represent the decapitated heads of losers in the sacred ball game. Certainly their helmets could represent the protective headgear worn by players of the dangerous game, which was played with a heavy rubber ball, weighing as much as 3¼ lbs.

A man holding a sort of censer in his hand is crushed in the coils of a huge snake which seems to be watching over a sarcophagus. The mysterious nature of the subject and the free style in which it has been carved out of a single undressed block of stone give this Olmec carving from La Venta an extraordinary expressive power, for the artist has used the stone's natural shape to add force to his curling design. The snake, which often represented the plumed serpent god, had considerable religious significance in the later pre-Columbian world. It was the symbol of the sun and a potent motif in Mexican mythology.

This statue in porous stone, known as The Wrestler, is one of the masterpieces of pre-Columbian sculpture. Its vigour of movement and attitude, and the sensitive use of relief to emphasise the muscle structure, create a particularly forceful impression. The man shown here has fine features, a beard and a moustache, whereas the more usual Olmec type is clean-shaven with heavy features. The position of the hips and arms has led some people to believe that he is not a wrestler but a ball-game player on the point of returning the ball.

The magnificent realm of the Mayas

*Even today, life in the tropical rain forest of
Middle America is an unending struggle for survival.
So how was it that a flourishing civilisation
was created there by a race of Stone Age men?
Without the wheel and with no metal the Mayas built
great cities, developed a brilliant artistic culture
and evolved a system of mathematics the equal
of any in the world. Who were these mysterious
people whose classic civilisation collapsed before
Columbus discovered America, but whose works
still arouse the wonder of modern man?*

When the Spanish *conquistadores* reached Yucatán, in south-eastern Mexico, they found tropical forests where primitive Indian tribes lived in thatched huts built of wattle and daub. Yet the same forests concealed deserted cities of stone, half-buried beneath the rampant vegetation. They were cities dominated by gigantic pyramids rising as high as 230 ft, with palaces that rivalled in size all but the biggest in Europe, all built by the ravaged civilisation of the Mayas.

The Spaniards had little interest in and no understanding for the past glories of their American con-

quests, and it was only in the 19th century that historians started to take an interest in Mayan civilisation. When they explored the forests they were surprised to find mounds covering buildings which had been ruined by the invading jungle. It seemed incredible that these great architectural creations could be attributable to ancestors of the primitive Indians of their own day, who roamed the forests or lived in isolated villages scattered across the Yucatán lowlands.

The historians tried to reconcile these vast cultural differences by producing explanations such as the theory that the great pre-Columbian civilisations had originated outside the Americas. They suggested, for example, that Mayan culture might have been founded by the ancient Egyptians, by one of the lost tribes of Israel, by Greek colonists, or even by the Scythians, the Chinese, or immigrants from south-east Asia. But the mysterious origins of the Mayas, and the baffling

---

This carved stone slab, typical of the style of sculpture at Palenque, shows a Mayan ruler with a crown of quetzal feathers. He is wearing elaborate ornaments – a breast-plate, necklace and belt. The profile, with a very high bridge to the nose, is typical of the Mayan people.

Looters who destroy the past

As scholars struggle to decipher the elaborate hieroglyphics of the Mayas, much of the most precious evidence is vanishing forever – destroyed by the greedy hands of looters.

Many of the valuable stone inscriptions have disappeared into art collections all over the world. And many of those that can still be traced have had much of their usefulness destroyed because there is no record of the site they came from.

In order to make the inscriptions more easily saleable and moveable, looters have sliced off the faces of heavy stone blocks in the jungles of Middle America, then cut up the sheets into small pieces with chisels and even sledgehammers.

As a result, not only has the knowledge of where they originated been lost, but sometimes the delicate – and often badly eroded – inscriptions have been chipped beyond repair as well.

Mayan cylinder vases have disappeared in the same way: into private collections via a brief stay in an art dealer's shop in Mexico or the United States. And these losses, say the scholars,

are particularly tragic since they often depict royal dignitaries and show scenes from Mayan life – such as ball games, processions and rituals – which carry hieroglyphic texts to explain them, so offering unique keys to translation.

Sometimes looters are so eager to strip a site that they will use force to try to keep archaeologists away. A Scottish expert, Ian Graham, disturbed a group of looters at work on a site at La Naya in northern Guatemala. Soon after, as the group were setting up camp to start their work of recording ancient Mayan texts, shots were fired, and one of Graham's assistants, Pedro Arturo Sierra, was mortally wounded.

At Naranjo, a Mayan site near the border of Guatemala and Belize (formerly British Honduras), half of the 40 known monuments have been scarred by looters. Often the precious carvings have been chopped into innumerable pieces, scattered across the forest by thieves who have been concerned only with what they could take away for profit.

---

grandeur of their architecture, ensure that even today they remain one of the most fascinating of ancient civilisations. It is hard to imagine anything more striking than these vast buildings, with their surprisingly modern lines, surrounded on all sides by almost impenetrable virgin forest. Sunlight shining through tall foliage into the damp gloom beneath reveals crumbled stairways and palaces, which have been invaded by orchids and are inhabited by chittering insects.

The country of the Mayas is in the heart of Middle America. Covering an area about the size of France, it

---

The land of the Mayas covered much of the present Mexican states of Chiapas and Tabasco, the states of Campeche and Yucatán, the territory of Quintana Roo, Belize, almost all of Guatemala and the western fringes of El Salvador and Honduras. Mayan culture reached its height in the most unhealthy part of this vast territory – amid the jungles and swamps of Petén, and in the forests of Chiapas.

spreads across Guatemala, Belize and parts of Mexico, Honduras and El Salvador. The Mayas occupied three separate regions: the southern highlands of Chiapas and Guatemala, together with the steamy coastal plain of the Pacific and western El Salvador; the tropical forests stretching from the Gulf of Mexico to Belize and Honduras but centred on Guatemala's Petén department; and the scrub-covered lowlands of northern Yucatán. From small beginnings about 2500 BC until the climax of their achievement 34 centuries later, the Mayas constantly struggled against the invading forest.

Farming by fire

Before the ground could be cultivated, it had to be cleared, and this was a difficult task. The method most often used then, and still used by the Indians today, was to burn off the plant cover. The Mayas' staple food crop was maize. But they cultivated several species of plants in the same field at the same time. This practice had the advantage of preventing the soil from becoming exhausted too rapidly.

Land cleared of tropical forest, however, is never fertile for more than a few seasons, and each field was usually cultivated only briefly, then abandoned once more to the scrub and the insects. Even so, the Mayas found time and energy to build the highest civilisation of pre-Columbian America. They were able to do this because, although their land was infertile, except along the river flood-plains, it was rich in building materials: limestone rock with a high calcium carbonate content – from which Mayan builders were able to make good mortar – sandstone and volcanic rock in the south, and hard stones used for making tools.

The Palace of Palenque was a maze of courtyards, porticos and rooms dominated by a high tower, probably used for astronomical observations. It was completely swamped in tropical vegetation when the American explorer John L. Stephens rediscovered it in the 19th century.

How the Mayas counted

As in modern mathematics, the position of figures in a Mayan number was vital. At a time when in Europe the Romans were using a clumsy system of addition (167, for instance, was CLXVII, which meant 100+50+10+5+1+1), the Mayas had a positional system even more concise than our own way of numbering. It used only three symbols – a dot, a bar and a shell shape representing zero.

Modern arithmetic, which was developed in India and the Middle East, is based on 10s, with the figure on the right representing units, the next figure to the left showing tens, the third column showing hundreds, and so on.

The Mayas, however, counted in 20s, and wrote large numbers in columns reading from bottom to top. A number up to 20 was expressed by a single hieroglyphic, as shown in the table. Each hieroglyphic was a combination of dots and bars, or dashes, each dot standing for 1, each bar for 5.

0	1	2	3	4
5	6	7	8	9
10	11	12	13	14
15	16	17	18	19

For numbers higher than 20, a new row was started above the first to mark the number of 20s in the total. Thus, the number 234 would be expressed by only two Mayan symbols: the sign for 11 (meaning 11 sets of 20, or 220), and the sign for 14, as shown on the right.

Similarly, the third row from the bottom in Mayan numbering stood for multiples of 400 (or 20×20), the fourth row for multiples of 8,000 (20×20×20), and so on. Our number 100,000, for example, would be written in only four digits, as it is on the right: the sign for 12 (meaning 12 sets of 8,000, or 96,000), followed by the sign for 10 (meaning 10 sets of 400, or 4,000), followed by two of the shell-shaped zero signs:

On dates, which is the form in which most large Mayan numbers have been found, the Mayas modified this 20-based system slightly to make the years easier to count. And they defined all their dates as the number of days since the start of their calendar, a date which many Mayan experts believe corresponds to August 11, 3114 BC. The significance of this day is still a mystery. But the modification they used in their calendar arithmetic is understood.

Under this system, the groups in each succeeding row had special names. The 360-day year, shown in the third row, was called a tun, and contained 18 months of 20 days each. The fourth row showed katun, *or 20-year periods, each of 7,200 days (20×18×20). And the fifth showed* baktun, *or 400-year periods, each of 144,000 days (20×20×18×20).*

This Mayan statuette shows a man playing a form of ball game. He is wearing a sort of safety helmet and a wide padded belt which was used to strike the heavy rubber ball. The ball was not touched by hand, but propelled by a swing of the hips.

Since the days of ancient Egypt, no people on earth have been more obsessed by time than the Mayas. It is curious that both these races, haunted as they were by the idea of eternity, should have been builders of pyramids. The Mayan cities, built in the virgin forest, were dominated by temples where priests measured the hours and seasons with mathematical and astronomical tables of a precision unsurpassed at that time even in Europe.

Deciphering the language of the Mayas

Their grasp of writing was one of the keys to their success. Mayan texts are found on stone tablets, wooden panels and pieces of pottery, as well as in all too rare books made of a kind of vegetable-fibre paper, impregnated and covered with a fine layer of lime. The Mayas used about 800 hieroglyphic signs, of which about a quarter have now been deciphered by language specialists. Thanks to their work, the names of days of the week, the months, the gods, numbers, and the points of the compass and colours can all be read correctly in Mayan texts.

Using the numerous inscriptions on monuments and others decorating pottery, as well as the three famous Mayan manuscripts known as the Dresden, Madrid and Paris codices (from the location of the museums now housing them), scholars have been making an intensive study of ancient Mayan writing. Still spoken by 2 million people, this language was written in a complex hieroglyphic script composed partly of ideo-grams representing whole words or ideas and partly of phonetic symbols for sounds – much the same as ancient Egyptian and modern Japanese. We do not know all that these people were trying to say, but more and more of the Mayan past is being opened to us.

Of their mathematics, however, far more is known. And what is known has revealed a degree of skill astonishing in a primitive people. They were, for example, familiar with the idea of zero nearly 1,000 years before the concept reached Europe from India through Arab traders who had opened up caravan routes across the deserts of the Middle East. The Greeks, for all their inventiveness, wrote numbers by using letters of the alphabet; and the Romans, for all their practicality, made do with a somewhat ponderous graphic system which involved writing four figures (VIII) to express the number 8. Both laboured under primitive numerical systems which can only have hindered their trade and scientific development. They were incapable of dealing with large numbers with the same facility as the Mayas, who could express any number by the use of three symbols: the dot, the bar, or dash, and a shell shape for zero.

It was to satisfy their interest in chronology that the Mayas developed their elaborate mathematical system. An obsession with the calendar, though not always to this marked degree, is a common feature of societies dominated by agricultural and religious festivals. An exact knowledge of the seasons and the period of maximum rainfall is, of course, essential to the timing of seed-sowing and harvesting.

No calendar can exist without careful observation

This ball-court at Copán was built about AD 775. At the far end it is bounded by steps with a carved stone slab at the top, and along each side are slopes edged with buildings which once had vaulted roofs. Three stone markers were set on the summit of each slope. Apparently the game, which was played by many pre-Columbian peoples, consisted of hitting one of these goals with a heavy rubber ball.

over long periods of the sun and the stars. The Mayan year was made up of 18 months of 20 days, plus five extra days, and was called the *haab*. The 360-day period was called the *tun* and was the basis of the calendar, but there were also a series of multiples. Thus 20 *tun* were 7,200 days, or 1 *katun*; 20 *katun* were 144,000 days, or 1 *baktun*, and so on up to a period which could cover more than 63 million years or 1 *alautun* – a total of 23,040 million days. This figure was written in only nine units, whereas our decimal system of writing numbers requires 11 units.

The Mayas used an extremely complex system to date important events. It was based on three different time scales: the solar year, the religious year and the Venusian year. The religious year of 260 days was

One of the great stone slabs at Copán, dating from the 8th century AD, has carved on it in high relief a Mayan sovereign. His face, treated in an almost realistic style, looks out from an elaborately decorated ritual costume and head-dress.

The Nunnery Quadrangle at Uxmal, built in the 9th or 10th century, is shown here as it was (reconstruction below) and as it is today (photograph opposite). The buildings are typical of the Puuc style of Mayan architecture, which flourished in Yucatán and is distinguished by the repetition of geometrical patterns in its carved decoration. Each patterned slab matches its partners with almost photographic precision. The complex contains a triumphal arch, monumental stairways, a central courtyard and four long, low palace buildings which have friezes of geometrical designs running round them and contain vaulted stone rooms. Beside this complex, on the right of the photograph, is the high Pyramid of the Magician, with its dizzying flights of stairs leading to the upper temple. The combination of temple pyramids and large central courtyards is a feature peculiar to Mayan town planning. Other distinctive features of the towns are huge squares between the buildings, where the population gathered to watch ceremonies performed by priests on the upper terraces of the pyramids. In the foreground of the photograph can be seen the remains of the ball-court of Uxmal.

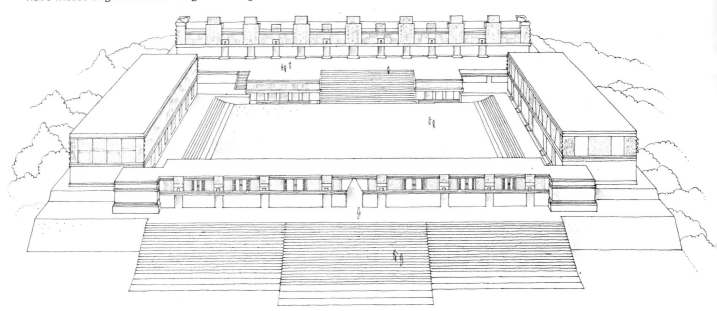

linked to the solar year and both were included in the Venusian year, which lasts for 584 earth days.

In addition to the *katun*, *baktun* and other multiples of the 360-day cycle, or *tun*, the Mayas used yet another time scale to link the 365-day solar year to the 260-day religious year. This 'calendar round' scale covered 52 solar years, or 73 religious years, and created a period corresponding to the idea which we express as a century. The object of the calculation was to ensure that particular ritual days in the religious calendar coincided with the same days found in the solar calendar.

Accurate astronomers

The Mayas realised at an early stage that if they wanted accurate data on which to base their calendar, they would have to continue their observations over very long periods. When the Dresden Codex was deciphered it revealed some astonishing facts about the accuracy of the Mayas' mathematical averages. For instance, calculation of the lunar month requires observations covering 405 full moons, in other words $32\frac{3}{4}$ years. The Mayas calculated that 405 full moons occurred in a period of 11,960 days. Today's astronomers make it 11,959·888 days. So the Mayas were out in their calculations by only one day every 292 years – or less than five minutes a year.

The estimation of the Venusian year – the time which the planet takes to make a complete circuit of

the sun – is just as extraordinary, for the observations involved are more complex. Mayan calculations seem to have been based on an overall period of 384 years of observations. They fixed the Venusian year at 584 days, while current calculations make it 583·92 days. This is equivalent to a margin of error of 72 minutes in each earth year, or six minutes a month. Such a degree of accuracy, to within 12 seconds per day, is mysterious in a culture which had no way of measuring time, not even an elementary system such as an hour glass or a water clock – and no astronomical telescope or other optical instrument.

If the Venusian cycle inspired Mayan mathematics it was probably due to the fact that Venus is the brightest 'star'. It is visible in the sky before the sun sets and continues to shine for some time after the sun has risen. This characteristic makes it possible to note the position of the planet above the horizon at the moment of sunrise or sunset. By careful observation, the Mayan astronomers could have found that over a period of eight earth years Venus completed exactly five cycles of movement in the sky, and that it then began to repeat the sequence. By dividing 2,920 – the number of days in eight 365-day earth years – by five, they arrived at the length of each Venusian cycle: 584 days.

The survival of the Maya observatory at Chichén Itzá, albeit in ruined form, has enabled modern archaeologists to check their results. It appears that these measurements contain a maximum margin of error of two degrees of angle, but the margin is often as

low as 0·005 of a degree. And the Mayas obtained these surprisingly accurate results without using any sighting instrument, such as the theodolite.

The Mayas used a date from which all periods of time were calculated, and their era seems to have begun more than 5,000 years ago, in mythical times when, it seems, the Mayan people were not independent of the surrounding tribes in Middle America.

Time out of step

The most difficult problem posed by pre-Columbian archaeology is, appropriately, concerned with time. It is to establish the correlation between the Mayan era and the Christian era. The Mayan builders dated most of their creations by counting the days from a single starting date, and these day counts can be read, since the hieroglyphics for numbers and days have been deciphered. So a precise chronology is available by which events in Mayan history can be related to each other. But not all scholars can agree on how to relate them to events in our own history. Even carbon-14 analysis of their artefacts has failed to show the exact

A high Mayan dignitary, wearing the superb quetzal feather head-dress and other royal regalia, grasps the hair of a man who is handing him his spear in a gesture of surrender. This bas-relief slab is at Yaxchilán and dates from AD 680. Open areas in the design are filled in by hieroglyphics.

relationship between the two eras. Many experts, however, now believe that the Mayan starting date corresponds to a day in 3114 BC.

The history of the peoples who created the Mayan civilisation can be traced back to about 2500 BC. From this time until about 300 BC is known as the formative period. This was followed by the so-called pre-classical period. The classical age, which came next, achieved its full flowering in Petén, and particularly at Tikal, which had become a major ceremonial centre by about AD 200. This period extended for more than 600 years, and the civilisation in Petén did not crumble until late in the 9th century.

Meanwhile, in Yucatán, cities appeared sometime in the 5th century AD. About 150 years later, a great renaissance took place in this area, and the cities of Yucatán took over from and continued the classical culture of Petén. Mayan civilisation in Yucatán was in full bloom from the 8th to the 10th centuries.

To distinguish between the classical and later Mayan periods, some specialists have called them the Old and

New Empires. In fact there appears never to have been a Mayan empire in the sense of a political unit. Rather, there was a confederation of independent cities, which had culture, religion, and a system of writing in common. Each, however, had its own government and set its own policies. Alliances certainly sometimes made their appearance, in response to some common danger, and were often cemented by royal marriages; but in general the links between these scattered cities were weak. Each city had its own distinctive style in architecture and in other arts.

Rulers like pharaohs

The highest authority in each city was an individual who, originally at least, must have combined religious and civil power. He was both high priest and war leader, as were the first Egyptian pharaohs in the time of the pyramids. This supreme chief was revered as half man, half god, as is shown by the magnificent burial site of the ruler of Palenque in the crypt of the Temple of the Inscriptions. The sovereign was surrounded by high dignitaries who formed the ruling class and lived in elaborate palaces. This ruling élite devoted itself entirely to managing the city's affairs and extending the knowledge which was necessary to establish the religious calendar and perform the rites. The scientific and artistic literature and knowledge of this class was extremely advanced.

The main body of the Governor's Palace at Uxmal looms beyond the throne of the two-headed jaguar. The building is more than 100 yds long, and stands on an enormous base which is twice as long. It is reached by a monumental staircase. The façade is nearly 30 ft high and crowned by a frieze in the geometrical Puuc style.

This short passage links the main body and one of the wings of the central building of the Palace of the Governor at Uxmal. It is built in the form of a false vault, or corbelled arch, and was originally open on both sides, but at some time it was walled off and columns were put up in front of it.

The central hall of the Governor's Palace, which is also roofed with a false vault, was made of concrete with a veneer of stone. Light enters the hall through three doorways. The vaulted interior is similar in shape to the inside of the huts in which the Indians of the Yucatán peninsula still live.

The power of this hereditary nobility rested on knowledge and ritual, which were vital to the continuation of life and society. The religious acts which these dignitaries performed on certain fixed dates were regarded as necessary in order to hold the world in its orbit and prevent it from falling into an abyss of nothingness. Sacrificial rites and rites of purification in honour of the gods of the rain and the sun were also considered essential to the prosperity of the agriculture on which the Mayas depended.

Beneath the ruler and his nobles, there was a relatively small class composed of specialised craftsmen. Then came the great mass of the ordinary peasants. The rural mass of the ancient Mayas did not disappear when the high dignitaries fell, nor when the Spanish *conquistadores* arrived. They are people whom the traveller can meet today in towns like Muna on the Uxmal road. They live in thatched wattle-and-daub huts in the villages of Yucatán, and still talk the old Mayan tongues, mixed with a few words of Spanish. Their huts are identical to those that their ancestors lived in thousands of years ago, which were the models for the stone structures of the classical period.

Apart from the often still baffling writings which have survived, Mayan civilisation is known only by archaeological remains: paintings, sculpture, pottery, jade and, above all, architecture.

'Stepped-in' arches

In architecture, the Mayas stood out from their neighbours in the pre-Columbian world because they were the only ones to have a type of roof known as the corbelled arch, or false vaulting, in which stone blocks are 'stepped in' to form an arch, each block slightly overhanging the one beneath. Mayan false vaulting – which resembles in shape the corbelled sandstone arches built by the Khmers at Angkor in Cambodia – was constructed with a remarkably strong lime mortar and can be found in most Mayan buildings erected between the 1st and 12th centuries.

The technique of building these vaults reached a highly advanced form in the golden age of Mayan civilisation. The facing of beautiful cut stone which can be seen from the outside is in fact a sort of permanent casing for a coarse concrete which fills the walls and

This frieze on the west wing of the Nunnery Quadrangle at Uxmal shows a carving of the type of mud or clay wattle-and-daub hut in which the ordinary Mayan Indians lived. Placed symbolically over the entrance of each room of the palace, these huts show clearly that the stone buildings used by Mayan dignitaries were in fact their homes, not just ceremonial meeting places. Inside, both hut and palace are the same shape. Modern counterparts of the huts that were copied in stone for the palaces – such as the traditional thatched wooden hut shown below – are still common in Yucatán.

roof space. And the interiors are much the same, in shape if not in grandeur, as those of the huts in which the Indians of Yucatán live today.

Some Mayan buildings were very large. In Petén, their temple-pyramids are as high as 230 ft, with a base of up to 130 by 130 ft. On the outside they slope steeply, with a dizzying stairway at an angle of as much as 60 degrees leading to the summit. At the top of this is the shrine of the Mayan gods.

Perhaps the most fantastically proportioned buildings of all were in Uxmal, the great capital of Yucatán. There, for instance, to support the building now called the Governor's Palace the Mayas built an esplanade nearly 200 yds long, 170 yds wide and 40 ft high, containing a total of some 450,000 cu. yds of material. On top of this colossal base, another terrace 130 yds long by 28 yds wide by 13 ft high carries the building, which is more than 100 yds long, 13 yds wide and almost 30 ft high. The whole building must have required nearly a million tons of material.

Then there is the artificial acropolis, or citadel, built at Copán, which covers some 12 acres and reaches a height of 125 ft with a total of more than $2\frac{1}{2}$ million cu. yds or almost 5 million tons of material.

Walls within walls

The vastness of these buildings is due in part to the Mayan practice of building each new edifice above and around its predecessor – a succession of buildings on the same site resembling a nest of Russian dolls.

Thus archaeologists digging at Uaxactún have found seven previous stages within the existing structure. This has been a valuable boon for researchers, enabling them to establish the succession of styles and the development of techniques.

The filling core needed for these colossal structures and all the smaller hewn stones and equipment were carried on the backs of men. Large blocks, such as the inscribed slabs, were moved on rollers. Although the wheel was known in pre-Columbian America (toy wheeled carts have been found in tombs), for some mysterious reason no carts were used in building operations. It is certainly not the terrain which explains this strange fact, for there were fine roads in existence. Uxmal was connected with Kabah by a 10-mile road laid down in a perfectly straight line, with a triumphal arch at the end forming a majestic entrance into the town. There is even a broad road linking Cobá and Yaxuná, which are 60 miles apart. The road is 31 ft wide and is laid down in three perfectly straight and level sections. When it reaches swampland, the road is carried on elevated causeways several feet high.

The religious significance of surviving Mayan buildings can be seen from the decorative motifs on their façades. Often, these show the stylised faces of snake-like gods. These grotesque faces, which were originally of stucco, are sometimes taller than a man and give the buildings a look of terrifying splendour. Sometimes they covered whole façades, as in the palace at Kabah.

The Mayas worked out their calendars with elaborate astronomical tables. This page, from a manuscript known as the Dresden Codex, shows part of the 260-day religious year. Above the drawings of gods linked with particular periods in the year are the bar-and-dot symbols of Mayan arithmetic.

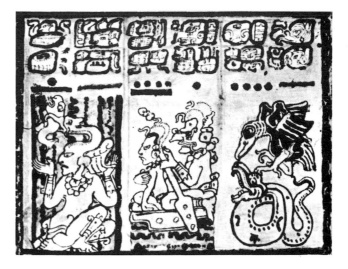

These stylised masks resemble a whole series of decorative motifs which are also found among peoples whose territory borders the Pacific. As the French anthropologist Claude Lévi-Strauss noted, these motifs existed in China 4,000 years ago, and among the New Zealand Maoris and the natives of Alaska and Siberia. There is a puzzling similarity between the Chinese masks, known as *t'ao-t'ieh*, which decorate bronze ritual vases of the Shang dynasty, on the one hand, and the snake-god masks in the land of the Mayas on the other. Some of these masks are almost identical. Should we see in them evidence of a common origin of these two peoples? It is thought that people from Siberia reached America during the Old and Middle Stone Ages by way of the Bering Strait. During the great ice age, Asian hunters probably passed over a

since-vanished land bridge from one continent to the other almost without noticing it.

The masks of the gods which adorn the Mayan palaces and temples are important for another reason. They are a prominent feature of what is known as the

The Caracol at Chichén Itzá was a Mayan astronomical observatory. The terraces and platforms of the base were laid out with great care to line up with important events in the heavens. At the top a spiral staircase inside the round tower led to a high observatory chamber. The chamber had precisely aligned loopholes through which sightings could be made, thus allowing the astronomers to calculate the angles of stars extremely accurately.

Puuc style, which is characteristic of the Yucatán buildings. The other feature of this style is the use in the design of simple and constantly repeated geometrical patterns. This is one of the most outstanding examples of mass-production in an ancient civilisation. The Governor's Palace at Uxmal, more than 100 yds long and 13 yds wide, is surmounted by an immense stone mosaic frieze, 10 ft high and running right round the building: it is more than 750 sq. yds in area. There are 150 snake-god masks on it, each showing eyes, ears, horns and giant fangs. And each elaborate face is carved to the same precise design.

Each mask contains 18 building blocks, and the masks alone required 2,700 blocks of sculptured stone. They are incorporated into a mosaic that has 30 pieces to the square yard, making a total of 22,500 blocks. More than half these blocks form a criss-cross pattern made up of identical pieces. These blocks had to be made absolutely regular, since a variation of even half an inch, repeated thousands of times over, would lead to disaster; thus, stone-cutters at the work-site where the blocks were prefabricated had to work to exceptionally high standards. Production methods perhaps resembled those of a modern factory. Some teams would have been responsible for rough-hewing thousands of identical blocks, which would then have been passed on to teams of sculptors. Experienced masons would have taken over only at the finishing stage. An organisation of this kind would have been possible only in a highly structured society with a powerful hierarchy and a centralised administration.

Decline and fall

For many years there was a tendency to regard the end of the Mayas as a complete mystery. There was talk of abandoned cities, epidemics and famines. Now, however, some scholars believe that it is unnecessary to look for any explanation beyond a certain lack of internal solidarity and a vague discontent among people subjected to the pressures of ever more ambitious building programmes. The discontented subjects perhaps found their opportunity when invading tribes, who were primitive but armed with a new and murderous weapon, the bow, penetrated their land.

Attacked by nomadic tribes

Invasions from the high plateaux were a regular phenomenon of Mexican life. Just as the barbarian hordes swept across the plains of eastern Europe to the Roman frontiers of Germania and the Danube, so nomadic tribes more than once attacked the great settled civilisations of Middle America.

Among the victims of such invasions may have been the inhabitants of the City of the Gods, Teotihuacán. Some theorists believe that refugees from Teotihuacán were on the move as early as AD 450, and that they built the huge monument at Kaminaljuyú, on the southern edge of the Mayan world.

As the shock waves of the invasions spread, the headlong flight of the city dwellers may have weakened the refined, complex structure of Mayan life. The ruling aristocratic élites would then have been toppled as the priestly clique lost authority and the sacred buildings fell into disrepair. Collective organisation would have disappeared, to be replaced by widespread anarchy. The forest would quickly have reconquered the abandoned land. As the collapse went on, writing and astronomy fell into disuse. Buildings were no longer dated. The spread of decadence can be followed by the last dates on monuments. At Copán the last is 830, at Palenque 835, at Tikal 889 and at Uxmal 909.

One Mayan community, however, enjoyed a spectacular Indian summer from 987. For in that year a tribe from Mexico's central plateau, called the Toltecs, conquered and settled in Chichén Itzá. The local population, defeated in war, quickly won over their conquerors by their culture; and the result was a brilliant revival, in which features of Toltec and Mayan life

The Temple of the Warriors at Chichén Itzá, with its 1,000 columns, is a high point of the Mayan-Toltec renaissance which flowered in Yucatán after the Toltec conquest. The temple was built in the 11th century and is remarkable for its huge roofed inner areas. Wooden lintels on stone pillars supported the vaulted masonry roofing. Lintels and roofing have long disappeared. Only the pillars and walls remain.

The priests at Chichén Itzá probably laid the hearts of the sacrificial victims on this reclining figure, called a Chacmool, at the top of stairs leading to the sanctuary of the Temple of the Warriors. The Toltecs left many such sculptures in the Yucatán peninsula.

were blended. In this corner of Middle America the collapse of the Mayas' classical civilisation was delayed by some two centuries. But the Toltecs seem to have abandoned Chichén Itzá sometime before AD 1224, and the final recipients of Mayan culture vanished. Their world may have been eaten away by attack from without and finally destroyed by discord from within.

From the 13th century to the 16th, constant outbreaks of internecine war marked the decline of a civilisation which had lasted more than 4,000 years. When the Spaniards landed at Yucatán in the early 16th century they were met by only the primitive descendants of what had been one of the most cultivated peoples the pre-Columbian world had known.

But the Spaniards were not concerned with what had gone before them, and virtually the only account of the people they found is that of the Spanish bishop Diego de Landa, who in 1566 published an *Account of the Affairs of Yucatán.* In this, he recorded the few tales which the local population could tell of their ancestors' achievements. But he had also been responsible, several years earlier, for organising a series of solemn ceremonies at which the historical, religious

and scientific writings of the Mayas were burned in the name of the Inquisition. We cannot know how much the world has lost by that fanatical deed.

Mayan civilisation is unquestionably the most fascinating pre-Columbian civilisation for historians and archaeologists – and for lovers of mystery. But in Mexico alone there are whole civilisations still to be explored. Almost entirely unknown, they could yield secrets as fascinating as those of the Mayas.

Archaeology in the Americas is still a young science when compared with archaeology in Greece, Egypt or the Middle East. It is still full of mysteries. The discoveries still lie ahead. The assembly of the jigsaw is just beginning.

HENRI STIERLIN

Enigmatic messages
of the Nazcas

*The strangest messages ever left by
man are indelibly scored on the flat, desolate
plainland in southern Peru. Drawn in lines of pebbles
across the expansive wastes are huge birds, animals
and geometric figures as if outlined by a
giant's finger. From eye level these great drawings
are invisible; they can be seen only from the sky.
Yet they were laid across the desert by the
Nazca Indians 1,500 years ago and long before
man could fly. What was their meaning?
And who was meant to read them?*

One of the most baffling enigmas of archaeology lies spread on the arid plain of the Nazca region, between the Pacific coast of southern Peru and the Andean foothills. It is made up of strange lines stretching across the desert as far as the eye can see, incomprehensible geometric shapes and huge stylised birds and fantastic animals, looking as though they had been drawn by a giant's hand.

The puzzle is made even more intriguing by the fact that often the complete figures can only be seen from

From the air, the tangle of lines, tracks and figures that pattern the desert floor seem the work of a mad geometrician. But the designs were drawn by the Nazcas at least 1,500 years ago. So far, nobody has been able to solve the mystery of the patterns or explain why the Nazcas made drawings which they probably never saw in their entirety.

an altitude of above 1,000 ft. Understandably there are some people who imagine that they must have been made by unknown extra-terrestrial beings, who came to earth some thousands of years ago and made contact with the pre-Columbian peoples. Of course, no plausible argument has ever been found to support the proposition put forward by these believers in helmeted visitors from space. Unless one is prepared to close one's eyes to the facts as they are known today, it is hard to imagine beings of higher intelligence travelling at the speed of light in times immemorial, or the Peruvian desert being used as an astroport by spacecraft thousands of years ago.

The Nazca lines offer enough scope for dreams without resorting to such fantasies. Vastness of scale and weirdness of design are as closely intermingled in this strange wasteland as in any science-fiction novel. Since cool prevailing winds from the ocean pick up

little moisture from the chill waters of the Humboldt Current, almost no rain has fallen along the coast for perhaps 10,000 years, though it is at a latitude where, normally, luxuriant tropical vegetation would grow. Furthermore, the erosion on the bare slopes of southern Peru is believed to be similar to that revealed by space probes on Mars; and NASA, America's National Aeronautical and Space Administration, have sent experts to study the area as part of their research into the possibility of life on Mars.

The extraordinary dryness of the plain has protected the ancient Nazca people's strange designs for at least 1,500 years; in a normal climate it is unlikely that they would have lasted until now. The lines are in fact two parallel rows of pebbles, containing iron and iron oxides. Too little rain has fallen to wash the pebbles out of place down the centuries.

As early as the mid-16th century, the Spanish

In the desert, between the Andes and the Pacific Ocean, there are scattered traces of several dead cities. Here, the winding courses of dry river beds contrast with the geometric regularity of man-made designs. Tracks and lines edged with dark stones seem to converge from all sides on the unnamed town in the lower left corner.

chronicler Cieza de León was intrigued by strange 'signals in some parts of the neighbouring desert of Nazca', but it was not until 1941 that the enigma attracted much scientific attention. The strange designs were first studied by an American, Dr Paul Kosok, from Long Island University. He examined the parched plain from the air, and discovered what he called 'the largest astronomy book in the world'.

His work was followed up by a German mathematician and astronomer, Maria Reiche. She is now in her seventies and has been studying the Peruvian desert for more than 30 years. She has criss-crossed it step by step, picking out hundreds of triangular, quadrangular or trapezoidal 'runways', networks of straight lines, sometimes running parallel to each other, sometimes in zigzags or star shapes. She has also found long wide

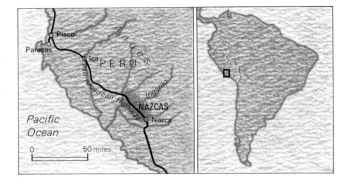

Some specialists believe that the world's largest astronomical calendar was drawn by the Nazcas on the dry plain of southern Peru. The site, which today is crossed by the Pan American Highway, lies at an average elevation just over 1,300 ft, and covers an area of about 200 sq. miles.

stripes crossing like roads or forming grids, circles and spirals of all sizes – and more than 100 giant figures of animals, birds and plants which are still clearly visible.

One of the most unusual aspects of the Nazca lines is the giant size of the designs, which cover huge flat areas or run unswervingly straight across narrow rises and deep ravines between 'islands' of ground surrounded by dried-up river beds. The total area covered by the designs is about 200 sq. miles.

Tons of small stones must have been moved to create the outlines of each line. And the positioning must have been done to carefully calculated plans in order to reproduce the patterns as if on a giant canvas. Maria Reiche presumes that they must first have been drawn on small plots of ground about 6 ft square, as she has found several of these near the largest designs.

Using each plan as a model, she believes the Nazcas divided it into sections and then reproduced each section on the required scale. This method allowed them to work out gigantic designs without needing any overall view of the work as it progressed. To draw straight lines they stretched strings from posts, lining up three or more in successive rows to keep the overall line straight. The remains of some posts have been found and dated by the carbon-14 method to AD 500. The curves are believed to have been formed using a series of small arcs placed end to end. Maria Reiche is also said to have worked out from the designs the unit of measurement that the Nazcas must have used.

A number of other theories has been put forward. The latest could well belong in a science-fiction novel if it were not for the fact that two of its defenders, Julian Knott and Jim Woodman, who are members of the International Explorers Society of Coral Gables in Florida, base their ideas on a painted Nazca ceramic. According to them this piece of pottery shows an airship. The two men and some of their colleagues in the explorers' society were convinced that it would have been technically impossible for the Nazcas to compose such large-scale designs without having an overall aerial view. But they could have obtained such a view by using a lighter-than-air craft, since materials to make one would have been available: vegetable fibre for the ropes and for weaving the gas-bag, and reeds for the basket.

So a group from the explorers' society made a primitive balloon using these materials. Sitting astride a swing seat below a cloth bag filled with hot air, in a few seconds they reached an altitude of over 600 ft

Buried beneath the sands, the Nazcas' cemeteries contain mummies like this one, which was disinterred from a tomb after being buried for 2,000 years. The feathered turban and fine cotton cloak embroidered in multi-coloured wools are evidence of the great skill of Nazca textile workers.

before being violently blown back to the ground by a sudden gust of wind. The accident brought the experiment to a premature end. However, as soon as the airship had been relieved of the weight of its passengers, who had fallen out, it rose to a height of some 1,200 ft and flew for a further 20 minutes or so, covering a distance of nearly 3 miles.

Other researchers have tried to find out more about the Nazcas by studying tombs in the neighbouring Paracas region. Scholars believe that one site in particular, known as the Necropolis, dates to the beginning of Nazca times and was used as the burial place for high-ranking dignitaries and priests from both areas. At the Necropolis site, more than 400 mummies, all wrapped in shrouds and wearing elaborate cloaks, have been found in a building under the sands. They are believed to have been buried there about 2,000 years ago amid complex funerary rites.

The bodies of these noblemen were wrapped in layers of very long, fine cotton cloths, richly em-

---

Maria Reiche, the German mathematician and astronomer, has devoted her career to the study and preservation of the Nazca drawings. After more than 30 years of research, she is convinced that the Nazcas created a giant calendar.

broidered with multi-coloured alpaca or vicuna wool. These embroidery designs show strange masked people who appear to be gliding or descending in a steep dive apparently with the help of many ribbons which can be seen floating around them. Could the Nazcas and Paracas have constructed man-carrying kites? The pre-Columbian drawings of southern Peru would seem to suggest this.

Some specialists on Peruvian archaeology share the views of Paul Kosok and Maria Reiche and think that the Nazca drawings are an astronomical calendar. Spanish chroniclers have indicated that heavenly bodies – especially Venus, Mercury, Jupiter and the Pleiades – were used by pre-Columbian priests to work out the calendar.

Survival was a challenge on this hostile dry coast, for life could only flourish in isolated oases near the rivers of the Andes, and even these rivers were often dry. The Nazcas took up the challenge boldly, judging by the works they made, which are still used by today's farmers. They built valley-wide irrigation systems, using the river waters so efficiently that they were able to grow two or three crops a year on their fields.

In so harsh an environment, it seems certain that the huge desert drawings must have been intended to help in studying water conditions. Paul Kosok thought that some of the lines pointed to the solstices and others to the equinoxes. The widest of the solstice lines, it is thought, points to the part of the Andes where the first rains fall. Even today many farmers still read the start of the mountains' rainy season in the stars, and wait anxiously for its bounty to pour down from the steep slopes of the Andes to the coast.

But the sandy soil of the desert is so poor that natural fertiliser is needed, as well as irrigation, to make it fertile. Guano – a thick deposit of droppings left by seabirds on rocky islets – is the fertiliser used in this region nowadays. In Nazca times, however, the major fertiliser was sardines. These, like all components of the coastal economy, are subject to the influence of the Humboldt Current.

The waters of the Humboldt Current – which is known at this point of its huge Pacific sweep as the Peru Coastal Current – are colder than those of the surrounding sea and rich in plankton. The fish which feed on the plankton provide the main source of food for the guano-producing seabirds. However, in some years an equatorial current known as El Niño, 'the Child', because it often comes at Christmas, disturbs the ecological pattern. It brings warm waters which kill off the plankton and the sardines. It also destroys much of the rest of the marine life near the coast, causing the seabirds to migrate or starve in their millions. It is presumed that the Nazcas read the news of coming difficult weather conditions from the flight patterns of seabirds, like those they drew on the plain, and one of which is shown flying southwards.

Like their remote ancestors, the Indians of Peru still believe in the magic power of totemic animals, and they see the shapes of these animals in the stars. The giant figures of the desert zoo are believed by some theorists to be reproductions of the shapes made by groups of stars. Some constellations could have been interpreted by the Nazcas as being their mythological ancestors. Or the shapes may have formed the signs of a pre-Columbian zodiac which only the greatest and most learned astronomers could use, because they alone could read the language of the stars. Another suggestion is that they could have been part of a

Seen from above, this long line of piled stones forms one side of a huge truncated triangle. Hundreds of straight lines, geometric shapes and outlines of animals and plants were drawn simply by arranging stones in lines, revealing the lighter-coloured soil between them. This remarkable task was performed by hand, since the Nazcas had no draught animals.

Drawn in one single line, this 50-yd-long spider is one of the most impressive drawings in the extraordinary bestiary at Nazca. Like the others, it was probably the totem of a caste which, at certain times, came to dance on the drawing. The spider could have been linked with rites of foretelling the future but may also have been the earthly representation of one of the constellations which the Nazcas are thought to have worshipped. Another possibility is that it was associated with a fertility cult.

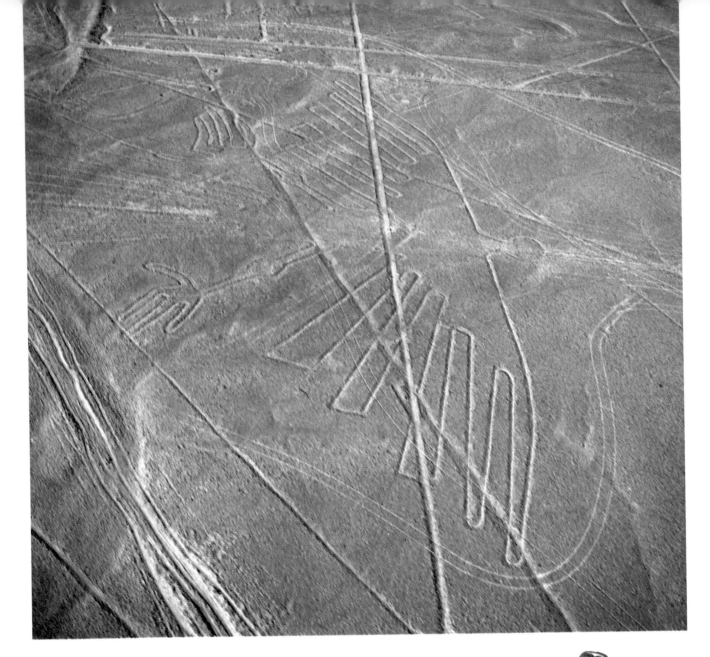

There are 18 of these bird shapes drawn on the desert along-side the Ingenio river. The scale of the drawings is colossal – from 30 to over 300 yds long. A 3·7-mile-long solar line runs across the 140-yd wingspan of this magnificent specimen. Similar birds are found on some of the Nazca pottery.

The Nazcas were extremely skilled potters. The beautifully stylised images on their multi-coloured pottery depict animals and plants and the activities of men and gods. One of their favourite decorative motifs was the hummingbird which, like the condor, is shown with outspread wings.

magical religious cult expressed in a theatrical ritual.

Certainly, agricultural work in ancient Peru gave rise to great festivals during which ceremonial dances were performed to the music of pan-pipes, and the beat of drums. These dances inspired motifs on Nazca pottery, and the symbolic drawings on the plain may be stylised versions of them.

As for the lines, they are thought to represent the

courses of the stars. Single lines, it is believed, are the axes of solstices (pointing to the sun on mid-summer day and mid-winter day) or of equinoxes (pointing to the sun's position in mid-spring and mid-autumn). These are less numerous than lunar lines, which seems to suggest that the moon was more important to the Nazcas than the sun. This would fit in with the theory that the lines are an astronomical calendar of some kind; perhaps the cycle of the lunar month was more important for farmers than the movement of the sun. The double lines, however, which occur more frequently, may have been sacred roads along which the long procession of the living travelled, escorting the souls of the dead of each clan. It is thought that there are still huge tombs buried near the drawings.

An explanation still remains to be found for the famous triangular, trapezoidal or quadrangular 'runways'. Here opinions differ and the controversy continues. Were they astronomical observations or places of assembly? Were burnt offerings made to the Nazca gods here? Or was it taboo ground, guarded by the figures of the spirits?

Technicians in the astronomy section of the Peruvian Air Force are trying to make a topographical plot of the Nazca drawings, using aerial photographs. But they also need to reconstruct the map of the sky as it was centuries ago, because, they believe, it is only by comparing the two that it would be possible to decide whether the markings really do constitute the largest astronomical map in the world.

A computer check made in the late 1960s by the astronomer Gerald S. Hawkins has sounded a discordant note, however, among the chorus of voices sup-

porting an astronomical interpretation of the Nazca complex. The measurements of 93 alignments and 45 stars were fed into the computer along with the key question: are there significant alignments of the Nazca lines with positions occupied by the sun, moon and stars since 5000 BC? The answer was disappointing: some alignments were found – but no more than could have happened by sheer chance. The computer found no statistical evidence that the Nazca lines had been designed as a calendar.

There is a further problem. Research in the area risks being affected by the depredations to which the site has recently been subjected. For a long time the drawings were neglected; but now they are only too famous, and they have been in danger of being ruined by the influx of vast numbers of sightseers. Some of the ancient marks have already been blurred by the tracks of feet and wheels. In response to a call by Maria Reiche, a committee for the protection of the site has recently been created. And Peru now bans walking or driving over the area except by special permission; instead, tourists can see parts of the layout from a roadside observation tower. In this way the government and scientists hope to preserve a fascinating chapter of pre-Columbian history – a chapter whose mystery, for the moment, remains intact as well.

SIMONE WAISBARD

Maria Reiche, guardian of the Nazca desert, stands in the centre of a spiral maze. Spreading out across the stony plain, the maze is, in fact, the tail of a giant monkey. Could it be the depiction of a sign read in the skies, or is it a fertility symbol?

Did a black hole hit Siberia?

*Explosions have scarred the face of the earth
often down the ages – by accident and by design.
None is more baffling than the blast that rocked
Siberia. Where and when it took place are
known precisely. But how it happened is unknown.
Was it a giant meteorite? An atomic blast from
a crippled alien spaceship? Or was it a
collision with the most chilling rogue body
in the universe – an object so dense that
it twists the very laws of time and space?
Did, in fact, a black hole hit Siberia?*

At 7.17 a.m. local time on June 30, 1908, something frightful occurred in the Tungus area of central Siberia. As though a catastrophic mid-air explosion had taken place, virtually all trees within a radius of 20 miles were blown down. As recently as the 1960s, the charred tree trunks, many of them with the bark torn off, could still be seen from the air, forming a striking pattern of lines radiating from the heart of the area where the devastating explosion took place.

Residents of the region who were alive at the time of the blast have reported that just beforehand they

The end of the world may have been perilously close in 1908. One theory about the Siberian disaster is that a small black hole – a mass so dense that not even light can escape its gravity – passed right through the earth. A larger one could have absorbed the planet, as the picture shows.

spotted a fire-ball crossing the sky that was so bright 'it made even the light from the sun seem dark'. From Kirensk, 250 miles away, a 'pillar of fire' was seen, followed by three or four claps and a crashing sound.

Such was the force of the explosion that horses were thrown down in an area south of Kansk, more than 400 miles distant. Equally remarkable were the flash burns sustained by residents of this sparsely populated region. A farmer, S. B. Semenov, was sitting on the steps of his house, 40 miles away, when he saw the flash. He instinctively lowered his eyes, but the heat was searing. 'My shirt was almost burned on my body,' he told later visitors. When he raised his eyes again, the fire-ball had vanished. Moments later, the blast hurled him from the steps, leaving him briefly unconscious. When he recovered, a great thundering sound was audible. His neighbour, P. P. Kosolapov, was facing away from the fire-ball and the first he knew of it was when his

This picture, taken 20 years after the explosion, still clearly shows the devastation in the Tungus region. On this hillside, 5 miles from the epicentre, trees had been flattened by the blast and scorched by intense heat.

ears burned painfully. A Tungus tribesman told scientists who reached the site long afterwards that a herd of 1,500 reindeer had been wiped out: 'The fire came by and destroyed the forest, the reindeer and all other animals.' In one herdsman's storage hut, everything had been burned including his clothing, and his samovar as well as his silverware had melted.

Five widely divergent explanations for this event have been advanced:

● The first hypothesis was that a giant meteorite had fallen, exploding from the intense heat generated by its impact. Such a meteorite struck central Arizona in prehistoric times, leaving a crater ¾ mile wide. Experts on early expeditions to the Tungus discounted this theory because they could not find an impact crater, but some scientists believe that a stony meteorite (as opposed to one of almost pure nickel-iron) within a certain critical size range would not survive its fiery passage through the atmosphere but would explode – perhaps even as violently as the Tungus event.

● In the 1950s it was suggested that a distant, highly advanced civilisation may have somehow set off a mid-air nuclear explosion. The blast did, in fact, take

place high in the air, and this was shown by the dissection of tree branches that had been growing in 1908. The upper surfaces of the layer that had been exposed to the sky in that year had been seared. In addition, recordings of fluctuations in the earth's magnetism at the time showed an effect strikingly like that produced by an atomic-bomb explosion in the atmosphere. Expeditions to the site in 1958 and 1959 reported that unusually high levels of radioactivity had been detected there. However, a careful study of the area in 1961 showed that report to have been spurious.

● The explanation many scientists still favour is that a comet head plunged into the atmosphere at such speed that it exploded in mid-air from heat generated by its entry into the atmosphere. Comet heads are widely believed to be huge 'dirty snowballs', formed of frozen gases, such as ammonia and water, mixed with dust and possibly particles of meteoritic iron. Despite scepticism by some scientists, a comet might approach without being seen. The gas and dust scattered in the explosion would have spread through the upper atmosphere, accounting for the pale 'white night' skies seen over Europe for several days afterwards.

● A theory put forward in 1965 is that an 'anti-rock', made of anti-matter, plunged into the atmosphere and was annihilated on contact with atoms of ordinary matter, producing a fire-ball of gamma rays and an explosion. This would account for the flash burns, the apparent absence of a mushroom cloud like those generated by ordinary chemical and atomic explosions, and the lack of any residual material.

● The latest proposal is that a tiny 'black hole' hit Siberia, passing through the entire earth and emerging in the North Atlantic.

Nothing in the art of the medieval alchemist or the contemporary science-fiction writer is more bizarre than the concept of a black hole. Yet in recent years a number of physicists have come to believe that they are a considerable, perhaps vital, part of our universe. A black hole would be a huge lump of matter that had shrunk or, more properly, collapsed, to a state so extremely dense that it had become invisible. Because of its density, it would generate gravity in its vicinity of such extraordinary strength that no light, nor anything else, could escape from it. Any light rays passing near would be irretrievably drawn in.

Gravity is the weakest force in nature. For example, it takes the whole mass of the earth to make a feather drift down. But if the earth were compressed to the size of a ping-pong ball, its gravity would become so concentrated that nothing could resist it – not even light. Visually, therefore, such a body would be a black hole.

Because of the extreme conditions within such an object, the laws of nature with which we are familiar would be overwhelmed; and, many theorists believe, crazy effects predicted by the relativity theory – and to some extent already demonstrated – would prevail. Inside the black hole, time and space would be interchanged, so that, like Alice's experience in *Through the Looking-Glass*, it would be no more possible to remain in one place than to stop the forward march of time in our world. Anyone who fell into a black hole would be stretched out like a string of spaghetti, then would disintegrate. Finally, even the atomic particles of the unfortunate person's body would lose their identity. Yet, theoretically, his or her image would linger, ghost-like, on the outer fringes of the hole, where the black hole's gravitational field is not yet strong enough to prevent the escape of all light, preserving indefinitely the last glimpse available to an outside observer.

In contemplating such exotic explanations for the Tungus event as anti-rocks or black holes, we realise how far our ideas about nature have gone beyond what we can see, hear and feel. The concept of anti-matter arose as scientists learned more and more about atomic particles, and about symmetries in systems of space, time and matter. In 1928 the British scientist P. A. M. Dirac, whom many physicists rank with Einstein, put forward a theory which suggested that there must be a particle identical to the electron but with an electric charge that is positive instead of negative. Four years later, such a particle – the positron – was discovered in laboratory experiments. It became evident that there were anti-particles that mirrored or corresponded to each type of particle. If such particles were assembled into atoms, and the atoms assembled into stones, people and worlds, they would constitute anti-matter.

Throughout our environment particles of anti-matter are constantly formed by the impact on atmospheric atoms of high energy particles, or cosmic rays, raining on the earth from space. The anti-particles can be observed by sophisticated laboratory techniques, but they survive less than a millionth of a second. For as soon as they encounter an atom of ordinary matter, and there are plenty of those in our atmosphere, they are annihilated, leaving only a tiny but intense flash of light at the invisible but highly energetic radiation wavelengths known as gamma rays.

Galaxies of anti-matter

While ordinary matter dominates our part of the universe, conceivably there are galaxies of anti-matter with their own anti-worlds and anti-people far out in space – anti-galaxies, so to speak. Light generated by anti-matter would be indistinguishable from our kind of light, so it would be impossible to identify an anti-galaxy through a telescope.

The possibility that the Siberian explosion was caused by a meteorite of anti-matter was examined by the noted American chemist Willard F. Libby, former member of the Atomic Energy Commission and winner of a Nobel Prize for his discovery of radioactive carbon dating. Libby and two other physicists observed in *Nature*, a British scientific journal of world-wide repute, that both anti-matter and matter would be converted into energy if such a meteorite fell into the atmosphere. It would be a far more efficient con-

The Tungus is a desolate forested plateau near the Tunguska river in central Siberia, 500 miles north-west of Lake Baikal. In summer, the land is swampy; in winter, it is frozen solid.

version than that of an atomic bomb, so a relatively small amount of anti-matter would be needed to produce a blast equal to that of 30 million tons of TNT – the estimated force of the Siberian explosion. They also pointed out that the disintegration of an anti-rock would briefly increase the amount of carbon-14 in the air, which is normally manufactured at a fairly steady rate by the rain of cosmic rays. If there was more carbon-14 in the air than normal in 1908 and soon afterwards, then wood formed in trees anywhere in the world in the following years would be unusually rich in that form of carbon.

The amounts of carbon-14 in successive rings of a 300-year-old Douglas fir from Arizona and a venerable oak from near Los Angeles were measured – and, indeed, the highest level occurred in wood found in 1909, the year after the blast. But the rise was only one-seventh of what it should have been if there had been a meteorite made of anti-matter. Libby and his colleagues concluded that the evidence did not prove anti-matter was the cause of the explosion.

In September 1973, two scientists at the University of Texas, A. A. Jackson IV and Michael P. Ryan, Jr., suggested that the 1908 devastation was caused by a mini black hole. A 'conventional' black hole is the residue of a giant star that has collapsed, leaving a superdense remnant with a mass more than twice that of the sun. In 1971, however, Stephen Hawking of Cambridge University had proposed that mini black holes might have been created during the initial big-bang phase of the universe's birth. Hawking pointed out that if the earliest period of the universal explosion were turbulent, there must have been areas of great compression, as well as regions where expansion was taking place. The compression would have squeezed material into mini black holes that would still permeate the universe. Writing in *Nature*, Jackson and Ryan proposed that the penetration of the atmosphere by such a mini black hole and its passage through the earth could account for all the reported effects. The theory, however, has never won wide support from the scientific world. For if such a black hole had hit Siberia, it would have emerged from the far side of the earth at some point, leaving similarly cataclysmic evidence of its passage. Yet no such place has ever been found.

Bewildering black holes

The more conventional idea of a comet – or a meteorite sufficiently insubstantial to disintegrate before it hit the earth – makes scientists happier. But no explanation satisfies everyone, and we are left with the real possibility of a recurrence. Should it take place without warning in a populated region and resemble a nuclear blast, could it trigger an atomic war? A better understanding of such phenomena could minimise the risks. The discussion of black holes as a possible cause of the

This yawning crater in central Arizona is the earth's most dramatic meteorite scar. Formed in prehistoric times, it is about ¾ mile across. At its centre, the crater is 620 ft deep.

If the earth were compressed to the size of a ping-pong ball, its gravitational pull would be so intense that nothing could escape it, not even light. It would be a black hole.

Tungus blast demonstrates the extent to which some scientists are rushing to explain various puzzles in astronomy and physics with this bewildering concept. Astronomical observations in the past few years have made black holes seem more of a possibility, although, as one physicist put it, they are 'as pervasive in theory as they are evasive in observation'.

The roots of the concept of black holes lie far back in the history of astronomy. In 1844, at the observatory in Königsberg, Prussia (now Kaliningrad, U.S.S.R.), the German-born astronomer F. W. Bessel found that the path of Sirius, the sky's brightest star, was slightly irregular. To casual observers it had always seemed to remain in the same spot, but being one of the nearest stars to the solar system, its motion relative to distant objects in the universe could be traced through a telescope. Sirius, Bessel showed, moves in a wavy line rather than a straight one. This suggested that Sirius has an unseen companion, and that the two stars were circling each other as they flew through the void, held in each other's arms by their mutual gravity. Since the mass of Sirius could be estimated, it was possible, using the laws of gravitationally controlled motion, to estimate the weight of the seemingly invisible companion. It turned out to be about the same as that of our own sun. Why could it not be observed?

Nineteen years after Bessel's observation it was seen. An American telescope-maker, Alvan Clark, spotted the companion while testing a new instrument. The star's intrinsic brightness proved to be one-four-hundredth that of the sun. The real surprise came when light from the star was analysed. By the early decades of this century it was recognised that the whiter the light from a typical star, the hotter, brighter and bigger it is. Small stars burn cooler, are dimmer and redder. But this faint star was as white as Sirius – which is whiter than the sun. If so white and hot, why was it so dim? The only plausible explanation was that the star was very small and, because it was the same weight as the sun, extremely dense.

Ton of matter in a matchbox

Sir Arthur Eddington wrote in 1927, 'The message of the companion of Sirius when it was decoded ran: "I am composed of material 3,000 times denser than anything you have come across; a ton of my material would be a little nugget that you could put into a matchbox." What reply can one make to such a message? The reply which most of us made in 1914 was – "Shut up. Don't talk nonsense".' Sirius's companion was a 'white dwarf' not a black hole, and with only one such object on the register, it could be dismissed as a freak. In time, however, other white dwarfs were found. In fact, they proved to be fairly common,

although so dim that only those close to earth could be detected.

The explanation became apparent in the late 1920s, when scientists not only began to understand atomic structure but also got their first inklings of what it is that makes stars shine. The sun, it was evident, had been shining for millions of years. But no one knew what process could possibly account for such an enormous and continuous output of energy. Einstein had proposed, in theoretical terms, a balance between matter and energy. His formula suggested that conversion of even a small amount of matter would release vast amounts of energy. Eddington and others considered the possibility that the fusion of hydrogen nuclei to form helium nuclei might occur within stars. Since the helium nucleus would weigh 0.8% less than the hydrogen nuclei from which it was formed, this small residue of matter would emerge as energy.

Collapse of a burnt-out star

If fusion – such as the conversion of hydrogen into helium – were responsible for energy generation within stars, what would happen when the fuel for these nuclear fires burned out? Stars are made of gas, and as long as they are hot inside – as long as their 'fires' burn – that gas tends to expand. The energy generated in their cores fights its way out through the star in the form of radiation, exerting an outward pressure that counteracts the massive weight of the star's own substance. The British mathematician R. H. Fowler proposed in 1926 that when a star has burned up all its fuel, this resistance to the inward pressure of the star's own weight vanishes and the star collapses upon itself, forming an object of great density – like one gigantic, frigid molecule. This would be the superdense stuff of a white dwarf.

In 1930 a young Indian, on his way to study at Cambridge, began calculating what forces within an atom resist compression. On his arrival in England, Subrahamanyan Chandrasekhar, now known as 'Chandra', showed his calculations to Fowler. He had come to the startling conclusion that, for any star much larger than the sun, there was no known force that could halt the collapse.

Contraction to a white dwarf was possible because atoms are hollow. According to the traditional description of an atom, it resembles the solar system, with a nucleus in place of the sun and electrons in place of planets. Like the solar system, it is largely formed of empty space. Chandra realised that when something is squeezed in a powerful press, there are forces within the atoms that resist. One arises from a basic law, the 'exclusion principle', that had been enunciated by Wolfgang Pauli, the Nobel Prize winning Austrian physicist, a few years earlier. The electrons occupy certain 'slots', not really comparable to planetary orbits, and only one is permitted in such a slot at any one time. Under high temperatures or great compression the electrons are forced out of their slots, forming a mass of independently moving electrons and atomic nuclei. But the electrons still repel one another in the manner defined by Pauli, and it is this effect that finally stops the collapse of a white dwarf.

Beyond white dwarfs

Chandra, however, calculated that the weight of any star much larger than the sun would overcome this 'electron pressure'. There are giant stars 50 times more massive than the sun. They burn so intensely that their lifetimes are limited to 10 or 20 million years. Countless numbers of them must have burned out during the history of the universe. What happens to them? 'A star of large mass cannot pass into the white dwarf stage,' wrote the youthful Chandra, 'and one is left speculating on other possibilities.'

The leaders of the scientific establishment reacted with indignation to his suggestion that there was no limit to the collapse. Eddington pointed out that if a star kept on contracting, once it had shrunk to within a few miles' radius, its gravity would become 'strong enough to hold the radiation' – that is, it would be a black hole. But Eddington could not accept this and refused to take the idea seriously.

The first clue as to what actually happens when a large star collapses came from analysis of the most spectacular event that the heavens offer – a 'supernova'. In 1885 astronomers had observed an extraordinary flare-up of a star in the great swirl of star clouds known as the Andromeda Nebula, which is the nearest galaxy resembling our Milky Way. For 25 days that single star shone more brightly than 10 million suns. Then it faded to such an extent that it was no longer visible through the most powerful telescopes.

Astronomers noted that in 1572 a similar flare-up known as 'Tycho Brahe's Nova' had occurred in our own Milky Way. Two astronomers at the Mt Wilson Observatory in California, Walter Baade and Fritz Zwicky, pointed out that the star associated with the nova had apparently vanished.

Baade and Zwicky theorised that a supernova marked the death of a very massive star whose collapse was so catastrophic that a large part of the star's substance was converted into energy, leaving something of considerably smaller mass. This residual star, they said, must have been compressed to such a degree by the explosion that it consisted almost entirely of tightly packed neutrons. These are electrically neutral, and can be packed together more tightly than protons, which, carrying a positive charge, repel one another. Since a neutron, when free of an atomic nucleus, eventually sheds an electron and turns into a proton, it seemed reasonable to suppose that, reversing the process, the compression of a sea of protons and electrons could produce neutrons.

Attention had been drawn also to the most spectacular remnant of a supernova in the sky – the Crab Nebula, which today still looks like the high-speed photograph of an explosion. By comparing pictures of the nebula taken over a span of years, it was possible to trace the expansion of its luminous gas clouds. Running this 'moving picture' backwards indicated that light from the original explosion must have reached the earth in about AD 1054. That was a time when the Chinese were keeping careful astronomical records, and in that year, according to chronicles of the Sung Dynasty, a star appeared so brilliant that for 23 days it could be seen in full daylight. If the Crab Nebula was a product of that explosion, Baade argued, perhaps it had left a neutron star at its centre. Indeed, a faint and rather strange-looking star was observed in that region.

There was a strong suspicion, however, that the neutron star was a mere figment of theoretical manipulation. The concept of a white dwarf, a nugget of which would weigh a ton, had been considered pure nonsense, but the idea of a neutron star, 1 cu. in. of which would weigh 1,000 million tons, was preposterous. A white dwarf was formed from the material of a star as large as the sun compressed into the size of the earth; but a neutron star, formed from a star somewhat larger than the sun, would be a comparable amount of material crushed into a body with a 5-mile radius.

When matter disappears

Even greater scepticism greeted the proposals of a young physicist at the University of California in Berkeley named J. Robert Oppenheimer, later renowned for his leadership of the atomic-bomb project. He and his students explored what would happen if the weight of the collapsing star was too great even for neutrons to resist. Put another way, what would happen if the compression were sufficient to overcome the strongest force in nature – that exerted by such nuclear particles as neutrons upon one another at close range? The calculations of Oppenheimer and his group culminated in a 1939 paper that he wrote with Hartland Snyder, *On Continued Gravitational Contraction*. There was nothing, they said, in Einstein's theory of gravity – the so-called 'general' theory of relativity – suggesting any reason why such a collapse should stop.

Visitors from outer space?

The most startling theory about the devastation in Siberia is that it was caused by a damaged flying saucer from outer space, disintegrating in a nuclear explosion. The theory has been put forward recently by the Australian journalist John Baxter and the American scholar Thomas Atkins, who followed up the work of Russian experts, including engineer Alexandre Kazantsev and Professor Felix Zigel. They claim that there is considerable evidence to support the theory of a nuclear blast.

In the first place, they say, the earth's magnetic field was disturbed at the time of the explosion, as it would have been by a nuclear blast.

Secondly, the pattern of destruction in the shattered forest is more consistent with the shock waves produced by an atomic bomb than with those of a conventional explosion.

Other clues were the extreme intensity of light at the time, and the later discovery of numerous tiny green globules of melted dust, called trinitites, which are characteristic of an atomic blast.

According to a Russian expert on the area, Professor Alexei Zolotov, the globules also contained metallic fragments of elements which are not found naturally in the area, and which are not part of the usual makeup of meteorites either. Baxter and Atkins believe that this metal could have come from a spaceship's hull or fuel tank.

Finally, the two men point out that plant mutations in the area after the explosion were similar to those at Hiroshima in Japan after the atomic bomb was dropped there in 1945.

Baxter and Atkins draw on the eye-witness evidence of people in the Tungus region at the time to complete their theory. Many of them described a large bluish object, cylindrical in shape, hurtling across the sky with a multi-coloured vapour trail in its wake. The noise of the object could be heard while it was still in sight, according to their evidence, and this, they calculate, suggests that it was travelling at around twice the speed of sound, or about 1,500 mph.

From all the evidence, Baxter and Atkins built up their theory, published in a book called *The Fire Came By* in 1976. This is the remarkable science-fiction picture they drew:

On June 30, 1908, an extra-terrestrial flying object (similar to the one photographed above over Yugoslavia in 1975) dived towards the earth from space to attempt a landing. Because of some accident aboard, its situation was critical. Having succeeded in entering the atmosphere, it flew in a wide arc and began its manoeuvres for touchdown. But it was too late.

Two miles above Siberia, the atomic fuel which powered it became heated to a point above the critical threshold and set off a nuclear explosion of about 30 megatons – equivalent to 30 million tons of TNT. This turned 25 miles of the earth's surface to molten rock, and burned people as far as 400 miles away from the centre of the explosion.

What sort of people were in the crippled spaceship? Where could they have come from? What could they have looked like? These are other mysteries lost in the debris of the Tungus.

As the contraction proceeded, the intensity of gravity in the heart of the star would increase, causing the collapse to run at an ever faster rate until finally the density would become so great that the gravity would be strong enough to prevent anything, including light, from escaping.

Because gravity, when very intense, slows time, the collapsing process would seem to a distant observer to slow down as the gravity field increased in strength until, on the outer fringes of the black hole, the process would appear to have stopped altogether. The progression to total collapse could take as long as the life-time of the universe. But to someone unfortunate enough to be falling into the stellar abyss, cut off from

all contact with the outside, the collapse would seem to be running its course in about a day.

The ultimate destiny of such a black hole, derived from the Einstein equations, would be infinitely powerful gravity concentrated in an infinitely dense, infinitely small spot where time and space have lost their meaning – what is known as a 'singularity'. Whether things really go to that extreme in the heart of a black hole is one of the basic problems confronting theorists today.

Surveying the heavens with radio antennae, astronomers at Cambridge University reported in 1968 that for several months they had been recording extremely rhythmic radio signals from four points in the sky. Each source generated pulses at a characteristic rate, all being in the range from one pulse per quarter-second to one every two seconds. Rhythmic phenomena were not new to astronomy, being typically associated with the spinning of the stars, planets and moons, but nothing was known to spin as fast as once every second. 'Our first thought,' said Sir Martin Ryle, leader of the British group, 'was that this was another intelligence trying to contact us.' Then, however, the scientists began pondering what would happen if a star collapsed to a superdense state such as a white dwarf or a neutron star.

Radio beacons in the sky

There is a basic law known as the conservation of angular momentum which is instinctively familiar to every figure skater or ballet dancer. In a pirouette, if the arms are extended, the spin rate slows. If they are held close to one's sides, the rate is fastest. Thus, if a star 'pulls in its arms' by contracting, its spin rate will increase. Many stars spin roughly once a day, and it was calculated that if they collapsed to a superdense state, their spinning would accelerate enormously. If such a collapsed star had a magnetic field of great strength – as seemed likely – and the field was offset from the spin axis (as with the earth's own magnetism), the star would emit beams of radio waves that, with each rotation, would sweep the sky like an airport beacon, accounting for the pulses.

Then came evidence that not all of the pulsing radio sources, or 'pulsars', are beeping at sedate tempos. From the Crab Nebula, radio astronomers detected pulses at 30 times a second. Could Baade and Zwicky, then, have been right? Was it conceivable that the peculiar star in the heart of that supernova remnant was, in fact, a neutron star, spinning 30 times a second? To test the possibility, special light-monitoring and stroboscopic television systems were aimed at the star. The astonishing discovery was made that it does, indeed, 'switch itself off' 30 times a second – an optical as well as a radio pulsar.

By now, scores of pulsars have been detected. With such powerful evidence for neutron stars, the possibility of even more extreme forms of contraction – black holes – began to seem reasonable. A number of physicists started thinking about how they could be detected despite their 'blackness'.

Remembering the discovery of the first white dwarf through the effect of its gravity on an easily visible star, they proposed that a two-star system in which one member was a black hole might be found. A further clue would be the detection of emissions from material falling into the hole. This material, being drawn in and compressed, would become so hot that it would generate brilliant X-rays before it vanished into the hole. Where a black hole was circling with an ordinary star, robbing it of gas, the X-ray emission should be particularly intense. An early hint that such X-rays were coming from certain points in the sky came in the 1960s, when it became evident that some celestial objects are extraordinarily brilliant at X-ray wavelengths. Four of the brightest were in the constellation of Cygnus, the Swan, which decorates the evening sky in summer. They were given numerical designations, the most powerful being Cyg X-1. C. T. Bolton of the University of Toronto, and others, pointed out that Cyg X-1 coincided with a two-star pair – one of whose members is invisible. The visible star, a so-called supergiant known as HDE 226868, is circling something once every 5·6 days.

In the same way that it was possible to calculate the mass of the invisible white dwarf circling with Sirius from its effects on Sirius, so Bolton and others have estimated that the unseen companion of HDE 226868 is eight times heavier than the sun – far too massive to be either a white dwarf or neutron star.

Not all astronomers are convinced that the existence of black holes has been demonstrated. But, as one of them put it: 'Either there are holes in the sky, or there are holes in the general theory of relativity.'

Black holes have been heralded as a possible answer to a basic problem in cosmology: what is it that holds the universe together, and binds the clusters of galaxies? Einstein's theory predicted that there must be enough mass within the universe to keep it from flying apart indefinitely. In other words, although the galaxies are flying apart, as though blown asunder by some primordial 'big bang', it appeared that they would not have sufficient velocity to escape one another's gravity. Their dispersal, like the flight of a ball thrown upward, does seem to be slowing. But it is not clear whether this means that the galaxies must eventually start 'falling back', in a contraction that some theorists believe will plunge the entire universe into a single black hole.

Invisible 'glue' of the universe

The trouble is that adding up all the material that can be seen or readily inferred accounts for only about 2% of what would be needed to hold the universe together and prevent eternal expansion. Black holes and the dark cinders of stars that remain after a white dwarf or neutron star has cooled might make up for the deficit.

It may seem a long and, in places, tenuous chain of reasoning that begins with a mysterious explosion over the Siberian tundra, and ends with the death of the universe. But it also seemed far-fetched to the astronomers of 16th-century Europe when Copernicus first published his discovery that the earth moves round the sun, causing men to doubt what they saw every day with their own eyes.

It is by such daring leaps of logic and of the imagination that astronomy advances. There is at least the possibility that black holes do exist, somewhere in space ... and that a tiny one fell to earth in Siberia, at 7.17 a.m. on June 30, 1908.

WALTER SULLIVAN

Gazetteer

of mysterious sites around the world

by Emmanuelle Hubert

*Exploring the past is like entering a vast
cave system with only candles to light the way.
The deeper the explorer penetrates its chambers
and its endlessly forking tunnels, the
more he becomes aware of the darkness
that surrounds his tiny pool of light.
The following pages show some of the places around the
world where explorers have tried to lift the shadows.
But every new discovery in archaeology gives rise
to new possibilities. And every new answer
suggests new questions, new mysteries . . .*

MYSTERIOUS SITES OF THE WORLD

Abalessa. The tomb of Tin-Hinan.

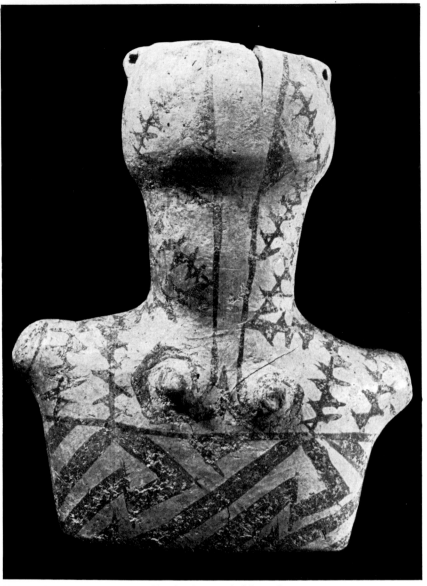

Maliq. Illyrian vase in human shape with painted geometrical decoration.

Albania

Maliq

(62 miles south-east of Tiranë). The Illyrians, the ancient Albanians, pose many problems for archaeologists, and a number of diggings have been undertaken at prehistoric sites since the Second World War.

At Maliq ancient dwellings have been excavated, proving that the Illyrians lived there from 2800 BC – well before the arrival of Indo-Europeans.

The Illyrians must have maintained relations with Mycenae, as objects characteristic of that civilisation have been found at the site. The pottery of Maliq, on the other hand, resembles that of Anatolia, in Turkey, and northern Greece. Curious little bell-shaped earthenware altars and vessels with handles and fluted bowls have been found which are unique to this area.

The Greeks and then the Romans settled on the coast of Albania and built cities there. Some of the Illyrians joined the Roman army or took up trades to serve these new colonies, but most of them did not become assimilated and sheltered in the mountains, leading a very primitive life up to quite recent times.

The excavations at Maliq have proved the antiquity of this Illyrian settlement, but so far little else is known about the people who once lived there.

Algeria

Abalessa

(34 miles west of Tamanrasset). The Tuaregs claim descent from a legendary Berber princess named Tin-Hinan and, according to them, her remains lie in a tomb near the village of Abalessa.

In 1925 a group of French archaeologists decided to verify this. They found a circular mound, some 80 ft in diameter and 3 ft high, at the place indicated. During the course of excavation they uncovered a carefully made stone structure consisting of several chambers, built in an architectural style foreign to the country and certainly one that predates Islam.

In the end chamber they found the skeleton of a tall woman (5 ft 8 in.) of the Caucasian race. She resembled an ancient Egyptian rather than a woman of European or Mediterranean extraction and wore a leather dress, seven gold bracelets on the right arm and seven silver bracelets on the left arm. Beside her, in a wooden bowl, were thin leaves of gold bearing the marks of Roman coins. Not far away was found an early Stone Age steatopygous statuette (a figure with distinctively large buttocks). It seems likely that this statuette was an ancient idol of some kind.

Fourteen small funerary buildings intended for the slaves surrounded the main building, which did not appear to have been built for use as a mausoleum. It seemed to be more like a fort, but built by whom? It may have been built by the Romans as, according to Pliny, they would have been in Abalessa in 19 BC. Would Tin-Hinan's forces have fought them in the desert?

298

Bahrain

Quala'at al Bahrain

(Northern tip of the island). Bahrain has been called 'the island of the dead' as it is almost entirely covered by some 100,000 burial mounds, both large and small, dating back to prehistory. Until recently it was thought that the pre-Islamic populations of the eastern coast of Arabia went there to bury their dead and that no prehistoric city, temple or palace existed on the island, which is largely desert.

Recent excavations have proved this to be incorrect by revealing the wall and houses of a town, a palace of unknown style and a sanctuary. It is now clear that Bahrain was the centre of a vanished empire which extended to present-day Saudi Arabia and to which the Sumerians referred in their texts as the realm of Dilmun, country of the rising sun, centre of earthly paradise, and the only region to survive the Flood.

The objects that have been dug up indicate the existence of commercial activity oriented towards both India and Mesopotamia. At one time subterranean canals piped spring water to irrigate the gardens.

The archaeological workings at Bahrain are still only in their initial stages. However, on the Arabian coast and on nearby islands traces of the same civilisation have been uncovered, some of them even older than those discovered at Bahrain.

The key site which would enable a date to be set for the beginning of this culture unfortunately cannot be excavated, for it is located at the women's bathing place, making it strictly out of bounds according to Arabian custom. On the surface,

shards of pottery, flint implements and obsidian blades dating from about 4000 BC have been found.

One day, through archaeological work, the history of the Dilmun civilisation may be revealed. At present it is one of the oldest-known civilisations in the world. There is a possibility that further discoveries might reveal the existence of an even older culture.

Brazil

Pacoval

(On the island of Marajó in the Amazon delta). In this inhospitable region at the mouth of the Amazon there are traces of a developed civilisation of Andean character. Archaeologists have studied some 60

Pacoval. Woman's loincloth in pottery.

man-made hills, built so that their summits are above flood and high-water levels. Some served as burial places, and villages stood upon others. The pottery that has been uncovered of the oldest period (about AD 1300) is of very fine quality, the most curious pieces being some ceramic models of women's loincloths.

This culture must have disappeared before 1450, for when the Portuguese colonised the region they found only primitive Indians living there. These people would certainly have been incapable of landscaping the hills.

The indications are that an unknown Indian group emigrated eastwards to settle in the Amazonas. They must have been skilled and had a strongly hierarchical society in order to accomplish such remarkable feats of construction. It is not known why these people came, or left. Perhaps the weakening effects of the climate were in part responsible for their disappearance. It is thought that they may have travelled on to the Antilles Islands in the Caribbean.

Canada

Fort Chimo

(Ungava Bay, 750 miles north of Quebec City). In this area there are rock walls dating from 500 BC, which intrigue many archaeologists. There are also piled-up blocks of stone which look like statues, though no chippings of stone have been found in the vicinity. Thus, the blocks may have been transported to the spot, but by whom?

The culture of the Eskimos who now inhabit the region appears to have nothing in common with that of the people who raised these stones. Eskimo legends tell of these stones having been erected by a race of giants whose language differed greatly from their own.

Some scholars believe that these mysterious giants could have been the Vikings who came from Norway. Others speculate that Indians who were members of the Dorset culture might have established themselves at Ungava Bay. As yet there is no proof supporting either of these two assertions.

Canary Islands

Hierro Island

(94 miles south-west of the island of Tenerife). It is now more than 100 years since a priest, walking in a remote part of Hierro Island, discovered signs of writing engraved on the side of a cliff. At the base of the rocky wall were seats of hewn stone, arranged in a ring.

Quala'at al Bahrain. Some of the prehistoric burial mounds.

Since then a large number of these signs have been found and studied, not only on Hierro Island but also on the islands of La Palma and Gran Canaria. It seems that these writings are of three different types. Some signs resemble those drawn in Europe by Bronze Age people; others are similar to Saharan rock carvings and Cretan writing.

These discoveries prove that the Canaries have been visited since ancient times. However, the discoveries do not reveal the origin of the Guanches, the people whom the French and Spanish found on these islands. Some of their skulls seem to indicate that they belonged to the Cro-Magnon race, which is thought to have emigrated to North Africa from Europe. Marvellous cave paintings found in Europe prove that the Cro-Magnon people were skilled artists, but no such paintings have been found in the Canaries.

Caroline Islands

Nanmatol
(Island off Ponape, 1,300 miles north-east of New Guinea). In the most inaccessible part of this island stand the impressive ruins of a Stone Age town. Blocks of perfectly hewn basalt form walls some 30 ft high.

A system of canals, or rather of channels, cut the mysterious city into small islands surrounded by high walls. Gates once opened and closed these canals on the seaward side. A wall had been built in the sea – perhaps to protect a port.

The present-day Micronesians

would certainly have been unable to carry out this type of construction. No one knows when this city was built and why it was suddenly abandoned by its inhabitants – some walls have been left unfinished. There is also the question of why a town of such importance was built on an island as remote as Ponape.

China

Shih-chai-shan
(In Yunnan Province, 30 miles south of Kunming). A Chinese general is said to have conquered the Tien kingdom of Yunnan around 329 BC. When he was prevented from returning home by another Chinese army he settled in Tien as its king and his men introduced the Chinese cultural influence into the region.

Nothing was known of this culture, which developed apart from the main Chinese tradition, until 1955, when archaeologists began excavations at the burial ground of Tien nobles in the Shih-chai-shan region. A large number of objects were found which had been buried surrounding the dead. Study of these has established the existence of a Bronze Age civilisation in this area, whose inhabitants also knew the use of iron.

The art of the Yunnan people was connected with that of the people of the steppes; their arms, for example, are decorated with animal bas-reliefs. But it is their bronze drum-shaped vessels which were used as containers for cowrie shells (a form of currency) which are of particular interest. Small figures were set on top

of these vessels, portraying aspects of their daily or religious life. On one of them a seated woman appears to be receiving offerings, which may be proof of the existence of a female-dominated society. On another a human sacrifice is portrayed.

Yunnan came under Chinese suzerainty at the end of the 7th century and was later conquered and colonised by Kublai Khan. Even if the majority of the population were assimilated it is possible that a portion was exiled. In south-east Asia and even in Polynesia bronze drums have been found, and it is known that human sacrifice has been practised in these regions for a long time. Could both the drums and the ancient practice have been introduced by the Yunnan people? But again, could a society living in a land-locked region have travelled so far without previous maritime experience?

Colombia

San Agustin
(250 miles south-west of Bogotá). One hour's walk from this small Andean village, in the dense forest, is an area a few miles square where there are more than 300 large stone statues. Some of them are as much as 14 to 21 ft tall. They have terrifying human faces, teeth like cats and some seem to be feeding on the children they are holding.

In the same area as these statues are the remnants of Stone Age temples and tombs. The temples were primitively buried, with just their approaches left open.

Designs drawn on the stones differ from those found elsewhere in South America, where the subjects are generally animals. At San Agustin they are geometric figures, squares and rectangles. Their repetitious nature seems to suggest a system of writing, but they could just as well be formulas or magic designs.

The strangest and most original monument, to be found at Alto de Lavapatas, is an arrangement of smooth boulders on the bed of a stream which has been made into a pattern of pools with interconnecting channels. It is decorated with carvings of human figures and aquatic animals such as reptiles and frogs. Although the nature and function of this strange monument remain hypothetical, it is thought that it

Nanmatol. Stone Age town wall, with a burial vault in the foreground.

San Agustin. Massive stone statue guarding a burial chamber.

could have been a place for curative or sacrificial ceremonies.

Carbon-14 dating has established that the monuments were made between the 5th and 12th centuries AD. Since no trace of a city has been located in the region it is thought to have been a place of pilgrimage, although nothing is known of the people who frequented it.

The statues have some affinity with those of Easter Island, and the other monuments are in some ways similar to Polynesian artefacts.

Egypt

Avaris-Tanis
(75 miles north-east of Cairo). The old empire of Egypt underwent a serious crisis when it was partially invaded by a little-known people called the Hyksos. By 1700 BC they had imposed their rule on the Egyptians and settled in the Nile delta where they built their capital Avaris. By around 1674 BC they were sufficiently well established to form the 15th Pharaonic Dynasty, but native Egyptian rulers succeeded in expelling them by 1570 BC.

Avaris has been located beneath the ruins of another ancient city which followed after it, named Tanis. The excavations at Tanis are incomplete, so the remains of Avaris have yet to be unearthed. These remains should eventually reveal more information about the Hyksos, who overcame the Egyptian armies with their superior equipment, arriving with horses and war chariots which were still unknown to the Egyptians. It is thought that they may have been a people from the steppes of central Asia, where horses were well known.

Ethiopia

Chabbé
(160 miles south of Addis Ababa). Chabbé is a very deep gorge on the open savannah, ranging from about 15 ft to 30 ft in width, and the local people say that for a long time it was a cave. Debris of a natural canopy does indeed prove that it was a sort of tunnel at one time.

The walls are covered with about 50 painstakingly carved reliefs depicting elegantly stylised cattle, whose bodies appear in profile, with the horns viewed from the front. All the beasts are female with the exception of a few calves. The layer of residue which covers these sculptures indicates in places that the carvings were executed some time in the remote past.

With the exception of the rock carvings at Harar, these carvings are quite unlike any others in Ethiopia. It is clear that Chabbé was a centre where fertility rites for the herds were held. But it is not known why all the animals are depicted headless, with horns springing directly from their necks. Above the horns, an elongated triangle pointing at each beast can be distinguished. And the cattle follow each other as though they were going to leave the tunnel.

Although the rocks in the area are of soft sandstone and are well suited to sculpture, it is only those in the gorge that are carved in any way.

Melka Kontourea
(On the River Awash, 30 miles south of Addis Ababa). In 1963 the traces of an ancient settlement were discovered on the banks of the River Awash. For thousands of years men used this area as a camping ground and left behind remnants of their implements on their departure.

When the river overflowed in the wet season, clay settled on these successive remains, sealing beneath it a portion of the past. Archaeologists have only had to scrape the site, bed by bed, to reach a settlement that goes back more than a million years. At this period the inhabitants were not so much men as very primitive hominids. Nevertheless, they used rudimentary tools made by cracking stones together, using the edges so formed to cut and scrape.

Chabbé. Cattle carvings on the rock face.

Melka Kontourea. Floor of a settlement more than a million years old.

At Melka Kontourea these implements and their stone debris have been found littering the ground all around a completely bare oval platform 10 yds square, with the exception of one side where five small circles formed by six to ten stones were found. This could not have been a chance arrangement: the stones must have been so grouped to serve a particular purpose.

It has been suggested that they may have been wedges to support the stakes of a shelter of branches or skins. But why then is there no trace of such a shelter on the platform? The hominids certainly did not clean their camp before leaving. This platform and the circles of stone may have been connected in some way with a religious ritual.

Tiya
(Near Soddu, 156 miles south-west of Addis Ababa). The stelae, or decorated stone slabs, at Tiya are among the many archaeological mysteries of Ethiopia. They are 16 ft high and are large, flat slabs with one side bearing reliefs consisting of uninterpreted marks and the outlines of a varying number of daggers, sometimes arranged in two rows with their points facing inwards. The significance of these daggers and their arrangement is not known.

The local people say that these stelae were erected by Muslim invaders for tethering their horses. But they certainly pre-date the Muslim invasion, which took place in the 16th century. They are vaguely similar to the Corsican menhirs (see p. 78) but the markings on them are unique. The form of the carved daggers seems to suggest that they may have been depictions of copper or bronze arms.

France

Douarnenez
(11 miles north-west of Quimper). The legend of the town of Ys tells of a flourishing city that once stood on the Bay of Douarnenez, with an embankment to protect it from high seas. A gate in the embankment was opened at low tide for the water from the river to flow out. It was then closed at high tide, and only the king of Ys had the key to it. The king's daughter was dissolute and perverse and stole it from him to give to the devil. The devil then opened the dyke gate and the sea flowed in and Ys was submerged. All its inhabitants were drowned with the exception of the king, who was able to flee, thanks to the intervention of St Gwenolé.

Did a town exist where the bay is now? At the beach of Le Ris, 1½ miles from Douarnenez, the presence of ancient structures, either silted-up or immersed, has been recorded. How old are they? The legend places the catastrophe in Christian times, but legends often modernise ancient events. It could possibly have been a Roman or Celtic town, or even built in the same period as were the megalithic monuments. Perhaps one day underwater excavations will answer these questions.

Forest of Fontainebleau
(30 miles south of Paris). This forest, which is now a popular recreation area, was an isolated region for thousands of years. It was a haunt of robbers, fringe dwellers and fugitives who sheltered in its caves and carved the walls with inscriptions, designs and abstract signs. More than 2,300 sq. yds of rock are decorated in this way.

Among the carvings are human figures with rectangular bodies, neck-less heads with sunken eyes and U-shaped noses. Their arms are outstretched, with the fingers spread like a fan, and often the legs are missing. A second group, in bas-relief, have their arms close to their bodies. In a third, the figures are dressed in skirts and have only three fingers on each hand.

The crosses, circles and hopscotch-like designs are almost impossible to date. They may be from prehistoric time, or they could have been drawn yesterday. All have been indexed and some are similar to designs which specialists have located elsewhere. However, there are some designs which are found only at Fontainebleau. These are the irregular latticed designs which have been deeply incised into the rock. They have been found in the most inaccessible places, in cavities where only an arm can reach. Why were these engravings made under such obviously difficult conditions? They were certainly not made recently, but how old are they? What message did their engravers wish to leave, and who were they?

Lebous
(11 miles north-east of Montpellier). The hunters of prehistory often chose to settle on promontories that were easy to defend, giving them two more or less perpendicular sides and a secure wall to their rear. This arrangement gave some protection from attack and enabled them to view the surrounding area without difficulty.

The Stone Age castle at Lebous, however, was of an entirely different nature. It is no longer standing, but its foundations, which have been recently uncovered, clearly show its layout: seven towers, a number of connecting fortified walls and a large enclosure into which the houses were crowded. All this was built 4,000 years ago without the aid of cement: the irregular stones were filled in with rubble, and the enclosure walls were made of a double thickness of rock. The towers were spaced some 25 yds apart and stood on the perimeter which measured about 50 by 75 yds. The houses or huts averaged 22 by 11 ft. One of them, much larger than the others, had a sort of roofed recess behind a hearth, in which human and animal bones have been found – suggesting cannibalistic rites. It is surprising that this is the only known castle in existence dating from this period, as the people of Lebous could well have had many imitators.

When invaders equipped with bronze arms occupied the region they managed to take Lebous, as the occupants had only slings to defend themselves. Impressed by this stronghold the invaders buried their chiefs in the towers, where their remains have recently been found.

Le Mas-d'Azil

(16 miles north-west of Foiz). During the course of excavations in the famous cave at Le Mas-d'Azil several thousand painted pebbles were discovered. They date from around 12,000 years ago, the period of tran-

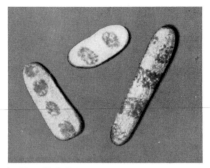
Le Mas-d'Azil. Painted pebbles.

sition between the Old Stone Age and the New Stone Age.

They are almost all oval shaped, ringed by a line of paint and decorated on one side with an abstract sign – a cross, a circle, a stripe and so on. Some of the signs call to mind characteristics of Aegean, Phoenician and Cypriot writings, while others resemble signs that can be seen on some of the earliest cave paintings, which date back almost 20,000 years.

What were these pebbles used for? Were they pieces of a game, coins, or stones endowed with magical power? The French prehistorian Edouard Piette, who discovered them at the end of the last century, believed that they were some form of primitive writing.

Provins

(45 miles south-east of Paris). At Provins there is a town under the town. A maze of corridors leads to

large arched rooms 16 ft high and decorated with numerous columns. The soot which covers some of the walls indicates that these rooms, or caves, were inhabited for some time. But who lived in them – and in what circumstances?

Some of these rooms must have served as warehouses for storing food in case of siege. These date back to the Middle Ages and are not particularly mysterious. On the other hand there are others, situated beneath them, of whose existence the medieval builders must have been unaware. They dug just above these earlier caves without breaking through to them, otherwise they would surely have taken advantage of the extra space.

These older caves are quite unlike those situated above them and consist of great halls more than 200 yds long which do not intersect or meet. On the walls there is graffiti similar to that drawn by Bronze and Iron Age people: suns, concentric circles and similar designs. However, fish and skulls have also been drawn on the walls and some signs have been deliberately scraped out.

What was the reason for this? Were the caves a pagan centre, later occupied by primitive Christians who attempted to obliterate the magic signs and drew the fish symbol used by members of the first Christian communities? It is not known why these great halls do not connect with one another.

Galapagos Islands

(About 600 miles west of the coast of Ecuador). In support of his thesis that the peopling of the Polynesian islands resulted from a migration from the east, the Norwegian Thor Heyerdahl has proved with his raft, the *Kon-Tiki*, that a very primitive ship can reach Polynesia from the coast of South America.

On the Galapagos Islands shards of unquestionably pre-Columbian pottery have been unearthed dating from about 2,000 years ago. There are about 2,000 pieces, and although it is not known how many unbroken items these pieces represent it is unlikely that there would be enough to prove a prolonged settlement. On the other hand, one or more ships could have run aground on these islands or taken refuge for some reason.

Forest of Fontainebleau. Latticework and other designs incised into rock.

Perhaps it was a port of supply. Whatever the reason, it is strange that the pre-Columbian Indians have left us so many painted vases and reliefs illustrating their daily life, but no illustrations showing any maritime expeditions.

Greece

Andikíthira

(25 miles north-west of Crete). In 1900 fishermen divers discovered an old wreck and its cargo of marble, pottery and other objects near the shore of the island of Andikíthira. Among these items was an encrusted bronze object of undetermined use.

It languished in the reserve section of a museum until 1955 when a curious scientist decided to clean it. He found that it was a complex instrument with cog-wheels fitting one into another. Finely graduated circles and inscriptions marked on it in ancient Greek were obviously concerned with its function. The object seems to have been a sort of astronomical clock without a pendulum.

The cargo has enabled the shipwreck to be dated around the 1st century BC. No Greek or Roman writer has mentioned the existence of such objects, but many classical texts are still unread and one of these could yield a description.

Mycenae

(47 miles south-west of Athens). Heinrich Schliemann, the 19th-century German archaeologist, had a particular interest in the great Greek epic poems of Homer, the *Iliad* and the *Odyssey*, and undertook to prove to the scientific world that Troy really had existed. Having succeeded in this he then went on to do extensive excavation work at Mycenae, again searching for evidence of Homer's heroes. His discovery of a large quantity of gold treasure in the Grave Circle was proof of the existence of Mycenaean civilisation, about which scholars were completely unaware.

Towards the end of the 15th century BC the Mycenaeans conquered Crete. By the 13th century BC they were established everywhere in the Aegean world. But then some great threat appeared and everywhere town defences were strengthened. Mycenae extended its fortifications and with great difficulty a well was hollowed out from solid rock, yielding water at the bottom of a subterranean gallery. This indicates a strong premonition of disaster: when a siege takes place it is essential to have a supply of water.

Men at Tiryns and other centres acted in a similar way. At Pílos, tablets in Linear B (the writing of the Late Bronze Age) recount how the bronze from the temples was requisitioned to make arms.

After the final tablets were written at Pílos there was a terrible fire: the catastrophe feared took place. In a few years the Mycenaean civilisation was annihilated.

India

New Delhi

The Iron Pillar at Meharauli, near Delhi, is a memorial to a king named Chandra, and stands some 22 ft high,

New Delhi. Rust-proof Iron Pillar.

with an average diameter of about 4½ ft. It is a solid shaft of wrought iron with an ornamental top and testifies to the metallurgical skill of its makers – there would be difficulties in constructing an iron pillar of such a size even today. Scholars have dated it at around the 5th century, and it has become famous because, despite all the years of exposure to wind and rain, it has not rusted.

Scientific study has revealed that the metal from which the column is made is full of impurities, which would tend to make it more prone to rusting. As yet no entirely satisfac-

Mycenae. Gold mask, discovered by Heinrich Schliemann in a tomb.

tory explanation has been advanced to explain why the metal is so well preserved.

Iran

Shahdad

(Dasht-e-Lut, about 440 miles south-east of Teheran). The desert of Dasht-e-Lut is an area where excavations have only recently begun, but it is clear that at one time in the distant past it was a cultural centre of some importance.

Shahdad. Incised seal from a pot tomb.

At Shahdad a necropolis has been discovered where red clay pots were used as coffins, but the skeletons have disappeared.

These pots date from 2000 BC or earlier, and contained small green steatite vases and other objects, including unbaked clay statuettes representing a goddess of vegetation. She has a woman's body with branches growing from it. Some of the pots are incised with what appear to be seals, and they bear signs of an unknown writing.

There is no trace of a town – only of temporary dwellings. The climatic conditions in this area would have compelled the people to move about. Often periods of extreme heat were followed by catastrophic floods. There is a possibility that the people were nomads who served as commercial intermediaries between the peoples of the Indus Valley and Mesopotamia.

Iraq

Tell es-Sawwan

(About 70 miles north-west of Baghdad). Only a few years ago the Sumerian civilisation was still considered the oldest of the great civilisations of the Middle East, appar-

ently having emerged in an almost fully developed state, without any evidence of a preceding period of growth.

The discoveries of Tell es-Sawwan have begun to shed light on the mystery of the origins of the Sumerian civilisation by proving that from around 6000 BC there existed in Mesopotamia a very advanced culture, although the people had not, at that time, developed writing. Excavations have revealed a city built from unbaked mortared bricks, which was well defended against wild animals by a ditch and walls. The houses, of varying shapes, with access through the roofs, were coated with plaster, then bitumen and finally a facing of gypsum. Silos were built for grain storage. The people evidently had a knowledge of agriculture, pottery, grazing and weaving. Numerous alabaster statuettes with inlaid eyes were found in the oldest tombs, and they indicate an extremely high degree of artistic development. There is also evidence of cults involving a mother-goddess and male sex organs.

Until recently it was thought that metallurgy had begun with the Sumerians, but at Tell es-Sawwan the discovery of a small knife and copper beads proves that this was not the case.

The site at Tell es-Sawwan was occupied for 1,000 years, which indicates the existence of a stable social organisation and the beginning of a form of urbanisation.

There are similarities between Tell es-Sawwan and Çatal Hüyük (see p. 145) in Anatolia, although nearly 1,000 miles separate the two sites, and Çatal Hüyük existed 1,000 years earlier than Tell es-Sawwan. Archaeologists see the culture of Tell es-Sawwan as a means of filling, in part, the considerable gap in our knowledge of the period between the New Stone Age and the beginning of recorded history.

Israel

Gethsemane

(Jerusalem). There is a very old church at Gethsemane which has been rebuilt several times over the centuries, going back to early in the Christian era. Tradition places it at the site of the tomb of Mary, the mother of Jesus.

Gethsemane. Funerary chamber with bench.

In 1972 floods caused extensive damage to the church which, because its foundations have sunk over the years, has become a sort of crypt. When restoration work was undertaken, a slab closure was discovered beneath a thick bed of plaster. Beneath this, three funerary chambers were found carved out of the rock.

One of the chambers had a sort of niche in the form of a bench where a body could have been placed, but all of the chambers were empty.

Syrian and Ethiopian tradition tells of three burial places being prepared in the Garden of Gethsemane, one of which was provided with a bench on which the body of the Virgin Mary was placed before her Assumption. Perhaps, then, the niche in the newly discovered chamber is the tomb of the Virgin.

Italy

Grimaldi Caves

(3 miles west of Ventimiglia). These caves were the subject of extensive excavation at the beginning of this century. They served as a shelter during prehistory and contained a considerable number of archaeological layers, each corresponding to a different period of occupation. The earliest period so far excavated is the Aurignacian, which dates back to about 35,000 BC. Skeletons of the Aurignacian period uncovered were of members of the Cro-Magnon race, to which the first true men known

Grimaldi Caves. Negroid skeletons.

to have lived in Europe belong.

The Grimaldi skeletons had been buried carefully, and their bones had traces of red ochre which had been ritually sprinkled over them at their funeral ceremonies. They were still wearing ornaments in the form of necklaces and bracelets of shells and animal teeth. In a ditch were found the skeletons of a man, a woman and an adolescent, buried together.

The most surprising find at Grimaldi was that of two fossilised skeletons, one of an old woman and the other of a boy. They had been buried together with their heads protected by a horizontal slab placed on two vertical stones. The shape of their skulls, the structure of their facial bones and the length of their forearms tend to suggest that they belonged to a Negroid race. If there were black communities in Old Stone Age Europe, where did they come from, or were they aboriginal inhabitants? When excavations were made of later periods, no traces of Negroid peoples were found.

Modena

(Po Valley). Aerial photographs taken near Modena have revealed the existence of buried structures which are, judging by their layout, an amphitheatre with a surrounding wall. Bronze Age jewellery has been found in the vicinity, and also burial places which date back to pre-Roman times.

It is quite probable that a town existed there at one time, as the whole region of Italy between the Alps and the Apennines was a centre of prehistoric cultures. Pliny the Elder, the Roman writer of the 1st century AD, writes in his *Natural History* of a flourishing city in the Po Valley called Otesium.

St Peter's Basilica

(Vatican City). Tradition, supported by texts going back to the 1st century AD, asserts that after St Peter had been tortured and killed, his body was buried near Nero's gardens. Afterwards, the Emperor Constantine built the first basilica over the apostle's tomb, where the present basilica stands. However, Nero's gardens are not situated in this area but a little further away, and searches near the location of the gardens have revealed a cemetery with a central tomb which was found to be empty.

Pope Pius XII had excavations carried out under the present basilica beginning in 1939, and beneath the foundations of a certain wall plastered with red, dating from the time of Constantine, the remains of an elderly man were discovered, wrapped in remnants of gold and purple material. The particles of earth stuck to these remains are identical to the earth surrounding the empty tomb in the cemetery situated near Nero's gardens. The body from the red wall is headless. The basilica of St John Lateran in Rome boasts many relics – including the heads of the apostles Peter and Paul.

It is possible that Constantine had the body of the first leader of the Christian Church moved from its original burial place to the area where he intended to build the first basilica. On the other hand, the body could be that of another Christian dignitary or martyr.

Sardinia

In Sardinia there are almost 7,000 nuraghi, dry-stone structures dating from the beginning of the Bronze Age. The oldest are like towers, with the inside reached through a narrow corridor. Others are corbel-roofed – that is, the roof is built up from overlapping slabs of stone. Still others make up complexes comprising several towers linked by corridors.

At one time it was thought that they were temples, but it has now been proved that they were fortresses in which people from surrounding villages took refuge in times of danger. Each nuraghe was visible from a neighbouring nuraghe, so that the defenders could communicate by means of smoke signals. Such a system of defence would seem likely to have been established to protect the island from foreign raids.

The puzzling fact is that the nuraghi are less numerous on the coast, from which danger was most likely to come, than in the interior.

After the Carthaginians landed, they settled in the largest nuraghi, from which they were later driven by the Romans.

Sybaris

(In Calabria Province, 62 miles north of Catanzaro). In the 7th century BC, Sybaris was a city renowned for its wealth and its inhabitants' delight in luxury and pleasures, which gave rise to the term sybarite. But the town disappeared beneath the waters and passed into legend.

Then the University of Pennsylvania prospected the area near the Gulf of Taranto where the city once stood and discovered the existence of structures buried 20 ft deep in water-soaked soil, which must be what remains of Sybaris.

Enormous sums of money would be needed to carry out excavation work, but this might be repaid if it revealed the temples and treasures of a city that was compared by the ancients with Athens.

Val Camonica

(62 miles north-east of Milan). It has been calculated that there are as many as 15,000 very old carvings on the rocks in this valley. They show the houses, religious practices, farming methods and a variety of scenes

Val Camonica. Rock carving.

from the daily lives of the people who carved them.

When the stones were first studied, it was noted that a large number of them were on rocks which had become buried. These engravings span a period of about 6,000 years, from the New Stone Age until the time the region was conquered by Rome in 16 BC.

The early carvings are similar to those at Mount Bego in France, so perhaps it is possible that the people who did them had settled there after being driven from Mount Bego by invaders. The inhabitants of Val Camonica may have taken refuge there in order to follow their own cultural activities and to avoid being assimilated by the local people.

Their art has been compared with the much older art of the Iberian peninsula. Were there minority groups in prehistoric times unwilling to accept changes who broke away from their main communities to settle in isolated regions?

It could also be possible that the engravings are the work of pilgrims who came to this high valley for religious reasons.

Japan

Takamatsuzuka

(20 miles east of Osaka). Between the 3rd and 7th centuries AD, during the period when Nara was the capital of Japan, it was customary for important people to be interred in burial mounds.

Takamatsuzuka is one of these burial places which has been recently uncovered near Nara, but it is distinguished from others by its interior decoration. The funerary chamber, instead of being painted with the usual traditional geometric patterns, is decorated with frescoes of men, women and children wearing rich clothing. Dragons, tigers and snakes are depicted in an entirely Chinese style, and the ceiling is studded with gold stars.

The man buried here was unusually tall for this region, and a large Chinese mirror was placed near him. It is thought that this mirror may have had some magical significance.

It is not known who he was. The tomb dates from the 7th century, a period when Japan welcomed many Buddhist missionaries. There seems to be no explanation as to why such

an individual style should have been adopted for the burial of this particular man.

Jordan

Petra

(About 90 miles south-west of Amman). In the heart of this arid desert area Petra, which was once a large and thriving city, lay undiscovered for centuries. Ancient authors had written of it but, like so many other dead cities, its location had been forgotten.

In 1812 a young Swiss explorer named Johann Ludwig Burckhardt was led by a guide through a narrow, deep gorge to some magnificent ruins. The cliffs had been carved into façades of palaces or temples in Hellenistic style. A door in each façade opened into a corridor that provided access to a bare room which was hollowed out of the rock, where there was sometimes an altar. The site that Johann Burckhardt had just discovered was the ancient city known as Petra. An English poet, the Reverend John Burgon, described it in a memorable phrase as:

A rose-red city –
half as old as time.

Takamatsuzuka. One of the frescoes from the funerary chamber.

Petra. Nabataean burial place with a temple façade, carved from the cliffs.

A people called the Nabataeans settled at Petra in the 4th century BC. The city, well protected by its cliffs, stood at an important caravan crossroads and the Nabataeans grew rich on tolls which they levied on goods passing through. Petra had a theatre, thermal baths, palaces and a system of canals for supplying water.

The holy place of the Nabataeans was at the top of a mountain peak and was reached by a stairway cut into the rock. This sanctuary has remained intact and consists of a platform some 45 ft by 20 ft, which was originally covered entirely with gold. A block of sandstone, raised on four steps, stands out from it, and it is thought that sacrifices were made here.

The Romans brought the Nabataeans' independence to an end, but Petra's prosperity lasted until the caravans took other routes. The city then declined and a series of invasions finally plunged it into the obscurity from which Burckhardt was to rescue it.

If the rooms hewn from rock were tombs it is strange that no human remains have been found in them. Their purpose remains a mystery.

Lebanon

Ba'albek
(44 miles east of Beirut). The acropolis of Ba'albek, with its ruins and its gigantic temples, is one of the most imposing sites in the world. The Roman sanctuaries of Jupiter and Venus succeeded earlier temples dedicated to the corresponding Semitic divinities – Ba'al and his partner the goddess Astarte, whose cult involved prostitution and sacred orgies.

These Roman architectural wonders, which were largely destroyed by an earthquake in 1759, do not pose any archaeological problems. On the other hand, one part of the enclosure wall, called the Trilithon, is composed of three blocks of hewn stone each weighing 750 tons. It is an amazing feat of construction, as the blocks have been raised 22 ft in order to lie on top of smaller blocks. Another hewn block, 13 by 13 ft and nearly 70 ft long and weighing at least 1,000 tons, lies in the nearby quarry. Did the Romans build the Trilithon or does it date back to an earlier period, and if so, how were these colossal blocks of stone raised into position?

Large numbers of pilgrims came from Mesopotamia as well as the Nile Valley to the temple of Ba'al-Astarte. It is mentioned in the Bible in the Book of Kings. It is possible that the vast underground passages beneath the acropolis were intended as shelter for the crowds of pilgrims.

Ancient Arab writings tell that the first temples of Ba'al-Astarte were built there a short time after the Flood, at the order of the legendary King Nimrod, by a 'tribe of giants'.

Mali

Arli
(375 miles north-east of Timbuktu). Herodotus, Pliny, Strabo and other ancient writers gave accounts of people called the Garamantes who lived in the present-day Fezzan region of the Sahara and travelled in two-wheeled chariots drawn by horses.

In 1932, near the straggling village of Djerma in Fezzan, several rock engravings were discovered depicting light chariots drawn by horses – proof that Herodotus was correct.

It was the first in a series of discoveries of paintings and engravings in which these same chariots appeared, treated in differing styles. A number of them exist in the Tassili N'Ajjer, in the heart of the Sahara,

Ba'albek. Colossal block of hewn stone.

Arli. Rock engravings.

which would indicate that the Garamantes may have been concentrated there. At Arli, some 625 miles south from the Tassili, two engravings found on a cliff show two-wheeled chariots drawn by horses.

Who were the Garamantes and where did they come from? The oldest representations of chariots have been dated to 1200 BC. At this time devastating waves of mysterious Sea Peoples broke on the nations at the eastern end of the Mediterranean. Did these people include the Garamantes? Some claim that the Tuaregs are their descendants.

Namibia

Maak Shelter

(188 miles north-west of Windhoek, South West Africa). In 1917, during a topographical mission, an engineer named Maak discovered on the side of Mt Brandberg a painted shelter.

The paintings depict a procession of people, led by women. They are of Mediterranean type and their elegance and posture are similar to those of the figures depicted in Egyptian frescoes. The figures have nothing in common with the aborigines of southern Africa.

The procession is dominated by a woman, known as the White Lady, dressed in skin-tight shorts like the Cretan bull-fighting girls, and carrying a lotus flower. She and her companions hold bows, and their wrists are protected by gauntlets. They all wear boots and some have red hair and fair complexions.

In Rhodesia there are similar paintings. It would seem that travellers or invaders may have come from the north-east of Africa to the southern areas. In one of the decorated shelters archaeological material has been uncovered enabling the painting to be dated to about 5000 BC, which was still in the age of pre-history in Egypt. However, the Egyptians are considered by some authorities to be a branch of the ancient Libyan peoples. Perhaps another branch emigrated southwards?

Peru

Chan Chan

(300 miles north-west of Lima). This extraordinary city, the capital of the Chimú people, who were later supplanted by the Incas, covers an area of 9 sq. miles with a strictly rectangular layout.

There were nine sections in all, each one surrounded by double or sometimes triple walls – with narrow doors as the only means of access. There seems to have been a road around the top of the walls which could have been reached only from the outside. It was as if the inhabitants had been prisoners under surveillance. Chan Chan in its prime sheltered an estimated population of around 50,000 people.

A very sophisticated and efficient system of canals, one of them more than 50 miles long, supplied the city with water. The houses had adobe walls with the lower part thicker than the top, no doubt to give better stability.

The city has been well preserved by the sands which encroached upon it, and because of the almost entire absence of rain. It is, however, a long way from being completely excavated. It is believed that there are still several miles of wall buried beneath the sand. The continuing excavations will no doubt give much more information about the city and its history. Chan Chan prospered from the 13th

Maak Shelter. Wall-painting showing the White Lady on the right.

Chan Chan. Ruins of one of the ten sections of the 11th–15th-century city.

century AD to 1470, when it came under the rule of the Incas.

There are legendary accounts of a founding ruler coming to Chan Chan by sea in a log raft. He could perhaps have come from the Far East or from Polynesia, but no similar cities have been in those places.

Poland

Biskupin

(140 miles north-west of Warsaw). The Urnfield culture, which existed during the 1st millennium BC, extended from the mountains of Lusatia to northern and western Europe. The civilisation was so named because the cremated remains of its people were buried in pottery urns shaped like truncated cones.

Practically nothing was known of this civilisation until the remains of an extraordinary wooden city were discovered. These had been preserved by the mud in which they had been submerged. The Lusatian town of Biskupin, once on an island, was encompassed by an oval wall of stone and clay and covered an area of about 5 acres. The inhabitants lived in over 100 identical rectangular houses arranged in 13 rows. The houses were built of oak and pine and consisted of a main room, a sleeping room and a

porch at the front where cattle were kept in the winter. Each row of houses was covered by a single thatched roof. A circular path 10 ft wide went round the inside of the ramparts. From this, diagonal paths paved with round wooden billets led between the houses. A 130-yd-long wooden causeway linked the island to the mainland.

It is clear that the inhabitants were

skilled at woodwork and their social organisation was well developed. Would the absence of any house larger than the others indicate that the inhabitants did without leaders?

Religion took the form of a cult of the sun and moon and the sacrifice of young people.

With their advanced techniques and dynamic social system, the Lusatians were a community of particular importance in European prehistory. Their culture spread far to the west, and some believe the Druids inherited their knowledge.

Romania

Cascioarele

(30 miles south-east of Bucharest). This site consists of a mound formed from the remains of a succession of prehistoric villages. A shrine measuring some 32 by 20 ft was discovered amongst the remains of some rectangular houses at the deepest level, which dates from about 3800 BC.

In this shrine lay the fragments of two columns which have now been restored, and it is clear that they were not part of the construction. Hollow, and made of clay, they had been painted on the outside several times with different decorations. A seat of rammed earth and the walls of the sanctuary also bear traces of paint. Around the largest column, which is 6 ft high, remnants of charred stakes

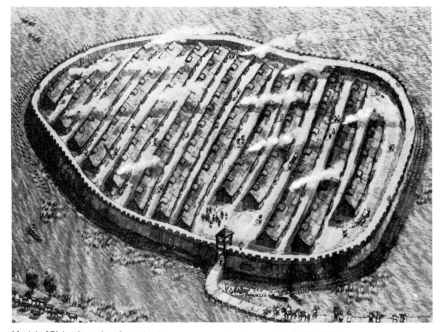

Model of Biskupin, a city of wooden houses preserved under mud for 2,000–3,000 years.

have been found. It is thought that these columns may have served as a support for a canopy. Seven horizontal rows of seven pairs of triangles, jointed side-to-side, decorated the larger column. The number seven could not have been a random choice: apart from being the number of days in a week, it is often associated by primitive peoples with good fortune. Is there a connection between this decoration and the calendar? What was the connection between the number and these columns, which obviously had some sacred purpose?

Tartaria

(220 miles north-west of Bucharest). In 1961 three terracotta tablets were uncovered here, bearing signs which are clearly not simply decoration. The archaeological bed in which they were found dates back some 8,000 years or more to the New Stone Age – a period much earlier than the appearance of writing in continental Europe. The signs are similar to others of about the same age that had been found at Troy and at Warka in Mesopotamia.

The Tartaria tablets were discovered in a hole which must have been used for a religious or magical ceremony, for it also contained small idols similar to those honoured in the Cyclades islands in the Aegean Sea. The presence of random human bones suggests that it was once the scene of cannibalism.

Could the signs have had some magical significance and could magic have played some part in the origins of writing, as it has with many other sciences?

Saudi Arabia

Mada'in Salih

(600 miles north-west of Riyadh). The Kaaba is the sacred shrine of Mecca, which contains the Black Stone venerated by all Muslims. This stone is probably a meteorite. Tradition claims that it fell from Paradise with Adam and was given by an angel to Abraham. This legend is the Islamisation of a cult of stone practised by the Semites of the desert.

The Nabataeans, in particular, have left remarkable traces of this cult. They came originally from the south of the Arabian Peninsula but moved to the north, prospering from the monopoly of the lucrative caravan trade between the interior of Arabia and the coast. At Mada'in Salih there is a sanctuary hollowed out of an enormous rock, which was built by the Nabataeans.

Corridors and rooms lead to the end of the temple where there is a block of stone which has been removed from the wall. On this stone they made sacrifices to the divinity of the place. The surrounding cliffs form a vast necropolis of family tombs, and in many of these sanctuaries there are similar sacred stones, some of which bear people's names and inscriptions. These stones were thought to be residences of a god and bore the name of *baetyl*, meaning 'house of the god'. The Black Stone at Mecca is the best known of all such sacred stones.

It is surprising that Mada'in Salih does not seem to have been the centre of a town. Only a few traces of houses have been found there. It may have been a sacred place where people came to bury their dead.

Spain

Elche

(20 miles south-west of Alicante). In 1897 the bust of a woman was found buried on a local doctor's farm. She has since become known as the Lady of Elche. Nothing else was found that could be definitely linked with this statue and thus enable it to be dated: no trace of any burial, temple or dwelling.

Elche. Ancient bust of unknown origin.

Mada'in Salih. Rock sanctuary.

Its jewellery is unlike that customary in Greek or Roman times and also unlike that of the much later Visigoth kingdom. It is possibly Carthaginian, for it was in the Elche region that Hamilcar Barca, Hannibal's father, obtained esparto grass to make ropes for his fleet; and the local population certainly maintained relations with the Africans. Judging by its style, the sculpture dates from the 4th century BC, a time of Carthaginian expansion in Spain.

The Lady of Elche appears to be slightly hunchbacked, which might be because of the weighty jewellery she is wearing. But why is there a hole cut in the back? Was the sculpture intended to be hung up? Was it a receptacle for ashes or some sacred object? None of these questions has been answered.

The Louvre Museum in Paris bought the Lady of Elche from the doctor, but in 1941 the Spanish government, which was very anxious to recover her, managed to exchange her for several valuable paintings, and now the Lady of Elche is at the Prado Museum in Madrid.

Santiago de Compostela

(Galicia). This far-western point of Europe seems to have played a mystical role in man's distant past. Santiago de Compostela attracted primitive men in the same way that it later drew the medieval Christians who made pilgrimages there to honour the remains of the apostle St James.

There are a number of megaliths and rock engravings round the town – evidence that it was a sacred place throughout ancient times. Men from far distant lands would have been able to find this furthest point on the continent by taking bearings from the Milky Way. It is not known, however, what these pre-Christians were searching for.

Sudan

Merowe

(200 miles north of Khartoum). The ancient writers speak of a rich and powerful kingdom south of the Nile – the land of Kush. The queens of Kush bore the title of Candace, and at times ruled in their own right.

The Egyptians were often in conflict with the Kushites, who eventually conquered the whole Nile Valley and in 715 BC established the 25th Pharaonic Dynasty, which lasted about a century. After Assyrian campaigns in Egypt the Kushites returned south to their own lands.

These people moved from their old capital Napata in the 6th century BC, probably after an Egyptian invasion, and settled further south at Merowe. The region was rich in iron ore, and the Meroites became famous for their ironwork.

From Egypt the Meroites brought the custom of erecting pyramids, but instead of the burial chamber being incorporated in the pyramid, it was hollowed out underground.

Merowe. Egyptian-style pyramids.

A number of these small pyramids exists, but only some of the more important ones have been studied. They served as tombs for the famous Candaces, depicted on the bas-reliefs as strong, formidable women. Also buried there were kings and other members of the ruling families. The many inscriptions in Meroitic writing have not been deciphered. Phonetic values have been given to the hieroglyphs and script, but the meaning of the words is still a mystery.

On the outskirts of Merowe there are ruins of Egyptian-type temples and the remains of sumptuous residences which were once surrounded by gardens watered by an ingenious irrigation system. Archaeological evidence indicates that although Egyptian influence was great, art of a distinct Meroitic style had evolved by the 3rd century BC.

About AD 350 the Meroites were conquered by the people of Aksum, in Ethiopia, and Christianised. Their empire disappeared, and perhaps they emigrated. The Chad peoples preserve the legend of a tall and clever race of men who settled in their country, 1,200 miles from Merowe, and who cast bronze using the lost-wax method, a process well known in the Nile Valley.

Switzerland

Augst

(6 miles east of Basle). The village of Augst lies within the perimeter of the old Roman fort of Augusta Raurica. In the early 1960s, while excavating a new school playground, a mechanical shovel unearthed a large quantity of silverware. Professor Rudolf Laur-Belart, of the University of Basle, immediately investigated the find and established it as one of the most important discoveries of Roman plate that has ever been made, dating from the 4th century AD. Eventually 257 pieces of silverware were recovered, including coins and medals, dishes, various eating implements, a candelabrum, a statuette of Venus and three silver ingots.

It has been suggested that the silverware belonged to the Roman Emperor Julian the Apostate, who set out from Augusta Raurica in AD 351 and never returned to this part of the Roman Empire. The treasure may have been buried on his departure and subsequently forgotten.

Syria

Tell Mardick

(44 miles south of Aleppo). Recently a library of 15,000 tablets covered in cuneiform writing, transcribing an unknown Semitic language resembling Hebrew, was excavated at this ancient site by an Italian expedition. So far the study of these and other archaeological remains has established the fact that between 2400 and 2250 BC there was a vast and powerful kingdom whose capital was the present-day Tell Mardick.

Sumerian and Akkadian writings mention this capital, but until the Italian discovery its location and significance were unknown. It was in the town's palace, which had been burned down, that the library was discovered. The city must have housed a population of 20,000 to 30,000 people, a considerable number for the period. Women played an important social role, unlike in Mesopotamia, and the queen was the second most important person in the kingdom. The main industries seem to have been weaving and felling timber for export.

There are still many tablets which have yet to be studied and they may well shed further light on the history of the Middle East.

Tell Mureybut

(50 miles south-east of Aleppo). Between the Old Stone Age civilisations of nomadic hunters and the New Stone Age civilisations of pastoral and agricultural peoples is a long period in the history of man about which very little is known. Tool making, religion and the way of life all changed. The old ways disappeared, leaving few clues with which to establish how these stages evolved.

At Tell Mureybut, remnants have been discovered of a solidly built village dating back 11,000 years – that is, 2,000 years before the traditional beginning of the New Stone Age. No doubt it was the nearby river which prompted men to settle. There was no natural shelter in the vicinity, so they built wood-framed huts filled in with clay which dried and made a solid shell. These are the first-known examples of real houses, as distinct from makeshift shelters. The same site was inhabited for a long time afterwards. There in about 8000 BC the cult of a mother-goddess appeared – the first-known representation of a divinity in human form.

Did Tell Mureybut play a crucial role in the history of man? Did its people invent the concept of permanent dwellings, and the idea of a god in human form? Or could the inhabitants have adopted the practices of earlier peoples, evidence of whom has not yet been uncovered?

Thailand

Ban Chieng
(450 miles north-east of Bangkok). On the site of Ban Chieng, near the Laotian border, Thai archaeologists have uncovered the remains of a civilisation dating back to 3600 BC which used bronze. Previously the beginnings of bronze metal working were thought to have been in Mesopotamia, around 3000 BC. Could the Mesopotamians have learned bronze-making processes from these mysterious people? What connection could there have been between the Middle East and the Far East at such an early date?

The objects found at Ban Chieng, bronze weapons and jewels, carved ivory objects and pottery, all of them beautifully made, bear witness to an advanced degree of civilisation. This is strong, though not conclusive, evidence that the making of bronze originated in the Far East. This metal was first used in China about 1300 BC but in Vietnam it only became known in the 4th century BC. It is surprising that such a valuable technique did not spread into surrounding regions.

Turkey

Hattusas
(95 miles east of Ankara). The ancient Egyptians both fought against and allied themselves with the powerful Anatolian empire of the Hittites. The Hittite capital, Hattusas, was protected by a massive dry-stone wall 3¾ miles round, some stones of which were 26 ft long and nearly 20 ft thick.

The Hittites, the first people to make extensive use of iron, had an extremely authoritarian system and obeyed an aristocracy whose foreign origins remain unknown. They wrote their records on thousands of tablets which scholars have deciphered. In the 14th century BC their power,

Hattusas. Remains of the Hittite capital destroyed 3,000 years ago.

based on iron, extended over a large part of the Middle East.

They were at the height of their power when they suddenly disappeared. Hattusas was completely sacked and burned down around 1190 BC. But it is not known who conquered the Hittites or what happened to them. One theory is that they founded the Etruscan civilisation in Italy.

Another puzzling fact is that, at the time of sacking and the fire, the brick houses of Hattusas were subjected to such intense heat that their bricks fused. It is difficult to imagine, given the weapons and fuels of the day, how such high temperatures could have been achieved.

Mount Ararat
(600 miles east of Ankara). The story of the Flood is not confined to the Bible; Armenian legends and the Babylonian *Epic of Gilgamesh* give a similar account. All the legends have a foundation of truth, for silt deposits have been discovered at Ur and various other Sumerian cities. These deposits belong to different dates so it is likely that floods were a familiar event which in men's minds led to the myth of the Great Flood.

According to the Bible, Noah built an ark and, as the waters subsided, this ark ran aground on Mount Ararat, situated in volcanic territory halfway between the Black Sea and the Caspian Sea.

Archaeologists and explorers have

combed the 16,945-ft-high mountain in the hope of discovering an ancient boat, and have uncovered fragments of a type of timber which docs not come from any tree that grows in the vicinity of the mountain. The timber is from trees of the Mesopotamian plains from which Noah is said to have come. These fragments seem to have been cut more than 4,000 years ago. To undertake further excavation where the discovery was made would necessitate moving an enormous amount of ice and would be an extremely expensive undertaking.

Mount Ararat. Biblical site of Noah's Ark.

Nemrut Daĝi
(350 miles south-east of Ankara). These spectacular ruins stand on an awe-inspiring site at the peak of a mountain. There have often been earthquakes in the area, but the enormous tragic heads lying among the ruins seem to defy the coun-

313

Nemrut Daĝi. Head of the colossal statue of King Antiochus I.

tryside and the centuries. The heads belong to 30-ft statues which have been toppled by earthquakes.

The origin of the statues is documented in ancient literature. They were made with the temple at the order of Antiochus I, king of Commagene, who ruled in that area in the 1st century BC, and claimed descent from both Greek and Persian kings.

He had a colossal statue of himself erected, and other statues of various gods, and he had a furnace altar built on the terrace which almost certainly overlooked the tomb where he must have been buried. The statues in their original state represented seated personages. These include King Antiochus, the Greek gods Apollo, Hermes and Helios; the Persian gods Mithra and Ahura-Mazda; and the Greek hero Hercules. Both eastern and western influence is found not only in the choice of gods but also in the style of the statues. That region of what is now Turkey blended and assimilated the different cultures that met there.

There is a particularly interesting bas-relief, called the Lion's Horoscope, in which the stars can be seen in the positions which they occupied on July 7 in 62 or 61 BC. Another relief praises the ancestry of Antiochus. But his line did not reign long, as the Romans conquered Commagene as early as AD 17.

Theoretically all that is needed to uncover the burial place of Antiochus and his treasures, if it is at Nemrut Daĝi, is an archaeological dig. However, the site has been so disturbed by earthquakes that such a dig would be an almost impossible undertaking.

United Kingdom

Bratton

(Wiltshire, 3 miles north-east of Westbury). Carved on the side of a chalky hill near the village of Bratton can be seen the figure of a horse nearly 180 ft long. There are other figures of the same type in the area, amongst them several other horses and a giant.

The Bratton horse, according to popular tradition, was created to commemorate the victory of Alfred the Great over the Danes in AD 878, and it is surprising that Alfred is not depicted astride his charger.

Bratton. Horse, 180 ft long, carved in the chalk of a hill, near the site of a Celtic camp.

It could possibly be an earlier work: the horse was an animal much loved by the Celts and was often represented by them in different ways. The Bratton horse is near the site of a Celtic camp later occupied by the Romans, Saxons and Danes and several battles were fought in the region.

The chalky downs are well suited to carving out such figures and the local people still occasionally make smaller ones, as well as maintaining those made in earlier times. The Bratton horse was entirely restored in the 18th century. There is still, however, the question of how such a large figure was composed with such accurate proportions.

Craig Phadrig

(Highland, 1½ miles west of the town of Inverness). At Craig Phadrig there is one of the most spectacular vitrified enclosures of Celtic Europe. It is a sort of oval granite fort which looks like a citadel with a basin-shaped depression at the centre, almost 9 ft deep. The enclosure is constructed from granite blocks which have been vitrified – turned into a glass-like form of rock – by temperatures of at least 1,300°C. No normal fire could have generated such intense heat.

'Vitrified forts' exist in other Celtic lands. How were they produced? What was the secret of this ability to generate such high temperatures?

Mousa. Fortified dry-stone broch, or homestead.

Mousa

(Shetland, 11 miles south of Lerwick). On this island stands the best preserved of a series of odd ruins that can be seen throughout the north of Scotland. They are brochs, fortified dry-stone homesteads shaped like thimbles. The Mousa broch stands 43 ft high, with 20-ft-thick walls. A long narrow passage, along which men and small livestock would have been able to worm their way, goes through the wall, leading to an interior courtyard 33 ft in diameter.

A study of the soil in the courtyard of the Mousa broch confirms the fact that this construction would have served as a shelter for pastoral peoples. But opinions differ as to who built the brochs. It has been suggested that they were built by the descendants of the builders of Skara Brae, a Stone Age village in the Orkney Islands, or by Scots and Picts fleeing from Roman domination. There is another theory that they were built many hundreds of years later by Norsemen, to serve as forts.

Silbury Hill

(25 miles north of Salisbury). This is the largest artificial hill in Europe. It is conical, more than 130 ft high, and measures 550 ft across the base. A ditch surrounding it was originally more than 120 ft wide and about 30 ft deep. The ditch continues towards the west in the form of a canal.

Excavations carried out in 1968–9 have established the fact that Silbury Hill was built in three stages around 2100 BC. The builders first constructed a foundation of clay and gravel, topped with earth supported by stakes. On this foundation they piled up materials from the nearby river and the entire structure was then covered with chalk. After this it

seems that the builders must have decided to extend their work, and the wide, deep ditch was hollowed out. It has been calculated that this great work would have occupied 500 men for ten years.

Artificial hills, just like pyramids, generally served as burial places. But when the centre of Silbury Hill was investigated nothing was found. Perhaps, as in the case of the Egyptian pyramids, the tomb was placed away from the centre of the hill in order to ward off desecrations.

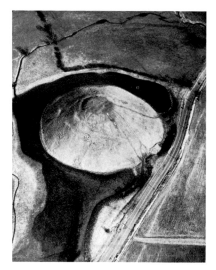

Silbury Hill. Artificial mound.

Skara Brae

(Orkney, 11 miles north-west of Kirkwall). During the middle of the last century, when the wind shifted the dunes at Skara Brae, stone houses with stone furniture were revealed under the sand. Excavations and fresh storms have revealed a perfectly preserved Stone Age village, 4,000 years old.

Contrary to what might be expected, the village was extremely

well organised. Paved paths linked the houses, and a sewer collected the dirty water piped from the dwellings. All the structures, made from unmortared stone, have been well protected by the sand dunes, with the exception of the roofs, which have disappeared.

The village consisted of a group of seven or eight houses all of the same design: one room with rounded corners, a very low entrance (3 ft 10 in.) which could be closed by means of a large flat stone, and a hearth in the middle, where peat ashes were found. There was no wood on the island and the various vessels unearthed were made from stone, whales' vertebrae and pottery. Colour pigments, no doubt used in body painting, were in bowls made from the vertebrae of marine animals. The inhabitants, who were sheep breeders, lived on milk, meat, fish, shellfish and whatever they could catch by hunting. One house, isolated from the others, seems to have served as a workshop where flint was shaped into tools and weapons.

What is unclear is why people capable of building such houses came to settle on such a remote island in a very severe climate, while Europe offered so many more hospitable places. It seems as if the inhabitants fled there suddenly, because of some threat.

USA

Monks' Mound

(Near East St Louis, Illinois). The valleys of the Mississippi and Ohio rivers, in Wisconsin and Illinois, were once a centre of activity for an obscure people called the Moundbuilders. They built mounds of earth, some shaped like animals, such as the Lizard Mound and the Great Serpent Mound, which is to the east in Ohio.

Monks' Mound is one of the largest. It covers some 16 acres – more than the area covered by the Great Pyramid of Cheops in Egypt. Study of the mound has indicated that it was rebuilt several times; the last rebuilding dates from around AD 1100. At its summit are the buried remains of the foundations of a temple 104 by 48 ft, which could have dominated the region.

Other mounds may have been used as burial places or had a military

Skara Brae. Perfectly preserved Stone Age village 4,000 years old.

have been discovered in other parts of the world, and the origin of the Hawaiians remains a mystery.

USSR

Issik

(Kazakhstan, 25 miles south of Alma Ata). For thousands of years caravans brought luxurious goods to Europe from the East. Central Asian rulers became rich on the duties they levied on these. Perhaps the duties were sometimes paid in gold, which would explain the recent discovery at Issik of a 5th century BC burial place containing 1,000 gold objects. Near the body was a silver vase engraved with 26 signs.

Some authorities claim that the engravings are indecipherable, while others consider them to be Armenian or similar to runes, early Scandinavian and Anglo-Saxon writing. But the burial place dates from the 5th century BC, when this writing probably did not exist.

function. Perhaps there was some Mexican influence. Why did the Moundbuilders abandon their sites? Pollution and overcrowding, some experts now suggest, pointing to accumulations of garbage, could have fouled the region's water supply.

Puuloa

(Hawaii). When Europeans first reached the Hawaiian Islands it was still the practice of the Hawaiians to carve designs on the smooth surfaces of the volcanic rocks. They explained that some were used for indicating roads, some commemorated important events and others had a religious or magical meaning.

The marks covering the hill of Puuloa belong to the last category. Some 15,000 can be counted over a surface more than 1,000 yds square, and on the surrounding rocks there are a number of similar marks in the form of simple cups, some with enclosing circles.

Until early this century, Hawaiian women came to give birth on this hill; and to ensure that the newborn child's life was long and happy they laid the umbilical cord in a cup in the rock which was specially hollowed out for this purpose.

Similar cups are found elsewhere, but there is no evidence to connect them with birth rites.

It is thought that the Polynesians colonised the Hawaiian Islands less than 2,000 years ago. They arrived with established beliefs and skills in rock carving. But no traces of these

Karmir-Blur

(Outskirts of Yerevan, Soviet Armenia). Between the 9th and 7th centuries BC, in the mountainous region surrounding Lake Van,

Karmir-Blur. Wine or grain jars half-buried in the storage-room floor.

known then as Urartu, a powerful kingdom prospered. Its people were able metallurgists and warriors who built citadels high in the mountains.

Their citadels were either of brick or cut into the rock, like the citadel of Karmir-Blur. The huge outer walls of the citadel had crenellated parapets and a square tower at each corner. About half the inner area was occupied by a palace of 120 rooms.

Among these were workshops, granaries and storerooms, many of which were underground.

In the subterranean storage quarters were found a number of very large jars, which could have been used for grain or wine. Superb pieces of jewellery, bronze and ivory objects and weapons were also found.

There are many of the elements here that appear in the famous story of Ali Baba in *The Arabian Nights*.

Maikop

(56 miles east of the Black Sea). A discovery at Maikop has apparently confirmed that the Greek legend of Jason and the Argonauts is true. The evidence is contained in a version of the story inscribed on a newly found stone. Scholars have identified the writing as Phoenician and have dated it between the 12th and 8th centuries BC. The language is that of the Abkhazian peoples of the Black Sea coast.

According to legend, the Argonauts sailed from Thessaly to Colchis, which is near Maikop. They are said to have been looking for the mythical Golden Fleece. Perhaps they were seeking the gold that was abundant in Colchis.

Yugoslavia

Bay of Dubrovnik

In the clear water of the Bay of Dubrovnik can be made out the remains of a long stone wall – the wall of a submerged town. According to legend, one of several towns named Epidaurus was in Illyria, at the very place where Dubrovnik now stands.

Tradition says, however, that the Epidaurians of Illyria settled on that spot after a first Epidaurus had been submerged by the waters of the bay. According to the same tradition, the founders of the vanished city came from Phoenicia. Excavation may yet reveal information about the first Epidaurus of Illyria.

Maikop. Inscribed stone that seems to commemorate the Argonauts' expedition.

Popovo Polje

(30 miles north-west of Dubrovnik). In the necropolis of Popovo Polje, as in other cemeteries in the area, there are a number of unusual funerary monuments. They are generally attributed to the Bogomils, a heretical Christian sect which settled in the region in the Middle Ages. The central teaching of this sect was that the material world was the creation of the devil.

The scenes and figures depicted on the sculpted stone coffins are enigmatic. There are joyous scenes of dancing, and animals such as stags and horses are portrayed. There are also carvings of the sun, the moon and other ancient symbols such as the swastika, the spiral (which signifies the passage of the soul after death), and a strange motif representing the female genitals, which may have been carved there in order to hasten the rebirth of the dead person. Some of the funerary monuments were not sarcophagi but columns ending with an Ansate cross, the sign of the planet Venus, which is now commonly used as the biological symbol for the female.

In spite of the frequent occurrences of crosses on all the burial places, these monuments do not seem to be Christian in appearance. But the Bogomils' heretical form of Christianity may have assimilated certain ancient beliefs. And if the Bogomils did not make them, then who did? Perhaps their origin lies in some cult of the magic.

Popovo Polje. Bogomil funerary monument.

318

Index

Acknowledgments

PHOTOGRAPHS: the numerals indicate the page of the book and the italic letters the positions of the photographs as follows: *b*, bottom; *t*, top; *l*, left; *r*, right; *c*, centre. **10** Equipe Vulcain. **12** Scala (National Archaeological Museum, Athens). **12–13** J. Guillard. **14** *t*, Archives Denoël; *b*, Explorer/Vulcain. **15** *t*, Solar-Filma; *b*, The Mansell Collection. **16** D. Rebikoff. **17** J. Guillard. **19** F. Patellani. **20** F. Faucheux. **21** Peter Baker. **22–23** N. Kontos (National Archaeological Museum, Athens). **24** Radio Times Hulton Picture Library. **25** F. Faucheux. **26** N. Kontos (National Archaeological Museum, Athens). **27** F. Patellani (National Archaeological Museum, Athens). **28** Explorer/Edouard. **31** Explorer/J. Valentin. **33** Triskel/Lozouet (Museo del Oro, Bogotá). **34** Vautier/Decool. **35** CDMO/J.-P. Vuillomenet. **36** BN/SRD/J.-P. Germain. **37** Vautier/Decool (Museo del Oro, Lima). **38** Lee Boltin (University Museum, Philadelphia). **39** E. Schulthess. **40** Rapho/R. Michaud. **43** Scala. **44** A. Saint-Hilaire. **45** Ch. Monty (Museum of Sana'a). **46** Explorer/Duhautois. **47** *t*, A. Saint-Hilaire; *b*, Private collection/Photo G. dagli Orti. **49** Ch. Monty (Museum of Archaeology, Addis Ababa). **50** Rapho/T. Spiegel. **54** F. Bruemmer. **55** UPI (Historical Society Museum, Bourne, Massachusetts). **56** *t*, Staatliche Museen Preussicher Kulturbesitz, Volkerkunde Museum Amerikanische Archaiologie, West Berlin; *b*, Musée de l'Homme, Paris/D. Destable. **57** *t*, R. Roland (Museo Nacional de Antropologia, Mexico); *b*, G. dagli Orti (Museo Nacional de Antropologia, Mexico). **58** F. Bruemmer. **60** J. T. Hopf. **61** F. Bruemmer. **64** Fotogram/H. Chapman. **66** Rapho/G. Gerster. **67** Aerofilms. **68** A. Gael. **69, 70, 71** J.-P. Germain. **74** *t*, M. Zanot; *b*, J.-P. Germain. **75** Magnum/E. Lessing. **76** J. Mohr. **77** P. Tetrel. **78** Magnum/E. Lessing. **79** A. Edouard. **80** Explorer/C. Noailles. **81** *t*, Cl. Olivier; *b*, Explorer/C. Noailles. **82** British Tourist Authority. **84–85** Agence Vloo/D. H. Tassaux. **86** M. Zanot. **87** Kadath/P. Ferryn. **88** Rapho/G. Gerster. **89, 91** D. Cockroft. **92** Ch. Lenars. **94–95** A. Rozier. **95** Paris-Match/T. Saulnier. **96** *t*, A. Rozier; *b*, J. Dumas. **97** Rapho/Languepin. **98** B. Villaret. **99** Paris-Match/T. Saulnier. **100** B. Villaret. **100–1** Agence Top/M. Desjardins. **101** J. Dumas. **102** B. Villaret. **103** Musée de l'Homme, Paris/D. Destable. **105** F. Matter. **108** Explorer/Moineau. **110** G. dagli Orti (Museo Nacional de Antropologia, Mexico). **114** Rapho/G. Gerster. **115** Vautier/Decool (Museo Nacional de Antropologia, Mexico). **116** G. Mairani. **116–17** Vautier/Decool. **117** Explorer/Moineau. **118** Vautier/Decool (Museo Nacional de Antropologia, Mexico). **119** Cedri/Salmer (Museo Nacional de Antropologia, Mexico). **120** Agence Top/Y. Métais. **122** *t*, The Mansell Collection; *b*, Scala (National Museum of Pakistan, Karachi). **123** Scala (National Museum of India, New Delhi). **124** Fiore. **125** J. Biltgen (National Museum of Pakistan, Karachi). **126, 127** R. Roland. **128** Scala (National Museum of India, New Delhi). **129** *t*, J. Biltgen; *b*, Scala (National Museum of Pakistan, Karachi). **130** Tetrel/J. Torregano. **132** A. Rozier. **132–3** CDMO/Gonnet. **134** A. and D. Zecca. **135** S. Waisbard. **136** A. and D. Zecca. **137** *t*, Tetrel/J. Torregano; *b*, M. Bruggmann. **138** S. Waisbard. **139** A. Rozier. **140, 143** Rapho/G. Gerster. **144** *t*, G. dagli Orti (Jordan Archaeological Museum, Amman); *b*, Rapho/G. Gerster. **145** G. Sipahioglu. **146** A. Mellaart. **147** A. Mellaart (Museum of Archaeology, Ankara). **150** A. Mellaart. **151** Magnum/E. Lessing. **153** D. Srejovic. **154** E. Schulthess. **157, 158** A. and D. Zecca. **159** *t*, Archives A. Metraux/Photo Ed. du Seuil, Paris; *b*, E. Schulthess. **160** M. Garanger. **160–1** Rapho/Languepin. **161** M. Bruggmann. **162** *t*, Paris-Match/T. Saulnier; *b*, Picturepoint. **163** H. Stierlin. **164** *t*, M. Vautier; *b*, G. Savoy. **165** G. Savoy. **168** Rapho/G. Gerster. **170** Magnum/E. Lessing. **170–1** Rapho/G. Gerster. **174** J.-C. Chabrier. **175** *t*, SRD/M. Chuzeville (Musée du Louvre, Paris); *b*, Musées Nationaux, France (Musée du Louvre, dép. Antiq. orient.). **176** G. Papigny. **177** Rapho/G. Gerster. **178** M. Carrieri (Iraq Museum, Baghdad). **179** British Museum (Dept of Manuscripts). **180, 181** D. Darr. **182** *t*, Sidoc/Leduc; *b*, Ch. Lenars. **183** *t*, D. Darr; *b*, R. Roland. **184** *t*, H. Stierlin; *b*, G. dagli Orti. **185** J. Dumas. **184** *t*, Explorer/P. Keel; *b*, D. Darr (Museo Nacional de Antropologia, Mexico). **187** Explorer/P. Keel. **188** Atlas Photo/W. Rozbroj. **191** Rapho/J. G. Ross. **194** *t*, Rapho/J. G. Ross; *b*, Editions Mazenod/J. Vertut. **195** J.-M. Grenier. **196** *t*, Agence Top/J.-Ph. Charbonnier; *b*, John Hillelson Agency/Brian Brake. **197** Ph. Francastel. **199** *t*, Rapho/Audrain-Samivel; *b*, Robert Harding Picture Library. **200** *t*, Editions Mazenod/J. Vertut; *b*, The Mansell Collection. **201** Magnum/E. Erwitt. **204** H. Lhote. **207** Agence Top/J. Guillard. **208, 209, 210** H. Lhote. **211** M. Bruggmann. **213** *t*, M. Bruggmann; *b*, H. Lhote. **214, 215** H. Lhote. **216** *t*, M. Bruggmann; *b*, L. Segarra. **217** Agence Top/Y. Métais. **218** M. Bruggmann. **219** J. Guillard. **220** Lee Boltin (State Hermitage Museum, Leningrad). **222–3, 224** R. and S. Michaud. **225** Lee Boltin (Museum of Historical Treasures, Kiev). **226–7, 227, 228, 229** Lee Boltin (State Hermitage Museum, Leningrad). **230** APN. **231** Lee Boltin (Museum of Historical Treasures, Kiev). **234** Mary Evans Picture Library. **235** A. Filippini. **236** Ch. Lenars. **237** Sidoc/G. Buthaud. **238** A. Filippini. **239** E. Schulthess. **240** L. Pellegrini (Queen Victoria Museum, Salisbury). **241** L. Pellegrini. **242** J. Mohr. **244–5** H. Stierlin. **245** Douglas Dickins. **246** Agence Top/L. Ionesco. **247** H. Stierlin. **250** *t*, B. de Andia; *b*, J.-M. Grenier. **251** *t*, Douglas Dickins; *b*, Agence Top/L. Ionesco. **252** *t*, MacQuitty Collection; *b*, Rapho/P. Koch. **253** Agence Top/L. Ionesco. **254** H. Stierlin. **254–5** Douglas Dickins. **255** H. Stierlin. **256** D. Darr. **257** *t*, B. de Andia; *b*, MacQuitty Collection. **258** G. dagli Orti (Museo de Antropologia de la Universidad Veracruzana, Jalapa, Mexico). **259** Fratelli Fabbri Editori, Milan. **260–1** Lee Boltin (Museo Nacional de Antropologia, Mexico). **262** *l*, D. Darr; *r*, Fratelli Fabbri Editori, Milan (Museo Nacional de Antropologia, Mexico). **263** L. Ricciarini/N. Cirani. **264** *t*, Explorer/Fiore; *b*, G. dagli Orti. **265** Tetrel/J. Torregano. **266** Fiore. **269, 270** D. Darr. **271** *t*, Explorer/Duboutin; *b*, Vautier/Decool. **273** *t*, Magnum/M. Riboud; *r*, Cedri/Salmer. **274** Magnum/M. Riboud. **275** *t*, Magnum/M. Riboud; *r*, H. Stierlin. **276** *t*, Vautier/Decool; *b*, B. Bansse. **277** *t*, Radio Times Hulton Picture Library; *b*, G. dagli Orti. **278** F. Roiter. **279** Vautier/Decool. **280** L. A. McIntyre. **282** G. Mercier. **283** A. Rozier. **284** L. A. McIntyre. **285** *t*, L. A. McIntyre; *b*, A. Rozier. **286** *t*, M. Bruggmann; *b*, L. A. McIntyre. **287** L. A. McIntyre. **290** Sovfoto. **292** Rapho/P. Koch. **293** USIS/SRD/J.-P. Germain. **295** G. Sipahioglu. **298** J. Laffay-Petit Palais (Museum of Archaeology and Ethnography, Tirana); *r*, Roger-Viollet. **299** *c*, Musée d'Ethnographie, Geneva; *b*, Ch. Monty. **300** Archaeology/J. H. Brandt. **301** *t*, Musée de l'Homme, Paris; *b*, Rapho/G. Gerster. **302** Rapho/G. Gerster. **303** *t*, R. Delon; *b*, M. Bouyssonie, M. Cluchat, L. Girard. **304** *l*, Giraudon (National Archaeological Museum, Athens); *r*, Atlas Photo/Lauros. **305** *l*, Musée du Louvre, Paris; *r*, F. Delfin Fernandez. **306** *t*, Musée de l'Homme, Paris; *b*, O. Langini. **307** Archeologia. **308** *t*, Magnum/B. Barbey; *c*, H. Lhote; *b*, G. Goldner. **309** Abbé Breuil. **311** *t*, Musée de l'Homme, Paris; *b*, F. Patellani. **311** *l*, Ecole Biblique et Ecole Archéologique Française, Jerusalem; *r*, Oronoz (Museo del Prado, Madrid). **312** Fotogram/Folco. **313** *t*, H. Stierlin; *b*, AAA/Photo Parrain. **314** AAA/Photo Picou. **315** Aerofilms. **316** *t*, Crown Copyright: reproduced by permission of the Department of the Environment; *c*, Aerofilms. **317** *t*, Musée de l'Homme, Paris; *b*, APN. **318** *t*, APN/S. Ozerski; *b*, R. Tournus.

COVER: Aztec calendar. This great stone disc, 12 ft in diameter, is carved with signs for the days, the months and the zodiac (photo Rome).

TITLE PAGE: Statues on the volcano of Rano Raraku, Easter Island (photo A. Rozier).

SECTION TITLES: **In search of fabled lands** (8–9): Christopher Columbus lands in America; engraving by Theodore de Bry (Giraudon). **Age of the megaliths** (62–63): Stonehenge (Rapho/G. Gerster). **Cities of mystery** (106–7): The city of Machu Picchu (Vautier/Decool). **Secrets of the pyramids** (166–7): The pyramid of Cheops (Roger-Viollet). **Vanished peoples, forgotten places** (202–3): Towers at Angkor Thom (B. Groslier).

DRAWINGS: The archaeological reconstructions in colour on pp. 72–73, 112–13, 148–9, 172–3, 192–3, 248–9 are by Gérald Eveno. The painting on p. 288 is by Denis Dugas. The drawings in black and white are by Pierre Brochard (pp. 19, 59, 86, 198) and Luis Camps (pp. 85, 88, 89, 127, 153, 185). The reconstruction of Durrington Walls (p. 85) is based on a drawing which appeared in *Durrington Walls; Excavations 1966–1968* by G. J. Wainwright and I. H. Longworth (Reports of the Research Committee of the Society of Antiquaries of London, No. XXIX, 1971). The plan of Mohenjo-Daro (p. 125) has been drawn after a plan in *The Indus Civilisation* by Sir Mortimer Wheeler (Cambridge University Press, 3rd edition, 1968). Reconstruction of the Bull Temple at Çatal Hüyük (p. 146) from a drawing by Grace Huxtable, courtesy Prof. James Mellaart.

TEXT: *Did a black hole hit Siberia?* is condensed from *A Hole in The Sky* by Walter Sullivan, which appeared in *The New York Times Magazine*, July 14, 1974. © 1974 The New York Times Company. Reproduced with permission. An enlarged treatment of this subject will be published in Mr. Sullivan's forthcoming book *The Edge of Space — The End of Time*.